The Silence of History

BY JAMES T. FARRELL

Doubleday & Company, Inc.
Garden City, New York
1963

All of the characters in this book are fictitious and any resemblance to actual persons, living or dead, is purely coincidental.

Library of Congress Catalog Card Number 61-12518
Copyright © 1963 by James T. Farrell
All Rights Reserved
Printed in the United States of America
First Edition

TO SURYA KUMARI

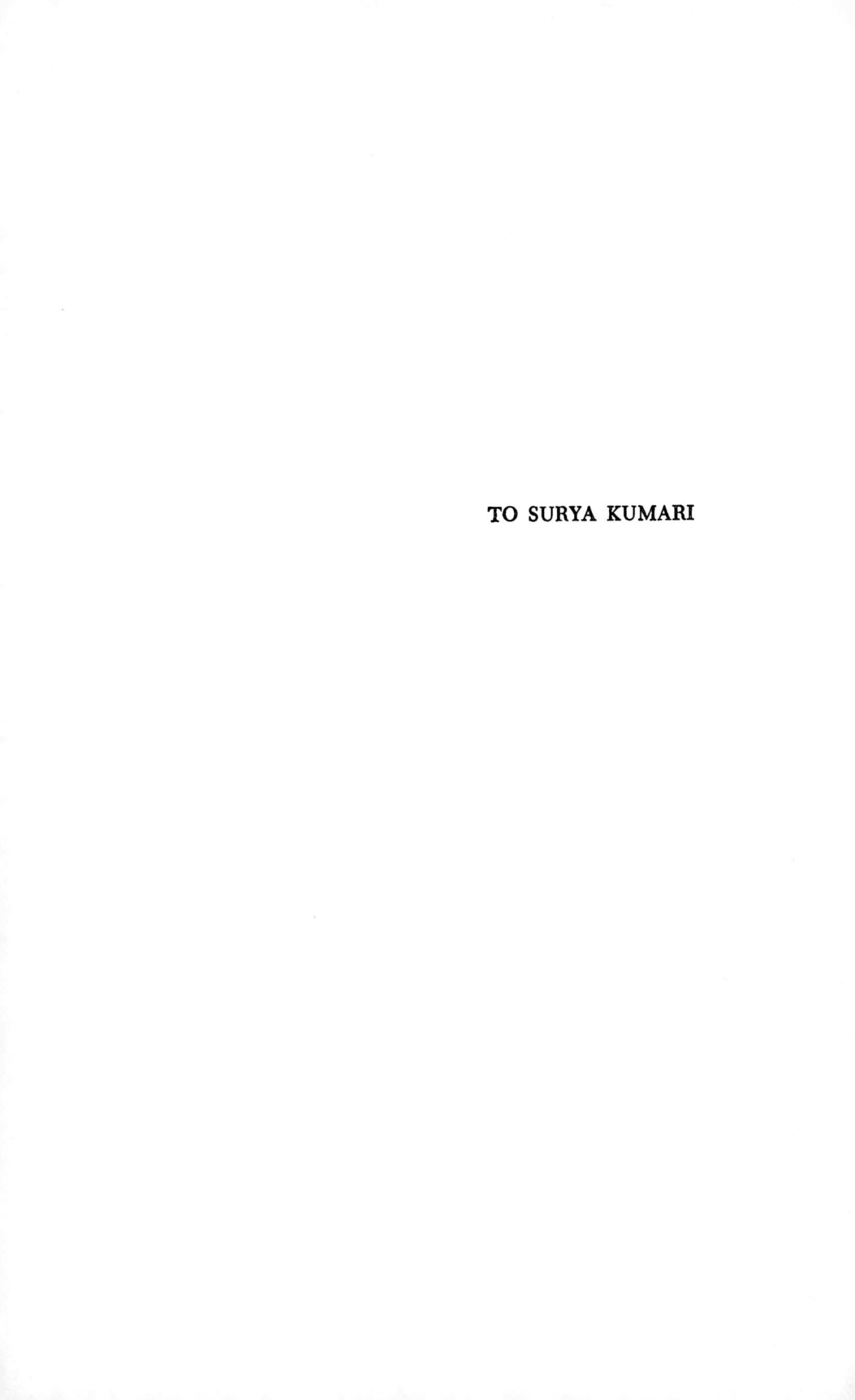

The Silence of History

Chapter One

I

His name was Edward Arthur Ryan, and in July of 1926, he was twenty-two years old.

He had looked forward to this summer with dreams and hopes that had sometimes been like sensitive nerves. But his dreams and hopes were—where? They were like the sigh of soft winds in trees of the park. A sighing song, monotonously sad, in the beaming sunlight, and the summer sun shimmering, winking, dancing gold in fragments upon the calm waters of the lagoon. Eddie was sluggish in an aftermath of accomplishment at the University that had been far beyond his expectations. Nine out of eleven courses were A. Nine sixes equaled fifty-four. Two fours were eight. Total sixty-two. Divided by eleven gave five and seven elevenths grade points. That's what he had accomplished. But his record won him little praise.

His good friend, Peter Moore, who lived next door, had congratulated him. Peter had also said that he merited high praise.

Praise was soft on your vanity, but that was all.

You liked it, praise.

He liked it. Yes, thought Eddie, he liked it—praise.

—Let 'em praise me when I'm dead.

Eddie had said this to himself several times before, during recent months. But he didn't, with certainty, believe that he actually meant it. No, not exactly, not strictly, because even though he might be giving way to the weakness of his vanity, he could relish it, and two times over, because of his scorn.

And still, he knew that he must be wary about this. Of course, in the case of Peter, the praise was genuine, sincerely meant.

Peter was genuinely Peter.

And lest he forget, there were few to praise him for what he was doing, there were few to care, there were few to understand.

These were facts that he must definitely accept as true. He was disappointed, a little hurt, possibly more than a little hurt. But his feelings about the matter were not all genuine. Could they be? He needed to push, he must push, his feelings farther than the range of neglect of all those who didn't really care a damn about him. If he didn't do this, then he would be weak, and this vanity would be a weakness. Weakness would mean his defeat. And he must fight any weakness in himself. Yes, and fight it until it was licked, and licked for good.

He believed his future depended solely upon himself. Any weakness that could destroy his chances must be fought, and beaten into permanent defeat. Any weakness that threatened him must be licked, goddamned cold, because he would have to win every inch that he could toward his own future.

Other than when he was in one of his moody fits, Eddie gloated with gladness about how the circumstances of his life had developed. He thankfully thanked all the stars, and all the gods there were, for the fight he must make to win his Victory of Success.

The summer morning played upon Eddie's mind, and he became quickly dissatisfied. He thought of nothing that he might do about this feeling, as it began to stir him into restlessness. It was a feeling which he would have quite often and at times even to a degree that was self-harassing, especially because it would, if only temporarily, rob him of confidence. Wasn't he sacrificing his youth, his best years of young manhood, to ambitions that were wild-eyed and crazy? Eddie asked himself this question with a depression of spirit; but in the innermost core of himself, he believed that he would fulfill his great ambitions, and that in being glum, gloomy, downhearted, he was playing to himself as a gallery. He had his private performance for himself, slopping and moping about the apartment.

The Silence of History

The summer morning was like gaiety, and the summer sun was full of an unspoken life that would sing in his mind, if it only had a voice. The wind across the street and inside Washington Park made murmuring music in the trees, in the branches, and in the bushes. He listened to the wind. He looked at the park, down from the window, and it was all greenness, and sunshine, and morning freshness of the clean, clear sky. The scene was familiar and it was new. The shining sunlight made it new. It was new because this moment, and this moment, and this moment, and this one, all had just been new. The new moments of the new morning, these made up now, and now made up this Tuesday of July, in the year 1926.

All that he had of Time was now, and now, and now, and now. . . .

Now was not an infinity, but rather a finitude of points.

It was a series of

Now, now^1, now^2, now^3 . . . now^x

And x equalled the last point in the series of points in a finitude of Time. It was the final now. This was the end of the series. It was x in parentheses, x in a bracket, x with a period after it; now, it was now^o and then OD. The zero was the end of the series of points of Time, and it meant no point of Time, which equalled *No Time*. And the "D" meant the Death of the points of Time. And that meant . . .

He was a romantic young man, and he wanted to live and find a love as big as all of the world, and as full of excited wonderfulness as this summer morning.

And he had hoped, summer after summer, and for nine or ten years, that one summer would be the summer of his life, and that on one summer morning, he would wake up to the day that would mark the beginning of the continuing wonder of his life.

And what this signified was that he would fall in love, with the right girl, the only girl, the girl who would love him, worship him, and understand him. Years of yearning would then and thus be ended in a tenderness of fulfillment. The end of longing would be like a moment that was as much forever as the sky was peacefully forever. A languorous silence would be music. Every minute, every second would be lived on clouds of wonder. Every dream would be a flowering fact. The silent voices of his spirit would become the choir of the music of his love.

Eddie was restless with years of unsatisfied romantic hungers. He was a very romantic young man.

II

Eddie Ryan had problems as well as yearnings on that July morning of 1926. He was beginning to feel uncertain about his job. This was his first thought on the subject as he gave way to an intermittent pacing about the apartment. But then he corrected himself. There had been some uncertainty, rising to more, falling to less, ever since he had started working for the Rawlinson Oil and Refining Company. And that had been sixteen months ago. Now he felt more uncertain than at any other time since he had begun to pump gas for Rawlinson. Deacon and Howell, the two supervisors, were riding him hard, and he was certain that they were both turning in reports that did him no good, and plenty of harm. He tried to get wrought up about his supervisors, but all he could do was to make a pretense at anger. After all, what did he expect of them?

Eddie was irritated by his own question. It broke the anger that he'd wanted to let loose, an anger of self-pity.

Yes, he was being sorry for himself. But he'd felt sorry for himself for a long time now, and with reason, good reason, and lots of it to spare. He could have easier conditions for his Battle of Life; but he meant more his Battle with Life. He could be free of uncertainty, of not knowing from day to day what to expect. But, on the other hand, he couldn't honestly claim that he had suffered excessively or unduly, and in any particular way.

There were too many points of view here, and he could keep changing his mind and revising, or even completely reverse what he thought. With this, a poignant longing came upon him.

Eddie heard the wind in the park, a caressing and gay purring, as if the wind were a maiden, beautiful but far away, who was

The Silence of History

singing into the summer wind a shy joy of life, a shy smile of happiness, a shy call of love. But it was only a current of easy speed, shaking branches and leaves, and echoing a pleasing monotonous sound of flattering friction.

It was only the summer wind.

And he was only Eddie Ryan.

He was sitting in the parlor, in the rocking chair set toward the wall, and a few feet in front of the first of the three windows that now admitted a deflected flood of the bright and clear morning light.

—Only the wind!

The phrase appealed to him so that he repeated it to himself four times, while his mind tiredly resisted his will, and would fill with daydreams the moment he would abandon will and thought, nervous worry about his job, and the spinning sad anger with which he would, out of the desperation of necessity, drive himself because the Tyranny of Time held dominion over him.

The rocking chair squeaked. It was old, and he could remember his grandfather rocking in it, sad-eyed, sad-faced, with a sad kindliness in his wrinkled expression.

But it was only the wind, and the wind spoke no language. The wind was feelingless. The grass, the trees, the sun and sky, all of the universe was feelingless, and the loveliness of the summer morning was something that did not know its name, didn't know itself, didn't know.

This affected him. His thoughts, however, were only a sign of that fact, an expression of the disillusioning and hurting awareness that could feel nothing and was without memory. There was no memory other than man's own remembering and his remembrances. There was neither reward nor any punishment in the world, except that decided upon by man.

It was his thoughts which caused all the trouble. They flattened dead his interest in Rah, Rah, Rawlinson and in the duties of his job.

But still, day after day, he had to report for duty, seven hours of working time.

SERVICE STATION ATTENDANT
Ryan
ON DUTY

There was no let-up, and there had been no release from the day-by-day, the . . . the . . . the day-by-day:

ON DUTY
Ryan

He didn't want to go to work today, and he didn't want to sell his time as he had to. Mastery of Time, his time, was the only condition of a future that was his best chance.

But his reaction was more direct and simple, more personal. He was fed up with the job, and he had to quit.

This thought was startling, and struck some nerves of fear in him.

His whole future depended on his job. He wouldn't dare to do it. He couldn't do it.

But if he could quit.

Eddie rocked. The rocking chair squeaked.

Yes, if he could quit, and be free, fully and wholly free.

The rocking chair squeaked, and he listened to the murmuring song of the wind, thinking of the freedom for which he hungered.

To be wholly free, to be fully free, to be completely free, yes to be free!

—Freedom—that's Time, owning my own time, Eddie thought.

And he didn't own his own time.

Again the murmuring summer wind. There was singing laughter in the summer wind. He wanted singing laughter in his life.

How could he quit his job?

It was crazy.

Crazy idea.

Eddie Ryan's education depended on his working and earning enough to pay his tuition at the University, and to help support

The Silence of History

his mother and his younger brother and sister. He gave his mother seventy dollars a month, which was half his regular salary, and, even though he lived at his grandmother's, he considered it his duty and obligation to help out his family. But he also wanted to do this, and was proud that he was able to, and could give such a relatively considerable amount of money. That was why he hadn't been able to think of college when he'd graduated from high school, a few years ago, in 1923. His father's second stroke had happened in September of his senior year in high school.

Now, his memory of all that had become bitter. Bitter? Yes, he guessed it was bitterness. It was anger, he was certain of that.

But what Eddie didn't recognize was how depressed he'd been during his entire senior year, how much of shame and of guilt he had carried as a burden upon his mind.

He was aware, day after day, of his stricken, broken father, dragging his right leg when he walked, as though he were dragging death itself along, as though, in fact, death were inside that pitiful helpless leg.

And this image was but one of many that Eddie had seen, and that had fallen into his memory. But as his senior year turned into days going by, gone by, more images fell into his memory. He'd forget them all, the fallen images of the real, the sad home over on Calumet Avenue. His father's eyes. Such a sadness of eyes in a face. Yet, their sadness was of his seeing. At the time, Eddie couldn't avoid feeling the estrangement between his father and himself; his instinct, his pull to life, his adolescent selfishness and dreams, these, and much else in himself and in his nature, were bound up with his awareness and his self-awareness. His whole life was going to be changed. He was going to be burdened. At times, he would think that he could have no future. Then, the future would become a daydream, or he would forget it, brush it out of his mind, away from his thoughts. But there was something else, and this wasn't, therefore, the only cause for the way he felt so often. Ambition. Take his ambition. What had happened to it? Why didn't he have it, his ambition? His ambition had been at the core of his sense of destiny, and his strong desire to believe that his life was a destiny. But in his senior year, at St. Basil's High School, Eddie had not retained the same feeling about his Destiny, himself as a child of Destiny. More simply, he began to think little of his future, but rather to daydream about it, and to trust to the hope of dreams as the means for his achieving, for his being or becoming a person of Destiny. It was like trusting to luck. At times, Eddie thought that's what it was, and that that was all he could hope for.

What was there for him to expect? This question, though he did not ask it of himself, was growing into him and into his life, during those high school days of a few years back. And in his thoughts and snatches of little conversations, he had often answered this question.

He had no chance.

Of his father, Eddie had thought this more frequently.

It was his father who hadn't had a chance, and even now, almost two years after his death, this conviction hurt Eddie, stunned him with the finality of meaning in those few words about his father's life.

—He never had a chance.

But his Uncle Dick had had a chance.

Eddie's face became clouded with grave reflectiveness.

Uncle Dick was sliding economically. He knew that much, but no more. His uncle kept his business to himself.

Uncle Dick's beliefs betrayed him. But he wouldn't take a tumble to himself before the facts.

The gravity of expression did not leave Eddie's face. It reflected, as a shadow of his mind and spirit, his feelings about the tragic, hurtful futility he felt in the life of his family. Only sympathy remained, that and memory. He could remember almost his whole life with them. He told himself that there was no bitterness in him because of these years. And he didn't want to hold any bitterness. When you were bitter, you couldn't prevent the effects of distortion on yourself and on how you saw. It was enough to live and strive today, without swimming in a dirty canal of yesterday's rancor. But there was anger and some bitterness that he had not assimilated. It was unfixed, fluid, mobile, and could fix his mind and emotions, like a gun, on

The Silence of History

many different targets. It was the anger and bitterness of his disillusionments, and of his pained and overintense feelings about the tragic fact of mortality. It was an angry bitterness that was, also, linked with his ambition, and the constant frustrations which he would feel because of it. He had no awareness of the extent and scope of this ambition, as contrasted with the modesty of the ambitions of so many others. He was restless with the slowness of the days, resentful of the time which passed while he did things he must do, but which he resented because he did not own his time for himself and his ambition, and for the study which this ambition demanded of him—at least, he was convinced of this, with a conviction as hard as solid rock.

Eddie had not been long in the parlor, although it seemed to him that he had been. He knew his own thoughts well on all these matters, and his mind worked quickly. His ideas came compressed, concentrated, accompanied by and partially embodied in images.

What this indicated was that Eddie was making a decision. He wasn't weighing alternatives, considering each of them fully in terms of what was relevant, factually; nor was he looking with straight-eyed practicality and self-interest. He was not being prudent, either. The fact that he had thought something, had told it to himself; this did not make his words irrevocable, nor, obviously, did private thoughts constitute action.

He was searching for a warrant to do what he was impelled, compelled to do for his own sake, because he felt that he ought to justify his decision by a clinching reason that would be more than personal, and would make it more than an act of his own doing that would seem like a goofy thing, or a retreat and a giving up of his education.

And he was struggling with a hurt sense of futility in life. Man was going nowhere but to the grave, and all of his achievements would one day be nothing, while he, while man, was cold and frozen dust, and winds were cold and coldly moaning and coldly whistling to nothing but a cold world, a cold universe of chilling, freezing cold space, whistling, moaning, singing a monotonous monotone beneath the shadowed cold rays of a sun gone dead, and cold with its own death.

He was battling with despair, and what was there for him to say, to think, to do but let life be awake in him, while despair should sleep a dreamless sleep.

In his mind, the cold winds of eternity were blowing.

—And by poetic license, Eddie told himself.

—There'll be no winds in the timeless reign of entropy.

And he remembered Mr. Wood, at a meeting of the service station attendants, saying:

—Sometimes, fellows, you've got to take it. You got to, chin up, stiff upper lip, eyes bright and looking straight, seeing straight, and that's the way to take it. It's the way that some of us like to style "The Rawlinson Way."

Eddie decided that, yes, he had to take it.

He rose from the rocker, and made a half-turn toward the three parlor windows. He saw, small-by-distance, a few human figures walking in the park in the foreground; and near the edge of the curb and the end of the park, he saw the movements of tennis players on a couple of the courts, which were set in a row, and in the enclosed caging of a structure of steel bars, painted green, and a crisscrossing of hard metal netting; perhaps that was also steel, he thought.

Eddie wanted to step to the window and stare out, in brooding melancholy. Instead, he moved to the phone.

For him, there was a hollow blackness in which Time had lost its breath. Time was like a heart that stopped in poised immobility and then became like heavy stone, frozen into fixity while it had been in motion.

A moment. Wait. Wait a moment.

Eddie was in a state of nervous fear about his job. If he lost it, he could lose all, that is, he could lose everything that was important to him. His future was at stake. It depended on his job. For he needed, he required a job which gave him time for attendance at classes in the daytime, preferably in the morning; and better yet, a job that made it feasible for his academic day to begin with an eight-o'clock class. His job meant pay enough for him to contribute something substantial to his mother's support, because his youngest brother and his youngest sister were still in school. Since he had graduated from high school, since June of 1923, he had never given his mother less than fifty dollars a month. He was giving seventy on that July morning, and had been ever since he had started at the University, over a year ago. Also he needed a job on which he had time for reading and study.

And Eddie had tied together in an asseveration of utter necessity his job and his attendance at the University.

He'd gone to the telephone, impelled to make this call. He'd acted with impulsive instantaneousness, and then, after getting Rawlinson on the wire, and being told to wait a moment, he had a near-panic. His mind went uncertain. He didn't know what to say to Mr. Wood. And his future could be hanging in the balance or on scales weighted against him.

It was serious; it was a crisis.

This thought came to him, and he knew that it had to be.

—But what had to be?

"All right, Mr. Ryan, here's Mr. Wood."

A sinking hopelessness. Words dying in a dark emptiness of mind.

"Hello, Ryan."

Mr. Wood's voice was normal, dignified, but cordial.

"Hello, Mr. Wood. I phoned; I wanted to ask to come over and see you about something, a matter, well, of importance."

"Certainly, Ryan, come right over. My office is always open to you fellows, and certainly to a fellow like yourself."

"Thank you, Mr. Wood," Eddie said, with an air of complete frankness.

"Can you make it here, and get to work at your station on time, Ryan?"

"That's another thing I wanted . . . to ask, Mr. Wood, that is, I'm shot from overwork. I'd appreciate it if you could send a relief man in my place this afternoon, and . . ."

"Yes, I guess I can. You're a good man. I can do that all right, Ryan."

"Well, thank you, Mr. Wood. I certainly appreciate . . ."

"Don't mention it, Ryan. And how long will you be in getting here?"

"Oh, about an hour, Mr. Wood."

"I'll see you then."

"Yes, sir, and thank . . ."

"That's all right, Ryan. You can always talk, straight-from-the-shoulder, man-to-man with me."

"Yes, sir."

"So long."

"Goodbye, Mr. Wood, and . . ."

There was the clicking sound of a receiver being put back on the hook.

". . . Thank you, Mr. . . ."

Eddie put the phone back on the hook.

Eddie sat for a few listless moments, wishing that he had not made the call, but he meant that he regretted having asked to see Mr. Wood.

He knew that he still had a drag with Mr. Wood. That would have been enough, if he hadn't been damned fool enough to ask Wood for an interview.

Then he stood up, snapping into alertness. He knew that he wanted the interview, but he wasn't sure why he did.

He had to get moving and he could think things over on the long ride by el train and streetcar.

He got ready to go in a hurry, and he was just about to leave, when his grandmother entered the back door, carrying a small brown bag of groceries that she had gone out to buy at the Mendelsen & Noble's Grocery Store on the south side of 58th Street and near the elevated structure. She came up the back stairs, a little woman, wearing a blue cotton dress with white dots.

"Are you at them books like a scholar, son?" she called. But not waiting for a reply, she continued. "I just ran out to get the food for your meal at work, son."

Eddie came into the kitchen, wearing his blue herringbone suit, his best one, and a tie with slanted gray and black stripes; his shirt was of white broadcloth, with an attached collar.

The Silence of History

He looked very well dressed, on the conservative side, except for his tie.

"Good Mother of God, son, don't let me be hearin' you tell me you're going to work dressed like you had gotten dressed for Sunday Mass. And son, isn't it early, you're off, going to work with the gasoline?"

"I'm going over to see my boss, Mr. Wood. I'm not working today."

"Is something the matter, that you're seein' your boss?"

"Oh, no, Mother. I just have to go over to the Main Office, and see Mr. Wood."

His grandmother had set her bag on the kitchen table.

"You didn't do something, you're not in trouble, son, with that good man you work for?"

Her voice had been grave, but it lightened with her next question:

"What's that you were telling me his name was, son, Mr. . . . Mr. . . . ?"

"Mr. Wood."

"He's a good man, whatever his name is, and I'll remember him in me prayers."

Eddie said nothing in response to his grandmother's words. But he stood in the kitchen, with a strange indecision, the indecision of sadness.

Through the black screen door he saw the blue sunny sky.

A new mood, near melancholy had come upon him. It was not any sadness about himself, but a fear and a feeling of guilt and sorrow for his youth, when his grandmother was old, she didn't know how old she was, and she couldn't possibly live long.

He should say something to her, now, because he didn't know how much longer he would have with her. He ought to talk, and his tongue was silent.

There should be questions to ask, too, questions galore.

Eddie couldn't ask them.

But as he looked at her, there was a shifting of his feelings, not in their sadness, but in their character and their effect. It wasn't his fault that he was young, and he would be old himself someday. His time would come too.

Life had the structure of sadness in its palpitations and its movements. It moved and moved on to death. To think of death in the summertime, on a summer morning of the good old, good old, good old summertime. . . .

Many questions wanted to ease their way into his mind. They had been there before, on the stage of his thoughts.

He didn't have time for them, now.

And she was alive and healthy. To forget the day when she would go, and to forget the day when he would go, to forget the condemnation of evil and all to the cold silence of six feet of earth, just below the surface. . . .

"I have to hurry now, Mother."

"When will you be comin' back home?"

"I don't know; don't count on me for supper."

"Well, son, I have a nice cut of sirloin steak to fry," she said, rather casually, and with no discernible sign of disappointment in her voice.

This gave Eddie an instant of eased sorrow. He told himself that his grandmother didn't seem to be unhappy about his not coming home for supper. And she wouldn't be alone tonight. Aunt Jenny would be home; she'd gone to work on the early shift this morning. And his Uncle Larry would be there. And his sister Clara.

But a clutching and guilty sadness remained, unremoved by these thoughts. He, too, should be here, and it was him whom she wanted home. She'd raised him, and she loved him, and it was sorrow he'd bring her by neglecting her.

"Well, son, you can have it another night. But sure it's not for the likes of the rest of them but you and me oldest son that I'd be buyin' and fryin' sirloin steak," she said, moving about the kitchen.

She was agile, and steady of foot, and she didn't at all look her age, although Eddie guessed that she must be well past seventy-five, and she might even be eighty. He didn't know her age; she didn't know it herself.

Eddie looked at his grandmother as she moved about. This he

did only occasionally. We can take people and scenes for granted visually, just as we do psychologically, socially, intellectually. And Eddie had been taking his grandmother in this way. In effect, he had been seeing her as much with residual memories as he did in any present moment with his eyes focused on her.

He caught her in vision as he crossed the kitchen. Like a kid. She went fast and light, she didn't yet walk like an old woman.

That was a relieving observation, and, while her hair had thinned a little, and lost a sheen it had once had, it was only graying, not gray yet, with more brown strands than gray ones.

And that was cause for hope, even if the hope were for only a while. We all could hope, only for a while.

She was thin and small, and while she had always been that way, she was not beginning to shrink with age, while her skin was getting dry and discolored. And her face. Old age had begun to shrivel and wrinkle the skin on it.

She was old.

But then, she had always been old to him, his grandmother. And for years, he had feared and worried about her, that she would get sick, and that she would then die. But it was summer, and he had always had less fear about her after the winter had gone, and there was the springtime and the summer.

—The good old summertime, Eddie told himself meaninglessly.

But people died in the summer, the good old summertime, and more than the young, the old died . . . in the good old summertime.

His eyes remained on his grandmother. She seemed to be more frail with age than she actually was.

But now he had to go.

"Goodbye, Mother," Eddie said, in a voice that was husky with the strain of an angry sorrow.

"Goodbye, son," the old lady answered, and all the years of her love for Eddie were in the sad tenderness of her voice.

Eddie pushed a kiss at his grandmother's forehead and left, the screen door slamming with a snapping, distinct sound after him.

The little old Irish woman, Grace Hogan, seemed to be talking to herself. Her lips were pale and purpled with the thinning strain of the many years since the day that she was born.

Her grandson made her . . .

—Sure he's me son, and let me hear the one that will granny me, she told herself, with a will and courage of spirit that were far beyond the strength of her old body, although she had not yet begun to sink into frailty and weakness.

Eddie went down the wooden back stairway, out of the yard, and turned right in the alley, toward 58th Street. The walk took about a minute and a half to two minutes, and during this period Eddie thought and observed more than was usual in so short a period. There was the sun. To say "summer sun," that would be bad, like bad writing. A summer sun could be any time, in the good old summertime. This sun, it was this morning's sun. It filled everything with warm, golden light that was like gladness spilled down over the world, and spilled even into back yards and alleys. It made the world seem like a place of glory where dreams were glory and glory could be real. The glad morning was moving into its late last hour in the almost unshadowed gladness of the sun. This was a day that could well become the day that his heart's desire could silently explode into wonderfulness.

Thus did the morning seem to him.

But the sadness of his heart was more than its desire. As he walked the short familiar path, he slid from his depression and sadness into a state of despondency; it was quick, so sudden that he was struck, for a second or so, with an intense fear that something dangerous, menacingly catastrophic, had happened to him. But then he quickly understood that this was a delusion. The ache of sadness, the angry anguish of his despair, the way he felt, this was no delusion. It was the reality of misery.

And it was thinking and feeling that made it so, the misery of a mind that knows that all things perish, and that perishing is only change.

We only perish into something else.

We perish from consciousness into what the sun does not feel, and what the wind does not sing, and what is not the vast and blind order of the vast sky.

It was only a moment's walk out of the alley, which was paved with cement, and was not a dirty alley, strewn with trash.

Hell, he had things to do besides weeping the blues of the universe.

Mr. Wood—what to tell him.

—Mr. Wood, I am depressed of spirit, melancholy, despondently descending into the pardonable platitude of the nadir of despair.

Eddie smiled, but with a touch of grimness.

Now he felt dull, and 58th Street was dull with familiarity.

There were three-story apartment buildings on either side between South Park Avenue and Calumet Avenue, and there was no grass, only black dirt and small stones and rocks in small, narrow rectangles of earth, which paralleled the sidewalk and lay between it and the curb. People were moving, a few of them.

He walked toward the elevated station a block away from the alley where he had emerged onto 58th Street.

And Christ, what would he say to Mr. Wood?

He couldn't think of anything to say.

And he knew that he'd be nervous.

And Time, he couldn't say that this was on his mind.

—The Tyranny of Time is the thief of youth, Eddie told himself as he came to Calumet Avenue.

He crossed catercorner to the other side of 58th Street.

He was in a mood of exalted pessimism.

And the day was so urgently beautiful. He wanted all of that vague beauty of the day, but he didn't know quite what it all was that he wanted.

He walked slowly past the stores on the north side of 58th Street, between Calumet Avenue and the elevated station in the middle of the block. There was a deadly smallness of life on the sidewalk and in the stores—mostly small ones, the drugstore, the tailor shop that used to be owned by Louie Bergman's father and uncle, the delicatessen store owned by that little Jew who must have died, Isaac. Some of the kids used to say that Isaac had consumption, and that he spit into the sweet buns and the bismarks; there was a new owner now.

Eddie had passed the delicatessen, but he recalled Isaac, a little man, as short as, or shorter than his Uncle Dick.

Eddie remembered how he used so often to feel sorry for Isaac, despite what many kids and some adults used to say about him.

He wore a dirty white apron most of the time, and kept his hat on in the store. Often he was in need of a shave, and it gave the impression that he was dirty. He seemed like a very sad man, too; his smile had been one of appealing sadness.

Eddie had come almost to the poolroom, run by the Greek.

He gazed inside, with casual haste. There were three or four fellows in the back where the tables were aligned in an even row. The front part was narrower, and before the Greek had bought the place from Bert Calkins, there had been a barber shop in the narrow front part of the establishment.

Eddie passed a number of people, and noticed others, going in either direction. He'd seen the people coming and going, entering stores and leaving them, but he'd given them almost no thought. They merely registered as figures on 58th Street, some recognizable, others strange.

But all that he saw was important. That meant the people, the shopping women, the old man, everyone he saw. And they, too, would share his final fate.

In the face of that stark fact, why did so many . . .

The thought did not need to be put into a completed sentence.

—Why?

—The petty smallness.

He was at the elevated station.

He said hello to Moe Moritz at the newsstand. Moe looked comic, but he wasn't. He was always hustling to sell papers, and he had a strong Yiddish accent.

Eddie shook his head, indicating "No," before Moe asked him what "papee" he wanted. They smiled at one another, and Eddie went forward a few feet, and brushed through the rather heavy swinging doors of the station.

Paying his fare at the window, on the ground floor level, Eddie wondered again what he would say to Mr. Wood.

He didn't know. He couldn't think of anything to say, and he was afraid that he wouldn't do any better when he was facing his boss at the Rawlinson offices.

Was he a damned fool?

He asked himself that question as he started up the stairway to the station platform.

Maybe he was. And at least, he'd done a damned fool thing by telephoning Wood.

Now. . . .

Eddie heard a downtown-bound train pulling into the station, and he bolted up the stairway, letting his intended thought fade away. And he found the relief of pleasure in this sudden, plunging, lurching upward on the steps with some approximation of his full physical power.

Eddie easily made the northbound, Loop-bound elevated train, which had come from 63rd Street and Stony Island Avenue, the end of the line for Jackson Park trains.

Was he going to ride to the end of his line with Rawlinson?

Chapter Two

Eddie Ryan walked up the marble steps of the entrance to the low, long, dark-bricked Rawlinson Oil and Refining Company.

Still once again, he asked himself what he would say to Mr. Wood, what he would tell him.

And Eddie felt as most workmen do, when they are entering the company building and are about to see their boss: he felt that he was there on sufferance, and that he was working for Rawlinson also on sufferance.

He went out of the sunlight, opening a screen door, and stepping inside the building. Before him was a long corridor, which looked even longer than its actual length. It was lined with open and closed office doors. He heard voices in a kind of drifting echo, a man's voice, a girl's, another girl's or a woman's. And he heard the sound of typewriters in use, and that of a ringing telephone. And he heard his own heels click on the marble floor.

He was a little nervous, but not so much as he'd been while riding over here on a 22nd Street trolley car. But he needn't have any fears. The way Mr. Wood had spoken on the telephone had carried assurance enough to give him a feeling of safety about his job. Yes, Mr. Wood's voice had been cordial.

Eddie had walked at a slant to his left, toward an open door which was situated about eight or ten yards from the building entrance, and entered Mr. Wood's outer office. He was made full of yearning by both the young and pretty girls sitting at their desks and typing, and by the well-watered, freshly green lawn beyond the window.

It was a brief yearning, like a silent, soon-expired sigh.

"Yes?" asked the pretty brunette sitting at the desk facing the entrance door.

Her manner was matter-of-fact; it almost disconcerted Eddie. He said that he'd come to see Mr. Wood, and gave his name and the number of his service station, 76. But as he finished speaking, Eddie felt a wrenching of his pride. The two girls might believe that he'd been called on the carpet and that he was coming in to be bawled out and possibly to lose his job.

The brunette wrote his name on a pad, and asked him, again in a matter-of-fact voice, to take a chair. Imagining himself awkward and graceless, he sat down in one of the row of chairs along the wall from where he could see the other girl, a blonde typing at a desk on the left side of the entrance. He could also look through an open window at a section of the lawn, green with a well-cared-for greenness; two sprinklers were within his sight.

He tried to look calm and at ease, so that these two janes—girls, he meant—couldn't think that he might be nervous or worried about his job.

He was worried. It was about his job, of course, but because the job meant his education, and his being in a position to help his mother, and Steve and Nora, his youngest brother and sister, so that they could keep on at school.

The brunette got up, came out from behind her desk, and passed by Eddie. She knocked on the door of Mr. Wood's private office and went in. Eddie sat frozen-faced, as if she held no interest for him because she was so trimly well built. But he wished. He wished.

For her figure, plump and soft, filled her print dress. And her legs, in silk stockings, had such shape—yes, he just wished.

She was back in a moment, saying:

"Mr. Ryan, please go in."

Eddie was inside Mr. Wood's office before he realized that he hadn't politely thanked the girl.

Sitting behind a long, flat-top desk in a large, bright office, with a big window admitting plenty of light and sunshine, Mr. Wood was an impressive figure. He was a well-built man of about six feet, tanned and bald-headed; his manner was reserved.

"Come in, sit down, Ryan," he said cordially, and not at all like a boss.

"Thank you," Eddie said; he didn't quite know what else to say.

A few months ago, he had still been dreaming of the day when he might be sitting behind a desk like Mr. Wood's, in an office pretty much the same as this one, or perhaps a bigger and better one.

—A few months ago, last year, not now any more. . . .

A few words silently spoken to himself. He didn't finish the thought, but he knew what he meant. He was changed. He felt the change in himself. He thought differently. He had learned, he was learning, and he couldn't believe, no longer believed, nor aspired to expired aspirations.

All this was but the quickness of an impression, while Eddie slipped into a chair. He smiled, and noticed the orderliness of Mr. Wood's desk. Everything seemed to be in the best possible place, the neatly stacked, small pile of letters and papers under the glass paperweight, the wire basket with letters on the right side, the note pad, the block of yellow paper, pens and finely sharpened pencils, a company manual in black-bound leather, loose-leaf books with information, other items probably.

"No, thank you, I don't smoke," Eddie said when Mr. Wood offered him a cigarette from a hand-painted box, probably made by Indians.

Mr. Wood took out a cigarette, lit it, took a puff, sagged back in his swivel chair, and seemed to wait for Eddie to speak.

He was fate and destiny to Eddie Ryan. He was the boss.

Eddie didn't know what to say; his mind went blank.

Chapter Three

Mr. Wood had been General Superintendent of the Service Station Department in Chicago for about a year and two months. He had been transferred from New York, where he had previously been a salesman and had then done personnel work. He knew several high executives, one of them influential with Walter C. Rawlinson, the founder and president of the corporation. Walter C. Rawlinson was nationally known as a very rich and powerful oil man, a sportsman with a string of horses, and the owner of an expensive and elegant yacht, which made him, *ipso facto*, a yachtsman. He was publicly known to be a sportsman-gambler for high stakes, a gentleman bettor. Rawlinson associated with men who were high up in the Republican Party, and with others who were among the most prominent men in America. He had been involved in a scandal exposed by a Senatorial Committee.

Mr. Wood believed in honesty and integrity as the best policy. It was his conviction that a man got out of life no more than he put into it, and he regarded his own experience as a confirmation of this maxim. For he had given the best of himself to the jobs he had held in the Rawlinson Corporation since he had started working there in 1910, when he was twenty-two years of age, as a clerk. Even then, Mr. Wood had believed that the oil industry was in the advance guard of progress, and that, in providing the fuel of the future, it would rise to new heights. The automobile was one of the greatest advances; it was an infant industry, but nothing on God's green earth could hinder it from developing and expanding a hundred times over, and supplying thousands and thousands, and hundreds of thousands of automobiles to be driven by Americans in the days and years to come. The market for gasoline and motor oil could only expand widely, in accordance with the law of supply and demand. He'd liked such phrases and had used them from his very beginnings as a young clerk, and as time went forward and he was moving up the ladder of success, he became more inclined to and more fond of using them. By almost constant repetition of them, he grew in the conviction that his grasp of economics was firm and pretty thorough.

Norton Wood was born in Smithville, New Jersey, a small town that was about a half hour's ride by train from Hoboken. He grew up an only son because of tragedies in the Wood family; Irene, a baby sister, had died of diphtheria when she was six months old, and an older brother, Willard, had been drowned at Atlantic City during a vacation. Norton could barely remember these tragedies, because they had occurred when he was between the ages of two and three and a half years. He scarcely remembered anything more than excitement, and his mother being terribly unhappy and her crying in sadness. However, he had heard much about both deaths.

Especially because of her bravery, Norton's mother had been the inspiration of his life. All of his success in life was for her, and for her memory. Her courage, never-say-die, never-give-up, never-complain philosophy had taught him the lesson of success and ambition, the lesson of the courage to win, and the lesson of the indomitability of hope.

Mrs. Wood had been a big, raw-boned woman, whose plainness of feature and appearance might have seemed epic in a pioneer environment. She carried herself with an air of courage and dignity; except in her own home with her family, or with the very few for whom she had a great closeness of feeling, she guarded the sorrows of her heart within herself. But the branded mark of sadness and tragedy had been stamped upon her by nature. She was as one of those who might forever be forlorn, but who uncomplainingly carried her sad misery through the years as though it were a heavy cross which was crushed upon her poor shoulders.

At home, she had sometimes spoken of the two dead children.

"What God wills, who am I to gainsay?" she'd say. "But there's no gainsaying the Will of God in feeling what I feel here in my woman's heart."

Whenever she spoke thus, she'd point her right index finger at her chest, or poke herself between her two sagging breasts.

And, gazing at Norton, she'd say:

"God left me you, Norton. He will always help you—if you help yourself."

Norton's father hadn't liked such talk, and he'd sometimes say, with the anger of dispiritedness:

"The deck is stacked against a little man. Them big fellows have the high cards."

All during Norton Wood's boyhood there were conversations between his father and mother, and he would listen carefully. He took to heart and remembered what his parents said, especially his mother. He knew that his mother was speaking as she was for him.

He loved his mother.

When he sat quietly, paying attention, looking at her—most of the time, not all of the time—he hoped he was helping give her some comfort.

The conversations were special ones, tacitly recognized as such by the two parents and by Norton. Always, these talks were held in the parlor. Mrs. Wood generally talked of Norton first, but then she'd speak of God, and of God's Will, of life and death, of fate, of the future and of what it was like, of what a man had to do, and what happened or could happen to a man when he was out in the world, earning his daily bread.

The general impact of these sermons, felt in the ever-extending years, had grown into Norton's character from the time when it was still being formed. They had become assimilated elements of himself, whatever he was.

This is what he came to believe while in his "man's estate," as he phrased it. This moral something was the legacy his mother had endowed him with.

When he had come to Chicago as a boss, he believed that this legacy was something else—that it was the lesson of life. His mother's inspiration, which was the gasoline for the pistons in the motor of his ambition, kept him running smoothly on the right road. To her, his mother, he owed a loving debt of gratitude, and he knew he could never forget it. She had passed on to the world beyond, where she was enjoying the unruffled peace and joy of the spirit, a rich happiness in the Land of the Lord. His sadness at her death had eased, but that was as it should be in the life of a man such as himself. Let the sleeping dog of sorrow lie like dead. And like Robert Burns, the Scotch poet, wrote:

A man's a man for a' that

Of course, he was no poetry reader, or no book reader of the nonessentials, either. He was a doer. When you couldn't be a doer, you taught, you read, you wrote. That was, except for a student who was getting himself an education in order to make something of himself, especially a young fellow like Ryan, who was studying at the University. For that young fellow was a genius. Pat Keefe, his predecessor thought so too and had put him on to Ryan. That was one of the few good steers Pat had given him.

Mr. Wood did read, not at the expense of work, but more than most fellows, like the company manuals and other material on technical operations explaining how you dug wells, pumped the oil, refined it, the whole shebang of what you did in order to get the finished products. And he read, or dipped into, other books, searching for practical lessons, bits of wisdom, suggestions for inspiring mottoes and morals, and for ideas and words to use when the occasion arose, such as, for instance, when he called the service station men to a meeting where they could be enthused, inspired, imbued with the right spirit, and thereby become better for Rawlinson O&R, and for themselves.

His father, Tom Wood, had been a man of medium height. Tom Wood had inherited enough money from his father, Easy Old Woodenhead Willie Wood, who'd had no wood in his head, but he'd had the nickname from childhood and liked it, because he was always addressed as "Woodenhead Willie" with great respect and affection. The old gent had owned a paint store which was profitable enough to have provided him and his family with a mighty comfortable living, and "Woodenhead Willie" had an eye, nose, ear, as well as a sixth, seventh, and eighth sense for a nickel, so long as it wasn't wooden, and for any other denominations of money that he could get his hands on. And he got his hands on enough of it, but less than the townsfolk believed. His reputation far exceeded his resources. Nevertheless, he did make money in real estate, insurance, in various deals of one kind or another, and also by playing poker. When he died, he left Tom Wood several hundred thousand dollars. But Tom Wood lacked his father's luck or his head for business and in the course of time the inheritance dwindled, as a result of bad investments, mistakes, and rash efforts to recoup losses which only resulted in fresh ones. His family did not go in want because of his bad business judgment, but neither was it rich and able to live in the style of the most well-to-do families of the community.

Norton's mother, Martha, did not suffer because of Tom Wood's financial ineptitude. She had no desire to enjoy the vanities of this world, and had she been rich, even a millionaire or the wife of a millionaire, she would not have indulged in the social frivolities of other women who were well-off. And, her tragedies had left in her a chill of death and eternity, and she often told herself that the life of men and women was vanity, vanity, and vanity again. But she did not regard as vanity the keeping of what one had, and using it well to get more. Handling money as her husband, Tom, did was like flying in the face of God. She thought, also, of her son. What the grandfather had left to the father should, in turn, be passed on to the son. It was only right that a man should do such a thing. Tom Wood's foolish and foolhardy schemes were sinful and wrong. But there was no telling what he'd do, and when he had enthusiasm like the fever, there was no stopping him.

"This fellow, Martha, is a mint, a gold mine, a genius who's gonna make Thomas Edison look bush league. He's got some invention, an automobile engine that will make an automobile run on the power of its own self-generating batteries, and it won't need no gasoline. It's got some new principle, different from those electrics that old ladies drive, and it will make an automobile go faster than the gasoline engines. Five thousand dollars, Martha, and in a few years, the Woods'll have enough money to buy up all of the State of New Jersey. Then I think I'll go into politics, and become somebody important."

Norton heard his father talking thus at the dinner table one night in 1904.

"And Nort, you'll go to Princeton, and get the polish I never had, or your grandfather. You'll be like the Crown Prince of the Wood dynasty."

"What's the principle of the thing, Dad?" Norton asked.

Tom Wood's face went blank. He hesitated a moment, and Norton became embarrassed for his father. This was another harebrained venture. He'd begun to hear tales and jokes about how Tom Wood was losing the hard-earned money which his own father had left.

It was this that Martha couldn't approve of, this that was wrong.

Tom did not always speak of what he did with money. But on those occasions when he did mention an investment, or an intended one, Martha Wood had little to say, and while washing her hands of the matter, she made it very clear to her husband that she did not approve. Such matters were for the man to decide, but with the help of God, it was always her hope that the man would decide wisely.

"I make wise decisions," Tom explained to Martha, after she had given him her familiar and often-repeated answer when he'd spoken of his five-thousand-dollar investment in the new electric motor for automobiles.

She wouldn't gainsay her husband's word, for who was she to be knowing the what and the why of a thing like that.

And Tom both counted on such a response from his wife and felt let down by it. She had no faith in him, and it was a trial and tribulation for a man to be wedded all of these years to a woman who had no faith and confidence in his judgment and character, a disillusionment to face, a source of discouragement which made it harder for the man. Not only his woman, but the people of the town thought little of his capabilities, and he knew

The Silence of History

what they thought of him, and the things they said behind his back. He knew it well and more than well that they said that Tom Wood was never the man his father, "Woodenhead Willie" Wood, had been. It was all part of the talk of the town. But to his face they were different, and they'd damned well better be. Or they'd settle with him, man-to-man.

But Tom Wood wasn't bitter or angry about this whole situation and his own position in life. While jokes were made about him, he was well liked, and the humor, bandied back-and-forth at his expense was not malicious in intent or malignant in consequences. The best that Tom Wood could achieve in life was to become something of a town "character," and the raillery and jokes and fun poked at him all helped to make Tom a "character." This was a substitute, by living caricature, for the colorful personality that his father had been. He couldn't be his father, but he could be talked about as much, and that was a form of prominence which Tom accepted as his due, because he was Tom Wood, the son of Woodenhead Willie Wood, and thus he was somebody instead of just anybody or nobody.

It was easier for Tom Wood to accept himself and the knowledge that he was regarded as something of a clown, even by good friends of his, because he had a dream. He saw himself as he would be when his dream became reality more than as he was.

—He who laughs last, laughs best.

His dream had to happen, had to come truer than true. If a man dreamed with enough faith, he could make his dream come true. Like that night, four–five years ago, when he had been playing poker at the home of Seth Smith, the undertaker, and he'd been having a streak of the goldarndest bad luck a man could have, and Seth Smith was one man that no man ever wanted to lose to, at poker or anything at all. Losing too much to Seth Smith would give any man the creeps. He wasn't the only one who used to get the willies when poor Seth would rake in the chips, with that grin on his face that seemed to tell you that raking in your chips was just a kind of preliminary before the big act of bringing you in in a big black box.

Tom could well remember, all right, that Saturday night, when he'd gotten proof that if you willed and wished enough, why, you got it. That Saturday night, he must have ended up taking thirty–forty dollars from Seth Smith.

It was about a year later that Seth, poor Seth, joined his past customers in the cemetery.

So, Tom often thought, he knew darned well what he was doing, and he'd get his whiz-bang cleanup to riches on one of his investments. You had to take a chance if you wanted what he wanted, which was like one fast, quick leap right straight over the moon. Something sensational, that was what it had to be for him, an investment in something that would make him the big pile he wanted, and make it fast, fast.

Over the course of the years, while Norton was growing up, Tom would constantly imagine his day of days to come, when his big dream would turn into the substantial reality of a fortune. He wanted a fortune. Through that fortune, he would best bestow honor on and show love to his family. This, also, was part of his dream.

He could play for stakes on the stock market, and he did from time to time, but his luck had been as rum rotten as his broker had been. He knew, though, that the market wasn't his answer. Real estate was another kind of shot to take, and he'd lost about three–four thousand there. But if he hadn't been badly advised and hadn't lost that three–four thousand, real estate wouldn't be the skyrocket he needed. That was it, the whole thing in a nutshell. He was out to skyrocket. What he needed now was what it took to send him skyrocketing up, way up above the clouds. Something new, sensational, something that made progress in the age of progress.

But what would all this do for him?

His failure had not been in trying, but in finding, and his failures to find had been made with an investment of between sixty and seventy-five thousand dollars, he didn't know just exactly to the penny. He guessed he could figure it out, any time he wanted to, and some day he'd get out all the stock certificates, receipts, the whole blankety-blank record, and add up how much it all came to.

Tom never did it.

When Norton was a little boy, Tom fascinated and enthralled him with stories of how they, too, would get rich, maybe as rich as anybody in the world, by selling all kinds of wonderful machines and things that would be much more fun to play with than any toy even Santa Claus could give him. Norton wanted the machines and things right away. Tom told the boy that he hoped to have something for him soon, but Norton had difficulty controlling the urgent impetuosity of his wish for the machines and things.

Norton waited for "soon" to come.

It never came.

He couldn't understand why his father had told him what wasn't the truth.

Tom was relieved when the kid stopped asking about the machines and things. He guessed the boy forgot. That was how kids were. Ah, there was no time in life like childhood days. How he missed those days that would never come back to him, ever again.

One lie was not sufficient to break the boy's faith in his father. However, more followed. Tom promised easily, and forgot to keep his word, without realizing that he was causing his son to feel betrayed. He wouldn't have viewed his failures as a breaking of his word; if these had been called to his attention he'd merely have pointed out that he hadn't gotten around to keeping his word, but would do it, just as soon as he had the time.

These promises, easily and glibly made and lightly forgotten, these broken promises and unkept words, gave Norton Wood his first and most painful disillusionments with his father. And being a bright boy, Norton, wounded in spirit and self-esteem, began to notice one of Tom Wood's inconsistencies after another. He wished that his father were different, were what a father should be to a boy. And a father should act differently from the way his own acted. A father oughtn't to be laughed at as his was, and ought not to make a boy ashamed.

The rift had definitely happened between father and son. It widened as the years went by.

Tom Wood was slow in perceiving his son's changing attitude toward him, and he was equally slow in his awareness that

Norton was growing up. When his son was no longer a little boy, Tom was still talking to him as though he were. And Norton could only react to such treatment by closing up in fits of boredom.

The years advanced for Norton, and the years receded for Tom. A phase of bitterness in Norton toward his father wore away into a settled attitude of indifference, softened and pressed down hostility, and irregularly occurring short moments of struggling sympathy to regain a closer tie with him. And then hopes of his father's changing, and a few futile tries at reforming Tom.

Norton worked in the store frequently, after school and on most Saturdays, and had he had no other reasons for deciding not to go into business with his father, the accumulating impressions of these experiences would have been sufficient. His father ran the store carelessly, and pretty much catch-as-catch-can, apparently without caring if he showed a profit or a loss. He didn't order promptly to keep in a good supply of paints, and he didn't seem to care about making sales, building up his business, or even keeping what business he had. Or rather, Tom cared, so long as it didn't interfere with his life, his other activities. Among these were poker games in back of the store. Every Saturday when Norton was working, and on many a weekday afternoon if he also happened to be in the store, Tom Wood arranged a poker game with some of his cronies.

With Norton and the helper, Kirk Jones, behind the counter, there was just about no need of Tom, and Norton quickly became aware of this. However, he was still a growing boy, innocent, and somewhat religiously inclined. Gambling wasn't right, or at least he wasn't sure that it was, and thus, that it wasn't a sin. But it didn't matter whether his father's gambling was a sin or not. Norton still held the poker games against his father. His father was gambling during the business day. And the old man wasn't building up for the future, retaining the money which one day should be the due and inheritance of him, himself, Norton Wood.

Norton's mother had helped to graft this last criticism of his father into Norton's mind. She had told Norton that it was "your birthright." And when his mother talked to him like this the boy could not have escaped being influenced and emotionally troubled. He tried not to be, but in vain. He tried not to think of his father wasting money that would otherwise come to him. A good father wouldn't do any such thing. He didn't have a good father.

Such feelings, however, didn't strike Norton as real, not as wholly real. For he couldn't dislike his father as much as he ought to, or in the way that he'd think he did, sometimes, in the store, and especially when he couldn't easily put his mind on anything else. Hell, nobody could dislike Tom Wood, not really dislike him. He was too good-natured and friendly, too uncomplaining, too jolly. He laughed away hard luck and strokes of ill fortune, and he did not harbor any grievances or ill will toward any man. He was a pathetic sort of a man, one for whom many people could have felt sorry but for the fact that he had enough money to live on, and, after the tragic loss of his two young children, he suffered from no further hard blows of fate and none of his mistakes and follies led to disaster. His failures did not bring him more than passing unhappiness, and he gave the impression of enjoying life just as much when he met with another failure and lost money as he would have should success and a killing have been his.

Tom Wood was a man who was liked, but not respected. Norton's predominant feeling about his father became one of shame and sometimes, in reaction, he would think about his own future, and resolve to be different, to make himself respected above all else, to have dignity, dignity above all other personal traits.

Norton's wish to become a man with dignity was one reason, but not the only one, why he came to the decision that he would make his way on his own, instead of playing leapfrog from Woodenhead Willie Wood to Tom Wood to himself. He'd become a self-made man, going out to win success in a bigger world, rather than coasting in Smithville, New Jersey, and finding himself compared to his father and his grandfather. With times changing, and more and perhaps bigger changes to come, an ambitious young fellow had to go out into the world if he wanted to make something of himself.

New York was close, very close, and New York was the

biggest world a young man could plunge into and start the battle for fame and fortune. Several times, on his own, or on errands for his father, he had gone to New York, and the visits were to a city which was Fairyland, but real, true, honest-to-goodness Fairyland, where everything was real, stone and cement and iron and steel and men who were successes and others who weren't, and dollars were coming in, dollars going out, dollars into profits, or dollars into losses. He saw New York as a wonderland created by men who had the vision of success, and the urge for fame and fortune. The skyscrapers, the hordes pouring in and out of them, the builders of the American and of the twentieth-century dream of success, and all of the activity of the biggest and greatest city in the world—he saw this as the doing of the men on top, the men with pluck, vision, ability, drive, and the will that he wanted to build in himself, the will to win the stakes of the game of life, the will to make everything bigger and better, and even to make stone and cement, concrete and steel, grow into towers pointing at the heavens.

Especially because of his father, seeing his father in the store as well as at home, hearing his father's talk of the big strike he would make on something new, something of the twentieth century and the new world of the twentieth century, and also hearing the anecdotes about Woodenhead Willie, Norton thought of the future, his own future, and found his own ambition in life. He would make his way up one of the ladders which the big men had built, for themselves and for others, for just such young fellows as himself.

His grandfather, Woodenhead Willie Wood, had not been one of the big men, but judging from stories told about the old gent, there had been something of the stuff of bigness in him. Norton knew his grandfather, who had died the year he was born, only from hearsay. But he had gotten a picture of the old gent from the stories told about him, a picture of his character, and not merely of what Woodenhead Willie had looked like. And as Norton Wood grew up, his idea of becoming a man and a success was one of character and character-building. To become a success in the world, a man had to have character, and the

The Silence of History

climb up the ladder was, in itself, character-building and character-creating.

The main reason why Norton was ashamed of his father was because he didn't think Tom Wood had character.

It was evident, and he had heard others say as much so often that the impression became fixed and had acquired a status of immutable truth.

—Tom Wood'll never be the man his father was.

—Only shavings off Woodenhead Willie, his old man, that's all poor Tom Wood is.

—Tom has the wood of Woodenhead Willie, but none of the head.

At first, Norton had been angry at those who spoke against and joked about his father. He didn't believe anything that anybody said against his Daddy. He had a wonderful Daddy, the most wonderful one in the world. And someday, his Daddy would show them all, show how wonderful he was. Tom's dreams stirred Norton. The boy waited for his father's dreams to come true, for those machines and things to be built by his Daddy, so that everybody would know about them. His father kept talking about the modern age, the new age, the new century, the future, the wonders yet to come, and the wonders that Norton would see when he'd grow up to be a man. The boy often became impatient with eagerness to grow to his manhood, and the seed of expectation was planted in him. His father gave him an idea of the world as a place of progress and change, of new things, of new inventions, of doing things differently and better, and of not sticking in the mud where you'd been born. As a little boy, Norton had thought that he'd never be a stick-in-the-mud. He thought of those who said things against his father as stick-in-the-muds. As he grew older his feelings toward his father changed, but the seeds of his ambition, first planted by his Dad, grew as he was growing. His father had had the right ideas, but the wrong way of putting them into practice. He felt more than shame about Tom Wood. He couldn't have expressed all of his other feelings, put them into words for anyone, but they were inside of him, part of his character. And at times, when Norton dreamed of how he'd go out into the world and fight his way up the ladder, he thought of showing them, the stick-in-the-muds. They were the ones who had laughed at his Dad, and he'd show them, show them for what his Dad should have been.

The time came when he left home for New York. Tom Wood was more visibly affected than Martha. She knew that Norton must go and make his way in life, and she knew that he would, with God's help and God's protective eye upon him. Tom, gray and fat, still talking as he had twenty years before, urged Norton to stay, to help manage the store, and share in the great plans which were going to come true any day now. Norton went away to New York, with his feelings chafed and with his ambition to make good. He ran errands, he worked as a stock boy, he was an office boy, and then he was hired by the Rawlinson Oil and Refining Company.

He gradually rose to the position he held when Eddie Ryan went to his office on that July morning in 1926.

Back in his home town, his father was old, fat, gray-haired, and had retired on the income from the small remains of Woodenhead Willie's inheritance. Tom Wood still dreamed the same dream that he had told to Norton when his son was a little boy. And he sat on a bench in the sun, telling other old men of his dreams and of his son who was becoming a big oil man, just like that with W. C. Rawlinson, himself.

Norton Wood's salary was $450 a month.

Mr. Wood's dream and ambition were as alive as when he began, a sallow boy, younger than this young fellow Ryan whom he hoped to straighten out with a man-to-man talk.

Ryan was ambitious.

What would the country come to without ambition?

This question rose in his mind as he took a puff on the cigarette which he'd just lit and looked at Eddie Ryan.

Chapter Four

I

Mr. Wood believed that honesty was not only the best policy, but, more importantly, that it was right. Since he had come to Chicago and taken over the Service Station Department, succeeding Pat Keefe, he was, at times, afraid that he was losing his faith in human nature; as he told Mrs. Wood, he never would have believed that this was possible, but he feared it was true. Almost from his first day in Chicago, he had been encountering cheating, lying, deception from service station attendants, and these were major problems with which he had to contend, "day in and day out." He'd drive to work in his newly purchased four-door Hudson, hoping that he would not find anything on his desk which dealt with any of his men short-measuring customers, stealing small sums from the company by one means or another, soldiering while on duty, or putting something over on the public, on him, or on the company. There were such mornings, but not too many of them. He'd been no babe in the woods when he'd come to Chicago, but nevertheless he had been utterly unprepared for the sheer volume of cases of this character, and having to deal with every one that came to his desk, bringing men in and questioning them, hearing them lie when he had irrefutable evidence right before him on his desk, having to keep firing men, becoming familiar with the cleverness and ingenuity as well as the bold-facedness of some of the attendants —all this had been a depressing experience. There were times when he would wonder what to do, and what to think about his men, about human nature. More than once he had asked himself whether anyone could be trusted.

Ryan, at least, was honest.

In the neat stack of papers on Mr. Wood's desk were reports on Eddie Ryan turned in by Deacon and Howell, the two supervisors who alternated, monthly, between the North and the South Side stations. He had thought about these reports, and had listened carefully to what both Deacon and Howell had said of Ryan.

—He's no good for Rawlinson, Mr. Wood, Deacon had said.

Howell had spoken similarly.

But Mr. Wood had also talked with Kalm, the collector, who was a sub-boss to the supervisors. Kalm, a good, hard-working, reliable young Swede, had spoken favorably of Ryan, and had said that he thought him honest, pleasant, damned intelligent, a pretty good man.

And Mr. Wood had gone through a couple of spotters' reports which didn't incriminate Ryan in anything in any way.

With these reports, and his own estimation of Ryan, he could not honestly agree with the conclusions of Deacon and Howell. He favored Ryan, he knew, and had hopes and plans for the young fellow.

Ryan was a good man.

"What's the matter, Ryan?" Mr. Wood asked, with what he considered his man-to-man approach.

Eddie faced his boss, thinking that there was a gulf between them, and it couldn't be crossed. Yet he found himself feeling a little sorry for Mr. Wood, and sympathetic toward the man.

"I guess I must be overworked," Eddie said. "I did too much. I overworked myself studying."

This was true and yet he didn't believe that it had anything to do with why he was here.

"I know that, and I've wanted to help you," Mr. Wood told Eddie in a voice that was understanding and almost gentle.

And suddenly Eddie thought that nothing was the matter— only himself. He had no real excuse for this interview. He'd have to think fast to keep out of hot water.

"I've scarcely taken a day off, and I went through four straight

The Silence of History

quarters at the University, and I've gotten an A minus average. I'm one of the highest men in the freshman class, and there's about a thousand in it."

"Yes, I know how you've been working to get yourself an education and to make something of yourself, Ryan."

In the neat stack of papers on his desk, there was one spotter's report, describing Eddie on a cold winter night, at the desk in the lonely station, studying with such intensity and concentration that he forgot to close up at nine o'clock; then, ten or fifteen minutes later, he'd jumped up and rushed through his closing chores, lugging in the display of canned goods, taking the hose off the pumps, pulling down the covers and locking the pumps, putting money in the safe, turning out the lights, and locking the station door. Then he had walked slowly away to catch an elevated train, lugging a black briefcase stuffed with books. This report had earned Mr. Wood's admiration.

Eddie had glanced off, waiting for Mr. Wood to say more. He was blank about what he ought to say or do. He didn't know why he had to do anything, because he still had his job, despite Deacon and Howell.

"It's a mighty good thing that you're making such a mark for yourself in your academic work, Ryan. We can only be pleased, here at Rawlinson, if one of our men distinguishes himself the way you're doing."

"Thank you, Mr. Wood."

"There's nothing to thank me for; it's your own accomplishment. All I did was give you permission to study on the job, and one reason I did was because you came and asked me, instead of trying to sneak it in. You know my rule, no reading on duty, and I'm strict in its enforcement, because when you men are on duty, that's our time, and we pay pretty good money for it."

"Yes, sir," Eddie muttered.

"And the reports on your station aren't heartening . . ."

Eddie grinned defensively.

"I got several reports that the air conditioner was filthy."

"It's clean now."

"It should always be clean. You know that, Ryan."

Eddie was tightening up inside.

"I don't know, Ryan," Mr. Wood continued after a pause. "Your sales are good for a small station, and there's no serious demerits on your record. I don't have complaints about the way you deal with the public, like rudeness, surliness . . ."

"Well, I try, Mr. Wood."

"There's an increase in canned goods and coupon books, and in flushing oil. The increase is due, mainly, to you, although your partner, Corlin, is holding up his end of the stick, too. All this shows initiative."

Eddie couldn't listen to Mr. Wood with great interest. But his mind wasn't locked up and stretched any more.

"That's what I like to see in you men. And at Station 76, I know that it's principally due to you, Ryan."

Eddie looked solemn because he was pleased by what he had been told, but he was also a little troubled. For he was drawn to Mr. Wood by admiration as well as by gratitude, and hoped he wouldn't do the wrong thing.

"Corlin's a good man," Eddie said, discovering his tongue, and taking the occasion to say a good word for his partner. "We work well together and trust each other."

Eddie meant what he was saying, but he was praising his partner because this was easier than saying he-didn't-know-what to Mr. Wood. He liked Corlin, but the difference between them was wide, and it was growing wider.

Mr. Wood nodded and told Eddie:

"Yes, if I didn't think Corlin was a good man, an honest fellow, he wouldn't be working for Rawlinson. But Ryan, there's something I have to say to you . . ."

"Yes, Mr. Wood?"

His mouth was dry now. He waited in suspense.

"You're different from Corlin, and fellows like that. Ryan, you're a genius."

Eddie was startled into awe. What could he say in reply? He wanted it to be true. If it only were!

But he had a happy doubt about Mr. Wood's amazing statement.

"I just want to get ahead, as far ahead as I can. I have ambitions," Eddie said, speaking because he felt he ought to say something, and wanted to say something that ought to impress Mr. Wood.

But that was silly. He had impressed Mr. Wood. He didn't have to do any additional impressing.

Wanting to get ahead had been his sincere ambition when he'd first gotten a job with Rawlinson from Pat Keefe. Now he didn't know what he wanted to do, or what he ought to say. Nor was there time for him to clarify his mind. He still wished to go on with Rawlinson, to work his way up from the ranks, clean to the top. And he was in danger of tottering into expressing his gratitude to Mr. Wood by giving way to the values which he believed he had rejected for life. It was in this state of sudden uncertainty that he realized why he had asked for this interview. He had come to quit his job, and to take a new chance. His awareness of this motive, which had been developing in his mind, growing beneath his consciousness, became clear to him when he unexpectedly said to himself:

—No, I don't want to quit.

Eddie didn't want to quit. Not only was his job safe, but he was in a solidly fixed position, and the supervisors who had been riding his tail, Howell, a dumb ox, and that sonofabitch Deacon, hadn't hurt him with Mr. Wood. He could stay on the job, and continue next fall at the University. He was sitting pretty.

Then why shouldn't he think of success? Why shouldn't he think of making a career for himself with a big corporation, such as this one?

And there was Mr. Wood, sitting at his desk, holding down a good job. He could hire and fire, give orders and enforce them with authority, and he had the prestige of a boss. He was somebody in this man's world. And Eddie was certain that Mr. Wood was on his way up higher.

He could be on his way up, too. If you had a good job in business, you were respected by nearly everyone. That was the way, too, to make good money, the route to riches.

Why should he attack business and middle-class values? Why should he refuse to make his way with them, but think of books and the search for truth, of injustices in the world, and take all the risks you took if you decided to spend your life trying to learn what was true and then saying it in public, and in fighting against injustice?

Who did he think he was—Bertrand Russell?

—I won't quit, Eddie told himself.

Mr. Wood sat watching Eddie, not surprised by his silence. It was to be expected that such praise would take him aback. Mr. Wood had said more than he had intended to, but he believed what he'd told Ryan.

Yes, that was his true opinion of this young Irishman.

Eddie's lucidity had become painful with both conscience and clarity. The feeling that he should talk, and frankly, was becoming a pressure, with an urgency that was almost a compulsion. He told himself that Mr. Wood deserved more than he had been given. Mr. Wood deserved more than Eddie knew he could give in return for a faith in himself that had never been so expressed in all his life. And Eddie knew that he was just about reduced to a morally defenseless position.

He was ashamed of himself, because of petty deceptions such as all, or almost all, attendants practiced. Because of the unsettling suddenness of his enhanced respect for Mr. Wood, and because of a released current of sympathy for the man, Eddie winced at the thought that he had cheated. What he'd done was small change stuff, like "pulling the pumps," or short-measuring on gasoline, for carfare and food from Jimmy the Greek's Restaurant across the street from the station. Or gypping a little to make up shortages, because every cent on the daily audit had to be turned in, and you couldn't run a station fourteen or sixteen hours a day without having some shortages. And then he did a little juggling of the sales of bulk motor oil and of cans of motor oil, in order to give Corlin and himself a slightly better record; you just about had to do some of this because of the pressure to sell more and still more.

No, these actions had caused no serious moral qualms until now, when he was sitting in Mr. Wood's office.

"Well, Ryan?"

Mr. Wood's simple question, cordially uttered, made it easier for Eddie to speak, and to do it confidently, with no strain in his voice.

The Silence of History 43

"I took on too much, I guess, Mr. Wood, and I must have brought myself close to the danger of having a nervous breakdown."

Eddie's voice seemed like the accented sound of sincerity. He sounded sincere because Mr. Wood believed him to be sincere.

And Eddie wanted to be both sincere and honest, but how could he tell if he was? He didn't know if he believed what he said, and even if he did, would that mean that what he said was true?

These were now intruding wishes, because he was, really, trying to excuse himself from any suspicion or blame as a consequence of how he really felt about working at 76.

And no—yes—no—yes—no—his interest in going on with Rawlinson was just about squashed dead. During the last couple of months, this had become an evident fact.

"Do you think you need a rest, Ryan?"

This he did want. Since classes for the spring quarter had ended last month, he'd gradually gotten to hate his job. And just as Mr. Wood had spoken, it had been on the edge of his tongue, almost, to ask for a vacation.

"I think I need one, Mr. Wood."

Now he had a clear road.

"I put myself through a pretty hard grind. It was a seven-day work week, and at the same time I went at all my studies hammer and tongs."

The apprehension that he might be on the verge of saying too much struck his mind. He went on, but with something of the feeling that he was plunging:

"I try to make it my policy to do more work in every one of my courses than any other student. Next year, after the summer vacation, it won't be so rough, because I'll be more used to it, and . . ."

"How long a vacation do you think you need?"

Eddie was too surprised to answer immediately. This was unprecedented. Attendants didn't get vacations. He stared uncertainly at Mr. Wood.

"Of course, I really do need one . . ."

Eddie abruptly stopped. He was pitched into floundering

hesitation. He didn't know how many days to ask for. Could he request more than a week? Two weeks? . . .

Through the window, past Mr. Wood, he saw the sunny luminousness of the air, the turning sprinklers, the dull neatness of the domesticated green lawn and, beyond the fence of gray wire, the railroad track.

The sky was blue and big and clear, and he thought of it as an airy freedom like the freedom he thirsted for.

—Two weeks, he told himself. Can I get it?

"Yes, I can see how you would. I think I'd get stale myself, doing as much as you've done," Mr. Wood continued the conversation.

"Well, I did push myself pretty hard, I guess."

"I know. And you held up your end of the stick until recently. Some of the things that were reported to me aren't like what you are, the kind of man you appear to be. For instance, going home and forgetting to lock the station door. . . ."

"Yes, I just can't . . ."

"Understand," Mr. Wood interjected, but with a grin both friendly and amused. "Understand how you could do such a thing?"

Eddie nodded in accord, and half-smiled.

"And another night, forgetting to lock the safe, and leaving the window open in a neighborhood full of darkies. And then, forgetting to take the hose off the pumps?"

"I just don't know how the hell . . ."

"Yes, Ryan, naturally."

A shadow of a smile played about Mr. Wood's mouth.

Eddie licked his now dry lips. Something was coming.

What?

"Ryan, if you take two weeks, will that give you a chance to rest up well, and come back to us shipshape?"

"Yes, sir," Eddie said, bewildered. Then he added: "Thank you, Mr. Wood."

"There's nothing much to thank me for," Mr. Wood explained. "I'll do whatever I can that's fair for any man, especially a good one."

"But I'm very grateful—you've been more than fair to me."

The Silence of History

Eddie knew that he meant his words, and he'd uttered them with as much relief as honesty.

This was the unexpected, the unbelievable. It was a new start, with the books erased clean, and with nothing lost. It was a gain for him, a climb of a couple of rungs up the ladder.

"You've been a good man, Ryan, one of my best—and I think you know that here, at Rawlinson's, we don't want to keep a man like you down. Show us the spirit that matches your ability and brains, and we'll bring you up, and you'll get a chance to go as high as your ability and record merit."

Eddie was happy with a mood like that of Victory, but only for an instant. Unsure and doubting thoughts seeped into this mood. The meaning of these thoughts was that he had made a mistake; and he knew that he had. For if he took this vacation, he was, in reality, pledging his word, and that was the same as a commitment of honor. And he would commit himself to giving his future and his time to Rawlinson.

He became a little lightheaded. He feared for his freedom, and that he needed, for his own future.

And yes, he had pledged his future to himself.

There was his mistake. It amounted to taking the wrong road, the road that went the other way.

No longer feeling lightheaded, he now verged on a fear that was close to helplessness and despair.

Mr. Wood had picked up a yellow pencil with an eraser on top, and was playing with scribbles and doodles on a scratch pad.

"You can take a two-week vacation, Ryan."

He couldn't do it. He didn't want to do it. He was sure, he knew, he was certain, that he must not do it. The pressure of urgency was demanding, and he must tell Mr. Wood.

"I think I'd better quit, Mr. Wood," Eddie blurted out.

He felt like a bastard, and wanted to get out of the office, quickly. But he knew he had to do it.

Mr. Wood gave Eddie a look of slow surprise.

"I'm convinced I need a change."

Eddie couldn't say any more; he was tied up in knots.

"But I don't understand you, Ryan."

And Eddie didn't know how he could really explain. He'd bargained his case, and was capable of the explanation, but he knew that he couldn't reach Mr. Wood's understanding.

He couldn't explain that his heart could not go into success. That's what it was.

All he could say was:

"I think I need a change."

There was a hiatus before Mr. Wood spoke, and Eddie felt strange in this silence of rising emotions.

"I've almost lost my faith in human nature," Mr. Wood quietly said, his voice dropping into dispiritedness.

There was nothing more to be said, it seemed. Eddie sat for a moment, feeling awkward about saying goodbye.

"If I need a reference, will you give me one, Mr. Wood," he then asked, with strained uncertainty.

"Of course, certainly. You deserve it. And good luck. I can only wish you good luck and success."

They shook hands and Eddie left.

Mr. Wood picked up a report on an attendant at a North Side station, who had been caught after having pocketed all the money at his station, claiming that he'd been held up.

"God, yes, what is human nature," he asked himself as he read.

II

There was a quality of newness for Eddie Ryan in the experience of quitting his job at Rawlinson O&R. This was one of the stimulants to a sense of exhilaration that he felt, riding on an eastbound 22nd Street trolley car. The car was more than half full of human dullness.

He was free.

Deacon and Howell and Mr. Wood, he was free of them. Reporting to work at 2 P.M., perhaps seeing a complaining expression on Corlin's face because of windows needing to be washed, or tops of cans to be polished, or something else that took up time—he was free.

He knew that he would have to get another job, but he had a hope that he could get one at National Oil of Illinois. Katy

The Silence of History

Dunne—she was about his third or fourth cousin—was married to a man named Phil Leeson, Superintendent of Maintenance at National. He never met Leeson, but he'd heard that he was a nice guy. Katy Dunne, before she married Phil Leeson, used to come to see them pretty often and once she'd stayed with them for about two months, when she'd been out of work. He hadn't seen her since he was a little fellow, but she used to like him then, and still must.

The trolley car stopped and started, stopped and started, and Eddie was impatient for the ride to end. If he read, the time would pass.

He knew he couldn't read.

Traffic, stores, vacant lots, people on the streets. He would catch flashes of a sadness of defeat and indignity, and he would have an upsurging sympathy for them. They were the victims of injustices which cause poverty, as his parents had been. Middle-aged women seemed so sad, and he felt the pathos of Time's thievery of the beauty of women.

But the sympathy and pity he felt were abstract, and his thoughts quickly turned inward, upon himself and his future.

Maybe he'd done a foolish thing, he reflected.

But he rejected this.

The trolley car had slowly emptied of passengers as they approached the elevated station between State Street and Wabash Avenue. He got off at the station.

Suddenly he decided to go downtown to the Crerar Library instead of going home.

It was symbolic, a kind of gesture, for himself and to himself.

He climbed the stairway for the downtown tracks.

Chapter Five

I

Eddie Ryan, by going to a library after his talk with Mr. Wood, was making a purely personal moral assertion. This was an act of faith on his part, following the rash risk which he had taken when he quit his job in such a seemingly offhand, casual, possibly stupid manner. In his own mind, this action was dramatic, but its importance to him was vital, fundamental, essential. His future, his hopes and dreams, the content of his life, were involved in what he had done. No one whom he knew could grasp the meaning of his conduct, except possibly George Raymond. He couldn't reason out and analyze for himself, in clear logic, the reasons why he had made the best, the right, and the only decision he could have made; and he saw his decision as one of Destiny.

The idea of Destiny was lodged at the core of his character. He knew the sufferings of brooding despondency, fits of despair, lonely moods of low confidence, when he feared that his ambitions were ridiculous and grandiloquent jokes, even delusions of grandeur. He drove himself as pitilessly as his will was strong over his body, his nerves, his appetite, over his entire being. With weak eyes behind his glasses, he thought he might be going blind, and feared blindness. But when this fear was active, the Tyranny of Time became even harsher in the conditions it imposed on him. If he were going to be blind, he must get more in than others, and get it in fast. He guzzled coffee, and stuffed aspirin into himself when his eyes were dry and burning with pain. He read and studied when tears streamed out of his strained eyes, and he could have moaned and wept in pity for himself. But he went on as long as he physically could bear the stabbing, sick pains, and the weary need for sleep.

Eddie didn't surrender to such thoughts of despair. He found emotional release in them, and he continued to use himself unsparingly. He was preparing to make his Destiny. The seeds of belief and conviction that he could do this were strong and tough in the sub-soil of his character. And he was getting close to knowing what that Destiny would be.

Eddie quit his job with Rawlinson Oil and Refining Company because he was close to knowing the direction he would take. His decision was made in the interest of his sense of Destiny.

Destiny and success are not equal to each other. A young man who has started to move in the direction where he will meet and contend with his Destiny is not a young man imbued with the ambition to become a success. Success can be won and lost many times. Or it can be gained and its fruits can be possessed for a lifetime, and unto many succeeding generations. But Destiny is not won and lost like a job, a fortune, a name or reputation. Destiny is a fate, to be lived with and to be fought. And Destiny in such a sense has a time schedule of eternity. The time that a Destiny lives is long, longer than the years in which man can sustain his weak mortality. The time for the flesh is all too short when the time of Destiny is eternity.

Thus it was with Edward Arthur Ryan, twenty-two years old, in July 1926. Quitting a job as filling-station attendant for the Rawlinson Oil and Refining Company was for him an event of such proportions that he would have been laughed at as a lunatic if he could have explained the meaning of his action.

What would he, and what could he, do with himself in the future? What would he make of his years before he became something? The meanings hung in these questions, and behind them. He grasped these meanings, and saw them sufficiently in the questions to know what he was contending with.

And thus, after Mr. Wood's fairness and concessions, Eddie had quit his job.

II

Eddie had worked a few days short of sixteen months with the Rawlinson Oil and Refining Company. During this period, he had become a good enough filling-station attendant. If he gave himself fully, in the spirit of George Babbitt, plus dear old Siwash, he could easily have become a hot shot, blazing a trail, showing, demonstrating, proving, and establishing beyond what was called peradventure of doubt, that he was doing everything the way everything ought to be done by one of those men-to-be-envied who were the subject of articles in *The American Magazine*. In other words, he could have climbed the ladder as the ladder should be climbed. And the fact was that he did do the things that counted in the record, and he did these well enough. The main achievement was to sell, especially motor oil. And before long he was sure of himself down under a car and unscrewing a crank case bolt, or shooting grease into the breaks. He'd heard so much about selling. George Raymond got good selling jobs, and his uncles Dick and Larry were salesmen, only Larry had good immunization against working. It didn't take Eddie ages without end before he learned that selling was easy enough, at least when you had something to sell which the public wanted. Motor oil was a necessary commodity. In any station you were bound to sell a certain quantity of it. By trying, asking every customer, and giving a sales argument when you got an opening, you sold more.

His experiences were sufficient to convince him that a lot of talk he'd heard about sales psychology was bunkum. By the time he read Sinclair Lewis' *Babbitt*, which was in September 1925, he was ripe for laughing at salesmen, and all the praise and build-up they got. *Babbitt* opened his mind to any number of details, phases, habits, manners and mannerisms, customs that were prevalent around him.

While he was reading *Babbitt*, he didn't want the book to end.

He'd taken two courses in history, Medieval History, and the History of the Post-Medieval World to the end of the seventeenth century. That was in the summer of 1925. In his neighborhood,

The Silence of History

just west of Washington Park, the University was unpopular, and some hated it. When he began attending the University, he became unpopular with a number of guys, and he even started receiving warnings to be careful lest he read too many books and go crazy. A few of the old women, and others as well, were convinced that the University was an A.P.A. institution, or, as the old women claimed, a place of the Devil.

He was little bothered by these revelations of ignorance and prejudice. That was the way some of the people were, and he saw why, in some cases at least. His grandmother, on his mother's side, for instance, was a peasant woman from the Irish Midlands, and she was illiterate, like his grandfather had been.

Eddie could see why others were the same way, for that was how he'd been. In high school, at St. Basil's, back in his senior year, a couple of the priests had advised him and the other fellows in his class against going to the University. He'd have been influenced not to go to the University if he'd had rich folks, and had been in a position to pick his alma mater back in 1923, when he'd graduated from St. Basil's. Opposition to him hadn't been so bad until he'd lost his religion last spring, and publicly said so, and had stopped going to Mass on Sundays. He'd become the talk of the neighborhood and there was still some talk about him, he guessed, but he heard about it only secondhand, and he should worry about what they said of him! Except for Dan O'Gorman and Louie Pearl, he didn't have much to do with any of the fellows in the neighborhood, and he hadn't had much to do with any of them during the last couple of years. He didn't hang around the corner of 58th Street and Prairie any more, but, at most, he'd stop for a few minutes on his way home at night, usually from work, or go to the Greek's Restaurant for coffee—and, and maybe he'd see some of the fellows.

Nothing would happen to him, and even if he were in danger, he'd have to face that music; but he was sure there wasn't any such music, and he was just as glad.

Hell, he didn't know how many cared, and probably it was damned few; life was changing and many people in his neighborhood were changing. And he, also, was changing. Life was change.

Life was whirl.

Eddie liked whirl better than change in this context. However, there was a wishful element in his preference for this word. That's what he sometimes thought he wanted—life as whirl.

It was new. Life was new for him. Each morning was new. It pushed out the light of a new day which he found rich in hopes, alive with dreams, and exciting with interesting expectations.

There were many days, in that period, when Eddie could not have said whether he was happy or unhappy, but often he knew that he was very unhappy, and that the world was full of sadness.

But life, with all of its sorrows and sadnesses, with the death of men, and the death of everything that Eddie came to accept, life and the world were also new, and the days were new. The world in which Eddie was living, and about which he was trying to learn, was new as well as sad.

III

It had begun to seem as though there were something Eddie had lost in memory, in that summer of 1925. Although he could have recalled the passing days of those months with such abundance of detail as to constitute a cluttering fullness of little things remembered, he had little to remember with pangs, with the faint pervasive sadness of beauties and joys known and gone, or with stronger emotions, the deep wounds of disappointments, or happiness, trouble, victory which is a landmark, a shining star of the heavens of one's life but gone into the unreachable as are the celestial stars. It was the kind of time sequence about which one says, "Nothing happened." This summary was not, however, accurate. Something did happen that summer.

He grew.

As Eddie grew, he began to think more about the world, the past, the present. He began to think about himself, and to see himself differently from the way he had before. He began to fill his mind with the stuffs of life, and to think about the quality of these stuffs. Areas of past time, which had been barren or but thinly populated and with few structures upon them, became expanding settlements. The world in which he lived inside of himself unfolded outward. There was a multiplying progression of meanings, not only in the many acquisitions of the story of history, but everywhere. There was more to feel and to feel about, and a greater thickness of emotion from day to day.

His life was endowed with purpose which was stretching to encompass everything, all of the world of time and history.

IV

At about eight-thirty, from Monday to Friday, Eddie left the apartment on South Park Avenue, where he lived with his grandmother, his aunt, two uncles, and his sister Clara, and, proudly carrying a black briefcase, he would enter Washington Park at 58th Street, to go across the park and out of it at 57th Street, for the walk to Cobb Hall on campus. He always had more books than he needed or could read in his briefcase, along with his big, black-covered, loose-leaf notebook.

No one morning was striking in its singularity in that summer quarter. And all the mornings were singular, for each in turn was emerged newness, and he was walking to where he would live, in his imagination, in the long centuries of yesterday. Purpose was strong, strongest, in the morning.

And Washington Park was the landscape of many associations, many memories, many dreams that never came true, many brooding boyhood sadnesses, many recollections of running, shouting boyhood play. Washington Park was nature to him, for Eddie was a city boy. It was the first frail green wonder of spring. It was summer and sunshine, and long nights of stars and trees become black shadows full of mystery. It was fall and turning leaves, with the glow of sad autumnal beauty. And it was winter when the withered grass lay dead over the crusted solidity of the hardened earth, and the air was full of noiseless, flying, falling snow.

From the parlor window, he'd looked at Washington Park at so many different hours, and in so many moods, and he'd seen the park in so many of its changes. His own moods were as one with the park.

And after the years of his growing up, he was walking in Washington Park, with the seeds of the rich green future growing in his mind.

Eddie had little time for dreams and idle thinking, but his morning walk across the park gave him an opportunity for a free play of mind, and for the flow of currents of consciousness on their own momentum. He would be expectant of the day's classroom lectures, and wasn't tempted to dally. The walk was a prelude to the day. The dew had not all evaporated and was sparkling, and sometimes colored drops would hang on blades of grass. The birds were nervous and singing in a sweetness of repetitions. It was all crisp and new-made, and the air sometimes seemed almost to be growing.

And Eddie had much to think about, more than he'd had a year or two ago, on more important subjects. He was particularly glad to be taking a course on the history of the Middle Ages. Those centuries seemed to him to have passed in slow time, and under a sun of the brightest yellow-gold, with the prayerful sounds of tolling Angelus bells, and of chanted Latin which expressed man's worship of God and his appeals before the Almighty's throne. And he thought of an atmosphere as still as eternity, and of moving changeless hours and days in which the silence was like the voicelessness of a whole world, lost in meditations of eternity where the silence of death becomes the silence of time and the silence of the soul in timelessness.

Eddie had other images of the Middle Ages, of the decline of Rome, and of an unnatural eerie darkness settling over Christendom and over the Eternal City. In 410 A.D. Alaric, King of the Visigoths, took Rome and sacked the Holy City. Of this he sometimes thought in the sense of great tragedy, the darkening of soul and hope, the end of a world, as though the light of the sun had gone dead, and the earth were a midnight. Augustine had written *The City of God* when the Eternal City of man, the majestic Rome of Caesar and Marcus Aurelius was dying, crumbling. History had given unto Caesar what was Caesar's due, the mortality of Caesar's work. Rome could fall, but in *The City of God*, "eternal life is the highest goal, and eternal death the highest evil," and for those who gained eternal life, there would be life without end in *The City of God*. Christianity, the Church, had saved mankind, and he could feel great pride, because he was a Christian, and a Catholic. The University wouldn't destroy his faith, and his friends and the neighbors need not concern themselves about that.

But could he gain eternal life in the City of God?

Questions such as this one shrank him from within whenever they occurred in the course of any reflections about Rome, Augustine, the Middle Ages.

He was small against the scenery of history, and why should he dare to dream that he could be big?

He must dare to dream.

But no matter how he dreamed, and how tall he might grow into bigness, wasn't this life but a trial? And what would the profit be if he should lose his immortal soul and life eternal in the Eternal City of God?

Eddie would manage to push the menacing uncertainties and danger of Hell from his mind.

He was alive, yet, wasn't he? And healthy. Wasn't he? Why couldn't he save his soul?

Look at Constantine the Great. He had finally accepted the faith and was baptized when he was at the point of death.

Eddie Ryan, carrying his black briefcase which was packed with books and notebooks, a student with life and death and past and present and future in his mind, and with other thoughts and hopes and dreams of a girl, a beautiful girl, of fame and faith in the future, walked through Washington Park, absorbing many passing details of the summer days that were one-by-one going by.

V

To be young and in the midst of a crowd of young people who are talking and jabbering, and to see pretty girls in clean, brightly colored summer dresses, this is to feel with poignancy the pathos of youth.

Eddie felt that pathos of youth.

The scene was the sidewalk before the entrance to Cobb Hall.

As a class hour approached, a crowd of students gathered. After coming out of Washington Park on the Cottage Grove Avenue side, Eddie usually picked up his pace. The street, with odd-looking flat buildings, was depressing, not conducive to thinking and dreaming as he'd done in the park. The campus was nearby, and the time for his nine-o'clock class close at hand. He would stride along. There would be other students on the sidewalk, and people bound for work. He wanted to join the crowd in front of Cobb Hall. He might meet someone, a new friend. He might meet a girl. This was his real hope, his reason for more haste.

While he studied at the U that summer, and on through almost half of the regular school quarter, Eddie aspired after a social life. He hoped to be bid by a good fraternity, and to participate in campus social activities, dating girls who were popular and who rated, until from among them he would find one with whom he'd fall in love, and in return find love. There were many remnants of his high school fraternity attitudes, and of the journalistically inspired jazz age and revolt-of-youth notions in his dreams of the college days that he would live and enjoy. And he imagined that by becoming a college student at the U, his social status would rise, and thus he'd become a more important person. When he matriculated, he read the syndicated columns, such as Arthur Brisbane's, as though these were nuggets of the wisdom of life, philosophy. Brisbane was famous, a powerful journalist with a national following, who made short-sentence, brief-paragraph profundities of platitudes about life, experience, and many other topics, including the Florida real estate boom. He had a way of making a commonplace have the sound of wisdom, as though his mind were familiar with all of the ages of mankind. Eddie also read the *Four Minute Essays* of Dr. Frank Crane which his Uncle Dick had bought in a set of small brown-covered books that fit exactly into a pocket, and that a man could carry without revealing that he had a book in his possession. And Dr. Crane wrote with brevity and inspirational punch.

It was necessary to look to the world, and to find in it the voices of those who knew the world, and could speak with the authority of their knowing. Their authority was a form of proof

The Silence of History

of the worth and the truth of the struggle for success which a young man such as himself would have to make if he determined to become somebody.

Eddie didn't know the world, and most of what he believed to be truth required acceptance on faith. When he'd been twenty and had read the newspaper column of Arthur Brisbane and the *Four Minute Essays* of Dr. Frank Crane, he was not only sustaining his faith but finding, in their words, what amounted to evidence that faith in himself and in his chance to succeed was true, true in the sense of being possible.

Some of his assumptions and expectations about campus life had been glimmered from newspapers, and when he'd begun college, Eddie applied to himself thoughts and notions that he'd read about student life, as well as about working one's way through college as a means of becoming a success, and the certainty of getting what you sought if you applied yourself and had ambition and faith.

The Eddie Ryan who stood in the crowd of students before Cobb Hall on those sunny mornings while the last of June passed into the beginning of July, holding his stuffed black briefcase, peering about nervously, as though he were clutching at faces instead of seeing them with his weak eyes, this young man was full of simple faith and simple beliefs. He believed in truth. His mind was open to accept truth, all of the truth that it could find to grasp. He wanted to know the truth, but he saw knowledge as something to be learned in books, not as what he would find out and learn by asking questions and seeing everything anew in the relationship to questions which, when posed, were challenging, and dealt with new and unsolved problems rather than with what was already settled. He had no desire to be unconventional, or to isolate himself from others because he would study and learn. He was not a young rebel, nor did he harbor any notions whatever that he would have to be a rebel. He wanted to like people and to be liked by them. He wanted to learn and to succeed. And he wanted to be respected for succeeding and for the manner in which he was trying to make something of himself, by working his way through college.

He stood alone, usually, in the crowd on those sunny summer mornings. Wanting to speak to other students, he was reticent. He could never predict when he would or wouldn't be shy in speaking to strangers of his own generation, and most frequently he couldn't speak. Often, Eddie didn't know if the compression of silence which affected him was shyness or was caused by the fact that he couldn't think of what to say, possibly because he knew so little psychology.

The wait in front of Cobb Hall was always brief. He had the class hour to look forward to, and Mr. Kraft's lectures were very good. The class period passed with imperceptible haste, and the buzz of the bell in the hallway was a surprise; several times, he'd had difficulty in convincing himself that it hadn't rung ahead of time. He'd come out for the few minutes of waiting between classes, hoping he'd talk to someone interesting, make a friend, strike up a conversation with one of the good-looking girls in class. There were at least six.

He wasn't making any friends, and he'd not progressed an inch toward knowing some beautiful coed, but it was the summer quarter. Many of the students were older than average, school-teachers who came only for the summer session, and he might have to wait until the fall quarter. The fraternities rented out their houses, and the majority of regular students weren't on campus. Eddie was looking forward to the fall quarter. Then he'd meet some fellows, be bid to a frat, and once that happened, he ought to have plenty of chances of meeting popular coeds, and dating a few who were eye-catchers. He'd been a Catholic League athletic star. The fraternities ought to want him. If the summer quarter were a social failure, that couldn't signify much.

And yet, for those few minutes in the morning, Eddie would usually stand alone, trying to be nonchalant and to look nonchalant, wanting to appear blasé to anyone who noticed him, and seeking, among the crowd of healthy-looking students, the face of at least one new friend, or the radiance of one girl's beauty that he could know with pride and justification was for him, and only for him.

But he found neither a friend nor a radiant girl.

VI

In the classroom, they could hear the steam shovel and other sounds of construction work from across the street, where a new building in the University building program was to go up. It was to be a hospital, the Billings Hospital or Billings Memorial Hospital, Eddie believed. The noise could be more than disturbing because it jarred the nerves, and the mechanical screeching and grinding was as inhuman as it was unusual. Sometimes Professor Kraft banged the window closed, and Mr. Thornton, who had the ten-o'clock class, was distracted and often looked to the window, or walked over and closed it. One morning Mr. Thornton, a thin young man with receding brown hair, closed the window and said:

"The machinery causing such a racket, thank goodness, wasn't invented by Leonardo da Vinci."

Some of the class tittered.

Both classes were large, with enrollments of about fifty or sixty. Instead of desks, there were chairs with an attached arm serving as a desk, and the great majority of the students had notebooks but none took as many notes as did Eddie. He sat in the last row on the right, bent down, often writing fast as the lecture proceeded, making an effort of concentration in order to keep listening to what was said while he wrote. Eddie didn't trust himself to remember, and he not only took notes of the classroom lectures, but also of the assignments he read nightly in the textbook. He was the busiest student in the class.

VII

After Professor Kraft's nine-o'clock class, Eddie went outside, and stood for a few minutes among the crowd before Cobb Hall. There was the reflex of hope that he'd meet someone, that he'd meet a girl. But his mind wasn't on this hope, but was rather fixed in its own thoughts and in remembered parts of the lecture.

Eddie was foggy with thoughts, and he had an absent-minded, bewildered look on his face of which he was not conscious. Rome, and the darkness in the mind of men when she fell, and Augustine, and Charlemagne, and the Holy Roman Empire, the excitement of learning, and the future he had to look forward to, when he would learn so much, when he would know things, and when some day he could write and teach and be a lawyer, too, and fill up every minute of his life usefully, and come to feel like . . . His flow of thoughts became like a bed of dry sand.

The bell buzzed, and he went back into the same classroom and the same seat for his next class.

The ten-o'clock class was about as large as the nine-o'clock one, but Eddie was the only student taking both. The instructor, Mr. Thornton, was in his thirties, and taught at a small college in Michigan; he was giving the course at the University for the summer quarter only. He had a habit of beginning or ending his lectures with a question to the class, or of interrupting in the course of his lecture to ask a question. After one or two students had answered, Mr. Thornton would resume lecturing, and give his own answer to the question he had posed. In this manner he was constantly helping the students to bring the material of the lectures and their reading into focus, to relate it to problems, and to keep alive what they were learning.

Mr. Thornton had asked:

"Was the Renaissance anti-traditional?"

"Did it overthrow the ideas of the Middle Ages?"

"Was the Reformation a movement for political liberty?"

"Did Martin Luther believe in freedom?"

"Did Calvin want men free?"

"Was Machiavelli a Machiavellian in the sense in which the word has come to be used in our own era?"

These and other questions brought to Eddie's mind ideas which he hadn't thought about, but he was beginning to understand that you had to do more than find out the answers to questions if you wanted to learn. That was what he had thought when he'd started taking these two history classes. He was also getting more confident, because when Mr. Thornton asked questions, Eddie found that thoughts came to him and that he could say something in response to these questions.

The Silence of History

Both of his teachers seemed to know so much, and every lecture had given him something that was eye-opening.

Instead of a question, Mr. Thornton began the lecture that morning with a quotation.

Immortal God! What a world I see dawning. Why can I not grow young again?

"That is a translation of something written in 1517 by Erasmus, Desiderius Erasmus, who was born in Rotterdam in 1466, and who, then, was fifty-one when he wrote what I have just quoted. He lived on almost twenty years more, and died in 1536. He did not find what none can, the Fountain of Eternal Youth, the quest for which sent Ponce de León across the ocean to what is now Florida.

"But the Renaissance, as I believe we have already emphasized, was like a new youth for men. That's how it derived its name, Renaissance—Re-birth."

Eddie left the classroom at the end of the period, inspired, divided in mind, trying to think, and lonely. He didn't know whether the Middle Ages and the Renaissance hung together, with one developing into the other, or were in sharp contradiction. He was fearful that they contradicted one another as historical periods and that he believed in the Renaissance. At moments he thought that he might be starting to think in opposition to the Church; he didn't know how far that could go, once you began to veer from the Church. Eddie suspected he had really begun to veer from the Church. And once started, where would the stopping be? But mostly he felt secure in his faith, and proud of it.

Eddie was more moody because, with classes for the day finished, he felt let down and lonely. Now, he'd walk back home, study or read or try to write, have lunch, of course, and work against the clock and the glum feelings with which he left for work. On campus, he could forget so much, and be so far away from the rest of his life and his past. But then, he had to go back. And the campus was so peaceful and remote that he could be in a university in the Middle Ages. The gray Gothic buildings and towers, the grass, cut and fresh with healthy greenness, the quiet, all this was so far removed from the depressing and rackety-rack-rack noises of his neighborhood, in which dullness had become like seediness.

And a loneliness, like impenetrable but unseen space, invaded his mind and he had a sense of himself as a living being who stood imprisoned in a land of the dead.

He stood among the crowd of students in front of Cobb Hall. They seemed to know only lightheartedness, laughter, and facile gaiety.

He thought of himself as different. He couldn't be as they were. In later years, he'd show them. They'd hear of him. They'd know of him. In years to come, he'd win the only way he could, by giving all he had to the great, big, giantlike, real-looking, terribly real will-o'-the-wisp he was chasing.

The chimes were tolling, ringing with a lightness like bells, a slow and solemn sighing of the notes of *Nearer, My God, to Thee*. He walked around Cobb Hall to Ellis, on to 57th Street, and then went to Cottage Grove Avenue.

And Erasmus had asked why he couldn't grow young again.

He was young. But what world was dawning, what time was being reborn? Back in high school, Marcus Hopper, an old man with silver hair and a silvery mustache that must have been curled with a curling iron, had looked out of the window at a gray winter day and said:

"That's true of all of us—of all men."

Marcus Hopper, a layman hired to teach them third year English, was dead now. He'd been reflecting aloud on four lines of Shelley which had been printed in the English textbook, and which they'd been studying:

> *We look before and after*
> *And pine for what is not:*
> *Our sincerest laughter*
> *With some pain is fraught.*

Chapter Six

He had slowly walked home through Washington Park, perspiring from the increasing weight of the day's heat, his mind in a meandering melancholy, with the thought of death a dark cloud which his mood pushed forward, a waving, shadow over the dark stream of his crazily wandering melancholy.

Eddie saw several people, and noticed them but casually. Seven, eight, nine rowboats were on the lagoon. A couple; a nursemaid, dense of face and with a thin line of ugly mustache on her upper lip; a golden-haired girl of two, three, he didn't know what age, running ahead of the nursemaid, returning to her with giggles; a little old man with a limp; a broadly built middle-aged woman wearing a dark straw hat with beads above the black band, and fortressed in a blue calico dress with large white flowers evenly patterned on it; a little old woman with a man's hat, who mumbled to herself; a man off to the right with a big collie on a chain; two barefoot kids, one with freckles; a neat man, fat and silver-haired, with the suggestion of calm written on his face; and a very tall man, so lean as to be funny, wearing a stained suit, and smoking a stogy with a manner subtly ostentatious—Eddie noticed these people. Each one of them was full of a remembered life and he knew nothing of it. He'd like to. A University student, he was separated from them, different, becoming educated. He wanted to be looked up to by people, but wasn't that high hat? He'd show them—not those people, but only fellows around 58th Street, and snobs, and girls who'd laughed at him and turned him down, and anyone who hadn't believed in him. And then what?

They'd talk about him, admire him, envy him. Every name mentioned in class today was of someone dead. The immortal dead, Nietzsche, the immortal sainted dead, Saint Augustine, and he was young. Erasmus at fifty-one had wanted to be young again. He was getting along, so why worry, Eddie Ryan?

"You back, son?" his grandmother called.

"Yes, Mother."

She was alone now. They were all gone. That was better. Uncle Larry sometimes sounded off about his curling up in a chair or for some reason that didn't matter. With Uncle Dick he couldn't say much, and the silence was a strain. Aunt Jenny blew up, and then she could go the square root of six ways plus to raise hell.

But coming home when they were all out but Mother, his grandmother, he could expect a few hours' peace until he left for the station. He didn't mind if his sister Clara were there.

He went to his bedroom off the dark hallway of the eight-room apartment, dropped his briefcase on the floor, and sat on the bed.

The bedroom was also dark, in shadow, because the window looked out across five feet of courtway at the side wall of Mrs. Nolan's apartment building.

It had been Eddie's room since May 1917, when they'd moved into this flat, but he always slept in the front bedroom when both of his uncles were away on the road. Eddie's disorderly and careless habits with things were apparent from the state of the room, with books stacked on the mantelpiece, a small desk by the window stuffed with papers and letters, and the closet cluttered up.

About fifteen or twenty minutes after he'd gotten home, his grandmother had lunch ready for him, pork chops, mashed potatoes, apple sauce, bread and butter, a cup cake and coffee. Eddie sat down at the kitchen table and began eating, without speaking to his grandmother. He was hungry. After his meal, he'd have a couple of hours for study and reading. As a consequence of the morning's lectures, he could only think of how much he

The Silence of History

didn't know, of how much reading, beyond what he was assigned in his classes, he must do.

His grandmother was little, and weighed perhaps one hundred pounds, with an almost beaked nose, small gray eyes, and brown hair in which there were but a few streaks of gray. She was wiry and strong for her size. She had forgotten how old she was, but she had come to the United States about sixty-one years ago, an Irish peasant girl of fifteen or sixteen, after six weeks on a sea which the Devil Himself had shaken something fierce. She was probably around seventy-seven years old.

"Son, you like your pork chops?"

"Yes, Mother."

Eddie had first cut all the meat off the bone, a habit he persisted in, and he was eating fast, another firmly acquired habit of his.

"I shunted down the steps, out of the alley, and over 58th Street to Mr. Katz's store, ah, he's a nice man, and I told his butcher, Mr. Herman, that I wanted pork chops for me grandson, not me daughter or the servant. He knew what I meant, indeed he did. Do you like your lunch, Edward, son?"

"Yes, Mother."

"Let anyone ever dare say I ain't given you enough food! Let 'em!"

Eddie smiled with amusement, affectionately. He finished his meal, and gulped the last of the coffee in his cup.

"Can I get you more, son?"

"Just coffee, Mother."

As she came toward him, he watched her, noticing that she walked firmly, that she had sagging breasts beneath her old polka-dot calico dress with a fading, almost indigo blue background, but he knew this anyway, and he noticed her wrinkled neck, the skin of her long face, which vaguely suggested parchment, and her talon-like hands with their long fingernails. Her fingernails were like claws.

She got his cup, and went, straight-backed, to the stove.

Eddie saw sadness in every movement of his grandmother's as she returned to the stove to get him more coffee, but this emotion was his, not the old lady's. She was happy in the moments for which she had waited out the morning. What a strong, fine, decent boy he was, growing into a man, and the way he was, was her doing.

Ah, and time was like the shake of a lamb's tail, no more than a good shake and he was a big, grown man instead of the little fellow who used to be so cute, and such a smart, nice, good little one. Could she ever forget?

She returned with the second cup of coffee, peering at him closely over the gold-rimmed eyeglasses which she had put on and pulled down forward toward the center of her nose. Ah, and the fine grandson he was, the fine boy, and as innocent as the day was long and as he was when he was a little fellow in white stockings, with beautiful long curls. And if that George Raymond stayed away wherever he was with the Devil Himself, her grandson, her son would stay innocent as the day was long.

"There you are, a cup of coffee, son."

Eddie thanked her, while she stood for a moment, hands on hips, studying him with an ache of loss for all those years, gone like the shake of a lamb's tail.

She saw Eddie in his first year, at three, four, and five years of age, but only in her mind's eye. There he was a young man, and time had gone by, whiffing by in a jiffy since Edward was a little fellow, a baby.

Ah, and there he was, she thought, turning away from the kitchen, a scholar, who could out-scholar the scholar, and she, herself, she had come to the latter ends of her days. 'Twouldn't be long before she'd be under six feet of ground in Calvary Cemetery, alongside of her man, Joseph, gone these many years, may the Lord have mercy on his soul.

And these days, she did be thinking that going out to her six feet of earth would be good, but for leaving her son, Richard, and her grandson, with none to be watching out after them as she could, and she the only one that could, and what else was there to be keeping her here on this poor Godforsaken crust of earth? What, yes indeed, what?

She often did be feeling and thinking this and such things as these, and whenever the Good Lord called her, she was ready to meet the Good Man. Such thoughts had been lurking in her

The Silence of History

mind even before Eddie got back home from being with the scholars at the school. Sure it was when there were mornings like today that thoughts were put into one's head, the Devil or the Lord, the white angel on your right or the dark angel on your left-hand side; if not one, another was sure to be putting something into one's head.

"Such a nice day, son," she exclaimed.

There was God's good sun shining in the sky, and it warmed your old bones, it warmed man, bird, and beast, and pierced all the way through your clothes, right to your pelt. And it was an old pelt, hers. A day 'twas to be running through the fields and the bush, picking flowers, and putting a flower in your hair to make the gossoons be looking at you, and not at Nelly Doosey or Katy with the peg-leg father, and with a rose in her hair and her head high with that rose in her hair, she'd turn a man face to the wall against Katy with that wooden-legged tinker of a father and that other one, what in the name of God was her name, Deasy, that Daisy, Leasy Doosey, she'd had eyes for Pa, all eyes. It's blind she might as well have been. And all for what was it? And all to come to the latter end of one's days, as she had come to the latter end of her own days, and to have the men throw the dirt over you when you are put down six feet under the ground.

All was the Will of God, and He was a Good Man.

And fine day it was, fine day indeed.

Eddie was impatient, but not by will or desire. For he was pulled a bit in opposite directions. Impatience was imposed upon him. Its source was within himself, but the cause, the spark which lit the source, was everywhere and nowhere; it was time. But no, that wasn't true. Time was everywhere. No, it wasn't. It was the shadows of the sun. If time were the shadows of the sun, these shadows were also ghostly shadows, reminding of death. They were shadows where the witches or gnomes, or the devils, could dance.

"I'm goin' into me room, son, and if you're wantin' something, call me."

"Yes, Mother."

Eddie left the kitchen quickly, and with his conscience blown clear. She didn't want to talk.

He'd been getting a bad conscience because he often didn't want to talk either, and he would ignore her, thinking his own thoughts, dreaming, studying, trying to write something on the big secondhand typewriter that he'd bought last March. They might not have her much longer. She was old, he didn't know how old, but old, nearly eighty, he guessed, and she must have many thoughts of death. He was afraid that he might ignore her, put off giving her any attention, and when he'd go out, to work, to a show, anywhere, maybe on a date, he might come back home and find out that she was dead. But he had to study, didn't he?

He had chosen *The Holy Roman Empire*, and Lord Bryce's book was big, over 500 pages, besides the notes at the back. He was a slow reader, he thought. Each book he read added five or ten or more to those he already felt he must read. Each class ended with additional books going on the unread list he kept in his head. He measured his reading speed by the swelling library of books he wanted to get to. One book was a mere grain of sand, a cupful of ocean water. How could he have time for all the grains of sand on the beach? How could he drink Lake Michigan dry, cup by cup?

However, once he got into a book and lost himself in enjoying it, or in studying, which was also enjoying himself, he didn't have such thoughts. That was something he was noticing about himself.

And in a few moments, he had lost himself in Lord Bryce's book, Eddie's mind began to play upon the descriptions, the facts, the thoughts of Lord Bryce. These were all enlarged, enlivened, embodied with feeling. Centuries gone, ages gone, dark-clouded yesterdays, time, men, deeds, cities, buildings, houses, ages of darkness in a sealed midnight of time that made a thick opaque blackness grow alive upon the stage of his mind, and that lived again for seconds or minutes.

The Dark Ages of the fifth century to the time of Charles, Charlemagne, the Emperor Charlemagne, changed from dark to shadowed darkness, and the journey of Charlemagne was like one into sunshine.

The crowning of Charlemagne in Rome, by Pope Leo III,

had been like the promise of happiness without end. But it had ended.

Eddie went on reading, feeling a heavy sadness about history, and almost tasting the loveliness of the summer day which came in through the window full of promise and of wishes to be fulfilled.

Chapter Seven

I

Grace Hogan came out to America in the year 1864. She was sixteen years old, and illiterate.

Grace had heard one thing or another thing said of America. In America, it was rich, they said.

And rich, to Grace, meant like Mr. Gordon, the landlord. And a fine gentleman he was, too. He rode to the foxes with the hounds, and what a sight that was for a person's eyes to behold. The way they would go leppin' over the fences on their fine horses, and the dogs, and fierce ones they could be, sure the poor fox would have to be foxy, indeed, to escape away with life and limb. And the coats, and the hats, and the boots of the gentlemen, and Mr. Gordon was the gentlemen of them all. It was acres and acres of land that he owned, sure and you see it all, there was so many acres and acres.

Rich, to Grace, meant a man's station in life, more than the money, but she well knew that to be a gentleman and rich a man must have money. Mr. Gordon did, indeed, and didn't he live like a king, in a big house fit for a king? But the likes of her and her sister, Bridie, who was two years older than she, herself, sure and how in the name of God could they ever expect to be rich? If it was English she was, or half-English, and not all Irish, God bless her father and her mother, and wasn't she often wishing herself that she could be half-English? Then she could play a lady, and the lady she would play, in fine clothes, and she'd say nary the word to the tinkers and the paupers, Jesus, Mary, and

The Silence of History

Joseph, *In the name of the Father*, the Good Man, Himself, let her be the lady in clothes fit for Mr. Gordon, and sure as the night follows the day, it's the lady she would be.

Gracie Hogan was the spit and image of her father, Timmy, 'twas said, and it was a good thing, the people said, indeed, that she hadn't been born a boy, because if the Lord had made her a boy instead of a girl, she would have been running her father, Timmy Hogan, more than his own flesh-and-blood sister, the widow May Bantry, ran that good man, and that was the truth, the truth indeed.

Little Gracie had had the deviltry in her, and it would be coming out if any other girl showed signs of thinking she was equal to or better than the Hogans.

When she was nine years old, the McNamara boy, Peter McNamara, cast slurs upon her own father, and she had scratched his face until the blood flowed, and Peter McNamara, two years older than little Gracie, turned tail and ran away from her, and he was screaming bloody murder, and the blood was streaming down his face, and there was she, herself, racing after him in her bare feet, chasing him to catch him, and to tear the flesh itself off of his face, if she could. That she would have done, but for that she was after falling in the field. Many times, a few, 'pon her word, she had beaten Peter in running races, and she was a swift one, swift as a deer, and she could run like the wind, she could, and that was the truth, even Father Corkerry, his reverence himself, had said that she could, and them were his very words.

—And it's saying it, I am, that Timmy Hogan's young one, she can run like the wind, it's fast as the wind that little Gracie is.

"Let me get these hands on that Peter McNamara," she had told Bridie.

And she had held up her hands, and her fingernails, sharp they were, sharp enough to scratch the Devil Himself, she was always liking to think, and to believe it to be the truth, indeed.

"Ah, sure, it ain't worth it, Gracie darlin'," Bridie had said, trying to calm Gracie down.

"I'll dig me nails into his flesh if I get me hands on him, Bridie."

Little Gracie had not acted in simple and uncontrolled anger.

She had been hurt. That was why she had become a nine-year-old fury. Peter McNamara's offense had been to speak against her father, such a good man.

The two barefoot, freckle-faced girls, nine and eleven years old, sat in front of the thatched hut that was home for the Hogans. The day was growing gray into the softness of a summer night.

"Sure and Bridie, look at how big God made the sky."

"Bigger 'tis than where the wild geese could fly."

"It's only the angels that can be flying to where the sky 'tis big."

"If I could fly like a bird, and me wings would carry me way up far, up there, Gracie, wouldn't I be hungry, and what would I do with nothin' in me stomach 'til I could fly way back here. Sure I'd starve with nothin' in me stomach."

"With me good feet to carry me on the ground, it's not for me to be needin' to be flyin' with wings way up where only the angels can fly to," Gracie said. "Ah, Bridie, look how big it is. Sure, and did God make the sky to be bigger than the world?"

"It could be as big as God, Gracie."

The little girls looked up with bigness of wonder in their eyes.

A dog barked from not too far off. The sounds of other animals carried in the darkening air.

From inside the hut, there came talk of their parents and their aunt, the Bantry one.

They looked at the sky in the hush of the twilight, drifting in upon all of Ireland that they could see and hear. They could feel it getting damp.

II

When little Gracie Hogan saw Peter McNamara again, she didn't carry through with her threat to attack him. To the contrary, Gracie smiled and talked to him, much as she did to anyone with whom she passed the time of day.

People were always after saying she looked like her father, and was the spit and image of him. Her mother she loved, and wasn't that what Father Corkerry was always after saying that a-one must a-one's mother? And God willed it. But her father—she

The Silence of History

looked like him. And was she proud! Indeed, that was why she would have torn the skin off of the face of Peter McNamara, why she would have, and scratched his eyes out because he spoke against her own father.

And when her own father heard tell the story of what she'd done, and what did Timmy Hogan do but take her up on his lap and hold her, petting her and telling her that she was needing a blue ribbon in her hair, and him petting her and kissing her cheek now and again. And sure she didn't mind the queer, strong smell on his breath. Wasn't he a good man and the best man in all of the world as far as Wicklow, Wexford, Dublin, Limerick, and Kerry?

She heard tell from the men talking, and the women talking, too, that they would be stealing sheep just as if sheep didn't cost a pence, not speaking of pounds. And America, which they said was the biggest country in the world and everybody rich as the Queen of England, and sure, wasn't she always going and forgetting the name of the Queen of England?

Timmy Hogan was called a good man, and good he was, "good enough," he said, to be hoping that when the Archangel Gabriel blew his trumpet loud enough to be heard all the wide way around the wide world, he would have Father Moline to his right, and Father Jackboy McGee to his left, but sober, and Father This, That and Henry as well as Tom, Dick and a Cardinal, and he would slip into Heaven, unbeknownst, maybe, even to himself.

There was a striking resemblance between Timmy Hogan and Gracie, especially in the similarity of their beaked, birdlike noses. Timmy Hogan was a very small man, and almost but not quite insignificant to look at; however, he was big-boned for his size. In later years, Gracie was much the same. And a tapering of hands, with proportionately long fingers, was another common characteristic.

Too many mouths to feed, and too little to feed them with, that's the same problem for many a man in many a place. That was Timmy Hogan's problem. Besides himself, Timmy Hogan had five mouths to feed, and the few acres he had as a tenant farmer did not yield largess and bounty. He was a poor man in a poor country, and he worked as do the poor. In his home, he had his wife, her older sister, Maggie Brenna, his son Paddy, and the two girls. Pneumonia had taken off a second son, Lawrence, not so many years after the Famine.

—If the pneumonia didn't take him, the hunger or America would, it's the Will of God, Maggie, his sister-in-law, had said.

—You say the truth, Maggie, Timmy had said.

To Timmy Hogan, the Will of God was just and mighty; the will of man was pitiful and weak. This was truth and fact in Timmy Hogan's life. Timmy could neither read nor write. What he knew of the world, beyond his own time and place, was what he had heard told. He knew a thing or two, and maybe more about this and that, about the things that he did know something about, or had heard tell of.

And there was a great variety of details and beliefs, superstitions, animals, birds, fowl, and one thing and another. But he was just a poor man. He knew an infinite amount of little details concerning the world of his sight; the lay of the ground; the lumps of land; the holes; the stony roads; fences; huts; chimneys; trees and bushes; the potato plants coming up out of the earth each year; the road to Mullirgar; the road to Athlone, with the steeple of Athlone in its infinite variety of changing shadows of clouds, and its changing glares and its deeper shadows when the sun was hidden like a priest sneaking off of a Sunday morning before he says Holy Mass; the raggedy pride of his neighbors and their boys; the purple-red line which made the nose of Richard Brown a sight to behold, and 'twas a sight to make a man laugh, the way Richard Brown's nose it sailed and struck; the song and sound of the creatures of the field, bird and beast and fowl that had been here in County Westmeath and in Ireland when Ireland was full of heather, and that would be in Ireland when Timothy Hogan, none less than himself, would be where all of the Hogans, who came before the Hogans who came after them, God have mercy on their souls, were all at rest. Their bones were asleep, sleeping in the quiet of the dead. No scholars, no gentlemen, and no gobeen men either, had there been in the Hogans before him, none that he had heard tell of. They had been of God's poor.

The Silence of History

But many a man was worse off than Timmy Hogan, and not the worst of men was he, or the best of men. He knew that the world was full of wonders that God had made to behold, the wonders in the West, and in the East, and in the North, and to the South, and the Will of God was not for the fathoming of the likes of him, or the likes of any man, be he prince or a pauper.

But while Timmy Hogan often thought like this, it was the truth, indeed, Timmy Hogan also had his many other thoughts and his dreams. He thought often enough of the Lord, but more frequently his mind was on the land. He dreamed of it, of owning land himself, and in freehold. If his dreams could still his knowing what was what, and the black despair which was in a dark basement of his soul, then Timmy would believe that he could one day, maybe, own land. Timmy's usual thoughts of the land were those that escaped from the cellar of his soul, black with despair.

Timmy Hogan believed that he had drunk a big cup of bitterness. And he could remember, 'twas well he could do that. Could a man ever forget the year of the Big Famine, with people dying like leaves falling off a tree when the cold autumn days are chasing after the summer that's gone? Ah, and hadn't he seen them dropping, and dying like starved dogs in the field. A man could well have thought that the Devil, Himself, had come from Hell to Ireland, to stay an immigrant, an immigrant bedamned, like an invading Englishman of the likes of Oliver Cromwell.

And could he forget the death of his son, Lawrence? With the world still as death, and with nary a whisper of the wind, and himself, standing alone, with his eyes like nailed upon the poor dead little boy, lying there in the shadows on the bed in a corner? The bed of woman's sins and sorrows, it 'twas. His own son, Lawrence Hogan, and it was like an angel asleep he looked.

But he was dead.

No, he never could forget the stillness in the cottage, and the stillness outside, and the stillness of the world. It was the stillness of death, it 'twas, like a spirit that had filled all of everywhere in the world.

Timmy Hogan had been stricken into dumb sorrow. It had been like being numbed with cold; it had been the numbing of

Time by the shade of death. Death like a silent spirit had stolen inside of him, and his heart was frozen stone cold. He was struck stiff, and could have been turned to stone, just there on the spot where he stood by the bed. His heart could have stopped beating. He could have stopped breathing. Yes, he could have turned into stone.

And he knelt down and prayed to the Blessed Virgin Mary. And he blessed himself as he got up off of his knees. He went outside, and his heart was heavy with the black sorrow of living, and he was full of the dark side of life.

There was somberness in the soul of Timmy Hogan.

And something of a like somberness his daughter, Little Gracie, seemed to have absorbed. It was not only in her father, but in the atmosphere of her life. And that was a social atmosphere, in which melancholy, somberness, unseen and unnamed, were of invisible substance.

It was the social atmosphere of a world well-populated with the unseen, alive with a life behind the life everyone led. Powers and mysteries, bones and spirits, God and the Devil, himself, angels of the Lord and devils who were the spawn of Satan and of Hell, the little people, ghosts of the dead departed, there was a nameless hovering in this world behind the world everyone lived in. It was in the air, it was behind the sky, it was hidden in the night. It was the subject of common talk, also, the invisible world.

Timmy Hogan had been born into this world, and so had his wife, and so had most of the people he knew. Gracie and Bridie, in turn, had come into this same world. They were growing through childhood in it. The visible and the invisible were, in many instances, equally real, and in some cases the invisible world was regarded as more real than the visible.

Life, in much of the visible and immediate part of Timmy Hogan's Irish world was mean and hard for most of the people. The anger and the hatred of the ignorant was cut deeply into their beings. A smoldering emotion slumbered in them, but it could awaken in meanness at any time. Most of the people in the small village were illiterate. They had a great curiosity about the wonders of the world to behold, but they feared their own

The Silence of History

curiosity. Servility had been dug into them, as it had been into their fathers and mothers, and it had seeded them with feelings and emotions that they could only hate in blind misunderstanding. Strongly clannish, they were as friendly to as they were suspicious of strangers, and many among them were great ones for talking. Sometimes, talk was more intoxicating than ale, and with the gab they could make themselves grow bigger than they were, and in a bigger world. Their suspicion was linked with their wonder of the world; they were more driven to know the truth of life without realizing what they needed.

"You say the truth."

"You don't say?"

These expressions were so commonly used that they had become traditional speech habits. Other sentences had also become habitual because the people needed to know; but they didn't know what knowing of the far-off was, or what the truth was about the world where there were foreign people and strange things. Liverpool and London, and Van Diemen's Land at the bottom of the world, which they heard tell was round, and Boston and New York and other places to which some of their own, their neighbors or some whom they heard tell of had gone out to. Letters and money came back from the wild geese. There was work to be had and money to be earned in these places; they must be better than Ireland, except, of course, Van Diemen's Land where the British sent the men in chains as felons.

All this made for much talk, and letters were read and reread, and many would say that they were growing up to go out to America.

Grace did not say that she'd be going out to America, but the thought came to her mind now and again. And she would suddenly be asking herself:

—And what if I do be goin' out?

Ah, she didn't want to be leaving her father and mother, and going out to America with all that she heard tell of the boat, and the pitching and tossing. She liked well enough when well enough was well enough so as to be let alone.

As she grew up, Grace Hogan didn't think of herself as an unhappy girl. She wasn't running barefoot, helping her mother in the cottage, helping her father in the field, and playing and working to be happy, because that wasn't why she had been put on the earth. God had put her where she was, and she had to be good so that her soul wouldn't burn in Hell. She didn't know it as such, but she was acquiring a fatalism of attitude, an acceptance of the lot of her own people. Bad luck, miseries, inflictions, punishments of God, the sly works of the Devil, the unseen spirits and forces and the Will of God—such were among the controlling powers that made the world the way it was. She didn't think this, but merely came to accept it, to respond as though she had been taught or had discovered principles of life and laws of the universe in the exercise of the unseen powers. And she knew nothing else but what she saw, and was told, and experienced.

The terrors of the unknown lurked in the dark of the night. Little Gracie never missed saying her night prayers on her knees, before climbing up into the old bed in which she and Bridie slept. She prayed for her parents, and for Bridie, and for all whom she knew, and she prayed for herself. And she prayed for God to protect her from any ill and harm from the spirits of the Evil World, from the Devil, Himself, and all of his little devils. She prayed, God protect her when she would be asleep, and her fear sank away. But Little Gracie became somewhat used to the evil spirits, and often she would see them in her dreaming. But she wasn't hurt or snatched up and carried off by the Devil Himself, or by witches and other spawns of the Devil. Indeed, God was good, and He kept her safe from the offsprings of the Devil. She went to confession many weeks, so as to receive Our Lord in Holy Communion, and she wouldn't be seen in her pelt, or be caught playing with the boys, who were growing up, like she was. But they had the devil in their pants. She was a fighter, and sometimes, she heard said she was a bad one, but she knew that she wasn't, and God, the Good Man, wouldn't think it was a sin because she would fight them that tried to make game of her. When she started to grow and the things you don't speak of happened to her, the gossoons came around and she could of had the pick of them. She chose Joseph Dunne, the second son of the six sons of Martin Dunne who had shook the hand of Daniel O'Connell.

Didn't his eyes melt her heart and wasn't he kind as the day is long? He was going on eighteen, but small for his age. But strong he was, and nary a one had nary a word to say against Joseph Dunne. He had a way with the horses and he had a way with the girls, but when he looked at her, his tongue was struck dumb and sure, the words wouldn't come out. And it was she who helped poor Joseph to find his tongue again. It was when they were walking in the fields together, and he talked of his queer dreams, of going out to America and of making her rich as a queen. And he'd be going out into the big, wide world where the wonders would make the eyes pop out of your head, and where earning only a pound or two a week was nothing at all. And she, herself, was beginning to think a thing or two, and she was after thinking that there were too many mouths to feed, and feeding these mouths was breaking the back of her poor father. And there was much talk of those that wanted to be going out to America, and the talk of those who didn't. And it was her own heart that told her why there was a silence in Joseph Dunne. Why, didn't his face grow red as a beet at the sight of her? And sure, he gave her the respect that the brazen hussies wanted like the redheaded McGurk one, the daughter of Red Top McGurk, whose grandfather took the soup, so 'twas said.

What place was there for a second son? There was nothing for Joseph Dunne, and he had to be going out to America, just as many another strong lad would be going. Her father had begun talking of her and Bridie going out, and it broke his heart to think of their going on one of the ships, but little there was for the two of them here in Ireland. Better off they'd be in America. That was what her father was after saying, and he wished that he'd gone himself.

She and Bridie were like one. But Bridie was the smarter, she knew. No one could learn a tune faster than Bridie. And she was always laughing and full of fun, with the gossoons chasing her. But she'd have none of them, Bridie wouldn't. Bridie was saying she'd go out because she had a dream that there was something waiting for her in America. It was something the Good Lord had waiting for her over the seas.

Joseph Dunne went out. That was a sad day, a sad day it was, indeed, seeing Joseph off, and she pledged to him. She went off by herself in the field. The tears came from her heart. She prayed to God and to His Blessed Mother to look after Joseph, and protect him, when he would be far away, over the ocean and in America. Her heart was heavy, far too heavy for her young years.

And she had to go out, too. It was the talk all about, going out to America because there were too many mouths to be fed in Ireland.

III

Six months after Joseph had left, Grace and Bridie went out to America. Timmy Hogan was able to borrow and raise the passage money for the two of them. He wanted them off because he loved them. Things would be so much better for them in America, and with so many of their own kind, so many Irish gone out, he had no need to fear for his daughters. There would be plenty to help them with a word of advice. And Joseph Dunne was there, and driving a team of horses in Brooklyn, New York. Leave it to Joseph to take care of himself. A fine lad he was, and a good one for hard work.

The two girls departed with a great sadness in their hearts. But Gracie and Bridie were young girls, and too full of freshness and eagerness for life not to hope, even though they were sad of heart.

Although it was the saddest day in her sixteen years, Gracie would not allow herself to cry.

And why must it be that she must be going far away, to another end of God's world, and Joseph had gone out there, and her sister, Bridie, was going with her, oh, thank God she was going, and Peter McNamara was gone, and the two Prendergast boys, and Johnny and Andrew Malloy. Why did she have to be going, when it was here, where she belonged, that she wanted to be staying?

In America, there was money to be earned, and food for

The Silence of History

hungry mouths. That's what she heard tell, and heard read. How was she to be knowing, and to be knowing that she would be the one to be earning money for her father?

But, yes, for him she could. For her father, she could. She could if she had to work the skin off her bones.

—And he's aged, he's aged overnight.

That was what she heard the mother of Paul Cleary tell to the mother of Limpy Larry McBride.

She wanted to cry her eyes out, and Bridie told her to cry. Bridie had cried. Gracie wouldn't cry. She had to go, and not be a burden on her poor father. It was God's Will, and He would look after her father, just as He'd look after Bridie and herself, and God would keep them all safe.

Gracie still wanted to cry. She felt the way she'd feel if her heart was being ripped right out of her. She was leaving her father and her mother, and all that she loved, and she'd be going to faraway America, where she wouldn't know the people, but for Joseph.

Sad, yes, and indeed she was sad. Her heart was heavier than her years. She was only a girl.

But 'twas the Will of God.

—God's Will be done!

And she didn't cry.

Growing up, Gracie Hogan had had many happy hopes, and she had believed that it would be better for her once she was grown up. She'd dream, before Joseph Dunne had won her heart, that she might think of another, a laddie who would get five or ten acres, or own a store, or she'd think that maybe she'd go into a convent, but she wasn't good enough to be a holy nun. And she thought of going out to America, too.

But when the day came, and she and Bridie were dressed to go, the two of them in new dresses of cotton their poor mother had sat up for nights by the light of a candle making, and carrying all of their belongings in a few bundles, and a sack of food, ah, and sure, she was full of a great sorrow.

The sun had come out early and bright that morning, and it lay warmly over the soft green of the fields, beyond the cottages, and she thought how she had run barefoot on many a morning such as this one, with nary a care in the world, and she had seen her father and the men, bent over in the field. And she remembered her mother, teaching her and Bridie to bake the bread. And she and Bridie kneaded the dough, and she could almost believe she was hearing again her Aunt Maggie talking of the poor people she knew who were sleeping in the earth, and the cows, and the pigs, and the sheep, and she could remember so much of many such mornings. She'd not be seeing such mornings here again, not till she came back, and many there were who never came back. No, she wouldn't be coming back. That she feared.

She was going out into the world she had heard tell of many is the time, and no child any more was she. It was like she was a grown-up woman.

And it was the last morning, and the last minute had almost come. Mother of God, she could scarce believe it, Jesus, Mary and Joseph, it was time.

Time to go off, to fly like the wild geese do be flying away to where there is food, and the sun is warm.

The cottage was full of people, relations and neighbors, and people from here and there and around about nearby the poor little spot that she and Bridie were going to be taking their leave of. There was talking and gabbing, tears and laughing, good wishes of Godspeed, prayer, and everybody was so nice, wishing well for her and for Bridie, and she and Bridie were being treated like real ladies, and important ladies. If it hadn't been for the people, you would have thought that there was mourning for the dead in the cottage, and it was like that, and her poor mother crying, and her father, poor man, she could see the sorrow in his eyes, and her brother, and all of her kin, sure, there was nary a one of them who didn't have an aching heart.

She couldn't be knowing how it all happened so quick, but quick it was, and there was herself and Bridie in Shamus McShane's cart, and her poor mother, the tears were streaming down her cheeks, and she was walking beside the cart, and then she was waving, and the tears were streaming out of her eyes, the whilst she stood, watching Bridie and herself being driven away. And her poor father, there he was, standing in the sun, waving his hand, and the tears were streaming out of his eyes, the poor man, he was weeping bitter tears for his two daughters.

IV

They were six weeks on the crowded boat, with the people going out crowded together, almost on top of one another, like cattle in pens. The ocean pitched and tossed, and many had the seasickness, even Bridie. But she was not sick, not a day. The storms and the waves, lapping up over the railing of the boat, were enough to put the fear of God in you, and the fear of God it did put into them all. Many a rosary was said, and going to sleep at night with so many of them, she prayed God to save her and her sister, and all of the people. There were the days when the water was calm as a dark pond, and the people all were out on the deck in the sun, and there was talking and getting acquainted, and singing, and it was six weeks she and Bridie were on the ocean coming out.

There had been crying and much misery and sadness when the ship had sailed out of Queenstown Harbor, but once they were on the stormy ocean, Ireland was out of sight, and whilst not out of mind, she was not so much on their minds. Gracie and Bridie were like the others, and Ireland sank in memory as in a mist. They began getting used to the boat, and they had the queer notion that they had been on the ocean, sailing, for a long time, a much longer time than was actually the case. They got to know people very well, and there was always plenty to talk about, gossip, and back home, and America, whom they knew in America, and where they were going, and many little doings and sayings of the passengers. There were people from just about all over Ireland, with many stories to tell, and the two sisters listened like they were all ears. The world was growing bigger for them. And the ocean and the sky, what a power God had to create the world, the ocean and the sky.

"The fish, Bridie, they lepped; they were leppin' out of the water," Gracie said.

Bridie hurried through the crowded deck to the railing to see the fish leppin'. She saw them.

The days passed. The ocean turned gray, and the waves wrinkled and roughened its surface, and they tore across the waters and hit the ship a blow that you'd have thought would knock it over on its side, and big splashes blew up on the deck. The boat was going up and down and rolling, and it was worth your life to walk from here to there. The people were sick, and vomiting all over, lying like they might be dying, and they had the fear of God in them, and many, they took out their rosary beads. Every minute the boat pitched, and took your breath away for fear of drowning. The days passed, long days, with the ocean to see and little enough place to walk, and it seemed that the voyage would never end, and that they had been on the ship for years.

But there was land. They saw it way off, little, nothing at all but a dark line, but there was such an excitement, and such talking and shouting. Slowly the ship moved toward the land, and there was America with the sun shining, and they all wanted to know how soon they'd be in America on land. Slowly, the boat moved forward over calm waters, blue and wavering with the streaks of reflected sun. And they came to the harbor, and so many ships, big ones, too, and little ones were docked, and the buildings, it was a sight, it took away your breath.

The ship docked, and they landed amidst flutter and fright, and it was like a left-handed madhouse.

They were trembling, too, for fear that Joseph wouldn't meet them, but he was waiting, with his brother, Denny, both of them dressed up in dark Sunday suits of coarse cloth.

It warmed her heart to see him, and Bridie's too. The two of them were almost ready to have a cold sweat lest they be alone and lost in America which was so strange and harsh, and they were so helpless and lost.

"I knew Joseph would be waitin' and it warms me heart to see him."

His face was shining with pride, and he kept saying:

"Sure and you won't believe it, 'tis a wonderful country."

The Silence of History

He finally got them to Manhattan, and gaping, and full of childlike wonder they rode on a horsecar. Gracie kept saying that she couldn't get over it.

V

Mrs. Dunne sat in the old rocking chair in her room, now and then rocking, and drifting memories came back to her. Her girlhood, and her coming out to America with her sister, Bridie, and Pa meeting them and taking the two of them to Brooklyn in a horsecar.

She'd sit and rock a little and think her thoughts of when she was young, and then she'd make her grandson's meal to take to work with him to the gasoline station. But first, she'd sit for a while and rest her old limbs.

The rocking chair squeaked on the floor, and she thought how there was no one left for her to talk with about the times when she was a girl in the old country and came out to America, no one but her sister who was a holy nun in Brooklyn. And Bridie was getting on in years, and was an old woman herself.

She was lonesome to see her sister, to talk with her, just for the two of them to talk and to see one another before they died. They would meet in Heaven, if the Lord was merciful, and sure the Lord would be merciful because He was a Good Man.

—Joseph, 'twould be a fine work for you, drivin' one of these.

She could hear her own voice, saying these words to Joseph, and may God have mercy on his poor soul, she could hear her voice as plain as the day, and that fifty years ago, fifty years ago if it was a day, sure it was more than fifty years ago, and that was when she heard tell of Mr. Lincoln, too, and the war.

—Little Gracie, Joseph had said, I'm drivin' something bigger than the likes of this, with a team of horses, and a big wagon with barrels of beer, barrels of it, and some of the folks in the old country should see Joseph Dunne today in America.

They had laughed, and they had near split their sides laughing at this and that, and she and Bridie, riding on the horsecar with all of their belongings, the two of them fresh from the old country.

And some man behind them saying:

—Greenhorns.

Sure she didn't know what the word meant, or that it was them that the man was talking about 'til Joseph got red in the face, and him calling to the man:

—If I had me driver's whip in me hand, it's another tune you'd sing, me lad, Joseph had said.

And sure, Glory be, there was almost a fight and she was saying:

—Fist him, Joseph, tear him apart limb from limb, and give me his eyes, turn them out of his head and gimme them in the palm of me hand.

The big man got off the horsecar, and it was something he said about the Irish.

—Ignorant greenhorns, the man had called from the sidewalk, and the car starting again, and it was a knife had cut the man's soul, Joseph's, may his soul rest in peace.

And that was when she and Bridie had come to America.

But she'd best be tendin' to her grandson's sandwiches for his work at the gasoline station.

Mrs. Dunne got up from her rocking chair and went back into the kitchen.

Many's the time she made sandwiches for Joseph's lunch and him going out on the wagons with the men.

If God, the Good Man, would let her see Bridie once before she was under the earth with Joseph, and in Calvary Cemetery.

Her eyes filled with tears.

While she cried, Eddie was downtown in the Crerar Library, reading, after having quit his job at Rawlinson's.

Chapter Eight

I

But Eddie decided that he really was living in his future, the first days, the beginning of it. It was like a voyage, Columbus' voyage, and he was sailing in a small boat out to a big and vast sea, and far beyond, across the waters that would often be wild and stormy, there was the safe harbor, and the new virgin land and virgin world. But he was still near land, the water was calm, and there was little wind up to push his boat farther toward the deep and the wild waves where his ship would toss and pitch and he would struggle to keep it safe and on course.

However, the comparison with a ship crossing the Atlantic Ocean, such as the *Santa Maria* of Christopher Columbus, didn't fit Eddie's journey to the future that did not yet exist. Tomorrow and tomorrow and tomorrow were not merely unknown. They were not, not in time, but there was only a tomorrow to be, and then another tomorrow and another and another, each of them to be, one after the other, and how he would fare in those tomorrows to be, or what he would become, depended on himself, on how he prepared himself, today, and each today as it came and went. And in today and today and today, he was living not for the day, and not even for himself as he was today, but as he would be tomorrow when it came, not tomorrow that was next day, the next today, but tomorrow that was far away in time. Tomorrow, in 1935, and 1945 and 1955, if he lived that long, and after 1955 when he would be past fifty years of age, and would have lived over a half century of todays.

The half centuries, and the centuries, that was what they all were, an addition of so many todays, of so many tomorrows that became todays, and then, became yesterdays. But yesterdays were gone, and tomorrow had not come, and there were only todays, and all of the todays "until the last syllable of recorded time."

Thoughts like these came and went in moments, in a few minutes of reflection, and then, with his mind shifting to something else, he would leave these thoughts unsettled like unanswered questions, but ones to which he would one day know the answer.

During the summer, while taking the two courses in history, he had begun to have many thoughts and questions and moods about time. Time was only minutes, succeeding each other in equal seconds that ticked away, and so many, sixty minutes, made an hour, and the hours made a day, and so on, into weeks, months and years, and that was as it had always been, and always would be until the end of time, the end of the world which was the time when there would be that "last syllable of recorded time," the last day, and the last hour, and the last minute, and the last second.

For in eternity, it would be as if there were no time, but only always.

II

Once he began attending classes at the University, Eddie's war with time became a minute-by-minute and, in a sense, a pitiless battle. He needed all the time he could have, and this realization and insight was one of his first in the process of developing his vast ambitions and learning how to work at learning, and to concentrate and apply his mind. Then, in a library, he happened to read a fragment on habit from *Psychology* by William James, and he grasped the relevance of James' theory of habit to his own problems. He began, from his first day as a University student, to work toward an ideal, which could have seemed inhuman and machine-like, because he ignored self,

The Silence of History

surroundings, whim, impulse, and accepted no excuse for himself. It cost Eddie much strain and frustration, pangs of loneliness, time with friends, sleep and immediate enjoyment. It put a mark of seriousness on his personality, which some few grasped, but which caused others to regard him with unexpressed resentment, admiration, contempt, desire to help or to impede or to ignore, and it even caused a few to think him crazy. But Eddie was usually unaware of all such reactions.

He had not suddenly changed in character, he had been intense from early childhood, but had failed to know this trait in himself for what it was. His intensity, and the grandiose ambitions it fed, even during his boyhood, had been a reason why he felt himself to be different from other boys, and thus, as having something wrong with him, something which often made him fear that he was a goof.

Eddie had gone to night school for five or six months, and he had done far better than he had been certain of doing in advance. He began discovering that he could understand when he read and studied with concentration, and he had the will power to discipline himself and use his time well in study. However, it was only after he had begun at the University that he started to *feel* himself growing and changing. This growth and change was far more rapid and touched deeper sources within himself than he knew, or than he could have known or understood at the time.

Eddie Ryan had begun seeking his education, first at night school, and then at the University, in a state of desperation. He had been without self-esteem, and he feared spending all his life as a nobody. He had been living in a social world in which dispiritedness was like an invisible thing, powerful but unfelt. His father died, a sick man and practically a pauper. His Uncle Dick was making less money as a salesman, and had not been able to afford to pay for the final year's tuition of eighty dollars at St. Basil's High School. His Uncle Larry didn't work most of the time, and he didn't like work. Uncle Larry believed that some day he'd become rich. God, Good Luck, Universal Harmony, the Times of the Universe, New Thought, Wishing and Believing in His Wishes, the Good in the World, some such force would make him rich, a millionaire. Eddie's older brother, John, was driving a truck, and his brother Leo had had to quit high school after one year, and was driving a wagon for the Express Company. In high school, the fellows he'd mostly gone with, and those in the high school fraternity that had been formed, had all come from families that were better off than his folks were. There had never been much talk of the future and what they would do in life. At the Express Company, none of the clerks or supervisors or wagon men on the trucks and wagons, had thought much of advancing, going up in the world. He had come to feel that in some way he was different from those he knew, and that he wanted more than they were getting out of life. But he didn't separate whatever it was that he wanted from success, which meant a big job, money, getting your name in the paper as politicians did. And if you succeeded, you would be envied as well as admired. That was becoming a big shot. He had come to think of those who were better off as looking down on those who weren't on their own level or above them. He had grown up in an environment where that was how people acted and seemed to feel.

His own boyhood dreams had been of fame and glory, and of money, and for years, these had been focused on baseball. For almost three years, he had been living without direction, getting by in high school, and then working the Wagons Department at the Express Company. He could get an occasional date, but he didn't get too many. He had dreamed and been bored and dull, waiting for classes to finish for the day; when he had started to work, punching a time clock at eight or nine or ten in the morning, he had been thinking of when he would punch the same clock at five, or six, or eight in the evening, free for that day of work that he didn't like. His feelings fell into vain dreams, of girls and of fame that he knew were impossible for him to attain. His desperation was not for more success, but for escape and for himself.

Since he had been a boy, he had had little in his life upon which to grow. He didn't know what growing meant and how

The Silence of History

it was different from getting up in the world. He had felt the pricks and cuts and slashes of superiority for years, and his failure to get dates with girls had been like fresh cuts on raw, hurt flesh.

Going to night school, and beginning to learn, Eddie had still been influenced and hurt by his own world, and the stamp of inferiority that his family bore, and he with them.

Eddie did not think of the University, precisely, as a means of escape, but it was such; it was an escape for a young mind and young feelings which had been swallowed up in the emptiness of too many passing moments, passing hours, passing days and weeks and months. The loneliness of that first summer quarter was often poignant, and he was hungry for companionship and for what he thought love to be. Yet it was better that he was lonely. He was unimpeded, unaffected by the notions, the attitudes and prejudices of anyone. His mind and spirit gathered momentum, and within himself, he did not live in vain dreams or the tears of dying hopes. Nor did he live merely in the world around him. He began to live in the time of man, and this was a gain. This was what he needed as a release from his desperation.

By October 1925, when the fall quarter began, Eddie Ryan had lost much of his desperation. Two years before, he would get up in the morning thinking of how he must get through the day at the Express Office before he could call his time or his soul his own. He lived waiting for the next date, the next movie, the next chance for fun, the next weekend. But getting up to be at the University for an eight-o'clock class, even on five and six hours of sleep, was different, a source of happy anticipation. It was really morning in the sense of what a morning should mean, a new day with fresh chances of living, with the desire to meet the new day, with confidence about using rather than wasting it and with many expectations, not only of learning and growing, but also socially and personally. And he awoke with his big hope of finding the girl he'd love, the beautiful girl who'd love and understand him.

This was Eddie Ryan in the fall of 1925.

III

On the first morning of the fall quarter, Eddie was ready at seven-thirty. He heard his friend Peter Moore whistle from the sidewalk on South Park Avenue, and hurried down the front stairs and into the sunshine to meet him.

The morning air was fresh, with a wind so slightly cold that its brush against Eddie's cheeks was almost like teasing. The shrubbery in front of the tennis courts and the trees behind the courts still retained most of their greenness, and the sound of the wind through the trees was like a coy playfulness of nature. A first mellowing of the new autumn was in the sun, and Eddie liked this. He liked the morning. He liked his new life, and all of its promise.

And he liked Peter Moore.

"I see you're ready bright and early, Eddie."

"I didn't want to keep you waiting."

"This isn't like when we were kids in short pants. If we're late, or don't want to learn, we're fooling no one but ourselves, and nobody will care. We're not like the rich fraternity boys living on a rich father's income, going because it's the thing to do, or for the social life. We're paying for it ourselves."

"That's so," Eddie said thoughtfully.

They had started walking to the corner of 58th Street, to cross South Park Avenue into Washington Park.

Both Eddie and Peter told themselves that they were actually on their way to school, as college students of the University of Chicago. Eddie's joining him reawakened Peter's happy feeling of wonder. They had known each other, Eddie recalled, for about ten years, and were good friends. Perhaps they'd share the future, and be friends for years, law partners. He took to this thought, and knew that Peter did, also.

On that first morning walk of the fall quarter across the park and to the campus, Eddie felt as though he were at the real beginning of his college life and career. The future was spread before him in the expected years of his stay at college, and these would be the best years of his youth, years of triumph and fun

The Silence of History

as well as of getting an education. The world and the future became new, and they shone in him with the hope of all the dreams and all the yearnings that he had ever had. All that he had been wishing and waiting for during the last few years was now becoming possible, and would be his to gain and to get, his to win. This was like the beginning of going out to win the world, the beginning of his place and name and fame in the world.

He saw a difference between Peter and himself, although Peter was one of his best friends, and they had grown more close during the last year or two as a consequence of the common ambitions they both held. Peter had gone to public schools, although he was a Catholic, and a good one, and after high school he had had to work for a year and save money before he could go to college. Eddie had been almost envious with admiration for Peter because he had not believed he could do the same himself. Peter didn't drink or go on dates, and, in fact, had not yet learned how to dance. He'd always been what everyone who knew him in the neighborhood regarded as a decent boy, with no bad habits, but, at the same time, not a sissy or disliked by other fellows. He had been a cheerful, freckle-faced kid, a good runner and high-jumper, a pretty good wrestler, and a more than fair indoor ballplayer, although he had never played much baseball or been good at it. He had never gotten into any trouble, and hadn't ever engaged in dirty habits, as many of the neighborhood kids used to. When there would be a session of such talk, Peter would listen and say nothing; he might blush now and then. Eddie, also, had not engaged much in dirty talk, and even after he'd been eighteen, and had begun to go out on dates, and sometimes to drink or even to get drunk, he didn't go in for what the boys considered to be dirty talk.

The two of them had retained a common sense of purity and of shyness, and they also had something of a common sense about the people of the neighborhood, and their feeling for these people. They observed more than the other kids, and in their conversation they would talk and laugh about some incident or comment they had heard, some little oddity which they had caught on 58th Street or one of the nearby streets.

Neither of them could have explained motives or underlying feelings, but they showed a common love of the people, a tolerance, and a sense of amusement about foibles and excesses. They had unformed, unrealized identifications with the people of the neighborhood, especially the Irish and Irish-American, and these people were all their own.

This was a bond between them which they didn't understand, nor had they sensed the reason for its existence, and, thus, for the feelings of friendship they felt for each other with a greater strength than they had either realized or expressed. They did not go around together very much, and in most instances their meetings and talks were accidental ones, but inasmuch as they lived next door to each other, and had since 1917, they saw each other often. Sometimes, they did go to church together, to Mass on Sunday, to confession, or to Stations of the Cross, on a Friday evening in Lent, or to some other Lenten services.

In a very vague or loosely emotional manner, they both grasped another common bond, the fact that neither of them had been raised by their parents, and in their parents' home. Eddie had been raised by his grandmother, and had lived with her since he'd been three years old. Peter had been raised by his aunt, Mrs. Nolan, who had been born near Cork, and had come out to America as a girl, settling in Chicago, and marrying Dan Nolan, who had become a contractor and had done very well, so that he was able to buy the two connected flat buildings on South Park Avenue in the early years of the century, a good buy in a good neighborhood, and the buildings gave the Nolans a very decent living. Peter's father was Mrs. Nolan's brother, a workman with thrifty habits. Peter was the youngest of four children, and had two older brothers and a sister who was neatly built and very good looking. He had never seen his mother, nor did he ever speak of her to Eddie. She had died giving birth to Peter, and "Pop" Moore had been too lost and hurt to raise his family. He disregarded the advice of family and friends to find some good woman to marry and give him and his children a home, for he couldn't think of another wife after Kathy, the red-haired spit of a girl he knew and loved as a child in the old country, had gone on to God and His Angels. He had loved her with a sense of worship, and like his own mother, dead and in her grave back across the seas in Ireland, the ground she had walked on was almost sacred because of her.

Mrs. Nolan had taken the baby, Peter, and from time to time, his sister, Maureen, also lived with the Nolans. Mr. Moore and his oldest boy, Stephen, had moved in with Billy McGlynn, a first cousin of Eddie's father, and Maureen also stayed at the McGlynn house when she was not with the Nolans. They lived on Kenwood Avenue near 47th Street, in a sprawling wooden house, which Billy McGlynn, a plumber who got a good spot at the Shafter Hotel in the Loop as chief plumber, bought with some help from his brother, Jack McGlynn, the lawyer; the latter had run in the 1912 primary for State's Attorney, but had lost because he was aligned with the wrong faction of the Democratic Party. But Jack McGlynn was a very successful lawyer, who had long had brewery and other business retainers in Catholic circles. He and Eddie's father had gone about and done their hell-raising together as young men. Two of Billy's kids, Al and Teresa, had been raised by their Uncle Jack. The other McGlynn boy, Jerry, had worked with Eddie in the Department of Wagons of the Express Company. The Superintendent, Patty Lynch, was another first cousin, both of Eddie's father, Dick, and of the McGlynns. Peter's other brother Johnny, who was four years older than he, had been raised on a farm, and had then come to Chicago, lived with his father at the McGlynns', and had been given a job at the Express Company. He began as a helper on a wagon, and, at the time Eddie was starting that first fall quarter at the University, he drove a double wagon which transferred freight among the various railway depots and the stations for the Express Company.

Peter and Eddie were almost like cousins and they had many mutual feelings which were never directly expressed. The Ryans and Moores were the poorer members of their families, and neither Peter's father nor Eddie's had been examples of success. Each had been a man for whom others felt sorry, and who had suffered defeat in life. Eddie's father, Dick, had died, poor and paralyzed, and Peter's father had lost his wife and was living out a lonely life. He was a gentle man, quiet and soft-spoken, with an air of sadness about him. Now and then, he would get drunk on beer, but he was not a troublesome or violent man, and when he filled up on beer or other liquor, he'd sit in quiet fogs of his own gloom and sadness, and think of his dead wife and of things that never were, that never had come true in his life.

Eddie and Peter both had sunken away in them something of a feeling of strangers, which they had acquired in their early childhood. Their ambition was fed by this feeling. They both had come to see that it was up to them to make something of themselves. Eddie had thought, and with no feeling of envy, that Peter was much smarter than he, and Peter had gotten very good marks in high school. In his first year at the University, Peter had not quite hit a B average of four points, and on the first morning of the fall quarter, as they walked to classes, Peter had spoken of how he hoped to raise his average. He'd complimented Eddie on his A's, without any jealousy, for he had no such feelings toward Eddie. They spoke of other things, classes, plans, the future, the neighborhood, the Big Ten football season, and seeing the games together, and they parted by Cobb Hall with a warmth of mutual feeling and respect, each glad that the other was a student, able to get an education and try to make a future for himself.

Eddie continued in the fall quarter as he had done in the summer, but he had changed his plans and cut his courses down to two, the history course under Professor Carleton, and an obligatory course in English Literature. Since he was working nine hours a day, and a six-day week, he thought it best not to take on a load bigger than he could carry.

Eddie had, at first, feared that he was backing out of a task and evading what might be hard, but, nevertheless, he had decided to postpone the Political Economy course which he had planned to take for a quarter. He continued to fear that he was welshing from harder work when he should have taken it on, but he knew he couldn't handle it well enough. When he quit night school, he had had the same fears, but somehow he'd known he was making the decision that fitted him. He had begun to understand a trait in himself, and to recognize its im-

The Silence of History

portance in his education. When he sensed that he was taking on more than he could manage, or that he was not ready for a book, project, problem, or subject, he would do best to postpone it.

This made the fall easier, and he had classes only from eight to ten o'clock on weekday mornings. This would give him a chance to do extra and collateral reading. In History and English you couldn't get enough out of the course unless you did that.

Eddie was also hoping that he would have a chance for some social and college life; he thought of this in terms of time. However, he was hoping, really, for something to happen by way of a lucky break, because whether he took two or three classes, he would be working until midnight six nights a week, and have to make an eight-o'clock class on the five weekday mornings. He vainly wished for some change that would give him more time on campus. But he had no intention of sacrificing his studies. To others, these, his studies, seemed so little; they were as nothing in the scale of events. But to him, they were momentous. They concerned his future, and that was his life to be. In making his decisions, the thought never occurred to Eddie to ask advice or counsel. He was on his own in life, and it was up to himself to make his way or falter and fail. He had determined that he must make his way, and, daily, he tried to harden his will and his determination not to falter.

As he left Peter in front of Cobb Hall, he proudly felt that now he was part of University life. He wasn't a nobody. He wasn't the clerk in the Express Office that he'd been at the beginning of the year—1925.

—You'll never be the man your father was.

—Ryan, you dunce, you ain't dumb, you're dumber.

He could remember many cracks and jokes, and thoughts and feelings.

Students were crowding into the old building. Voices, cheerful, gay, and happy laughter. The voices and the laughter of girls. Everyone was young, and they all looked happy. The talk of the students, moving to classrooms, sounded like a gush of gaiety.

Eddie had entered Cobb Hall, self-absorbed, thinking that now every day would be rich and possibly it could even be wonderful. The chatter, the laughter, the senseless boom of talk broke upon him as he walked in a shuffling crowd of students. And it was like a realization full of sunlight. This was college. Happy minutes of youth. A time of hopes, of dreams, of learning, of making friendships that could last for life, of falling in love. A time when every day and every hour could be new.

Girls, in the richness of their first bloom, smiling with the naturalness of roses in unfolding red petals. Young fellows, many with a bland air and a manner of assurance as they talked and laughed at jokes and quips.

Eddie thrilled with his high hope, even though he felt so alone! Among students like this, he'd get everything that he wanted and expected to find.

Yes, this was the University of Chicago. Cobb Hall. And he, Eddie Ryan, was a student, beginning a college career. A year ago, or even back on last New Year's Day, the University of Chicago had seemed impossible, beyond his reach.

And now he was here. A student.

The class in English Literature was being conducted in a room on the second floor. At the head of the stairs he saw a tall, well-built, good-looking student with a fleshy, ruddy face, broad shoulders and long arms. It was Fox, who had been a center on the Lindbloom High School football team, and he was wearing a maroon sweater with the white numerals 1928 on the front, his sweater for freshman football. They had been together in Professor Kraft's history class last summer and had said "Hello" to one another two or three times.

"Hello," Eddie said, with open, eager friendliness.

Fox stared at Eddie as though he were invisible, and turned away without speaking.

Eddie halted for a fraction of a second, abashed and hurt by the slight. He hoped that no one had noticed it, no one going to the same class as he.

—Goddamn snob! he told himself in wounded anger.

He went to his first class, still stung by the thought of being cut. Also, he was bewildered.

Why?

Why had he been snubbed?

A depressing gloom hung in his mind all through the two classes that morning. He listened attentively, but the gloom persisted, and he was acutely conscious of a loneliness of spirit.

Miss Patrick, a graying, round-faced woman, with blotched red cheeks, was the instructor of English Lit. 103; Peter had had her, and said she was really good, and that Eddie "ought to like taking a class with her."

Her voice was rather dry, matter-of-fact. She smiled as she began speaking, but only for an instant, and then her face became unconvincingly stern. Her first sentence produced some laughs and giggles. Warning that she wanted no hands raised, she said that she wondered how many in the room were taking her course because they loved great and beautiful writing, and how many were present because the course was required. The present was a practical age, and many students came to the University not to acquire a liberal education, one which would provide them with the means of living more richly in themselves, but of learning whatever would help them get ahead. They seemed to think that a University was a sort of higher trade school, and that was a great pity. What a shame if anyone should allow himself—or herself—to go through life and never to learn and know, in Matthew Arnold's phrase, *all that is thought and known in the world.* Then, Miss Patrick's voice softened, and became musical, almost singing, as she quoted:

I wandered lonely as a cloud
That floats on high o'er vales and hills.
When all at once I saw a crowd,
A host of golden daffodils
Beside the lake, beneath the trees,
Fluttering and dancing in the breeze.

She assigned for the next lesson, Wordsworth's *Preface to Lyrical Ballads,* mentioned that Wordsworth's *Preface* had its origin in emotion recollected in tranquillity, and that it was "the first and last of all knowledge," and "the image of man and nature"; she spoke again of the poem, *I wandered lonely as a cloud*, the field of daffodils, ten thousand of them, which later flashed

> *. . . upon that inward eye*
> *Which is the bliss of solitude.*

Miss Patrick went on to speak of some of the writers whom they would take up, mentioning the names of the Romantic and Victorian poets. Eddie liked what Miss Patrick said, and guessed that he'd get something out of the course.

But the class was dismissed after about twenty-five or thirty minutes, and Eddie found himself alone and lonely, remembering the sting of the slight which he'd received from Fox. He left Cobb Hall, not knowing what to do with himself for the next half hour, until the nine-o'clock history class would start. The humiliation to which Fox had subjected him left him depressed and feeling out of place, as though he didn't belong on campus and were an interloper with no right to be there, even though he had been admitted as a student and had paid his tuition.

Others in his class had quickly scattered and he found himself standing alone on the sidewalk in front of Cobb Hall. From behind the gray and differently shaped buildings, he heard the jarring pulse of pneumatic drills, the fitful starts and stops of tractors, the dropping of materials, the hammering, pounding, and whirring of engines for digging and other construction work, all going on in the continuing process of putting up the new Billings Memorial Hospital on the other side of Ellis Avenue and the Midway, and his thoughts flashed to the summer so recently gone, his morning class hours, his usually confident expectancy for the fall term, his happy belief that somehow his personality would be seen for what it was, and that he would become popular and socially respected, even important, once the fall quarter had begun.

It had begun.

And the first student he had spoken to, other than Peter, had snubbed him as though he were some grasping, climbing, pushing Jew or Polack, an undesirable and an inferior.

The weather had changed very slightly, just sufficiently to

put the faintest tang of autumn in the air, and this he liked. He saw the movement of the early morning life on campus. Young men and women walked at a pace which suggested leisure, ease, and naturalness, with the movements of those who were contented or happy. There was so much less nervousness, tension of body, and shuffling of shoes here than there was in the Loop during those long and finished months when he had worked at the Express Company and had gotten off an elevated train at Congress and Wabash, and then had walked on to Dearborn. His own moods had affected how he saw and whom he saw for instants in the rushing crowd of workers who tramped in a herd to their offices or wherever they worked, and who were subordinated to the stern ticking of a clock. Even with the rackety-racketing, nerve-punching noises of the building machinery, the campus was quiet, as another world might be quiet.

Eddie looked about, with eyes of darting nervousness that peered with a consuming hunger and searched with the compulsion of loneliness. He looked as though he were seeking a face, a form, a person who must be seen now, and as though he were absorbing what he saw, gulping it into himself to keep forever. And there was a suggestion of dreaminess, also, in his restless eyes. His eyes were tired and bloodshot. For several nights, he had stayed up after getting home from work, reading Sinclair Lewis' *Main Street*, which was affecting him almost as commandingly as had *Babbitt*. He smiled, thinking of lunkheaded characters in *Main Street*. He thought of Fox.

He'd read more of *Main Street* after classes, and perhaps finish the novel. There was now always much for him to look forward to. There would be books to read from now on until the end of his life.

That was, unless he went blind.

But he wouldn't go blind.

His mind became a big blot of fear. What could he look forward to, if he were to go blind? The fear was a black stain on his feelings, seeping down farther into his mind, and eating at his confidence and hopes. For a few seconds, he felt as though doomed. He glanced about. But how bright the morning was. How soft the sun was. Soft with the new and still gentle autumn.

The grass had not yet withered on campus. It was green and shining, and it was a healthy green because of the morning dew. And the coeds. He searched for words with which to describe some of them to himself. They walked in the sun and brightness of the autumn morning. They were bright as morning. A blonde, radiant to him, was walking on the diagonal path, westward. Would she come in his direction? And be in his history class? The blonde passed off onto Ellis Avenue.

Students were gathering in front of Cobb Hall. Eddie looked eagerly about, compelled by an impulse which he did not feel. His feelings had faded away within him. He was waiting for the next class, for what it would bring his mind, but he did not understand this.

The last moments passed, the bell rang, and the students were swelling into the old building for the nine-o'clock classes. Amidst the usual bubbling of talk and laughter, Eddie went slowly into Cobb. His desire was like determination, and it wore the mask of grimness. The desire in him was a call of mind, of feeling and imagination, for the breaking sunshine which nourishes growth in the inner person. But not knowing and understanding this, Eddie kept looking about with almost stupid eagerness.

As he entered the classroom, the thought came to him that what he learned here at the University was all that would count in the long run.

He found himself a seat near the window of a big first-floor classroom.

He was at the University to learn, but he was hoping that an attractive coed would sit close by and he would get to know her.

That hope didn't come to pass. Only male students took seats near him. Three rows away, in the middle of the room, sat a girl with long brown hair, simply made up, with delicate features and nearly olive complexion, Eddie saw a very appealing and poetic beauty in her, and wished that he'd found himself sitting closer to her. His luck. Four classes in a row, without even having a halfway presentable girl sitting near him.

Just as Eddie was beginning to think about his bum luck, he saw a skinny redhead, almost six feet tall, walking quickly toward the empty seat across the aisle from the girl.

The Silence of History

A lucky, skinny redhead, and Eddie didn't fancy the guy's looks, none whatever. The redhead was too skinny, and thin-faced for anyone to call the guy good-looking. Nor did Eddie like his gray suit with white stripes. Not quite a Polack suit, but what was it? Eddie couldn't offhand think of a phrase to describe the suit, but he didn't like it.

And he would have found more to dislike in the skinny redhead, plenty more but for the quickly jarring surprise of the buzzing bell, and the simultaneous entry of Professor Carleton. He wore a lightish blue suit, immaculately pressed and looking stiff upon his tall frame. His face was prematurely settled rather than aged; or such was the impression he created. Having burst into the room like one who was late and in a hurry, he spoke rapidly and nervously about the general scope and contents of the course. His accent was Eastern and cultivated, and Eddie guessed that it must be a Harvard one; he was not good in matters such as accents. Eddie had a very good impression of Professor Carleton. That first class hour passed with unnoticed quickness, while the course was broadly outlined. The events ran from the Great French Revolution to the beginning of the World War. Professor Carleton's language also impressed Eddie; he spoke well and clearly, with ease and elegance.

Eddie began keenly to look forward to his history course, both to the lectures and the reading which he would do.

By the end of the first day's second class hour, he knew that the quarter was well launched as far as his courses went. He'd enjoy them, and do well in them, he felt.

Eddie's life became all work and no girl, no play. The classrooms at Cobb Hall, one on the first floor, and the other on the second; occasionally, Harper Library, after the nine-o'clock history class; and the filling station; these were the places where Eddie Ryan was preparing himself, was actually waging his battle for the future. These were the places through which time, some of his time, fell into the hole of yesterday. And these were the places where he was happier than he was able to recognize.

Each individual moment when he had a thought, he knew that he was thinking, and what he was thinking about. But it never occurred to him that this activity of mind was both a part and a rewarding consequence of his education which could barely be said to have begun. He knew that a major purpose of education was learning how to think, and he believed that he was making some progress in the development of his ability to think. However, he saw this only in direct reference to the content of what was taken up in the classroom.

What Eddie did not realize was that he was living more and more with his mind an active, functioning, operating part of his full person, just as his heart and other organs were functioning and operating.

There were different parts of his life, separate environments which had no connection with each other, except that Eddie was spending part of his time in them. There was his home; there was school; there was work. In his mind, these were not separated, disconnected, unrelated. The opposite was true. To him, these were but parts of the world, and they were full of connections and relationships, like cross references in various subject matters. Eddie didn't know that he was living with more intensity than many whose lives were, superficially, more varied, and who were having fun and good times. They were not giving themselves to all work and no play. Alongside of them, Eddie seemed the dull boy. He cast a smaller and more distorted shadow upon the visible earth. Those who cast more comely shadows must be more fortunate than Eddie. And it was so, theirs were the comelier shadows. To those who judged the shadows, Eddie was a young man with an unattractive shadow, a shadow unlike the rest of the shadows. He could cast no comely shadow, no lovely shadow. He was in flight from the shadow world, in search of that which was substance.

And he did not know that the more Edward A. Ryan was and became Edward A. Ryan, the more wrong would be his shadow in the world of the comely shadows.

He was living beyond the dancing shadows of the present. His mind was reaching out and into what could only be tumult and which did not balance into work and play, or into dullness and excitement. He was reaching out to life and he had no measures, no scales, no rulers, no containers which could control this living.

This was growth. He was growing, and he could not know for what destiny. He could not then have known that growing was a tumult carried into the unknown, unborn nothingness of the future that was only the hope of what he wanted to be and the mystery of what was to be.

The tumult of the substance was the feeling, the thinking, the living out of what the shadows merely reflected in outlined, wavering darkness against the light.

Eddie walked home alone after his first classes of that autumn quarter. And in the parlor, he sat down before a typewriter, and wanted to write something, a diary in which he would put into words, as though to last forever, what had happened since he had gotten up on that same morning.

But he did not know what to write. At the center of the top of the white, lined sheet of looseleaf paper, with two holes on the side, Eddie typed out, in upper case, the word:

DIARY

He typed the date on the right-hand side of the paper, up near the top.

He sat, struggling to bring something into his mind which would be expressed by words, and which would mean what he wanted it to mean.

He sat.

In sudden hopeful excitement, he typed:

This morning I began

He stopped typing. He looked at his few words on paper, at the typewriter, around the room.

He did not know what to write after the verb "began." He could not think of what to write, and bring himself to type whatever it might be.

He sat looking at the big, secondhand typewriter, and the white paper in the roller.

He heard his grandmother moving around in the back of the

apartment. She was singing a sad song, monotonously. He could not catch the words of the song, and heard only her voice, so monotonous and sad.

He looked at the paper.

His lips moved, and he read to himself, silently:

—This morning I began

Eddie couldn't write any more, gave up trying. Then he read restlessly and in snatches. One of the poems he read was Matthew Arnold's *Dover Beach*. He liked it, but couldn't decide why. Then he read Arnold's poem *The Future*. Life, the world, man became generalized, and as he read, it was as though the meanings were, also, far away, lost in other and earlier times, as well as in the future. The world seemed empty of people, except for the past, Matthew Arnold, and himself, and he followed the lines as though he were hearing Arnold speak, and, at the same time, he might have been Arnold, or in Arnold's mind when the poem was written. And then, the images and lines asserted themselves upon him, and he visualized the meaning of the words, but with some vagueness. A girl, and Rebekah by a well, and a herd of sheep, a desert of Araby. Time was an actual river, flowing through a somber world; he read aloud the two lines:

*But what was before us we know not
And we know not what shall succeed*

His mood became one of melancholy, and in his mind there was a growing dimness like the darkening atmosphere of a dejected day with a dejected gloom of heavy gray in the sky.

He put his book down on the floor, and sat, reaching for some sad thought which was hiding from him in his own mind. But the thought went unfound; it was like an invisible spirit permeating the air, floating through the atmosphere, unseen, yet seeing, and he imagined himself standing, alone, in a world where the air was gray and still, looking with a wish and drive beyond his power, wanting to call out for the spirit to tell him its knowledge, its answer to the sealed mystery of life and time.

And death.

The River of Time, he thought, was the River of Life and of Death. It flowed with fast, rich "deliberate aslowness" of *The Hound of Heaven,* and by its banks men stood, helpless and forever and always helpless. Only man was not standing by the banks of the River of Time. Man was carried along by that river.

And even the weariest river winds somewhere safe to sea.

He wished that the world were Swinburne's world, Swinburne's *Garden of Proserpine,* and that the softness of nothingness, that sleep which was like a dream that was no dream, nothingness that was a dreamless dream and a sleep with no waking, that this were the end.

But Hell was a pit of darkness with the silent, always running, red flames, and souls were burning, only burning in a silence where their cries were never heard, loud cries shouted in darkness, the agony of dying alone, but never dying, and that was life living forevermore. To burn and burn forever, moaning in the pains of Hell, knowing everything that had ever happened, knowing, helpless in the hot and licking flames of the burning black coal of Hell. But if Adam and Eve . . . if Eve had not heeded the snake, or was it that Eve had let Adam . . . let Adam . . .

He was halted for the word he should use. "Screw her," or the four letter word, or "jump," "get Eve's tail," or "get a piece," or . . . or . . .

If Eve and Adam hadn't had coitus, or copulated . . .

Thoughts of Time were melancholy, and Time was a flowing river, a ticking away, a dropping of the grains of sand, one by one by one. Time was sad because the meaning of Time was death, your own death.

Eddie had become drowsy, and let out an uncontrolled yawn which interrupted the flow of his thoughts. He felt dull and heavy. He let his eyes move vacantly about the parlor. The room was getting shabby. There were tears in the rug, and the wine-red coloring was faded. The chairs were scratched.

Another yawn came. Eddie thought that he ought to sleep. There was time for a nap. He wanted to sleep.

But he started to read the next day's history assignment, and persisted in it, fighting his sleepiness.

Chapter Nine

Socially, college life did not develop for Eddie Ryan as he hoped that it would. The University was a big one, with some thousands of students, and there were about a thousand freshmen. Among them, Eddie Ryan passed unnoticed. He walked to campus in the mornings with Peter Moore, attended classes, and then, occasionally, he would go to Harper Library to study or read, but on most mornings, he returned home after his last class. He read, studied, tried to keep a diary, and on some days, he wrote a book report, term paper, or other papers for his classes. His grandmother fixed lunch, and made him sandwiches to take to work, neatly wrapped up and tied. And then, there was his job at the station.

There was a uniformity about Eddie's days, and a regularity in his life. Most days seemed to be very much alike, and they were in their pattern of events. With the start of the autumn quarter, Eddie slept four to six hours a night, from Sunday to Thursday. He was often tired, but he drank coffee, sometimes to excess, to keep himself awake, and his mind more alert. When he had eyestrain, he increased the quantity of coffee he drank, and added aspirin as well. He would worry about the liberties he took with his health, but should he go blind, wrecked health would not make much difference, and perhaps a shorter life would be a benefit, a blessing in disguise. If he should lose his sight, his capacity to learn would be severely reduced, and he was racing against the possibility of such a disaster.

Eddie's fears that he might one day go blind had been roused in 1924 when he had gone to a specialist at Michigan and Monroe in the Loop, Dr. Stanford. About two weeks after he'd started attending night school, he'd had pains of blinding intensity in his eyeballs, and other, throbbing pains which ran in lines all the way back through his brain. He could remember a rainy Sunday in about the middle of October when the pains had been murderous, so sharp and pulsating that he had told himself that the pains of death could not be any more excruciating. He was still working at the Express Company and had started working a seven-day week, in order to get the extra day's pay.

The office was never closed, and was spoken of by wagonmen and their supervising bosses as a Stopover on the Way to Hell. On weekdays, the place was noisier than the Devil has any right to permit, because wagonmen and route inspectors came in, and a full staff of nine clerks as well as three wagon dispatchers shouted into the telephones, and there was plenty of additional shouting. But on Sundays, the office was quiet. Three clerks and three wagon dispatchers were on duty, handling the movements of the motor trucks, electrics, various horse-drawn vehicles, and tractors and trailers, in transferring incoming and outgoing shipments and taking care of occasional emergencies, such as a corpse.

Mickey Logan, nicknamed Funny Puss Jeff, handled special motor trucks, and therefore held the title of Chief Wagon Dispatcher, with no extra pay for the "Chief." He was theoretically in charge of the office, and also had authority over the clerks, or at least over those who didn't work at the other end of the long table with Hans Schmidt, of German descent but called the "Dutchman," and Blubber Cannon, who had once had Funny Puss Jeff's job but now was on the new tractor board. Funny Puss and Blub hurled insults back and forth at each other, often under the pretense of humor, but they had no use for one another.

Funny Puss had told Eddie that since he was going to school and trying to get himself an education, and was helping his mother, he could have work every Sunday. Most of the clerks didn't want the work, even though they would earn an extra day's pay.

Compared with other days of the week, Sunday work was easier, and Eddie liked it better, since he had come to accept the permanency of a seven-day week. He could get in some studying, because there wasn't too much work to do, and the pressure felt on weekdays was relaxed.

But that Sunday when his eyeballs burned with pain was Hell for him. Eddie kept trying to study his sociology textbook, but the pains became an agony. The strain of reading was too great for his weak and watering eyes. He closed the textbook, as though in admission of defeat of the spirit.

Lou Young and Charlie Norman, who were on the wagon and truck, both told Eddie several times to quit trying to study when he had eyestrain, there was no use in a man killing himself for anything. Young felt almost as badly as Eddie because he'd drunk too much beer and home-made brew the night before, and he hadn't gotten to bed until about three o'clock in the morning. Mickey Logan said that at least Young had had some fun getting himself into a passed-out condition, but Ryan, what sense did that make? When you were cold, you didn't have any fun, that was a goddamned sure thing in this man's world, and if you didn't have any fun while you were alive either, then, Jesus Christ, you sure were one poor sorry hell of a bastard.

Eddie kept looking at the clock and despondently thinking how long the day was, how much more time he had to stay and suffer, and of his misery. He'd told himself that he couldn't last it out until six o'clock, and he longed for that hour, and for his release. He was almost ready to let himself pass out and die.

Why did he have to pay so much just to get an education? Why didn't he give up, give up on everything?

But what do you do when you give up?

That Sunday had seemed like one of the worst days in his life, and had been spent in nausea and blinding pain. He was left in a nerve-shattered condition, and was jittery and restless for a couple of days. At the Express Company, he was kidded because of his excessive nervousness, and told that a whore only cost two bucks, and he'd better go get himself one.

A few days later, he went to see Dr. Stanford, a specialist who charged him ten dollars and fitted him with new glasses, but also told him that he couldn't use his eyes as much as he was. It was Eddie who had asked the question about blindness, and the doctor's answer had left him in a suffering state of ominous doubt. Dr. Stanford didn't say definitely that Eddie would go blind, but he did say that by thirty-five, Eddie's eyes could be very poor ones, very poor, if they were overused. Eddie said that he had to use them. The doctor warned him, and observed that Nature always took her revenge. Eddie asked if he had a chance of being able to use his sight for study and reading for more than fifteen years, or until he would be thirty-five. A chance, yes, but who could say for sure? The doctor advised Eddie to plan a life where he could work and be happy without having to put too much of a burden on his eyes.

"I can't, Doctor. I can't."

That had been on a gray afternoon, Funny Puss Jeff had given him the time off to have this eye examination, but he'd told him, for Christ sake, to hurry back.

Eddie had walked out of the building entrance on Monroe Street, after his visit to Dr. Stanford's office, with feelings that he couldn't possibly describe. He imagined himself in the future, a man of thirty-five blind, living with the world in darkness, and this was almost as though he were thinking of his doom and death. If he couldn't use his eyes for study, he'd end up like most of the men at the Express Company. His future would be ended now if he couldn't use his eyes.

Eddie had turned onto Wabash Avenue, and was drooping along southward to Van Buren Street, with a dazed expression on his face, his mind lost in despairing dullness.

Why did he have to have lousy eyes?

He saw all right now, and there were no pains. How could he believe that his eyes wouldn't always be the same?

There were no answers for him, nor was there much more to think of. What could he ask, and what could he think that would give him better eyes? He could pray and ask for a miracle. But prayers couldn't help him. God no longer worked miracles.

There was only one question for him to answer. To do or not

The Silence of History

to do, that was the question. To go on, use his eyes as long as he had them, to wear his eyes out in the best way he could, or else to abandon hope and resign himself to the life he'd have to live as Eddie, Edward Arthur Ryan.

Eddie's thoughts were drenched in pathos. He was creating a mental image of himself as one who bravely and courageously fights with destiny, who risks all and heeds not the cost, who takes the hard and unsure course, who loves a hero's glory. But what kind of hero was he? Why should he dream of any fame, and think that he ought to risk going blind in the prime of life, seeking that fame? Who cared if he should make something out of himself? And how did he know that he could make the name Edward A. Ryan famous and remembered after he died? No fellow his own age ever spoke of such glory, that was, none whom he knew. If he dared to speak of his dreams and his hopes, he'd be laughed at.

—Ryan, think you'll ever amount to anything? Hans Schmidt had asked.

To become a salesman and make fifty or a hundred bucks a week, to get an easy and soft job with lots of free time and dough in his pocket, that was one thing. But fame and glory, to become a name that would be imperishable, that was something of another order entirely.

Dr. Stanford had told him to get a job which didn't call for any great use of his eyes and to plan a future in the best possible way for saving them. But he wasn't blind yet, nor did he have any strain, any pains. How much could happen in fifteen years? Inventions, discoveries, new cures, and how could he be sure?

It was the uncertainty that had almost floored him, the fearful uncertainty that he'd carry with him for years, it was that which was the most terrifying for him, at least now and during the days and months and years before him when he would be studying, year upon year.

If he could go on and forget, and hope, not given in to terror, then he could face the danger with bravery, with high courage.

His work was so long and so short. Joy and sorrow were timeless, not actually, but a screen for time. You forgot time when you were happy, because you forgot yourself, and when you were miserable, you forgot the world and were too much with yourself.

He wanted to laugh, to stride along, as though he were without a care in the world, a picture, a walking image, an essence of nonchalance in motion.

Eddie drew himself up with an awkward movement which he knew was awkward, and felt he'd made himself a little ridiculous to anyone who noticed.

He had then crossed Adams Street, and had begun to walk with a brisker gait, celebrating a change of mind. The thoughts he'd just had, sob-sister thoughts, were like fading dreams which had stolen in upon him while he'd been taking a tired nap. And his mood and brooding thoughts grew strange in his inexplicably sudden state of false elation.

It was about three-fifteen, and he had to work until six o'clock. It wasn't a school night. He wished he didn't have to go back to work; perhaps he should have taken the day off, or at least the afternoon. But money talked. He was saving, bit by bit, but how small the bits were. His savings account was nineteen dollars. Still, every dollar counted and added up, so long as he could leave it in the bank. He'd be seven to ten years studying, and then he wanted to do his post-graduate work at the University of Chicago. He saved for the day he might have enough to go to the University during the day.

Climbing up the winding steps from the loading platform, where freight was piling up, going back to the office to work out the rest of the day, Eddie's spirits sank, and he was depressed with what he was, instead of enthused by the hopes of what he wanted to become.

As he had entered the noisy office, with the clerks shouting into telephone mouthpieces, Funny Puss Jeff and Blubber were shouting insults at one another, but Funny Puss paused long enough to tell Eddie that he'd been gone a long time.

"I couldn't help it. I had to wait until the doctor took me for an eye examination," Eddie said.

"You can't learn nothin' by gettin' better glasses to read more, Ryan," Blubber yelled at him from the tractor board.

The Silence of History

"Nobody missed him, that's how smart he is," Hans Schmidt called out.

Eddie clenched his teeth but said nothing. He couldn't understand why Blubber, and a lot of the others, the wagon dispatcher and route inspectors, didn't like him, and could get such pleasure in trying to hop on his tail. Eddie didn't realize that these men were ridden by envy because they all felt so small. The mere fact that he had graduated from high school was a cause for envy, a source of many of their belittling wisecracks and of the contempt they would show for him. Some of them had not even finished grammar school, and they all wished that they'd had some education. Then they could have done better for themselves in life. That's what they thought.

And when he started to go to night school, Eddie had demonstrated that he wanted to get the hell out of the common trap in which he and they were caught. They admired him and were resentful because he was trying to go beyond them.

Before he quit the Express Company to work for Rawlinson, Eddie had become largely impervious to what most of the men said or might think of him. In spirit he was outside of and beyond the company. Except for a passing moment, he had almost no dislike for the men. Eddie did not persist in any dislikes of people, and often he would feel sorry for them, because there was something, or many things, about their lives, which were too bad, just too bad. He saw them all, spending their lives doing the same things, the same work that they were then doing, and saying the same things, and telling the same jokes. He wanted to escape.

And he did escape.

However, it had been while he was still working at the Express Company that he had first been seized with the fear of blindness.

A young man cannot learn such news about himself, and make the decision to study at the risk of going blind around the age of thirty-five and be calm, equable, and like other young men of his time and age. He cannot go on along the road he had just chosen, and be nonchalant, unaffectedly courageous, fearless, and as casually defiant of his fate as the shadowed image of a young man on a black and white screen in a motion picture theater, who is romantically foolhardy, senselessly brave for success and the fair damoiselle.

Eddie's antagonist was himself, his nerves and senses, whose agonies and strains would result in pain that he would feel, and eyes that, he now had to dread, might lose their capability to receive images of light and register them in his brain. And his antagonist was also whatever in the world would impede his onward course. This was his fate, his destiny, and the price which it seemed to place on his meeting it and conquering it was heavy.

And all good Americans, presumably millions, were cheering for Eddie because he was going to do the American thing in the American way, only harder, and he was taking a chance of giving up more than his youth and the pleasures of youth. But all of America did not know of Edward Arthur Ryan, and that small percentage which did was concerned with other affairs and interests. Someday, all of America would know of his struggle, and then it would cheer him. So he thought.

But he couldn't do it as the movie stars did it. He couldn't be recklessly brave without fear, without doubt, without his moments of somber and depressed thoughts, his moods when sadness not only filled his mind, but also was the shroud of the world. There were times when he wanted to cry out to God across all of the spaces of the sky, to ask why and to say that it shouldn't be the way it was, it shouldn't be for him to have eyes too weak for the burden they must bear when others had perfect eyes, which they didn't need or think much about.

And he tried to fight such brooding moods. He wanted to be brave without as much as batting an eyelash. He wanted his struggle to be spectacular and heroic, for that was the kind of life he wished for himself, and that was the kind of a person he would be, if he could. But the terms of fate, of life, were plain and prosaic, and the risks were great. The risks were not to be talked about with many, for it was crazy in their way of looking at things. And yet he wanted to talk, and to be lauded, praised, patted on the back.

Eddie could not explain what he meant in a manner which

The Silence of History

would win the interest of anyone who did not know and like him. For he spoke only of a personal ambition, and he couched his words in the usual ones of success, getting-ahead, climbing to the top of the heap on the ladder. But that was not what he meant because it was not what he felt. He did not merely feel that he was going to get rich and be an important man of wealth. He felt that he was going to do something, but he didn't fully know what it was. He could and did say that he was going to study law, practice law and go into politics, and he also hoped to teach, and to write. But he felt more than that which each or all of these aims might suggest. He felt that he was going to get deeply into life, and that he was going to achieve some kind of destiny. More vaguely, he felt that he would be important in some sense, some way, and that he was going to pursue and gain knowledge which was the key to power. He did not ask himself what he meant by power; he did not question the meaning of this word. He felt the sense of destiny which had been in him since his early boyhood. What he was living through to achieve was life and light, and if he did not do it, there would be neither life nor light. He felt that this was his justification. To sacrifice his ambitions would be to accept a kind of darkness, even though it was not a physical blindness.

There was almost a year, less than three weeks short of one, between the visit to Dr. Stanford's office and the first day of the fall quarter. Eddie's fears about his eyesight had diminished and were diffused through his thoughts and moods. He had had moments of the most shattering anxiety, when he had wanted to quit, and to cry out against the fate that forced him to suffer as others did not, to suffer for doing what was supposed to be right, and a reason for winning encouragement and admiration. It was for such actions that he suffered, not for sinful or evil conduct. And sin and evil were the reasons why people were punished, were they not? This was what he had acquired as a belief while he'd been growing up.

But his eyestrains and his moods passed, and he had good days, when he used his eyes as much as he could in study and reading, without pain. He would forget the danger ahead, and go on assuming that he would have his sight for his whole lifetime.

However, a whole lifetime was too brief for him, and it was going, racing by. He was taking the Cash and letting the Credit go, but not the Cash that Omar Khayyám meant, the pleasures of the moment. These were the Credit for him, while the Cash was what he could put into his mind. He sometimes thought of the particular quatrain out of FitzGerald in which the Persian poet had used this metaphor, and he would sadden with the awareness that he was missing so much of youth and fun, like kisses and all of the sensuous and emotional pleasures and fulfilling feelings which must come from love, the joy of good times, the knowledge of girls and their bodies, so painful to him to see and not to know, not to have, while everyday and everywhere, fellows his own age were going out with girls, girls young and lovely, and indescribable in their first blushing youth and development, with their bodies formed or forming, their breasts quivering under their dresses, their bodies slender and full of grace, their legs shapely, and their faces like lights upon the sea of the world, with bright clear eyes, and soft tender skin, and smiles on their faces which were the smiles and the laughter of life. They could laugh as youth and life could laugh, new and growing, with the dew of spring mornings and the softness and languorousness of spring days in their laughter, and in their eyes, and in their bodies.

And others knew these girls, and shared the laughter of life in the springtime of their years. But he was missing this.

This, he believed, was the Credit which he was letting go. At least, he wanted to believe it. He was not convinced that it was actually true, or even true at all. He was a failure, a flop with girls, and he didn't know how to amuse them, interest them, win their hearts, as certainly his friend George Raymond did, or as many others could, even fellows who weren't in George Raymond's class.

Eddie felt a slow-growing sense of separation, from old friends, from his environment, and his past. This was vague, and he did not understand it with full clarity, any more than he understood much about who he was, and where he was going in life, and time, and society. He was absorbing, finding his way, not judging on the instant what he read, learned, thought, whom he met,

The Silence of History

and he carried his past and his environment with him to the University. He was no young rebel, and did not feel a need to rebel, but only to learn.

So he was in the fall of 1925.

He was fighting the future, fighting for the future, fighting for something in that future which he only sensed, for some value beyond just money or having his name known. It was a most vaguely sensed quality of life, something that was like Shelley's:

The desire of the moth for the star
Of the night for the morrow
The devotion to something afar
From the sphere of our sorrow.

He read this poem of Shelley's and recited it to himself. He thought of a girl, and of more. He was living to find "something afar." He also read and reread Shelley's *Adonis*. And in the filling station, in class, anywhere, unpredictably, he would be moved by the lines:

Who waged contention with their time's decay.

He'd think of himself finding some way, his way, to do something like that, to wage . . . *contention with their time's decay.*

Every minute, he felt a need to be working toward that future, toward "something afar," and toward the waging of that contention with time's decay. If he had to go blind doing it, he would, but in himself he wept silent tears for himself, as though he were Adonis.

Chapter Ten

I

Gradually, day-by-day, Eddie had been changing and growing, more than he knew or could understand. He was happier in hopes than he was grim in determination. The hopes were the sunny surface, flashing and glinting with dancing dots and spots and streaks of golden sunlight, and the grim determination was the cold current, running fast and far down.

Eddie's growth and his will for the future had not as yet brought him into conflict with himself or with the values and beliefs that he was bringing with him out of his short past. All that he must sacrifice could be time, and the risk of his eyes. This was what he thought. He had vague premonitions of more, but he never thought about what they might mean, and they were but the result of moods and melancholy broodings.

Thus was Eddie Ryan in October 1925. Up to that time, his life had been one with more sorrows than joys, and he had not known much happiness. The sorrows which he had known and witnessed had been big; the happinesses had been little. He expected that his happiness would become big. And he liked to think of himself as already happy, and to imagine that others thought of him as someone to be envied, leading the college life, going to dances and parties, knowing keen and much-sought-after coeds, acquiring the manners and blandness of a college man who rated socially and was somebody, taking on polish and becoming sophisticated. He wanted it thought that he was happy. Not to be happy, not to have good times, not to be socially accepted, these were all signs of incapacity, of something wrong with yourself, something which stamped you as inferior. And he had so frequently suffered from such feelings that he could no longer bear them, or so he thought.

Eddie had almost no time for any such campus life, and didn't know how to find it and become a part of it. He was shy about approaching others, and proudly sensitive of being snubbed. He couldn't be sure of when to nod and say "Hello" outside of a classroom, and would pass by someone who sat near to him in one of his courses. During the first days, he had received a couple of additional rebuffs, besides the one from Fox. It was bewildering to know how you decided which students were worth speaking to, and which ones weren't? He couldn't understand it. But being snubbed and ignored hurt him, and he was quickly becoming conditioned to avoid repetitions of this same thing. He was careful about talking to anyone, and those fall days became lonelier ones than the mornings of the summer quarter had been.

Eddie had looked forward to seeing the home football games, and arranged with his partner, Jameson, to come to work late on Saturdays, and to make up the time on other days. The old man wouldn't agree to working both Saturday shifts, and taking Sundays or Mondays off. It was settled how the shifts were to be worked, and he wouldn't agree to any change. Eddie thought this a dirty trick and selfish. But he didn't know that Jameson's main reason for refusing was his sick wife, who would have terrors alone in the dark, and who became distressed and like a frightened child if the old man wasn't with her. Jameson, Eddie thought, was mean and, like many old men, just as stiff as a board. Eddie also believed that the old man was dominating him, selfishly using and taking advantage of his need to work the afternoon shift on workdays in order to attend classes and also, selfishly refusing to make any concessions on weekends by taking an afternoon shift. Jameson might have made an arrangement to have a relative or neighbor in and succeeded in accustoming his poor wife to his absence, but he was under enough strain and pressure. And he was tired at night, even though he might nap before supper. His back would ache and his bones would grow weary. The years were penetrating bone and muscle, even though they had not weakened his will and independence.

Jameson also liked Eddie in a manner the youth couldn't understand. To him, Eddie was "the boy," "the kid." He was a good and decent kid, and ought to be kept that way. With guidance, and some stiffness of treatment, Ryan would stay a good kid, but he was the kind who could go wild, and squander his chances. Some reins had to be held tight on him, or he'd run away, and maybe get himself into trouble. A kid who worked like Ryan was overdoing it, and if you overdid things in one way, you could just as easily overdo things in another way. Kids were like that. It was human nature, and he had been around long enough to know a little something of human nature.

And Jameson believed that he had a responsibility to watch Eddie, to guide and help him. For when he'd been given the kid as a partner, after his friend and former partner, Mike Moore, had to quit because of a bad heart, Pat Keefe had come around to see him and had spoken of Ryan.

—Jamesy, I got a kid I want you to take in place of poor Mike.

—Pat, I don't want no more of them goddamned kids, not in this station—them black tarts are out walkin' the streets every night and you can't have no young kid here. You can't take a chance. You know what happens just as plain as me.

—Yeah, but this kid's different.

—What do you mean, different? At that age, they got too much in their pants and too little upstairs.

—This kid, his name is Ryan, he's got to work an afternoon-night shift so he can go to college.

—A fraternity boy, is that what you're gettin' me?

—No, Jamesy. You'll like Ryan. He's not cut out to work in a station.

—Then why in the name of blazes should I have him?

—He's a genius.

—I never seen a kid that was that, Pat. They don't come around this neck of the woods.

—He is, I'm certain of it. That's why I took him on. I had everybody and his brother telephoning me to get their friends a job, and six times as many requests and applications, ten times as many as I could fill. I kept some mighty important men

The Silence of History

waiting with their applicants, and took Ryan ahead of anyone. He's cut for bigger things than you or I will ever know, and he's a good, clean Irish boy, and we can be proud of him. A steady hand like yours will help him along. He's got his head up there in the stars.

Jameson had growled that he'd take the kid. Keefe was the boss, of course, and could have ordered Ryan to the station without consulting Jameson, but the Old Man was like a law and a tradition at Rawlinson's, and no one ever went against his wishes. It was known that he was the most reliable and honest man in the service stations, and grouchy as he could get, he had a heart of gold and a faithfulness like that of an old servant.

Keefe thanked Jameson for being willing to accept Ryan as a partner. He told the Old Man that Ryan needed help because he was a dreamy kid who studied and thought, but would be reliable, and was the kind of young fellow they wanted.

—Some day, he might go up so high, Jamesy, that you and I will go to him for a favor. That's how promising he is. You're the one man I got who can help him and take care of him the best, better than any other of my men in the stations.

—Well, I'll damn quick find out how smart he is and how good. There ain't a thing can happen in this station that I don't know about. My friends come around and tell me what goes on when I ain't here. This is one station that's always going to be honest and run proper, as long as I'm around, and you know that, Pat.

—I sure do, Old Boy.

That was how Eddie was assigned to work with the Old Man.

When Keefe lost out, and Mr. Wood was brought in, one thing Keefe did was to convince Mr. Wood about Ryan, and Jameson knew that Mr. Wood had the same ideas about the kid that Pat Keefe had. In fact, Mr. Wood was likely to help the kid go up higher and faster because he had drag with the big shots in the company, back East, so Jameson had heard.

Jameson had given his word to take care of Ryan, and he believed that he was performing a duty to the company, as well as helping Eddie. He complained and found little faults, but then, he would soften up and speak to Eddie in a gentle voice.

He'd do the extra cleaning with the idea of leaving the kid more time to study his books at night, and he had come to take great pride in the boy; while he didn't know in this man's hell what they meant by them words like genius, he knew a promising kid when he saw one, and Ryan was a promising kid, who was going somewhere up in this world, if he didn't foul himself out of a chance.

My God, the kid came to work every day with a briefcase chockful of books, and his friends said that at night, when business was dead, you could see him standing up over the desk, studying his books, night after night, and they didn't know how a kid could study that way. And Ryan kept up his end of the stick, and sold oil, too. Since Ryan had come to the station, flushing oil sales had gone up a couple of gallons, and that was a sign the kid was on his toes.

Jameson knew how a young fellow liked a night out and a good time, and he had no objections to that, within limits, but with the kid, it was a different matter. He had a responsibility and he thought it best not to give way on certain matters. It was better for Ryan to have a hard fight now. That would make a better man of him, and he'd value his future success all the more.

Eddie, ignorant of the Old Man's motives, and of the exceptionally high regard in which he was held in the office, was silently resentful and began to want a change. He tried to dislike Jameson, but he couldn't. He would always catch a note of pathos and sadness in the Old Man's walk, or in his soft gray eyes, or in his voice, and his anger and dislike would crumble in him. But all the more, he knew that something would sooner or later have to be done, and he'd have to declare his independence from Jameson. It was pretty mean, not agreeing to let him take off Saturdays, after the football games. What fun was there in seeing his first college football game as a student, and then rushing to Saturday night work at the station while most of the students were going on to a night of fun and dates, to parties and dances, the good times of youth and the gaieties of student life? For over a year, he'd been driving himself, working while others of his age were out with girls and having good times. He had no girl, no dates, none of the carefree good fellowship that others knew, and of which he'd known a little during his last year of high school, until he'd started night school in the fall of 1924.

—A kid like you don't need to think about them fraternity boys with rich fathers supportin' 'em, Jameson had told him. You watch where you're going, take a little advice, and you'll go so far past them in life they won't see you in the distance.

This remark had struck Eddie as very curious, but he'd liked it. He'd agreed with it, but he was young, and he wanted fun and romance, the kind of youth he'd had far too little of, the kind of good times that were supposed to give you lifetime memories.

By fall, he had begun to fear that all he'd be at the University was a grind and a drone, the kind of student who knew nothing but what was in books, and whose entire college career would be spent with books.

—You always got your nose in a book, his Uncle Larry had said to him several times.

And Freckles Dolan, one of the older guys who hung around 58th Street had told him after Mass one Sunday:

—You read too many books, Goof, and they'll lock you up in Dunning or Kankakee—you'll spend your life in the booby hatch.

He knew better and was happy with books and study, and already, he had come to realize that his life would be too short for him to read all the books that he must read and wanted to read. But he couldn't stop dreaming and wanting and all of the girls he had ever known and wanted to love, and had wanted to love him, had left him with the image of the girl he sought, the girl who would give him love and purity and beauty of living, and he wanted to find her, dance with her, kiss her, walk in the moonlight with her and feel that the glory and the grandeur of the world was in the conquest of their love, and that their kisses were full of shining silver of the moon, which filled the night with the dancing and glistening beauty of all of life and time.

Eddie had hoped for this with the faith of his hungers, even though he had no girl. He imagined, every day in fact, that he'd find one. And there would be the football games, and a date, dancing, and the moonlight with love.

Jameson's firm refusal to work the full second Saturday shift was robbing him of this dream. The Old Man could stay on for him while he saw the games, but then, after the games, Eddie would have to come to work. Sunday mornings were busy and a number of customers came in for Jameson to drain their cars. He'd been doing this for years, and they expected only him to do it. He couldn't work seventeen hours on Saturday, and be on his toes at seven A.M. on Sunday morning.

Eddie even saw in what the Old Man said, and in his keeping special customers, a way of protecting himself and his record with Rawlinson. That was all the Old Man had, and as Eddie often heard, plenty of good men were walking the streets. He could more than see a case for the Old Man, and he thought of Jameson's age, and felt that, perhaps, he had no right to ask such a favor of him.

Eddie went to the football games with Peter Moore. They both had loved sports all through boyhood, and enjoyed playing or watching. Peter was going out for the track team, and he had specialized in high-jumping, although he was also very fast as a runner, and could well stand a chance as one, at least on the relay team. Eddie wished he could go out for freshman football, basketball, or baseball, and hoped that the athletic authorities would look up his high school athletic record in the Catholic League, and know of the reputation he had had. He was not heavy enough for college athletics, his weight being around one hundred and fifty-five pounds, but he was worth a man twenty pounds heavier and an inch or more taller because of his broad shoulders, in which there was much power, and his long arms. He hoped that, somehow, he would manage to get the help, or to make arrangements which would give him time for athletics. Perhaps his right knee, injured in high school, and again in prairie football, was in good shape, or he could wear a steel guard, or even have an operation performed on it. He'd stand a chance of making some of the teams because he had shown enough ability in high school.

From early boyhood on, Eddie had dreamed of athletic glory and fame, and his dreams lingered with him. If he could find

The Silence of History

the time to play, maybe he could win a Rhodes Scholarship. This, too, was a dream of his.

Eddie had not outgrown the idea of school spirit, and he wanted to feel it, express it, and believe that it was important. This was one of the preconceptions which he had brought with him to the University. But school spirit was linked up with his dreams and visions of glory, because he did not want merely to be one who cheered others in loud bursts, but he wanted to be one of the cheered. He saw school spirit and college tradition as one who would, if he could, be part of both. He did not belong with those who acclaimed; his place was among those who achieved and were acclaimed. And he'd had this feeling concerning himself ever since he had been a little boy of six or seven.

Eddie sat among the students with Peter and a few of Peter's friends. One was Abe Lustig, a big, dark-haired, raw-boned, homely young man from Milwaukee, Wisconsin, who had already jumped 5 feet 11 inches as a freshman high jumper, and might one day break the world's record. Abe was supposed to be a genius who got straight A's in science, in which he was majoring. His only interests were high-jumping and science, and socially he was shy and awkward. Since he was a Jew, he wasn't eligible for membership in the Gentile fraternities, but would have turned down bids from them, as he had from a Jewish one. He had never learned to dance, just as Peter hadn't, and was oppressively shy with girls. He was self-contained, and needed few friends and little relaxation. Living in a rooming house near the campus, he made his own lunch, and ate it with Peter, who carried lunch to school every day in his briefcase.

Eddie and Abe took to one another, and although they didn't have much to say, they communicated a feeling of mutual respect which both caught and accepted. Both Abe and Peter Moore appealed to Eddie, to an important aspect of his nature, and he felt genuine comradeship for them. He respected their seriousness, simplicity, and innocence, and often wanted it for himself, and wished that he did not have so many counter-impulses, desires, and inclinations.

Usually they sat about halfway up in the north stand, in the midst of students, and Eddie felt a real satisfaction, a sense of accomplishment, but he couldn't get himself to let go and cheer, and he only mumbled the words of songs to himself, because he sang so badly—he was totally unable to carry a tune. But the school songs stirred him, and he wanted them to mean much to himself and to other students. There was a need within him, like a vacuum, which the songs seemed to fill. The *Alma Mater Song* evoked a solemnity and seriousness of mind, and he felt himself as one who had become a part of the University and who would strive and struggle to make himself a part of its traditions.

*She could not love thee half so well
Loved she not honor more.*

Then he would leave with Peter and Abe, and his mood would sink, falling into its own darkness. He would part from his friends and walk to the Midway, where he caught a bus to take him to work. It was a lonely experience, one of the loneliest he had ever had, the slow walk from the Reynolds Club, where he could hear a jazz band playing for dancing students, past the tennis courts, the various dormitories, and across the Midway to Woodlawn Avenue, where the bus would stop. The years before him seemed like a long road of sacrifice, and he wondered how many such years there would be, and for how long he would go on, leading this lonely life of his.

For two straight Saturdays this happened. Darkness had set in when he reached the station, and Jameson, who was all ready to go, spoke for a few moments about the events of the day at the station, asked about the game, and then left.

The football games loosened Eddie's sense of purpose, and weakened his powers of concentration. He was still developing his habits of concentration, and he was far from having attained a minimum of knowledge, which could serve as the foundation for an embedded intellectual self-assurance. He was prey to distraction; pleasure, intoxication, a happy or exciting break in his routine, were as much of a torment as a refreshment. He had to struggle with himself to grind on in his merciless routine of study, study. His mind would rebel against the will he tried to impose on it.

He was very restless, and was sorry for himself. He was missing life and love. He managed to study, but with less consistent concentration, and he went outside often, to look at the sky, at the moon and the stars.

II

Eddie had made a good start in the fall quarter. From the first day, he had kept up with his reading assignments, and done regular, almost daily, collateral reading. Both of his courses could have been easy, if he had allowed this, but Eddie did not think in terms of getting by, nor confine himself to his assignments. The courses were mere springboards for him to dive into a river of knowledge, and to swim as far as swiftly as he could. And he began swimming fast the moment he hit the water.

But he became restless and dissatisfied, because he felt himself to be bound and hemmed in, restricted on a long, daily grind, and very lonely. He was not making friends on campus, and none of the fraternities found out about him, and sought him out. He met no girls, even though they were like a swarm on campus, and he could not walk about so long as five minutes without seeing one or more, even a bevy of them. For many others, the campus appeared to be such a friendly place, but for him it was lonely. He attended classes, and sometimes went to Harper Library for books, or to read and study there for a few hours.

Eddie was overstimulated intellectually, and otherwise locked up in himself. His full release came from his mind and the physical activity which was required as part of his duties as a filling station attendant. He was happy, and would have known that he was, had he only allowed himself to do so. However, he could not do this. He kept thinking that he ought to be bid by a frat, and know club girls who were popular and sought after, and he ought to be going to dances and parties, and be recognized as somebody, and he ought to be known as having been a pretty damned good Catholic high school athlete, and damned promising varsity material; he ought to be in the swing of things, socially.

But he didn't know how to make any of this happen, and he knew that if he were to be living such a student life, he couldn't study as much, and he would have to sacrifice precious time. And he didn't think he could like fraternity boys, and campus big shots as he liked Peter Moore and Abe Lustig, and he couldn't value a big boy like Fox, because he was a dumb center and a frat man, or guys who were somebody because they had cars and money to blow, maybe raccoon coats, and clothes bought at the Hub, Rothschild's, Marshall Field's, or one of the other best places down in the Loop, because they had an old man who was in the bucks, and he couldn't value and like guys who sat next to him in the classroom and walked by him on campus as though he were an Eskimo whom they'd never seen before, and he couldn't value rich boys who would treat him like an unwanted Polack or inferior if they knew the story of his family and how his father had died, just about a pauper, and he couldn't like the frat boys who dressed with careful carelessness, and shook hands with the college handshake as though they were bored, and let conceited and insulting words drop out of the side of their mouths.

How could he like the girls he wanted, the snooty blondes, who looked at you and never saw you, the girls who liked you for your slow, affected, don't-care gait, your being the son of some man who was rich, your fraternity pin, your drawling tone of voice, your way of calling your old man the "Governor," the "Pater," the "Lord of the Exchequer," your way of dancing as if it didn't interest you, talking as if it were a condescension to speak.

And yet he wanted such people to notice him. He wanted it because he had been part of it in grammar school and high school, and it was the world of those who were something and his was the world of those who weren't much. He wanted it because he had been ashamed of so much, of his grandmother smoking a pipe and not being able to read or write, of his mother dressing like the scrubwoman's cousin and his father driving a horse-and-wagon and not being a businessman, and dying like a sick pauper, of his aunt's drinking and cursing, of his having had to graduate from high school without paying his senior year's tuition, of the times he had not been wanted, had been ditched by other kids, not invited to parties, turned down when he phoned girls for dates, and of all the pretending that he and his family were more than they were, and were just like those who were better off.

Only a week or two of the fall quarter went by before these shames of many years began to crop up in his thoughts, and he would think that he might be snubbed, and that all of those he knew, his old friends, the girls who had refused him dates, and had perhaps laughed at him, and many others, could laugh again because he was a student at the U but no different socially.

He had gotten A's in the summer quarter, and Miss Patrick was praising him in class before the first week was ended, and after the first quiz in History, Professor Carleton had looked at him, and told the class how very few of them wrote well enough for a college student, and he knew that Professor Carleton meant that he was one of the exceptions. Once in the classroom, his feelings of shame and inferiority, or, as Freud wrote, his "inferiority complex," were forgotten, and at times he'd forget himself, in thinking of the lecture or the questions on subjects under discussion. But after his interest in class, there was the emptiness he usually had when the bell rang.

A few times, he stood in the crowd before Cobb Hall, and heard snatches of talk about dates, dances, parties after the football games, and he wished he were not at the University. He told himself that he didn't belong where he was. But he quickly corrected himself. He didn't belong with the frat boys, club girls, at parties and in the campus social life. He should give up hoping, and come here to study, and learn with drive, and stun them, anybody and everybody, by forcing them to recognize him.

But he was sliding away from a boyhood feeling of showing them, and he was developing a strong power drive. What he was beginning to tell himself was that he would find, and develop, grow, have power within himself, and that he would win the world with power. It was the growing of sinews of emotions and will in his own character; it was the strength to be more alone with himself; it was a force of mind and energy. The first surgings of this he had felt, faintly and episodically.

In the history class, Professor Carleton had begun with the French Revolution. The lectures and reading overexcited Eddie, and he was living the violent grandeur of those days, wishing that he had been alive at that time, wondering if he would have been brave enough, and what he would have done, what his place in history would have been.

The French Revolution as it was described and analyzed in class and in Eddie's readings, cleared his mind of platitudes, fragmented impressions, like torn bits of old letters or notebooks, remembered clichés and lurid, melodramatic scenes of unmotivated mob violence and senseless, savage murder and brutality. Eddie's notions of the French Revolution had come from *A Tale of Two Cities*, and Rafael Sabatini's *Scaramouche*, his history lessons in third year of high school, and scraps of remembered allegations and facts from newspapers, magazines, and movies. And he had thought of the French Revolution as an outburst of mob violence and of feeling against the Church, which had resulted in persecutions. Napoleon he had seen separately from the Revolution, and he'd never thought much of a connection. But he'd never thought much, or scarcely at all, of the French Revolution until he matriculated at the University. Eddie had few real ideas about history, but a fair number of generalities, prejudices, distorted impressions, and subjective admirations and antipathies, and these, like odds and ends stuffed into an attic, were what history had meant to him. This in spite of the fact that he had acquired, mostly in a random and unintended fashion, much information about the events of history, dates, facts, chronological sequences. He had seen history as beyond him, solemnly dramatic and in books which usually had a dull colored binding. He was only in the process of losing this preconception when he began to take Professor Carleton's course. And his awakening memory was one of the most important events of his life. It was something which was happening every day, and which had been happening for over a year. And because of it, he was able to bear the strain, the grind, the restraint, the loneliness of his life better than he otherwise could have. The youth with thick

The Silence of History

glasses, and a touch of wonder in the far-away, dreamy, absent-mindedness of his weak eyes, with curly hair and a thin boyish face, who looked far too young to show the determination suggested by his chin, or the sensuality which his lips bore witness to, came and went at the University, carrying his briefcase stuffed with books and notebooks, spoke little because he was too shy and didn't know what to say, and was spoken to but little because he somehow didn't inspire others to approach him, this youth Eddie Ryan, seemed like a dull grind, as innocent as he might be uninteresting.

Eddie was growing. The roots of his growth were beginning to push up into his consciousness, and break through, as into sunlight and air. He was expanding from within. Eddie was becoming a new, a different Eddie. And also, as he grew, his loneliness could only become more poignant. Growth could only separate him more from those he had known who were not growing.

And Eddie was having sex on his mind too much. He could fight sex impulses in himself for years, until he got married, couldn't he?

But how did he know that he ever would get married? Judging by his whopping successes in getting dates, how could he describe his future prospects as promising, or should they even be considered as prospects at all? Whatever the prospects were, marriage was and would have to remain years off in the future. How could he not go nuts if he should have to practice celibacy all these years? And if he shouldn't, or didn't, then he'd be guilty of a mortal sin. This was clear, beyond all doubt, and there were no moderating circumstances. But merely to think of this put him into a slough of gloom.

It was hard, damn hard, too damned hard to be a Catholic, and he found himself wishing, as he had often wished in boyhood days when he'd been tormented by the fear of having made a bad confession, that he weren't a Catholic. It was harder to be a Catholic because you knew, too clearly, the lines between what was and what wasn't a mortal sin. This was why he sometimes fell into his dark moods, and became so glum and gloomy and full of pessimism. He knew too clearly the difference between a sin and what wasn't a sin, and between a mortal sin and a venial sin. He knew what he should do, and what he shouldn't do. And how could you live and avoid occasions of sin? If you didn't avoid them, you were, sure as hell and high water, going to commit sin, at least he was. And if he did avoid them, he would commit sins of thought and desire, and these, also, could be mortal sins.

It was sex, the sixth commandment, *Thou shalt not commit adultery*. It set you in a battle with yourself, and you never won it, or lost, either. The war didn't stop, and forgetting was only a truce.

Eddie knew that it was best not to think of the whole question, and that was what he tried to do. Whenever he was able to throw himself totally into study, he succeeded, but that wasn't always possible, not for him, or, perhaps, not yet. Here was one of his problems, the battle of his own will over himself. He had to make his mind obey his will, and he wasn't a saint, and knew that he never would be one.

He didn't only daydream of girls and love, romance, and of "The desire of the moth for the star," but, also of sex and laying a girl, except, no, he didn't like the word "laying." What substitute did he like? He didn't know, he couldn't be sure.

And every night, he saw the girls go by, alone, or sometimes in pairs, walking slowly, not strolling, but merely taking slow, very slow steps, as though they didn't at all want to be walking, and had no place to go, no destination. The way they walked was like wearing a red light, and he guessed this made it easier for guys to approach them, and it was a means of attracting the attention of men in the cars always zooming by on Michigan Avenue. By eight o'clock, they started coming out, and as the clock ticked close to eight, he'd start to get a little nervously distracted, and he'd begin looking up from his books, wanting to see them outside, hoping for something to happen by chance, or just to happen, half-thinking that maybe he'd speak to one, and tell her "Yes, Babe, come back at midnight and stay right there on the sidewalk, and I'll be ready, Babe, ready to get right out of my shoes."

The Silence of History

He kept imagining himself doing this, and getting it done and over with, so he could concentrate more easily on study. He didn't do it. Night after night passed. He still didn't do it. The fact that it would be a sin was not the only reason why he didn't, and he was inclined to believe that the fear of sin was the least of the reasons. A venereal disease, the clap or syphilis, would be a lousy kind of bad luck to catch, and he was afraid of that kind of bad luck, especially of syphilis. There was safety and he kept meaning to buy some Merry Widows at a drugstore and he'd forget, or be too embarrassed at the prospect of walking into a drugstore and asking for them.

And wouldn't it be sordid, paying, getting, getting off? And he didn't do it, but only thought of it, imagined it happening, planned to do it and then he couldn't, and he'd be breathless and sweating under the armpits, and his heart would start up like an overworked engine, palpitating, and he'd be helpless, like someone afraid of ghosts, like a hick, a yokel, helpless, quivering, and almost dizzy. It would go, he'd relax, resume his studying, and be glad and proud of himself.

There was masturbation, but he'd beat that, and stopped it before he was twenty-one, and that was one of his best victories, because it had used to leave him disgusted as well as ashamed and guilty about a mortal sin.

A few of the girls became recognizable; they were regulars, on a beat. One was the little, light tan one with the shabby white collar on her cloth coat, and the pointed nose, the black bobbed hair and bangs. She was almost a beauty, and she'd come every night, sometimes with a taller, darker, blacker one who wore a black cloth coat and high, high heels that made it difficult for her to walk, and funny to watch. The littler one, when alone, or else the two of them, would stand outside, near the corner, and wait, with their eyes peeled on the passing automobiles.

The sight of the two prostitutes waiting to be picked up would work upon his blood and titillate him. He would try to keep his eyes on his book, but he kept watching, and hoping that the pickup would happen very quickly. It usually did, but on a couple of nights, the wait was about a half-hour, and Eddie was distracted with interest. But he was more sad with pity than he was excited as the two of them stood in the dim glare of light from the station sign, and the automobiles hummed and hummed, and the girls waited, shifting their weight from foot to foot, turning their heads, moving a few feet in one or the other direction, tapping a toe or heel on the sidewalk, swinging a pocketbook, gesturing, and waiting before the eyes of every passing stranger who must have known on sight that they were two whores waiting for trade. If they turned toward the station, he'd avert his glance in strangely shy embarrassment, and he'd wish for the pickup to happen quickly, immediately. The sight of them would pull at him, until he was helplessly sorry and sad, and full of a pity that he couldn't very well express.

And there were others, a hefty blonde, middle-aged and hideously made-up; a skinny white girl who seemed to him sad to the marrow of her bones; a kinky-haired, buxom black girl who wore a white fur piece and looked somewhat like a dolled-up African savage; a fat white woman who always laughed loudly and coarsely; girls and women, pretty and otherwise, strangers he saw for a minute or less, whores in the night out to sell the use of their bodies and organs as he sold gasoline and motor oil.

Gradually, he was becoming less physically affected and roused, and more moved and hurt by the sight of them. They were girls and women, and he wanted girls to be creatures who walked in sun and brightness and were the image of all the beauty of the world. They hurt him with the heavy impact of prosaic reality of life which seemed leaden with disillusionment.

Thinking of the whores, seeing them, going home after he had closed the station, snatches of poetry, verses, lines, phrases would come to his mind.

. . . she was made to bruise and bless
Swift as the swallow along the rivers light.

And many times, this line from Byron would run through his mind:

With silence and tears.

III

There was one fact about Eddie Ryan which differentiated him from so many others, from most other people whom he knew, but Eddie didn't even think of it, didn't know it or even perceive it as a fact. He couldn't realize it as such.

His mind and his emotions were more active than the minds and emotions of people he knew, more so than those of a majority of the students who sat in the same classrooms as he did. He was thinking more, feeling more, responding to others, to what he read, to what he heard said, to his own memories and flow of thoughts and feelings, without let-up, day after day. Nothing was casual to Eddie, and even the casual details of work, the people he serviced, the figure of a man or woman passing by on the sidewalk in front of the service station, people on a bus or an elevated train, an odd pronunciation of a word by a customer, a chance and unexpected remark, all this he was hearing, catching, absorbing, and soaking in like a sponge, and anything which he caught with his senses or which even flickered for an instant in his mind, could affect and influence him, awaken feelings like light flooding a room. Any human being can be so affected, but with many, powers of absorption close up. There are different intensities in people, and intensity is not a separate trait but rather a changing, an ever-changing energy of the consciousness, a force of response and of all the play of the living awareness of a person.

Eddie's intensity was not revealed in quick responses, but rather as a steady force of energy within himself. As such, it could deceive him and others. A few years earlier, when he played end with St. Basil's High School team, he had seemed so slow, one of the slowest men on the squad, yet in a game, he would always get where he should be in time, and when covering punts, he would be down the field, even on one of Kid Coyle's fifty-yard boots. His intensity was like the unexpected speed he used to show on the gridiron.

IV

His future. It meant and it would have to be more than success and fame. It must be less of the world and more of himself soaring above and beyond the farthest star.

And didn't this seem like a preposterous joke on a dark day in October, when the rain was cold and each drop hitting your face was like a mean sting. The visible world was a terrible swamp, the sky was dismal and the low clouds were streaked with dirt. People on the sidewalk seemed pathetic, and many hurried along. Open black umbrellas moved like toys simulating weirdness. The day was just miserable all around, and it made people look as miserable to him as he felt.

He got off the bus at 42nd Street and Michigan Avenue, and walked with lowered head toward the station a block away, carrying his heavy briefcase, and thinking of the long damp hours that separated him from home, sleep, and the end of that long day. He was tired, and the dreariness of the day was settling inside him.

Entering the station, he said "Hello" dully, Jameson's delayed return greeting sounded very grouchy to Eddie, and caused a brief sinking of his spirits. But he perked up with hope. The raw, mean day meant lots of time for himself. And the Old Man had the pot-bellied stove going, shedding warmth across the station. There'd be plenty of time for study this afternoon and evening. He went inside one of the closets to change to old clothes, and put on his company overalls. The room smelled of the old, used, oily and grease-smeared overalls which were hanging on the hooks. It was mildly depressing. Eddie hurriedly made the change of clothes, and came back into the station.

The Old Man stood looking at the sodden day through the glass of the front door. Jameson turned as Eddie walked forward, putting on his black-topped Rawlinson Company cap, but didn't speak immediately. Catching an angry, but also hurt, stare in Jameson's small gray eyes, Eddie's thought was trapped in his mind for a moment. He had been thinking that Jameson was an old man.

The Silence of History

"Come on, come on."

Eddie opened his mouth to speak, but the Old Man continued:

"Youth! You young fellows! I don't know what the hell's happening to this damned world."

"What's the matter?" Eddie asked, finding his tongue.

The Old Man scowled but was silent. Eddie could feel himself getting tense with anger. His lips stiffened, he was pale, and he could almost feel his self-control ebbing out of him.

"Don't be so lazy, goddamn, shake a leg!"

"What the hell. . . ."

"Oh, here, take the money. Everything's done. Take this," Jameson said with an intolerant lack of patience; he handed his belt and money changer to Eddie.

What could he say of the man's conduct when it was so inexplicable, and utterly unexpected. He buckled the belt on and Jameson shoved a roll of dirty bills at him.

"I don't know how you'd manage without me to protect you."

"What did I do?" asked Eddie.

"You don't watch your business. You don't watch what you're doing."

"I do too!"

The Old Man stuck a hand into a striped overall pocket in the back by the right hip, and drew forth the cap of a gas tank, dull with lack of polish and marked with tinges and touches of rust.

"What's this?" he snapped.

"Where did it come from?"

"Where did it come from? Where in hell do you think? Where did I get that? It fell out of the sky like a hailstone or chip off a comet, I guess."

"You don't have to get so damned cranky," Eddie said.

"Who the hell you talking to?" Jameson blew out loudly and his anger was a simulation of meanness.

Eddie didn't want to call the Old Man. He was afraid. Maybe he was. His growing loss of control was like vertigo.

The pause between them was but an instant.

A honking horn jarred both of them out of the quarrel and into a reawareness of their duties as Rawlinson employees. The Old

Man started to belabor Eddie for not being on the ball, then shut up and turned to run out to the waiting dark-colored automobile, the make unrecognizable from where Eddie stood.

Eddie took a couple of quick steps, then brought his right foot down hard on the stone floor, and stood rigidly still.

—Why the goddamn . . .

"The goddamned Old Fart!" Eddie let out in a rage.

Eddie's blasphemous outburst was like an explosive release.

The Old Man was pumping ordinary gas into the black car. He came rushing in with two dollars which he handed to Eddie.

"Seven gallons," he said.

Eddie gave him the change, and Jameson hurried out to the customer.

Eddie stood in a confusion of distress. He didn't know what to say next to Jameson, or what the Old Man would say. He didn't want to have more hard words but he might have to. And if not now, then another time.

Sad resolution was forming in his mind as the Old Man came back into the station and the dark car drove out of the driveway.

"I have to hurry now and do some shopping. I made out the audit. Watch your change."

"Yes," Eddie muttered, half under his breath; Jameson's voice had been crisp and curt, but with pathos.

The Old Man had crossed the station, and he disappeared into the little toilet room opposite the front door.

Soon, Eddie heard water running in the sink behind the closed door of the toilet. The Old Man would be out of the station pretty quickly, in a few minutes. Eddie, almost nervously, wanted him out. He never did feel fully at ease with Jameson, and every day, on reporting for duty here at the station, he would be in the same kind of state of uncertainty and embarrassment about his job and the Old Man, but some days it would be more, others less. Something was missing between him and the Old Man. Jameson had the jump on him, and took authority into his own hands, although they were now equal in status and position, and they shared responsibility for the way this station was run.

But Jameson took over and acted like the boss, and would never listen to Eddie, but rather told him what to do. This re-

The Silence of History

lationship gnawed at Eddie in a small but persistent manner. For long, he'd wanted to change it, and didn't know how. There were Jameson's feelings.

It was postponed, Eddie thought, hearing the water still running in the wash bowl. He was half regretful.

He could tell himself:

—Wait, the day will come.

But Jameson liked him. That voice of his, a moment ago, was not without hurt, the pained hurt which had become a mark of life, like the indelible sign of confirmation on the soul.

There was a wrench of what was more than sorrow, or pain, or sadness: it was a wrench of life, a wrench because of what life should not be.

An automobile drove in to be serviced, and Eddie hurried out to it.

He was glad for several successive cars, which prevented more talk with the Old Man. Jameson called a "So long" to him as though there had been no scene, and Eddie believed that he was passing the episode off into forgetfulness as he talked a heavyset, frowning man into having his Oldsmobile drained.

Eddie caught a glimpse of Jameson trudging off along the dirty slickness of the wet sidewalk, a little man growing slowly more dim in a gradually increasing distance of oppressive, dismal, dirty day. A man walking, an old man walking away from work, on a day when all the dreams of the world had died the death of vanishing shadows. The world was heavy with itself.

But Eddie had a crankcase to drain.

A pelting rain came down from a sky which was sagging with its own useless weight of leaden time, and loosened on him the careless insulting power of wind and weather and of what went on separate from all the dreams of youth, the desire to hope, to believe:

That nothing walks on aimless feet

And that, particularly, Eddie Ryan wouldn't walk on aimless feet. And not walking on aimless feet, as Jameson walked, he would carry within himself:

The mighty hopes that make us men.

He wanted to keep feeling like that; but being drenched, he had the feeling of being very dirty. He quickly washed his grimy hands, changed clothes, overalls, and shoes; he kept an extra pair of old shoes for such emergencies as this.

The station was warm, and Eddie's depression melted in the heat which radiated from the pot-bellied stove.

If little things tried his very soul, what could he and all his hopes be worth? It was merely a miserable and rainy day, getting dark early.

Eddie studied history, but his interest was neither as quick nor as keen as it had been during the previous weeks. In Professor Carleton's class, they had covered the French Revolution, Napoleon and his fall, and had gone on to the Congress of Vienna, the Holy Alliance, and the period of conservative reaction which had set in upon Europe after the Battle of Waterloo. The image of Napoleon was in his mind, and thoughts of lessons concluded lingered in his memory because they had dealt with the Emperor.

When the Revolution broke out, Bonaparte was only twenty.

The afternoon light had all but faded into the murkiness of premature October darkness. Eddie had switched on the station lights, inside and outside, including the overhead Rawlinson sign at the edge of the driveway by 43rd Street. The rain had slackened into a slow, pitiless, steady, silent drizzle. The day seemed to be ending without even having begun. It was not night, but rather night had escaped the day, robbed it with a lack of concern, as cold as the rain had been; it had come too soon, and squashed day with a relentlessness that was like the extreme of unrelenting conquest. Darkness, ahead of schedule, had expanded quickly, seeming to rob time of its qualities of being time, as death robbed men of the qualities of time.

It was about seven minutes after four. It was unacceptably early. Lights went on in more windows along Michigan Avenue, not only to see by, but also to give brightness where a glow of life was sought.

Eddie was studying, but with his mind resistant to full concentration. After Napoleon, after *la gloire*, Eddie had believed that the next phase of European history, the Holy Alliance and Era of Metternich would sag in interest, and be too dull to ap-

The Silence of History

peal to him. He'd expected that his will power would be tested, and he hadn't been sure that he'd come through the test with his colors flying at their highest.

The Old Man had affected him because Eddie couldn't understand why Jameson had started lighting into him. You couldn't say it had been fair. He had been ready to stand up to Jameson, and yes, he had stood up, and he was willing to forgive and forget; he had already done that. But the unfairness of the old guy, the way Jameson had snapped at him, kept cropping up in his mind. Not only didn't he like to admit being hurt, but he feared that if you let anyone hurt you, that was a weakness in your armor. And Jameson had seemed to bother him.

The way he behaved, he was letting the Old Man run him, lay out rules and instructions, boss him. To let someone order you around wasn't a sign of strong character, and Eddie Ryan, Edward Arthur Ryan, must have, he had to have a strong character.

For a long time, weeks, since September, and perhaps even earlier, he'd had the feeling that there'd have to be a showdown. It was like fear, like weakness, his disinclination for the showdown.

Thoughts like these, when he came to think of it, had come pretty often to his mind, and they kept coming back, and coming back, and he knew that sooner or later something would have to happen, and something would have to be done about it. Putting thoughts like these out of his mind was only postponement. And what he was postponing was the assertion of his own independence.

Napoleon Bonaparte probably hadn't been any taller than Jameson. Jameson was acting like a Little Napoleon with him.

Eddie lowered his eyes to his book.

And Napoleon Bonaparte lingered in his mind, a name, and an image more vague than a ghost, a ghostly hero who should have won. When the Battle of Waterloo had been reached in Professor Carleton's course, Eddie had found himself wishing and hoping that Napoleon would be the victor. Then, for a moment, it was as though history had ended. He'd walked out of the classroom full of a brooding sadness, a sadness that was like a fog. Then he'd told himself that Napoleon had lost the Battle of Waterloo and had died in lonely far-off exile on St. Helena, but his glory was imperishable. Napoleon had won the battle of fame and glory.

He felt more about Napoleon than he thought, and he was still learning, and had much more to learn before he could think about Napoleon, or about many other historical figures, questions, theories, and issues before he could know many answers.

And Napoleon was one of the figures in history about whom he wanted to learn more. You gave up hearing about Napoleon, and if you wanted to say that somebody was crazy, you could say that he thought he was Napoleon. That was how great Napoleon was. Of course, he believed that Napoleon had been maybe the greatest man who'd ever lived. And he liked Napoleon the way you like some characters in history, and don't like others. But he wanted to know why. The rise and even the fall of Napoleon absorbed and compelled his interest because it was so dramatic.

It was a story of so much greatness and glory, of such a meteoric rise and sudden fall. Napoleon was Emperor of the French, and you liked the French, better than the English, or the Russians, or the Germans. It was that, and fighting against odds, and it was a fame and glory so far beyond what you could ever attain for yourself.

Napoleon had just been Napoleon. Eddie wished he could be like that, that he could have energy and coldness, could work the way Napoleon could, and carve for himself a name as Napoleon had done.

He wished that he could be a great man.

Behind the ghost of Napoleon's image lingering in his mind, there was the ghost of Eddie's secret hopes and wishes of what he wanted to be.

The last faintness of daylight had gone. It was dark like night and the cold drizzle continued, filling the dark air with dots and falling lines of gray. The cars went humming, honking, swishing by; some had skid chains, and left the echo of a monotonously ringing sound repeating itself with irregular frequency. The chains *ding-ding-dinged* in Eddie's mind, and he was meaning-

The Silence of History

lessly conscious of them as he continued to stand by the desk studying. The immediate scene, the part of the world where he was physically present at these moments, was, like the friction of chains on the cement street, meaninglessly present in his consciousness. The real present was Europe of the Holy Alliance and the Restoration, and St. Helena where the once Emperor Napoleon lived on in guarded exile while his glory and his power were no more. Eddie was grasping at this past, at characters and events, and the meaning which it embodied. What had gone could not be brought back, Napoleon's eve of glory, or the Europe which had been, before the Bastille was stormed on July 14, 1789. The illusion grew upon him that all of those years from 1789 to the death of Napoleon in 1821 had not vanished, totally and completely; they could be regained, awakened for him, as though he were and had been a spectator of the actual events of history which he was studying.

There had been few cars to interrupt him. He had shaken the ashes in the stove and put in fresh coal. He ate a sandwich and washed it down with water.

Soon, a black Ford two-seater coupe was driven into the station and parked.

—What the hell's he coming around for now? Eddie exclaimed to himself.

Deacon, one of the two supervisors, had driven into the station. Looking up from the book on the desk, Eddie waited, but Deacon took his time—his usual delay before getting out of his car. He always seemed to fumble with something or other. Eddie believed that Deacon had taken a correspondence school course in psychology and leadership.

But Deacon's psychological monkey business did make you nervous; the guy was a boss.

He came from somewhere on the North Side, had started in pumping gas, and had been promoted to an inspector, a supervisor earning two hundred dollars a month, who visited a regular territory of stations daily, made up the money bag to be picked up by the armored truck, checked over the daily audit, jacked up the attendants, gave orders about keeping the stations clean if necessary, and performed supervisory functions. Deacon's promotion had been the consequence of drag, or so went the rumor, and Pat Keefe hadn't had any use for him. Neither did some of the attendants. His manner was often snotty, and he ragged and kept on the tail of some of the men, but he didn't turn in bad reports unless he believed positively that he had to do it. He was certain that all attendants sometimes pulled the pumps, that is, gave short measures of gasoline, but if this was kept within limits, he was like the three dumb monkeys. He himself had pulled the pumps, to make up shortages, or for a meal or an extra buck once in a while, and that was only human. But robbing, going root-tootin' wild and gypping damned near every customer who came into a station, that was being a hog, and hogs belonged in the stockyards, not in a Rawlinson Service Station. He regarded himself as regular, as regular a fellow as his job allowed.

Deacon dragged out the fumbling in the Ford coupe, finally getting out of it, and walking the very short distance to the front door.

"Hello, Ryan."

"Hello, Mr. Deacon."

The greetings were spoken as though with much cordiality, but were instinct with a lack of it.

The supervisor was dressed to get a baggy stylish effect, and his dark gray suit and light gray top coat were loose-fitting. His gray hat was slanted to the right, with the brim turned down, and enhanced Deacon's plain, angular and homely features with an air of personality; the rakish hat took away the sissy effect of his big, horn-rimmed glasses.

Deacon was a young man who wore his clothes as part of his character and personality. He carried his conceit in these clothes as much as he did in himself. He was slender, taller than he seemed, and his gestures, carriage and walk were all singularly graceless. When he looked at some people, and definitely at Eddie Ryan, he appeared to be smirking and full of the contempt of superiority.

After the greeting, Deacon stood for a short moment, as though powerful in the silence of his authority and position. Eddie waited, wondering what Deacon had on him, or was going

The Silence of History

to gripe over and show himself to be a boss about. Deacon glanced about the station. It was clean and orderly. The Old Man always would have made sure to that, and Eddie didn't have much to do in keeping the station in the proper condition.

"Lousy night, ain't it, Ryan."

"Yes, it is, Mr. Deacon," Eddie said.

—Why in hell are you out in it, snooping.

"Excuse me, I got to take a good crap badly."

Deacon said this as though he and Ryan were quite intimate, and the toilet were a common source of that intimacy. He crossed over to the toilet, and went inside.

Eddie was almost disconcerted. While Deacon remained in the station, he must wait in suspended time, on guard that he did not say the wrong thing, and unable to escape the feeling that he was or might be under scrutiny as an accused or suspected employee. His movements seemed unnatural, and he felt a caution and a guilt which was waiting about within him.

The station, in one instant, became like foreign soil, and he like an alien who was there on sufferance. His dignity shrank into a dwarfed monstrosity of ugliness in his spirit.

For an instant, he felt small, close to nothing.

Through the window, he saw the dreary night, the dark buildings across the street, like shadows heavy with weight and material substance, broken by the rectangles of lighted windows, and a reflected play of moving shadowy light from a few passing automobiles. And with a slight adjustment of his glasses, he saw the visible side of Michigan Avenue. His sense of loneliness was a disconnectedness, a sense of separation of everything before and about him. It was a feeling related to where he was and what he was. He was a stranger in what was so unstrange to him.

Scarcely a minute had passed. But he resented its waste, even though it was only a minute.

Eddie went back to his study, and stood over the desk, with a fountain pen in his hand, ready in case he wished to make any notes.

Napoleon and Metternich, Talleyrand and Tsar Alexander, Louis XVIII, and Stein, he knew them better than he did Deacon. And Paris, Vienna, London, Berlin, St. Petersburg, these were more understandable to him than the corner of 43rd and Michigan. The minutes of life here on the corner were falling into the rainy night. But the minutes of life of all the men in the history he was studying had fallen away, too, as in a night. Only their minutes had fallen into history. What were these living minutes falling into?

Napoleon, the minutes of his life had fallen, but not into darkness.

The toilet door opened. A moment before, Eddie had heard the flushing sound of water. But he had heard it meaninglessly as a sound closed away from him, and echoing from a wall on the far side of his concentration. His nervousness and anger had quickly subsided, he feared that they would rise again, come upon him and beset him.

"Ryan," he heard, and the tone of Deacon's voice was a snotty one.

Eddie turned from the desk, hoping that Deacon would have little to say, and would leave quickly.

"You do a lot of reading here in the station while you're on duty, don't you?"

"Studying, it's study for my courses at the University. Mr. Wood gave me permission to."

At the moment, Deacon didn't like Ryan. The sight of Ryan reading had hit him when he'd opened the toilet door, and dislike had flared up, as paper will when a match is put to it. But Deacon knew that he must keep the controls on himself and stay in low gear.

—I wish I had more men like Ryan in my stations, Mr. Wood had said two or three days ago.

Deacon had noted that Mr. Wood never said anything like that about him, and he was doing a good job, while this kid Ryan hadn't been with Rawlinson six months yet, or anyway no longer than that. Deacon didn't see where in Hell Ryan was all that smart. What was he, Whirlwind Ryan?

But he was uncertain about his attitude toward Ryan because of Mr. Wood. Deacon's respect and admiration for Mr. Wood were most genuine, and since last June, when Mr. Wood had come in to replace Pat Keefe, the new boss had shown plenty of times that he had a lot of stuff on the ball. And he was a pretty keen judge of men. Deacon himself owed his promotion to Mr. Wood. There was a man to look up to, and be guided by, the first in Joe Deacon's life. His own father was a Presbyterian minister, and he smarted and burned with shame because of his father's profession and name. To be known as "the minister's son" had pierced more deeply than had the taunt of "Four Eyes." Deacon had cause for suffering such silent humiliation. Boys whose fathers were businessmen, or lawyers or doctors could more easily be popular than he. Four-Eyed Deacon had two eyes to see with for himself and two more to see for his father and for God. So some of the boys spoke of him in Ravenswood and in various North Side neighborhoods. He had to prove over and over again that he was a regular kid, and not a goody-goody snitcher, but proof and demonstration did not always win him a place equal to that of many of the other boys. For the mere fact that he was a minister's son could frighten many kids. He was a remote reminder of Hell's fire, punishment, a walking inspiration to fear. He was Bad News from the Bible.

None of the kids, who made of him a walking stigmatic, grasped the cruel unfairness heaped upon him. Joe was a threat, a warning, and reminder of the burning fires in Hell.

—Aw, you can do it and get your old man, I mean Reverend Deacon, to pray you out of Hell and where'll we be, gettin' our asses burned all to blisters?

Tommy Hope, undersized at twelve, told this to Joe in an alley when Joe was urging that a group of boys get three girls who would show what they had if the boys would do the same.

Two days later, Joe Deacon had been told by a ten-year-old kid, who'd seen everything through a window, that Tommy Hope had arranged for the exposure party with the three girls in a basement, and had sworn everyone not to tell a word of it to Joe Deacon. He'd cursed Tommy Hope with every blasphemous and obscene word he knew, but retained a measure of control; he hadn't announced that he would drop-kick, punt-kick, and double-kick the living shit out of Tommy Hope, and then gone looking for him instantly. That was what he wanted to do.

"They just looked at each other, and Tommy Hope didn't know what to do with his little dingle," Young Newcastle, the kid, said.

Joe Deacon laughed meaningfully.

Young Newcastle gawked at Joe in slow-growing awe.

"You mean, you, you . . ."

"Weinie. I've put my weinie where a weinie goes."

The awe became admiration.

Joe Deacon crossed his legs, leaned against a strong wire fence, a homely boy with a mop of blond hair, and with the glasses he hated on his big nose. Joe could see, all right, that Young Newcastle, not a bad little goof, believed him, and didn't at all suspect any bull or crap. How easy some kids could be fooled, and not only Young Newcastle, either, Tommy Hope would fall, hook, line, and sinker, and he'd be the biggest fish that Joe Deacon had hooked.

Deacon's uneven teeth showed momentarily in a harsh grin, the best he could do for a smile at that moment. Trying again, he couldn't smile, or even grin. His features were merely twisted and distorted in a grimace that lasted no longer than a breath.

"Yah gonna kick it outta him, Joe?"

"Maybe. If he's worth it."

If he busted Tommy on the jaw, that would be the end of it, and he'd be respected. He was half-tempted, no, tempted to do it, bust the hope and hell out of Tommy Hope, but he knew he wouldn't. Joe wasn't afraid of Hope, but he was of his old man, and the Reverend John S. Deacon had administered three whalings to Joe, one per fight about which the Reverend had heard. Each whaling had been successively more severe than the previous one, and, as his father put it, he could decide which cheek he'd turn, the Lord's cheek, or the Devil's cheek, which was a back-end one.

And Joe Deacon didn't think he wanted those cheeks at the back end to burn any more. Not even the Devil would want that from his old man. Nor was it the fear of a burning backside alone that kept Tommy Hope from getting a poke on the nose

The Silence of History

that wouldn't be anything to hope for. Joe wanted to do things differently.

—The Lord's way, he gagged to himself.

Not the Lord's way, really and truly, but the lording-it-over way, that was what he meant.

He, Joe Deacon, didn't want to be the lone wolf, the kid all by himself because his father was the Lord's man, and once he made the kids understand that his father's being a minister didn't make him an advance J.C., the Lord, and that he had a harder time of it than they did, then everything would be different, the way he wanted things to be. Then Tommy Hope would say he was sorry and apologize. And it would be Joe Deacon, not Tommy Hope. They wouldn't know, none of the kids, that he'd batted an eyelash with any green-eyed jealousy. They'd see, or they'd think and believe, that it was nothing to Joe Deacon, a kid more important than they were, and not afraid, one hell of a hell of a hell of a minister's son.

Joe refrained from taking a solid poke at Tommy Hope, and Mrs. Hope, Tommy's pain-in-the-neck, important-lady-of-church-affairs-and-everything mother, wouldn't be coming to see his old man to find out, oh, dear, what had been done to her precious hope, Tommy.

With a boy's quickness to forget, Joe Deacon's thoughts were all chortles. The joke was his; he owned it, all of it. The chortles came up out of him and he was loudly horselaughing, all the way down the alley.

So he was "the minister's son?"

What was Tommy Hope?

He horselaughed louder down the alley.

Tommy Hope was "Mrs. Hope's son."

He walked off, hands in pockets, peering with contempt at the street and the stones and rough-edged bricks of the buildings, walking with no destination, beginning to dream of how he was going to make Tommy Hope pretty sad and weary, hopeless, and then, he was dreaming of growing up, his mind pushing time aside like a snowplow cleaning a street after a storm, and he was on a clean, clear street, walking along just like he owned it, and he did own it, because it was the street of his manhood.

He was striding now, and watch his smoke. He'd fart it out of his ass, smoke blown bull's-eye into the nose of Tommy Hope.

Before Joe Deacon reached that manhood, which he had been so impatient for in his growing years, there were many more hard and hurting experiences. Not until he was crowding his nineteenth birthday did Joe Deacon lose the stigmata of "the minister's son." This was success, big success for him. He gained acceptance among many of his own age. It was what he had been impatiently waiting for, his goal, and his achievement. And overnight his father changed like a tire going flat, and Reverend Deacon wasn't the minister who could whale those back-end cheeks red now. He was a man gone meek in the not-too-profitable service of God, fussy, always repeating himself with the same jokes, the same sermons, the same conversation at the table, a minister gone bald and slack of muscle, and exuding failure in life as though it were an odor of stale food. And he had, in short pants, sometimes been terrified by his father, and for reasons other than the whalings on the cheeks; his father had spoken as Joe imagined God would have; his father had spoken God's words of doom, of that awful last Day of Judgment, and of the burning punishment that the sinner would suffer, forever and forever and forever always, which was eternity. While still young, Joe heard too many sermons of his father, and then the Reverend John S. Deacon was brimful of hell-fire and the damnation of predestination. At that time, Reverend John S. Deacon was in possession of brown hair so dark that it looked black; he was about an inch or so above medium height, with a fleshy body and a face which was slack and frequently set in frowns. When he stood before the lectern, the frowns and scowls were as though they had become solidified grimness, and a number of the brethren and sisters felt from warm to hot at the sight of him. The usual attendance ranged from seventy-five to three-fifty, and an occasional four hundred, and the proportion of those who were pre-affected by the sight of the man of cloth, even before he began his sermon, was correspondingly changing. The sermons of that time had the brethren and sisters feeling "the everlasting bonfire." Joe Deacon's soul burned every Sunday, and it burned when the Reverend talked about his

The Silence of History

sermons and practiced them. Joe felt as did the boys and girls who called him "the minister's son."

In Chicago and its suburbs, the Devil took advantage of Reverend John S. Deacon's fiery thunder of words about the heat in the nether geography of eternity. Satan pulled the brethren and sisters away from Sunday morning church services. The attendance gradually curved downward, as though toward Hell. And the Reverend stoked the fires with more sticks, and more sticks, until one could have wondered if God were creating sufficient sticks to supply the timber wood for the roaring flames of the Reverend John S. Deacon's holocaust in Hell. He complained and lamented the abandonment of God as exemplified in the decline of his Sunday church attendance.

The Reverend's ambitions were lofty. In order to fulfill their loftiness, he would have to loft himself. He would be the kind of man who lofted himself to loftiness.

—Oh, I say, my brothers, and I say to you, my sisters, look up, look up to God.

This was one of his favorite means of making his sermons an inspiration, of imbuing them with the loftiness which he saw as his mission, his vocation, his role, his dedication, and the essence of all that he was preaching and all for which he lived.

When he would utter this sentence in a sermon, as he did so often, he would lift shining eyes to the ceiling as though he were seeing through it, and his vision extended to the throne of the Maker of men and the Dispenser of their fates and destinies. And his fleshy face would shine, too, with the benignity of a man who was shining in the divine grace of God. His voice would quaver and the very words seemed to shake with gratitude to the God who would save the soul of Reverend Deacon himself, the stoker of souls for the blazing blisters of Hell.

He would become more of this earth as he lofted himself through the process of time that was moving as mercilessly as Hell's fires were burning, moving mercilessly to the Day of Judgment, when the lofty would be in loftiness and the rest would be but the timber for flames the like of which had never been seen by human eyes on the earth that God had given for man during his life of sinning and strutting where vanity was vanity and all was that same, sure, selfsure vanity.

He would loft to a better church, a richer one, and to a higher position, and his bank account would loft as would his home and the black suits which he wore.

But the Reverend Deacon did not loft himself from these lesser loftings to higher loftiness; he brooded, and he worried, and fell into long depths of silence.

The brethren and sisters became fewer, and the collections at Sunday services jingled in deadly muted monotony.

The Reverend Deacon's home did not become Hell, or like Hell, under the circumstances of diminishing returns, but neither was it Heaven. It was the home of a minister who was growing poorer.

In addition to his own, there were four other mouths to feed, appearances to be kept up, and Reverend Deacon found life unloftily annoying. Duty was duty and man had his duty, just as woman had her duties. That was God's will and God's way. The wife who didn't look after home and hearth and kith and kin, could surely look forward to that coming day of burning days, and the wife of Reverend John S. Deacon must perform her wifely duties according to those ways and that Will of God, and thus, she must obey and serve Reverend Deacon and not complain. He told her that before she ever complained, she should think of the Armenians.

—They are starving, dear Martha.

Mrs. Deacon spoke of this subject, the starving Armenians, to several of the ladies at a church social, but one of them, Mrs. Haggershrift, said that her sister's sister-in-law, Gladys Bell Mansonby, was married to an Armenian and he owned three six-flat apartment buildings. And he wasn't starving and if you saw Gladys Bell, you wouldn't say that an Armenian starves his wife. Mrs. Deacon told the family of this at the dinner table, the Reverend, Joe, his kid brother Calvin, and the snot-nose kid sister, Hester, but the Reverend didn't approve of a woman of good American background and heritage marrying an Armenian.

"Why are they starving the Armenians?" Hester asked.

"I suppose God wants them to starve."

The Silence of History

"God doesn't want anybody to starve."

"Then why doesn't He give the starving Armenians something to eat, Papa?" Calvin asked.

"When you die maybe you can ask God," the father said.

"I'll ask Him," Hester said.

Reverend Deacon, who was in his shirt sleeves, looked at the dark-haired little girl with the shiny, fine, saucy eyes; obviously wanting to say something authoritative and reprimanding, he didn't speak and almost smiled.

They were eating fried hamburger steak and fried potatoes; it was food, and probably good for the soul of every member of the family, because it wasn't very appetizing, and when eaten, it was not the source of any pleasure. Hamburger was cheap, and that was why it was on their plain table. And they ate it, falling into a dreary silence, as so often they did while partaking of God's victuals.

Mrs. Deacon was a dreary woman sitting at the dreary family table. She had begun to grow stout and her days were spent in the same round of domestic chores to be attended to, and church tasks which her husband assigned to her. She did one thing after another, as she always said, and that was more or less her life, one thing after another. Mrs. Deacon was not an unhappy woman, precisely, nor was she a happy one either. On her round face there sat an expression of dull contentment. However, this was but a mask, and the feeling which it vaguely reflected, was a deception. A woman cannot live without either joy or sorrow, except at the price of her nature going dry. She must feel, have feeling in her life, or else she becomes a woman whose nature is full of dry sand where there could have been bubbling springs. And although her features were placidly resting in a cast of dull contentment, the dry sand in her was suggested by the pouting tenseness of her closed lips, and the lackluster of her eyes. She had married because of her mother's desperate fear that she miss out and become an old maid, as much as for any other reason, and she had never come to know what she wanted in life, or what she might be like. Reverend Deacon treated her as a servant more than a wife, and the children were not close to her. She couldn't be close to herself.

As circumstances worsened, and the Reverend drove away his Christian sheep with words of fire and brimstone, his wife would whine and complain, and then subside into meekness. He would blame his wife and family, and take out on them his disappointment, but this did not improve his lot, and a crisis was upon him. If he continued as he had been doing, he would burn into ashes his means of livelihood, and then what chance had he to loft himself? He had to stoke the fires of Hell or else become a seedy minister, blistered by the flames of the fire he made and kept ablaze with the souls of others. He was in danger of burning himself up.

Thus, the practical sense of the Reverend Deacon asserted itself, and he gradually shifted from the agonies of damnation to the God of service and success and the gospel of Jesus Christ, our Lord. The gradual change of the minister-father was a bane and a boon to the family. Hell hissed less, and he practiced unctuous smiles more frequently. He talked more of service and success, and less of the souls burned like black, destroyed flesh in flame. Economic circumstances slowly improved in a new church, and Reverend Deacon was away from home more often, doing his duty by trying to associate with businessmen, speaking, usually for fees of $25 to $50, and trying his new, modern, up-to-date means of lofting himself.

Joe Deacon worked at odd jobs after school while attending high school on the North Side, almost was drafted to fight in the war, got a job in a Rawlinson service station when he was twenty, and at twenty-eight he was the Deacon who came out of the toilet while Eddie was studying history, and the October darkness was full of cold drizzle and a rawness which was uncomfortable to human beings.

He lived in his own apartment, and his family had moved to Aurora, Illinois, where his bald-headed father was still striving to loft himself, increased weight and all. Joe finally found it useful to be a "minister's son." This had helped him get his job with Rawlinson and to advance from the ranks. In Mr. Wood, he had met a man whom he could admire and look up to as he'd been unable to look up to his own father.

He was no longer ashamed of his father, especially since the

The Silence of History

Reverend Deacon was in Aurora, Illinois, and the old man had, at last, made a little headway in becoming somebody more than just average.

The twist of Deacon's thick lips was derisive, but not quite the sneer it could be taken for. And it was defensive derision. Deacon scarcely knew Eddie, and the general impression of the latter, in the main office, suggested that he was a good, clean young fellow, a boy scout. Deacon, recalling that boy scouts were ambitious, eager to succeed, and accepting most of boy scouting except for notions of purity, temperance, and sexual continence, was afraid that Eddie would be what he himself secretly might want to be, and become what he should become.

"What's in the book, Ryan?"

"History."

The derision became a sneer, but Deacon changed this quickly to an insipid grin which was not without contempt. History, the idea of history vaguely aggravated Deacon, as it often does those who are lacking in sufficient education, and especially when they are coming up in the world. Deacon was such a one. A high school graduate only, who had wasted his natural brightness and protected himself from being considered a goof or a sissy, he harbored a hidden rancor against history and many other subjects of knowledge which excited the highbrows, because they weren't regular fellows. Of what use was history, and would it help you get ahead in the world? His attitude was not unusual, and was caused by fear and a limitation of confidence in himself. History was linked with his boyhood days and the Bible, as his father had spoken of and preached about the Old and the New Testaments, and in history where there were so many famous and brave men that he felt small merely thinking of it. These attitudes were very vague, and thus more than half lost from his mind, but his fear of history became derision of and antipathy to Eddie, and he walked across the service station to look at Eddie's opened book and notebook in a mood of disdain which had no foundation other than sunken fear.

Eddie wished that Deacon would leave, and apprehensively wondered what was coming.

"Metternich," Deacon exclaimed in a loud dismissal of the

Austrian statesman and diplomat, or of history, or of study, or of Eddie, or of something.

"He dominated the period after the downfall and abdication of Napoleon, and you can't understand what happened to Europe in the nineteenth century unless you know something about Metternich," Eddie said.

"How much gas and oil did he sell?" Deacon asked, each word a slicing cut.

Eddie was gripped with a hard silence. He couldn't answer and he could feel himself rising to a fighting mood.

"Nobody in our outfit is against you getting your education, Ryan," Deacon said, falling into an easy insincere smile while his dark eyes were searching. "But be sure you tend to business here on the job. Do that and we'll get along and have no trouble."

"I tend to business," Eddie said, flustered.

"I didn't say you didn't. I'm just saying to be sure and keep on doing it. We want to take first place here in the city. It's good for all of us if we do. You can see that?"

"Yes."

"Well, so long."

Deacon slouched out of the station and slowly went the short distance to his car.

Eddie had mumbled a "Goodbye," and stood still for a few dumfounded seconds. His anger was suppressed and he wanted to let go with it.

Before Deacon stepped on the starter to drive out of the station Eddie went back to the desk and bent over the textbook, as though resuming his studying. He read words, but their meaning didn't register.

Deacon drove out of the station. Eddie heard the engine.

Eddie glanced up the moment he thought that Deacon's car was gone. He saw the slanting rain, grayish in the station lights.

Deacon was gone.

Eddie drew a nickel out of his money changer, and went to the telephone by the side door. It wasn't a dial phone. He dropped his nickel in, gave the number, heard the sound of the ringing, and a cheery masculine voice answered:

The Silence of History

"Brennan, Station 108 . . ."

"Ryan," Eddie cut in.

"Oh, hello, how are you, Ryan?"

"All right, Brennan. Deacon's out snooping. He left here, going south."

"Thanks. I'll watch and pass the word on, Ryan. So long."

"So long."

Eddie went back to his history textbook to study.

V

The cold drizzle dried and ceased in a rough wind that made the cold a blowing force and banged the Rawlinson Oil and Refining sign. There were very few customers, and the volume of traffic on Michigan Avenue was small. At moments, Eddie, bent over his book, heard only the wind and the banging of the sign. Two or three of the girls came out, but quickly disappeared. Eddie caught the loneliness of the scene made desolate by wind and cold. Time scarcely moved while the wind roared with unsubdued fury until its force was spent and silenced against bush and stone.

And Eddie studied.

Napoleon had died in bitter exile on St. Helena. Waves must have smashed against the stones of that island lost in an ocean of water and an ocean of history; and the winds must have screamed across St. Helena as though in literal mockery.

Napoleon had heard many winds loud with the rage of ocean storms, but their vehemence and shattering roar had only been the shame of the silence of history.

That was defeat, a silence full of shame that had no noise, no blast, no screech or scream from the depths of the world, no hording humans, a silence no explosion of the spheres could penetrate.

Defeat was death with the heart pumping, blood flowing, eyes open and all of the senses, organs, functions, muscles, all of a man functioning in life.

On St. Helena, Napoleon must have heard the wind, and

heard the ocean waves rushing and breaking on rocky shores, and he must have heard the silence of history.

Eddie thought of the phrase, "the silence of history." And he heard the clang-banging of the Rawlinson sign, and the hard blowing and whizzing of the mass of wind. He was in the silence of history. And so was Deacon and old man Jameson, and his family, his grandmother, and uncles and aunt, and his dead father, and all of them, the dead and the living.

—Deacon isn't Napoleon, Eddie told himself as a Packard drove into the station.

Rushing out to service the customer, a fancily dressed Negro, Eddie felt the cold prongs of the wind. He pumped ten gallons of gasoline into the car.

He was far away from history.

Maybe he was only a gas station attendant.

Eddie couldn't sell any oil, collected, walked back into the station, while the sign still slammed and rattled and the wind whined inhumanly.

Why did he think he could break the thick silence of history?

Chapter Eleven

I

Eddie was fed up. He couldn't go on as he had been doing. He must have a change.

When he would wake up, his head still thick with the tiredness of sleep, this was how he thought.

His grandmother had been saying to him, and often:

—Son, you're studying too hard to be a scholar. Sure, and you don't want to be getting yourself sick.

Eddie's Uncle Larry had gotten a job, which, by then, was unusual. Eddie didn't know what he was earning, but it seemed to be a good job with a shoe factory in Racine, Wisconsin, and he covered a number of Midwestern states, Wisconsin, Michigan, Illinois, Indiana, and Ohio. He had a larger territory, and he was due at the Hotel Muehlebach, in Kansas City. Eddie hadn't forwarded his mail for several days, and knew that he must do it. His Aunt Jenny was supposed to, but she had been careless about this for years. Eddie promised he'd do it, and was prompt, but for the past few days it had been as though he lacked the will to take the six or seven letters off the mail rack on the wall, near the front door, write the forwarding addresses on them, and drop them in the mailbox at the corner.

At the filling station, he had the same feeling about several chores which were his to do, which he more or less liked because he could daydream or think as he performed them and the time passed easily and pleasantly. But suddenly, he had become resentful about his cleaning, and several times, the decision to do necessary chores had been almost beyond his will. And he'd become more careless, also, about collecting from customers, and screwing on the caps of gas tanks after pumping in gasoline. He ran shortages four or five times during each of the two weeks previous to the October morning on which he awakened so fed up and so strongly feeling the need for change.

Eddie was getting more careless and forgetful of little details. His education depended on his job, and his having a good record, because it would have been utterly impossible to study as he did if he lost the privilege of reading while on duty. Eddie's record was important beyond this necessity, for one of his plans was to stay with the company after completing his education, and to try to work his way up as close to the top as possible.

But it seemed that he might be slipping.

The very small rows with the Old Man and Deacon had affected him, perhaps more than was warranted; he took them as warnings of more to come. And, more important, Eddie was living with no let-up; even on his day off, Monday, he studied and drove himself.

These were small matters, but trifles which expressed the pressure of conflicts that were developing in himself and in his life. He wanted much and got but little. Day by day, Eddie was giving his youth, and, taking his third successive course of history, he had begun to absorb a poignant sense of the cruel speed of time. Was he giving up his youth, or losing it? He was gambling, risking days and years for success and a place in the world, and all his sacrifices were for a hope and an ambition which was pushed far ahead in the uncertainty of the uncertain future. Was it all worth the cost? Would he be able to go on paying such a price as he was paying, and survive?

Something was wrong, and Eddie was fed up.

Sleepily, Eddie washed while his grandmother was preparing his breakfast. He found another dark day with the likelihood of gloomy, depressing weather.

Hell, he ought to give up. He was fighting a losing battle. He was trying to do too much. His eyes couldn't take it. Maybe his health couldn't.

Eddie's mood was sinking downward, falling lower and

The Silence of History

lower. It was a bad mood, and through it he was giving himself release, discharging a surplus of feelings and expressing to himself the pangs of a great loneliness of spirit which he didn't want to admit to himself.

Breakfast was ready when he went out into the kitchen, and his grandmother, such a little thing of a woman, said:

"Oh, this weather, son. It gets in the marrow of me bones."

"Yes," Eddie said.

"You dress warm today for your work, son."

"I will."

The early morning was dark and heavy. It was too cheerless a morning for his mood. Eddie longed for sunshine and brightness, as though it could feed all the hungers of his heart.

Eating breakfast, Eddie thought of Deacon. Deacon didn't like him, he was sure of that. But why? He hadn't done anything, had he, which should cause Deacon's dislike?

But neither did Eddie take to him. Fair is fair enough. That's what his grandmother often said.

And the Old Man, Eddie was irked by him, and his airs of being the boss. That would have to be stopped. But Eddie didn't want to say anything to him. It was as though he were afraid. He was afraid of him, wasn't he? Yes, he must be. That was his reluctant answer to his own question. It had to be fear when he was reluctant to put his foot down and tell Jameson to cut out his preposterous bossiness.

And what kind of character did he have if he was afraid?

But Eddie didn't want a row, and it wasn't important. What difference did it make? He was going in his own direction, and that was all that counted.

"You're quiet this mornin', son."

"What?"

"Are you well?"

"Oh, sure. I was thinking about my lessons," Eddie told his grandmother.

"You shouldn't be doin' so much as you do. You don't get your good sleep, son."

"I'm all right, I'm healthy."

But was he, and would he remain so if he kept up his pace?

That was bothering Eddie. What could his constitution stand? And his eyes? Sometimes he'd thought he might die young and in vain, before he had done all that he wanted to do, and learned and seen enough of the world; he would die a failure, an unknown. His father, he had never had a chance. Had he?

Eddie finished breakfast, and felt better physically and quite awake. It was a bit early for Peter Moore to whistle from the sidewalk on South Park Avenue. He thought of reading a few short poems while waiting, but he was restless and very troubled in mind.

He got his briefcase ready, put his coat on, and looked out of the front window at the slowly lifting dark gray thickness of the drab new dawn across the street in Washington Park.

The morning looked as lonely as he felt.

Eddie thought of Napoleon on St. Helena, as he had done the night before, while on duty at his station. His soul was somewhere, seeing and watching the world, wasn't it? If he were in Heaven, he should be happy in the fame of Napoleon on this earth. And shouldn't he be in Heaven, not in Purgatory? He had received the last rites of the Church.

Would he know that a boy in Chicago, on a day massive with gray sadness, was thinking of him? Boy? He was a young man, twenty-one, one who had reached man's estate.

Who was Napoleon's fame and glory for?

For him? For him, that was, as well as for others. He was about to puzzle over this question, when he heard the whistle of Peter Moore, and he rushed out of the apartment, yelling a "goodbye" to his grandmother.

"It's unpleasant, isn't it, Ed?" Peter said.

"Lousy."

They set out as usual, and in a moment were inside Washington Park, and could hear their feet crunching on the gravel walk. Eddie wanted to talk with Peter, but he didn't know precisely about what. His problems had become lost in a mood that was like a dense, obscuring fog. He was unhappy. That was something Eddie didn't like to admit, even to Peter. Why should he be unhappy, if it weren't his own fault? Admitting his unhappiness, complaining about it, that was confessing to a lack of

The Silence of History

stiffness of his upper lip. It was more, of course. One of the many reasons for his unhappiness was that he had no girl. If he didn't have a girl, wasn't that because he couldn't get one? There was much Eddie wouldn't admit. He didn't want to be seen as he was, but as an illusion which he wasn't.

They talked about Professor Carleton's history course, and Peter said that he hadn't done too well in the course, getting only a C. Eddie's pleasure and sense of superiority were a little cheap, for he was expecting to get an A, and he'd no sooner felt superior than he was a little ashamed of himself.

"You're doing wonderfully, Eddie—I admire you."

"That's all I do—it's my whole life, Peter."

"Yes," Peter said thoughtfully, after a pause. "It must be hard on you. It is on me, and I'm not working. Men aren't equal in life, are they, Eddie?"

"No," he answered quickly, before he gave himself any time to think of the question; then he thought of his father.

All men are born equal—but are they?

It was a sentence from the Declaration of Independence; he'd never questioned it.

"Some can run faster than others; some are richer; some can learn better; the boys on 58th Street in my cousin's bunch seem to be able to climb better. Equal to what?"

"I don't know," Eddie said reflectively, trying to think about that sentence, and Peter's quick, almost nervous comments.

"How much is true of what we were told and grew up believing?" Peter asked.

He had asked a question that was ripe within Eddie's mind, yet he hadn't thought of it. Instantaneously, he became angry and excited. But he didn't speak. He didn't know much. He'd have to think. There were *Babbitt*, Babbittry, suspicion of books and ideas, suspicion and hatred of the University, and much else.

"People are ignorant, Eddie."

"Yes."

"They can't help it. How could Pop ever learn much, I ask myself?"

"And my old man."

"You and I are the first in our families to go to college."

"I was first to graduate from high school."

"My older brother, he went to Armour Tech. I'm second."

They were walking on across the damp ground, and taking an irregular course to avoid some puddles.

"And on campus, what are we? Almost like the Jews, I guess, Eddie. Irish—from where? They don't know."

It was getting lighter all the time, but the weather remained cold and damp.

When they got to the drive near Cottage Grove and the park exit, their mood had changed. They went on, saying little.

II

Eddie's old man, who spent so many years of his life as a teamster, had never failed to smile with gratified pleasure when he said:

"Horses turn their back on it."

He'd meant work.

Eddie sometimes thought of this remark of his father's. There were plenty of times when he wished that he could turn his back on it, for good. But he was back at work now, after having had three days off. He didn't want to hurt Old Man Jameson, but his need for a change had become so urgent that he had asked Mr. Wood for a transfer to another station; the reason he gave was that because of his heavy schedule he'd like to work at a station which closed earlier. He had also asked for the three days' rest, and Mr. Wood had agreed to both.

Now his three days were memories without any particular significance. They must have done him some good, for he got more sleep than he'd usually been getting, but not so much more that he had wallowed in bed.

Eddie had asked for a few days off because he had sensed that he must not go beyond his limits. But unless he learned, he would remain Nobody. And more than other men he knew, the Old Man, and many at the Express Company, there was the thought of his father, who went to his death in the spiritual anguish of a proud man, poor and knowing that he was beaten, defeated, and living out the final days of his defeat. He suffered

The Silence of History

as Eddie had never seen anyone suffer. That was failure lived to the final apoplectic moment in a world that was pitiless and indifferent, and that talked of success and happiness while it pronounced, in contempt, the judgment that any man who failed had only himself to blame. Tragedy became shame. Eddie had been ashamed of his father.

He couldn't allow himself to fail. Knowledge was his great hope, and he was starved to know and to learn, far beyond his needs for the knowledge that could make him a success, save him from failure. He had given himself to the task of studying. But sometimes, Eddie thought of fellows he knew. They had good times and fun. They did not worry about the passing days: they did not feel, as Eddie did, that each minute must be a sum of "sixty seconds' worth of distance run." He had tried to be as they were. He still made the pretense that he was. And he desired to make that pretense real. There had been Saturday nights when he had stood over the books laid on the station desk, and couples would pass outside, or a car would stop by one of the station pump islands, and a fellow and a girl, or two or three couples would be in the automobile. And he was working and studying. He had no date. He had no girl. He would walk back into the station and to his books, slowly. Eddie could only be sad and want to complain and cry out against the stars and the moon, and all of space, and all of time.

Eddie had taken the big risk for a big try. At that time, that is, in October of 1925, he did not realize that he was taking the total risk. But he was. And his conduct, his actions were those of a young man whose choice in the game of life and destiny was the biggest of all choices.

Actually, it was not merely success in life which Eddie was seeking; it was destiny. He was not simply trying to get on in the world and up the ladder, to become a Mr. Wood, or someone above Mr. Wood, or a Jack McGlynn, his father's first cousin, the lawyer and politician. He wasn't even trying to be another Walter C. Rawlinson. He was embarked on the road of destiny of Eddie A. Ryan. It would be a long road, and it led far, far beyond the range of his vision.

The strain Eddie suffered from day to day was that of destiny, not of overwork and restriction of impulse and pleasure. This he didn't know. He was not conscious of the full weight of his emotions. He had not separated success and destiny. They were one and the same in his mind. But he asked for his destiny, and he gave every minute, and every incident and episode, the meaning of destiny.

However, Eddie had his three days. They were a truce between himself and the meaning of the minutes of time. He could spend them on campus, and he did. He could be like almost every other student, and he tried to be just that. The campus could be his world, the place through which his time flowed, and it was measured, hour after hour, by the cadences of the chimes. He was free to use his days as he decided, three of them in succession. Then, he must go to the new station on Wabash Avenue, and have a new partner. He'd have to put in seven hours a day, seven days a week, but he'd be through at nine o'clock every evening. And he'd be away from Old Man Jameson, and that had to be, or he'd either have lost his self-respect or kept quarrelling with him. Eddie was sorry because he saw, fixed in his mind, a clear image of a little man, broad and browned, gray, a little tight-lipped, meaning more than he said, speaking curtly, almost angrily, but intending kindness and friendship, giving himself the airs of bossy importance because he was not important and was only the equal of twenty-one-year-old kids like Eddie, living for little pleasures and many duties, and bravely pretending that the years were not pitiless and pregnant with the seeds of death.

But Eddie kept pushing this sorriness, the hurt of pity, out of his mind for those three days. Old age and death were remote, when he spent his entire days on campus and saw so many who were young, students, and he was still young. Now and then, he would discover himself thinking that neither the other students nor he could grow old, or, at least, not for so long a period that it would be virtually forever. The campus grew larger for him, and became a world of its own, an island set apart from all of the world that he knew. By the end of the second day, he was serene, and knew a kind of happiness, even in loneliness. The only pressure he felt was what he put on himself, the pace he set for study.

Peter Moore did not take his lunch and they ate at the Commons in the Reynolds Club for men. The room was big, the walls were paneled, and paintings of eminent University men of the past were substantial ghost images on the wall. Abe Lustig joined them, and a few acquaintances of theirs. They talked casually, of whatever subject occurred to someone, high-jumping and flaws in Peter's style when he left the ground to go over the bar, and the way Abe sliced his legs in a scissors, going over the bar, and Professor Donald J. Lenner whom Peter Moore was having in his Poly Sci. course, and the football season, in which the Maroons weren't doing too well, and Abe saying that he'd been reading *Creative Chemistry* by Edward E. Stossen, and he was quite dubious of Stossen's contention that the atom was as far beyond our reach as the moon. Rutherford, the British scientist, had spoken of "the bewildering rapidity" with which fundamental discoveries were being made, and Peter Moore asked him "for instance." Abe said that Rutherford had changed a few atoms of nitrogen into hydrogen, and gave a few other examples of scientific discoveries, and then he said that if the energy of the atom could ever be used it would be tremendous, more so than a high jumper over the roof of Bartlett Gym. Ed didn't talk much. He couldn't have on scientific questions, and furthermore, he didn't believe that he expressed himself well about ideas. He was looking forward to taking a course in public speaking.

Peter Moore had classes, study, track work in the gym; he also played intramural touch football. Eddie was alone much of the time during his three days. He saw many coeds who were well above the minimum beauty requirements. He'd look at them. He wouldn't know what to say, or how to get acquainted. He was shy, but shyness did not fully explain how he was. There was his pride. He didn't want to be turned down. Nor did he want to be hurt any more, because he had been hurt too much already. This was bound up with pride, but was more than pride. And unlike George Raymond, he didn't have a line. He couldn't give himself a fictitious personality.

Eddie looked at all the girls worth looking at, and the campus was pretty full of them. Many of them were so beautiful to him. And he liked to look at their legs, slender and shiny in silk stockings. He looked a lot.

In Harper Library, there were also girls when Eddie went to read and study. For his term paper in English class, he had chosen Wordsworth's poetry, and he read poems and dipped into a few books about Wordsworth. Miss Patrick had stressed nature in Wordsworth's poetry, and had spoken often of *The Preface to Lyrical Ballads*. Eddie read it for the third time, and he gained from it a sense of poetry being related closely to life, reflecting it, and distilling some of the concentrated values, the essences, as it were, of thought and feeling. And that taste in the arts was an acquired feeling, developed by long intercourse with them, and that poems were written for men, not for poets. Accepting these ideas, Eddie was able to read with more confidence, and not be afraid that he'd be wrong, or that he wouldn't be able to write his term paper without fearing that he might be all off unless he gave back to Miss Patrick what she had said in class. He could do his own thinking.

Reading in Harper Library, taking some notes, trying to think as he read so that he should have ideas, enough of them, to put down when he came to writing his term paper, his mind sometimes wandered, and he had many chance thoughts and feelings. Eddie wished that he didn't have to be bent over books in a library but that he could be off having tea with a pretty girl. He wished that his term paper were already written and that he'd been given an A for it. He wished that his family were rich, and that he didn't have to work his way through college. He wished that he could travel, go to the "back country" where Wordsworth had lived, walk as he had walked, in country woods, and along country lanes, see fields and trees as he had, think as he thought, and then write as he had. These and many wishes came and went as he read, and he thought of himself, and related to himself and to his life one or another line that he was reading. It seemed to Eddie that by reading poetry then, when young, he was giving himself the notes for melodies of his spirit in the future, and preparing for the way he would live and what he would be like in the future, as well as writing a term paper. If he could read and understand Wordsworth well, he could feel more of the quality of passing minutes.

*. . . For I have learned
To look on nature, not as in the hour
Of thoughtless youth; but hearing oftentimes
The still, sad music of humanity . . .*

That was sadness, and, yes, "Thoughtless youth," didn't feel and carry such sadness within itself. Did he? Yes and no! Yes. Before he had known many or really any "aching joys" of "thoughtless youth" he had heard

The still, sad music of humanity

This music grew sublime in nature.

*One impulse from a vernal wood
May teach you more of man,
Of moral evil and of good,
Than all the sages can.*

That didn't seem true to Eddie, but Wordsworth knew much of vernal woods, and of the surrounding Mystery of Nature and of life and their capacity to heal and restore your spirit: wasn't this something of what Wordsworth had meant?

He'd written that in 1798, the year during which Napoleon Bonaparte had gone to Egypt. Napoleon had probably never heard of Wordsworth, and had not seemed to care for poetry, except for Homer.

Eddie couldn't be serene like Wordsworth. The serenity he felt, while reading him, possessed the sad music of pathos rather than of humanity.

It was his pathos.

And Eddie went home with the day gone dark; the wind was sweeping the wide Midway as he walked halfway across it to wait for a bus.

A dark scene that was sad, merely sad, rather than "the sad music of humanity." His day had been a day well used, with much happiness, or at least forgetfulness which wasn't unhappiness. It had gone. The night had come, lonely and cold, and in a tired sinking of spirits, he had become depressed. What was he out to win?

Eddie didn't want to go home.

He wanted to stay at the University.

A big, lit-up bus appeared, looking clumsy and ancient. He boarded it and rolled on toward home. Washington Park appeared grim and deserted in the darkness. It was the bare, gravelike memento of a day gone by. South Park Avenue was forsaken, and full of ghosts of memories from his boyhood.

Tomorrow is another day, his grandmother was always saying, as were many others, millions of others.

Eddie's three fine days passed and he went to his new station.

III

Old Man Jameson wasn't at all unfriendly as Eddie had feared he might be when he stopped at the 43rd Street station to get old shoes, trousers, and other personal articles which he had left there. His manner was one of disappointment and great regret. He seemed hurt, injured in spirit when he told Eddie that he shouldn't have done what he had, it was a mistake, and all Jameson hoped was that Eddie watched what he was doing and watched himself at his new station. He spoke as though he were accusing Eddie but, at the same time, he forgave, and would bear the sadness of his great betrayal with true and full forbearance.

Eddie tried to explain that he had not asked for the transfer because of him, or of any gripes he had, but simply on account of the hours. He couldn't have gone on, working the same hours and studying, Eddie told him, or rather tried to tell him, because Jameson was not interested, and did not really listen to him. He interrupted to tell Eddie that he had made a big mistake, and only hoped that he wouldn't come to regret it.

Eddie felt a little sorry, but what could he do? And even though he wished, or half-wished that he had not gotten the transfer, he was sure that he had acted in his own best interest.

It was embarrassing for Eddie, and he sensed that it was for the Old Man. He stood, moving his lips slightly, as though he wanted to talk to Eddie and couldn't. Between them there was some of the unspoken sadness of the world.

They shook hands and Eddie left.

Eddie's new partner, Corlin, was a young fellow of about twenty-five or twenty-six, married and the father of a ten-month-old boy. He and Eddie were both feeling nervous suspense when they met. Quite obviously, the wrong partner could foul a guy up, and Corlin had as much need for the job as Eddie had, if not more. He had come to Chicago from a small town near Columbia, Missouri, in about 1920, and had worked at various random jobs, but none had suited him as well as that of filling station attendant. He liked his hours, even though he worked a seven-day week, and prior to Eddie's coming, he and his partner had usually worked two successive shifts, afternoon and the next morning, and had then had twenty-four hours off. But Corlin liked the idea of working the morning shift and being home every night. However, the fact that Eddie was a student had worried Corlin, he later said. They quickly took to one another. And Corlin agreed to a plan of Eddie's for him to work both Saturday shifts, and for Eddie to take the Sunday ones, when business was slow and it was dull and boring, waiting around the station until time was up.

It didn't look at all as though Eddie had made the mistake which Old Man Jameson had spoken of with a solemn regret that covered the wound he felt because he believed that Eddie had deserted him.

From the beginning, things moved smoothly at the new station. Eddie was always prompt in reporting, and occasionally he'd get to the station a little ahead of time, permitting Corlin to leave early. Corlin liked that, and it actually was to Eddie's advantage, because he could get his chores done and sit down to study. And Eddie was rapidly learning to read and pick up where he left off when interrupted as well as to concentrate and yet keep himself in instant readiness to jump up and rush out when a customer drove in. He had read that Julius Caesar could do more than one thing almost simultaneously, and one of his reasons for interest in and admiration for Bonaparte was his capacity for his work, his memory, his ability to sleep for only a few moments or hours, then rise and pitch into his work, whatever it was. Eddie would have to develop habits of this kind successfully if he was ever to achieve his ambitions. This desire, he knew, had, in itself, become an ambition, an end, and he was trying to make himself a storehouse of knowledge. He didn't think of the separation of knowledge into departments and, already, in term papers, reports, themes, and tests, he would use the material of one class in what he wrote for another. He quoted poetry in history papers, and cited history, the French Revolution or Bonaparte, for Miss Patrick. He did this, perhaps, to impress. But this was only superficial, and Eddie was actually revealing the way in which his mind worked. He had been the same in sports. What he learned in football, he had used, on occasion, in basketball, and he had used his basketball experience in football, especially in catching or intercepting forward passes. Peter Moore had seen him play a game of basketball in his senior year, when Eddie was captain of St. Basil's heavyweight team, and he'd said afterward:

"Eddie, you play half the game with your feet off the floor."

The footwork Eddie had picked up in basketball had also helped in football. His athletic reputation at high school, which was the stuff of which legends are woven, was based on his so-called dogged fighting spirit, but the fact was that it was also a result of his using his head, and of learning fast.

Corlin and Eddie got along from the beginning. They talked naturally, called one another by their first name, and Eddie never, from his first night on, checked up and made an audit before closing up, unless he feared that he was seriously short. Trust and confidence in Corlin's honesty worked a counter-response of trust, and this was psychologically good for Corlin because, after all, he was a small-town boy in the big city, and he had had to be keenly suspicious, and protective of his self-esteem.

Corlin had come to Chicago with cautious distrust because of all that he had heard about big cities, and he had never completely lost his suspicion nor had he come to feel that he was a Chicagoan, although he tried to be and believed that that was what he had become. Even his home life was affected,

The Silence of History

because besides being a Chicago girl, Mrs. Corlin had graduated from high school, and her father was a minor official in a large corporation, with twenty girls under him. Corlin would have liked to have gotten a better job, a white-collar job, but he couldn't have earned as much money, and they were saving up to buy a Ford.

Bill Corlin seemed to Eddie to be a decent guy, and there was no reason why he shouldn't have trusted him. Corlin trusted Eddie in turn. There was less business than at the 43rd Street station, especially after six P.M. To Bill, it was a relief not to work those dull evenings until nine P.M. when the station closed, but to Eddie the dullness was opportunity. He was beginning to believe that boredom was a weakness of character, a lack of interest, energy, ambition, and curiosity. It was a waste of that which was most precious of all the possible benefits of life—time. About a year had passed since Eddie had read, in a wonder of excitement, the "Conclusion" of Walter Pater's *The Renaissance*, and what he then felt and thought was expressed in a beauty of style he never hoped to equal. No moment should pass in boredom. No minute should escape from a human being's life wasted and unused. Each moment should have value and quality: To be dull and bored was to squander God's greatest gift.

Eddie got off to a good start, and forgot the immediately past months, and Old Man Jameson, who probably let memories of Eddie go dry and turn to the dust of his own past.

Eddie could now study in conditions of less disturbance and greater relaxation. His time and his program were more concentrated, pulled together, with less waiting time in which he had to make an effort of will to study or otherwise to use every minute profitably.

Eddie gained other opportunities, also. On Saturday afternoon, he no longer needed to hurry from Stagg Field and the football games to work. The opportunity to have a Saturday night date was given him, if he should be able to get one. He could and did go to the dances at the Reynolds Club, held immediately after the games, but few girls danced with him, and he didn't know what to say to those who did.

Eddie continued setting his own pace of study, and not one

day passed but that he did not learn and absorb. He was learning from books, and from life. The job he had was teaching him more about business, and thus about economics, than he realized at the time.

In order to keep their jobs, Bill and Eddie had to sell, and the more they sold, the more solid they could feel themselves to be with the company, but there was, nevertheless, no feeling of really solid security for either of them. They didn't know when there would be a change in policy, bosses, plans of the company, which would affect them and their jobs. While they were on duty, they did not know when they were being watched and by whom. Any customer could be a spotter. At any unexpected minute, a boss could come in and take them by surprise. They worked alone, but with the possibility of unseen eyes upon them at any moment of their working time. One slip and they might be fired, and they could even be discharged without their knowing the reason why. They didn't know what reports about them went into the main office, and were never certain of their status. From day to day, they came to and went from the station with suppressed uncertainty about their jobs, and while they had learned to forget this, it hung within them as part of their daily living and of themselves.

The whip of money was poised over them, and it affected their inmost feelings. The contant handling of money had many unrealized effects upon them, and how they acted about money was one of the measures of their character. Neither of them was totally honest. They "pulled the pumps" to make up shortages and bought their meals from the restaurant across the street, owned by Jimmy the Greek, out of the company cash which they handled. This required them to cheat customers out of a few cents here, a few cents there, to give four for five gallons of gasoline to some customers who did not watch carefully while they were being serviced. If they made a personal telephone call, they used a company nickel and that five cents, also, had to be made up at the expense of customers. They contributed, thus, to their own fear, and were, in part, the agents of their own anxieties. They increased their actual income by from about five to twenty-five or thirty dollars a month in this manner, and their guilt was only a muted one.

Eddie was, perhaps, more troubled by guilt than most attendants, because stealing was a sin, and he knew that there could be no excuse for this in the eyes of God. The small amounts he stole made his sin only a venial one, or so he believed. And he sometimes had to cheat because he would grow absent-minded in his studying, would service customers while his mind was on his books, and he'd forget to collect. Two or three times, Eddie was gypped by professional short-change artists who went around to stores and gasoline stations, asked for change for twenty-dollar bills, and so befuddled you that they managed to go off with ten or twenty dollars clear. About three weeks after Eddie had started working with Bill Corlin, he came to work one weekday afternoon, and found Bill upset and defensive.

"We're twenty bucks short," Corlin said.

"How in Christ's name did that happen?"

"I don't know. I know I didn't make any bulls like that and yesterday when I left we were about four bits over."

"Did you check up this morning when you opened up?"

"No, I didn't. There was a rush of trucks and before I had any time to think of checking up, I must have pumped fifty, seventy-five gallons. Then I thought what the hell, we always run pretty even."

They looked at each other. Bill was a wiry little fellow, tanned and skinny, but very strong. His eyes were fixed on Eddie with uncertainty, suspicion, and he was very tense. Then Eddie remembered the guy who'd driven in when he had a run of customers and a crankcase drain on the previous afternoon. The man had been dressed like a sport, and talked fast, in a way to set you back before you opened your mouth. He'd gotten change for twenty, and then for two tens, and had talked to Eddie all during the exchange.

"Jesus Christ!" Eddie exclaimed to Bill.

"What is it?"

"I got taken, Bill, by a short-change artist—the goddamn sonofabitch—if I ever get near that fast-talking bastard . . ."

Eddie described the incident quickly, and recalled that immediately after the guy had driven out of the station, he'd told himself that he must have been cheated. He didn't seem to have as much money as he should have had. But Eddie had been too busy to make a check-up at the time, and when he'd handled the succession of customers, he wanted to get at his books.

"Are you sure you was taken?"

"Yes, Bill, I am. That's the second time. I got screwed the same way last summer. That time, it was ten bucks."

Bill relaxed, and a smile of sympathetic friendliness came on his face.

"Tell the auditor to go drown himself, Bill, and let me make up the audit today and throw in the petty cash. I'll have to make it up, and if anything happens, and Jackson or that fat-face, the other auditor, come around and find us short, I'll say I was rooked and to take it out of my hide."

"We're partners, Ed, and we stand together, don't we?"

"Yes, Bill—but I was dumb, and you've got a wife and kid to support. I wouldn't want you to pay for my being a goof."

"I got taken once the same way."

"The next short-change artist who comes around here gets slugged, if I catch the bastard pulling that game. Right between the eyes with a right, that's what that bastard will get."

Bill smiled.

"It's a tough break, but the world won't end, and we can make it up. Some of the drivers who come in in the morning and sign for gas will help me if I tell 'em, and we're due for a new load of gas in Tank A. We always get three or five gallons over on a new load. Here, let's put the dough in fifty-fifty, and take it out when it's made up. I'll put up ten and you throw in ten and we'll be safe if the auditor comes around. We're due for an audit. Tilson told me to expect the auditor when he came this morning to make up the money bag."

Tilson was a "blind" collector, a close-mouthed and quiet young fellow of about twenty-five, who always told them when to watch their step and what they had to do to save him from sending in a report on them.

"I haven't got ten on me, Bill; let's chance the thing and use the petty cash. If anything suddenly happens and you try to pull your ten out, you can be misunderstood. And I'll say it's my responsibility."

The petty cash fund was twenty-five dollars.

Bill was impressed and touched.

"But what'll we do? We won't have any dough to speak of when we make up the audit. I didn't make it up today, but waited for you to check it over again with me."

"We'll check, and hold back some gas sales for my shift, and use our petty cash."

They did this. They were almost twenty-two dollars short.

"I'll make up some of it this afternoon, Bill, and if we get audited, then I'll say I was fooled by a short-change artist. I'll say it happened just before the audit."

Bill agreed to do as Eddie suggested. They were held responsible for every cent, and no shortages were allowed.

Eddie's quick admission of responsibility for the twenty-dollar shortage won Bill's respect to the degree that after that day, it was as though Eddie were manager, deciding how to run the station, and all of his suggestions on business were followed by Bill. Eddie had gained by leaving the Old Man, and was, in fact, managing the new station, and building up its business and Corlin's record as well as his own.

IV

Eddie was often cheerful, and almost no one who knew him realized the strain of his effort, the intensity of his life, the physical and social limitations which bound his days, the widening of mental horizons and the feel and depth of time for him. When he reported to work, he was often smiling, joked with Bill Corlin, and was at ease as he had not been when Old Man Jameson was his partner. The Old Man had acted almost as though he were his guardian; he could not help doing this, but it was depressing, and put unseen weights upon Eddie. He had not reported for duty at the 43rd Street station smiling or joking, accepting his job as part of his life, of his normal routine which he could accept and handle with a feeling of any pride or dignity. He could have neither pride nor dignity, working with the Old

Man, because Jameson needed to add to his own and he had only Eddie as the object for his self-enhancement. This Eddie felt through his own reduced sense of himself.

These feelings were gone, and Eddie was having good days at his new station. He was studying more than he had been, and he would leave work, sometimes stopping for coffee and pie in the restaurant near the elevated station at 58th Street, and sometimes going straight home to continue his studying. Eddie thought that he was unhappy, more than actually being unhappy. And he was more unhappy for others than for himself. He had been unhappy for the Old Man, and he was unhappy for some of the members of his family; for his grandmother, who was an old woman and illiterate, and often very lonely; for his mother, a widow, whose greatest pleasure was church and wakes, and whose children were growing up and away from her; for his Uncle Dick, who seemed to be going downhill in his career as a salesman; and his Uncle Larry, who could be like an old woman in his nagging of Eddie for always having his "nose in a book"; for his Aunt Jenny, who couldn't stay sober for too long a period and was given to fits of hysteria as well as to an incurable habit of borrowing and wasting money; for two of his brothers, who seemed to Eddie to be destined to spend their lives working at the Express Company where a man had little hope of going far; for the Negroes who lived in run-down wooden houses near his station and some of whom would come to buy four and six and ten cents' worth of kerosene for the lamps they used to light their homes instead of the electricity they couldn't afford; and for many, many others.

And the days passed, each one full of all of the excitements you feel when your mind, your feelings, your nerves are awakened.

But, also these were days of a growing sense of separation for Eddie, separation from family and from his whole past life. He saw his former friends less and less, and his childhood and adolescence were becoming a source of poignant, nostalgic memories, of regrets, of sad dreams that had once been dreamed as though they would one day come true, but were dreamed again with sorrow because they had not come true and never would. Eddie was learning that there was a hardness of time upon minds and emotions, upon nerve and muscle, and that some grew in time while others stood still as though yesterday could never die. This was a hardness that was like part of the nature of the world, of the way things were; it was something in the coming and passing of dawn and night, of the torn pages of the calendar, of the ticking of clocks which measured the minutes away, one by one; this was destiny and the destinies of people.

Everybody didn't get ahead in the world. Everyone wasn't going to get ahead. And Eddie was fighting to be one of those who would. He was a young man going somewhere. He was living a destiny, not merely a life.

This set him in a vast loneliness, which he did not understand, and which would sometimes come over him like a sadness born in the sky, the stars, in all of the vast extent of far-off spaces.

He would feel himself then to be utterly and only Eddie Ryan, forever, as long as he lived, Eddie Ryan, looking at the unapproachable and beautifully shining stars, looking, looking, and lonely with the miles and the light distance of years between himself and those far away planets of celestial beauty.

And Eddie was still but twenty-one.

Chapter Twelve

I

Eddie was unaware of how fast a mind could grow, and he did not fully appreciate his own pace and change. As in the summer term, he received A in both of the courses which he'd taken in the fall quarter, and he was ready to take a full schedule of three classes a quarter, starting in January of 1926. The history course of Professor Carleton had been one of quivering excitement, not only because of the Prof, but, also because of the subject matter. The course had brought him close to the present, that is to contemporary history. The class had gone on from the Metternich era to the 1848 revolutions, the reactions, the Second Empire, the rise of Germany, the role of Bismarck, the Franco-Prussian War, and the evolution into modern twentieth-century Europe, and the events leading to the unchaining of the World War.

One day in November, Eddie had come home after class, and sat down at the typewriter in the parlor and written a diary note. The first sentence read:

Socialism is inevitable.

Another day, as he walked out of Cobb Hall, following Professor Carleton's spirited description of the Agadir crisis, Eddie told himself:

—There will be a second World War.

These thoughts came to Eddie like illuminations and he did not immediately work out his reasons for holding to them. Yet

The Silence of History

they rang in his own mind with a conviction of truth, and he believed them.

My God, how much he hadn't known!

And how much he didn't know!

It would take him years to acquire even a small portion of the knowledge you must have, if you wanted to have any glimmering of an idea of what the world was about, and what history had been about, and of the way so much of it had happened. He hadn't known, for instance, the great importance of economics in the career of Napoleon, and why, because of economics, the Emperor Napoleon had had to establish a "Continental System" or else lose to England, as he'd lost. One of Professor Carleton's best lectures had been his exposition of Napoleon's "Continental System," as the only way of bringing England to her knees, and he could see that the Napoleonic wars had really been between France and England, and the whole continent of Europe, or almost all of it, might in the end have benefited if Napoleon had been the winning general at the Battle of Waterloo. Professor Carleton had worn a powder blue suit on the morning when he'd lectured the class on why the "Continental System" had been Napoleon's most powerful and necessary means of fighting England.

Professor Bertram Carleton was more proud of his powder blue suit that morning than of the lecture he delivered. The suit was newly purchased downtown at Rothschild's, and had been delivered the previous afternoon, after Professor Carleton had spent two impatient days waiting for it. His impatience grew out of fear that it wouldn't come, and that he would not have his so-important new suit for his date with Ramona Hilford.

She was plump and in her mid-twenties, the daughter of Professor Hilford, who taught European and American history, and who could have been a big man but for his big family. When Bertram Carleton had first come to Chicago, after taking his doctorate at Harvard on the French Revolution, and making a Grand Tour of Europe, he'd rented an upstairs room at the Hilford home on Harper Avenue, where he had both enjoyed and been distracted by the Hilford home life. There were kids from ten to twenty-five, the house was always in commotion, and he wasn't able to give the time he needed to study and reading. Also he and Professor Hilford were chess enthusiasts; they were guiltily falling into the habit of playing every night. Mrs. Hilford objected to this waste of time, lack of sociability and conversation, and the extra burden which was placed on her. Professor Carleton might well have been given his walking papers but for Ramona, who intervened in his behalf. At first Ramona annoyed and angered her mother, but quite soon, Mrs. Hilford, weighted down as she was with kids and duties, as well as out of the socially natural attitudes of a mother, saw opportunity beginning to beckon.

Ramona was neither pretty nor homely. She was, in consonance with American conditions, well-fed and plumply developed. Her mother had anticipated later health attitudes and health foods, and Ramona had been brought up on fruit juices, salads, and vegetables. Failing to agree with and share her mother's enthusiasm for the orange, the tomato, the cucumber, the carrot, and other such edibles, Ramona became an unhappy child, but this was modified by the pleasures of candy, ice cream sodas, banana splits, and other sweets. She was bright, quick of mind but lacking in originality and imitative. She had developed an interest in history because of her father, and besides liking to read books on the subject, she helped him with the writing of his papers and books, and occasionally did research for him. She was a grammar school teacher in a school out in the Grand Crossing District. She'd begun with much hope of doing good, but was gradually surrendering to routine and habit, and she had begun to worry about her own future. Was she going to spend all her life teaching kids and become an old maid? Her father had influenced her. He was an outstanding man of vast erudition, and almost a perfectionist in his conception of historiography. There was always more to be learned about a subject before it should be written about, and too many academic men, he was fond of saying, rushed into print with a haste that was indecent for scholarship. If she married, and she wanted to, Ramona thought she'd like a man in academic life, but she had never found the right one. She knew many, and her father was always bringing young graduate students home for con-

The Silence of History

ferences or inviting them to dinner, not for Ramona's sake, but as part of his own role. Her mother thought in more practical terms.

Ramona had been growing bored when Bertram Carleton came as a boarder in the fall of 1924. He was young, only about twenty-nine, and, at times, he looked much younger; he had a fine sensitive face, and a falling blond curl that any girl would like to touch. Her father considered Bertram Carleton to be a young fellow of brilliant promise, and although shy, Carleton spoke with intelligence, and such fine diction. Already he was an assistant professor at the University. There were no serious obstacles in Ramona's way, nor was there any reason why she shouldn't find Bertram a young man of interest and attractiveness.

And she so found him.

Bertram Carleton was slow in responding. But finally he did respond. He wanted love, and feared what he wanted. There was his career, and his name to be made, and he could not allow any tendency of the heart to interfere with the future that he was so eagerly wishing for himself. He was afraid of marriage but, also, he was a very lonesome young professor. This, perhaps more than any other phrase, suggested how Bertram Carleton frequently regarded himself.

—A lonesome young professor.

He told himself that this was not only what he was, but it was what he must be, and what he must remain for years and years. Otherwise, the ambition which was the bread and butter, the love and hope, the faith, the all, the be-all and end-all of his character, that quiet ambition which had come to possess him, could never be achieved. It was an ambition which had taken hold of him as an undergraduate student at Harvard, and which was responsible for his switch from Literature to History. He was to become one of the greatest, if not the greatest, Napoleonic scholar of his time, and to rank with great Napoleonic and historic scholars of all time. Why Napoleon Bonaparte? Bertram Carleton never asked himself this question, even when he was in a dangerously probing mood; he never sought any personal reason within himself and his own character. That he admired

Napoleon, the energy, will, capacity for decision and courage of the Corsican, he knew fully, and he believed that there was much in Napoleon to admire. But it seemed to be the unity of will and reason over emotion which Bertram Carleton regarded as the essential source of Napoleon's greatness. Napoleon possessed these traits to such a degree that he was not merely a commander of soldiers in an army, in the sense that a general was; he had been a commander of life, and of history.

Napoleon's capacity to command was perhaps, Bertram Carleton often reflected, the answer to what Plato had written of the war in the name of the human soul. Perhaps this might strike some as curious, and especially so if it were seen as growing out of the ideas of his great teacher, Dr. Irving Babbitt of Harvard. Napoleon had represented the new order of the two planes of man, spirit and matter, upper and lower, and of the age of romanticism. To all who had followed to imitate him, Napoleon had been the man of unified will and nerve, combining old and new, and thereby representing and revealing intellectual force of such strength that it became fate, changed quantity into quality and, as it were, to moral force.

This was one of Bertram Carleton's ideas, and he had many more. His nature rebelled against the moody belief that his plan for the future would only be fulfilled in a successful and brilliant manner if he pursued it step by step, with controlled patience, and as a lonely scholar.

He thought of classmates and colleagues, of the younger men on the University faculty, and observed how many of them were married, or engaged and planning marriage. Among them were a number whom he respected, and who he believed would become big men making their contribution to the growth of knowledge. These men did not all contend that marriage would thwart or limit their careers, and among them were those who gave evidence of a happiness which he did not know. Some were buying homes. Families were being raised. He was invited to dinner, and found a cheerful colleague, sitting back, often serving booze which was illegally bought, and almost radiating contentment.

Sid Ehrman, in the Department of Political Economy, had

The Silence of History

spoken of the subject one spring day when they sat having lunch at the Quadrangle Club, which was the faculty club on the campus. Sid Ehrman was interested in economic history, and was planning to make a serious study of both mercantilism and the physiocrats. At lunch, he and Bertram Carleton had talked of the economic problems of France during the days of Napoleonic rule, and especially in 1804, when Bonaparte became Napoleon I. Ehrman was a thin, small, aggressive fellow with a deep black mustache, restlessly roving eyes, a very quick mind and varied interests. He was married, and didn't complain about it. Sid had serious and big ambitions in the academic world. Bertram left lunch thinking of this fact, rather than of their talk about economics and economic history. He left the Quadrangle Club alone, and walked slowly across campus, toward Harper's; he had a few hours. But it was springtime, and the air was full of sun and the sap of love and of life. The girls, the youths, the grass, the bright living air, all were innocent of time and of the past. In the springtime, young girls walked as though they never could grow old, and youth laughed as though death were but a false rumor, and the sun shone as though it were forever pressing soft colors upon the world.

Thus did Bertram feel, and he strolled along, the lonely scholar who had become the lonely man.

He planned to do a massive work of from five to six, or even nine volumes, on Napoleon and the period of Napoleonic Glory. It would be more than a biography of Napoleon I; it would be a biography of his times and background, and thus of modern life, of the roots of the twentieth century.

But to achieve this great work, he would be forced to live out his life as a lonely scholar.

His eyes turned to a blond, blue-eyed girl whose body was slender under a clean pink dress and whose eyes were like the happy laughter of a world where even the blue skies were a laughing brightness.

Maybe he was a fool?

Bertram bore the suffering emptiness of a lonely life as he walked across campus. But he was not in love, except with the day, the weather, the springtime; his suffering emptiness was the greater because of this fact. There was a vacuum within him, and he feared, with the varying conviction of inner certainty, that no achievement of scholarship, no intellectual and academic distinction, would ever fill that emptiness. The pangs of personal love and living had not been many for him in recent years, just as in his studies, his readings, his classroom lectures, and the papers he had begun to write for professional journals, he had not focused on personal life. Even Napoleon's private life was public and open, the object of study and of public discourse as and when historians wished to discuss it. His aching emptiness was all the more distressing and disturbing because it was almost as new as the smiles and the bright faces and tender skin, and the healthy bodies of passing coeds which were revealed provokingly beneath spring dresses.

Historic objectivity, the fascination of ideas and their priority over anything human, that was contrary to pleasure, below the neck. Yet the absorption of traits and attitudes from Napoleon as a result of much reading, study, reflection, testing, produced a defenselessness before the quick onslaughts of physical desire; the spring day had dropped Bertram below the neck, and Napoleon was above his neck.

There had been spring days during the time of the First Empire, and the women had gone out to Longchamps, he guessed, in their carriages, and Napoleon Bonaparte had not lacked life or love, nor had the Emperor Napoleon been a monk. Bertram had the absurd fear that he was playing out a dream of being the Emperor Napoleon, and he suddenly felt a little foolish as he strolled on past the crowd in the center of campus, and turned south toward Harper's.

Bertram went up in the elevator and became the lonely but also dissatisfied scholar, sitting in a leather chair, with the window open upon the spreading sun across the grass of the Midway. He sat in a swivel chair with four-by-six note cards before him, and with a monotonous regularity, he wrote on these cards, but he could not have fully explained why, other than to say that it was habit, a trick of the trade, the way he had learned to study.

Bertram could think like Napoleon but he couldn't act like

The Silence of History

Napoleon, and quite obviously he wasn't like Napoleon. His saturated study of Bonaparte had affected him in the sense of having a divided mind, and of not, therefore truly knowing himself and his own thoughts.

Bertram Carleton was increasingly beginning to regard his own career and future in Napoleonic terms. Among the attitudes which he believed he had absorbed was that of Bonaparte toward women. Perhaps Napoleon had loved Josephine, and in a way, Marie Louise, and Countess Walewska. But none of his women had deterred him from his course, influenced his mind and judgments, interfered with the coldly intelligent methods in which he pursued his star of destiny and glory. And this concentration of purpose, cold and reasonable, was one of the features of the Emperor Napoleon which attracted Professor Carleton.

It was a day on which he didn't want to study, but then, the whole idea of study to Bertram was one of perseverance and sacrifice, and he always encountered more or less resistance and disinclination to work. It took on the character of duty. The day was seductive, through the opened window, and Bertram's thoughts were tempted to stray, again and again, with the result that his study took on the features of a struggle with himself.

Bertram Carleton had had more than one such experience during the years when he was launching himself as an erudite young historian. By October, when Eddie was taking his course, Professor Carleton was a man of such weakened defense that he could be conquered without much trouble, and Ramona was conquering by quick inches.

On the morning when he wore his new powder blue suit, he did not know whether he would or wouldn't propose to Ramona, and he wanted both. He was full of fear that he would propose, and he was joyfully hopeful that he would, and there was an intense play of joy and fear, of hope and despair lest she should or should not accept him. Professor Carleton's nervousness in class, of which Peter Moore had spoken, was not only related to but had been intensified by his personal conflicts, especially those which involved Ramona.

It was a smoky morning, with nothing suggesting variance in

the fuliginous universe. It was another morning, another day. Professor Carleton had gone to bed wishing for different weather, but the best laid schemes of men and lovers, as well as mice, and as well as Napoleon Bonaparte's, "gang aft a-gley."

There were his classes. Romance gave way to pedagogical duty and to the smoke-colored Chicago air. Perhaps he should wait until another day when the context and arrangement of the world was like love's old sweet song. So he thought.

But had Napoleon ever waited to seize the right moment?

Of course, Ramona was not Wagsam, nor Austerlitz, and God forbid that she be Waterloo.

Walking to campus, he carried a briefcase and looked quite well dressed and distinguished. His gait was nervous, too quick, too much that of a man in an almost frantic hurry, as though by the speed of his walk he could hasten the passage of time, advancing it more quickly to that moment when he would see Ramona. But he became very conscious of his running walk, and deliberately slowed down. He'd only be ahead of time for his eight-o'clock class unless he did, and he'd have to sit at the classroom desk in Cobb Hall or find some way of passing the time until the bell rang.

The atmosphere was still a rather thick gray, a dawn fog, but gradually it was lightening. As usual, he saw people on the sidewalk, bound for work.

Most of them would go to the Illinois Central to catch an I.C. train for the Loop, and, as usual, he was quite glad that he didn't have to do the same, and go to an office.

What a bore an office would be!

But offices were essential. How could life, civilization, continue without them?

He knew all this full well. And nevertheless, he could not but think—what a horror! To spend the best days of your life in an office.

Some of those whom he saw bound for offices must think similarly about his life, or they would if their attention were to be called to it.

And even though he thought it so horrible for men and women to have to spend their days in offices, the early morning, during

The Silence of History

which the host of office workers were to be seen on their way—the early morning was possessed of its peculiar, its singular interest, which was akin to charm, or, no, more to fascination. Among many unknown people, there was an unexpressed sense of unity, an unmentioned recognition that they were all going forth to the same kind of work which helped to keep the world, the social world, going along through the minutes and hours and days, and it was this which made history possible.

Many of those whom he'd notice would seem new, but others were becoming familiar, and he was developing curiosity about them—who and what they were, and what they did and what they were like. There was a tallish, well-built woman, not more than twenty-five or twenty-six, he'd guess, although he was not very reliable at guessing a woman's age, and she had a vigorous manner about her, as well as a handsome face. She usually wore a tan suit, of good material and quality, and every second or third morning, she wore a different hat. She carried several different pocketbooks, also. Bertram Carleton was proud of his keen observation because he noticed so much about the tall woman.

In the case of this woman, he guessed, with quite a decided certainty, that she would like him to speak with her, and if he should, she'd certainly answer him cordially. That was his distinct impression of the young woman, and he was of the inclination to make her acquaintance, and satisfy his curiosity as to what she was like as a person, and, perhaps, take her out occasionally. She had a look of intelligence about her, she dressed well, and on some mornings, he had observed that she was carrying a book.

On several different mornings, he had been on the verge of speaking to her, but had been held back by some shyness or restraint which he didn't quite understand, and he had resolved that he would speak, greet her with a "good morning," and make an effort to get to know her. But he had not done so up to the morning when he was wearing his new powder blue suit, and was in the throes of his confusion and personal conflict about Ramona. And on that morning, he walked like a man in a great hurry, and she like a young woman in equal haste. He did not catch the smile she gave him, but passed on his way, and she went her way. He had gone on about a half-block before he knew that he had seen her smile. Yes, he had, but he'd failed to notice it at the moment.

He turned about to look back but she was not in sight, and he went on his way, trying to still a rising excitement within himself. There was Ramona, and she was no stranger. That young woman who had smiled at him was a stranger.

But stranger?

We are all strangers to one another, and he knew the dead better than the living. He knew Madame Récamier much better than he knew Ramona, and he knew Napoleon better than he did President Coolidge.

He had seen a few other familiar faces on his walk, and the number of people on the street seemed to be increasing as he went on toward 57th Street. There was almost a stream of people pouring toward the I.C. station, walking with methodical haste, as though their movements were part of a ritual. He fancied that he perceived something grim about the way they moved, a grimness in their bodies as well as in the expression of their faces. He did not see many smiles on the faces of those people. He failed to catch suggestions of joyfulness in movements. Collectively, they created an atmosphere of disciplined grimness of which they were undoubtedly unaware.

He would think of these people in contrast with men and women of past times and periods, and he would think more of differences and contrasts than of better and worse, and of the ideas and conceptions of progress. What was better or worse? And what did it mean to speak of the judgment of history? He was a historian, and was his judgment supreme? These people came and went, lived and died, and the work of the world went on, and that led to history, but how much could history say? He had put much of himself into these and other problems, and he'd abandoned personal feeling in order to understand and describe what had been the meanings and fears beneath the superficial daily flow of life. And these people he saw and passed, they were part of that daily superficial flow, and they were swimming in it

The Silence of History

in a quest for happiness to which they gave various names—love, power, home, success, wealth.

When he'd told Ramona of such thoughts, she'd nodded as though she understood perfectly and agreed fully with him. But some doubt had hung in his mind, and he had retained it. He was not at all convinced that she did understand him and did agree. But how many would? A number of his colleagues couldn't.

The historian must do what Napoleon had almost done, and what Balzac had aimed to achieve.

Coming to 57th Street, and swinging right to walk westward to the campus, he thought of Balzac. He quoted to himself:

Ce qu'il n'a pas pu achever par l'épée, je l'accomplirai par la plume.

Bertram had thoughts of Ramona, and she was on his mind rather than the lectures he would give in his classes that day, one on "the Continental System," and in another course, a continuation of his lecture on the Enlightenment and the men of the Enlightenment.

He walked on, slowing his pace, principally because he did not wish that colleagues think him excessively nervous and restless.

Balzac and Napoleon—who was he to compare himself with them? But he was not doing that.

As for his lectures, these he would manage. There were plenty of four-by-six note cards in his briefcase, and he lectured best when he spoke extemporaneously, for he was daily thinking anew about these problems and these points, and there was no doubt of his having material at his command.

It was Ramona.

Bertram knew more surely that he would propose today, and he was sad and glad. He was walking at a good clip again, along 57th Street, and prospects of the day were cheering him up, like light faces of students who listened and even doted on his words, and the few, such as Ryan in his eight-o'clock class, to whom he talked; the day would pass, as he engaged in his professional activity, and settled the destiny of his heart.

And he looked well in the new suit. He knew that.

II

Bertram Carleton was not unduly vain, but he had his full quarter of vanity, and when he appeared at the eight-o'clock class in his new seventy-five dollar suit, with a linen handerchief in the upper side pocket, he was anything but modest and displeased. He felt that his appearance was quite impressive.

Bertram Carleton had often been anxious before a class or lecture, but once he was with a group of students, his anxiety was dissipated, and he was confident and sure of himself. He was extraordinarily erudite, had a quick command of words, facts, and ideas; he could close out any personal difficulties and wishes, and for the class period, he was able to concentrate on the subject of the lecture, with full command of what he knew. His nervousness, his clownish antics, his undue pacing of the aisles and front of the room, his sprawling sitting on the desk, his ungainly getting on and off it, his minor contortions as he lectured, constituted an undisciplined and but partly controlled use of his body as a means of calling attention to it, especially on the part of the young girls. He failed to realize that he did this, or rather, he but partially knew it, with the result that he found small outlets in petty and seemingly motiveless movements of hands, arms, and body, as well as in groans, sighs, grimaces, frowns, and a senseless play of eyes and eyebrows when students were as students so often are—stupid.

Bertram Carleton relaxed pleasantly, with a sense that he would forget without difficulty the problems which he had been giving the bum's rush out of his mind on that walk to class.

Bertram's feeling there had some parallel with that of Eddie Ryan who, likewise, was able to make the world and his own problems go as into sleep while he focused and concentrated on the subject of his studies. Other problems were of less weight and moment, and Eddie knew that the world must be pushed out of mind for his own interests or the world would rule him, enter and control his mind, and, thereby, the mind of Eddie A. Ryan would belong to the world and not to its rightful owner, Eddie A. Ryan himself.

The Silence of History

Eddie did not know that Professor Carleton possessed a trait similar to his own, nor did Professor Carleton know that Ryan, a promising kid in his class was, in that one sense, as he was.

The buzzing of the bell. Professor Carleton sat at the desk and went through the formality of taking the attendance. This done, the lecture could begin.

There was a shuffling of feet, movements in the seats, and small gyrations on the part of the students. A few flirted; a few, including a substitute tackle on the varsity, closed their eyes and tried to sleep soundlessly and unnoticed.

Professor Carleton took a half-used piece of chalk, idly tossed it in the air, caught it, and glanced about with eyes that should have been penetrating and frightening.

"We went a certain distance of history yesterday, didn't we . . ."

Professor Carleton stared about the room.

"Didn't we, Mr. Kemil?"

Kemil was the second-string tackle, but no one could call him a second-string tackle and believe in varsity. He was a broken first-string tackle, although a young man of virtuous Christian inclination, and an angelic desire to sing *Onward Christian Soldiers* and other songs of morbid Christianity for the soul.

Kemil said "Yes" to Professor Carleton in sleepiness.

"We didn't go ten yards in four downs, though?"

Kemil was dumfounded. A few students laughed openly; others restrained their impulse or laughed into a handkerchief.

"Who can tell? No one ever invented the gridiron sport for Napoleon Bonaparte."

"No sir. He couldn't have made an end run. He was too fat and small."

There were outbursts of laughter in various parts of the room.

Professor Carleton sat on the desk, tossed the half-used piece of chalk lightly in the air, caught it, and looked at Kemil, and then randomly at others, his eyes slightly amused.

"You have tackled men behind the goal line, I imagine, Mr. Kemil?"

"Yes, I tried. Them frogs is all small and I imagine I would play just a smashing game of tackle against any of 'em with Bonaparte-Napoleon at quarterback."

The question and repartee seemed funny, and the class awakened to smiles, giggles, and laughter. Professor Carleton restrained the amusement on his own broad and rather handsome face.

"They didn't have no Big Ten League then, in them days," Kemil said, provoking a fresh eruption of laughter.

"I believe that's an accurate statement," Professor Carleton replied.

The laughter rose.

"Of course, if they had, and I was playing defensive tackle, I'm sure I'd of ruined Napoleon as a quarterback, behind the lines, every time—unless he has some mighty good blockin' to protect him from defensive tackles."

Kemil spoke with ponderous, professional seriousness.

Almost the entire class was in uproar, and Professor Carleton expanded, almost glowing. The big oaf, Kemil, was so good-natured and unconsciously funny in his stupidity that he was positively charming.

"Napoleon played a different kind of quarterback," Professor Carleton said, when the class had quieted down some.

"But the Duke of Wellington was a mighty good tackle, wasn't he, Professor?" Kemil asked, and the class was shaken with laughter by Kemil's wisecrack.

Professor Carleton waited for the students to subside, and finally, when the class was quiet, he cleared his throat, and began his lecture.

"Was the Emperor Napoleon I, and before he acquired or usurped, if you will, that title, a mere war lord, glorying and gloating in war, and dedicated to the science or art, or the practice of butchery, as one may choose to characterize war?"

Professor Carleton began slowly, and with only a slight strain in his voice. For Ramona was but a dim acquaintance, shadowy, and to be seen in time more distant than the actual number of hours until he would meet her at Hyde Park Boulevard and Stony Island Avenue.

However, when Professor Carleton had spoken of Napoleon

The Silence of History

as merely a man of war, he'd seen recognition light up in many faces. That was what these young people thought, as their fathers thought, and as their fathers' fathers had thought.

"In a sense, it's true. General Bonaparte, leader of the Army of Italy, the Emperor Napoleon I, was a great soldier, a military genius. This is widely accepted, by critics as well as those who admire him. We have already considered some of his military exploits and I have discussed Napoleon, the soldier, the general, in contrast with earlier great captains, and with Frederick the Great, whom Napoleon much admired, and many others, Julius Caesar, Hannibal, and Alexander the Great. Napoleonic war was a new form of war, and developed its new and great book, *On War*, by General Karl Von Clausewitz. Napoleon had perfected the war of the people, of the nation, and the French Revolution had made this possible."

Much of this, of course, had already been explained, analyzed, developed in the preceding lectures, and in the reading assignments which he had given to the class, day by day. Catching the number of blank faces, Professor Carleton was able to decide that a large percentage of the class hadn't read all of the assignments, if any; this would be temptation to despair, were he not accustomed to students who didn't read enough, and, in consequence, failed to profit from his courses, and from the study of history, as they should. This was, he could not hold back in his own consciousness, the irony of Napoleon's fame and glory.

The name was known, Napoleon Bonaparte, Napoleon I, the Emperor Napoleon, and a few facts, at least proportionately few. But what glory was there in that?

When he did his work, and it would be completed, a big shelf of books, how many would read and study his work?

Professor Carleton thought of how little these young men and women knew about Napoleon, and how they would never know very much about him, nor understand him, what he was, and what his historic achievements were. That was Glory. To have your name known by many when you fell into undistinguished dust, and to be understood by few, and fewer than a few.

Such thoughts rose at the edge of Professor Carleton's mind while he continued with his lecture, and he was depressed for a moment. He was giving more of himself, trying harder, sacrificing more than the candle of life was worth.

He continued speaking as though that candle of life were worth all.

"The world of Napoleon Bonaparte and of Frederick the Great, these were two different worlds, and the differences were measured by time—time and change, not time itself as time, or time *quo* time, but time as the span of duration in which events happen, new generations take the place, the position, the prestige, power, and authority of older generations, and life and progress, or progress so-called, goes on.

"Napoleon was a different kind of monarch from Frederick the Great. The difference in military strategy, which I have already discussed with you ladies and gentlemen, is but one of the indices of this difference.

"These many differences I have, in one way and in another, been seeking to focus in your attention."

Professor Carleton liked to see the attentive, questioning, watching young eyes, the trancelike interest on some faces and the alert intelligence on others. He was stimulatingly aware of his effect and influence upon the class, of the respect with which his words were received, of the mastery and control, the power he was gaining over these students' young and fresh minds.

"Now, ladies and gentlemen, let's think of a general, a perennial question, one that is as hoary as the oldest proverb about a nervous wife, but hoary as it be, this question is an important and insoluble one. For it's likely, and who knows but that it might even be fortunate, that some questions and problems are and will forever be—insoluble."

Interest had quickened as a consequence of these last words, and he stepped up onto the square platform on which the desk rested, and sat with awkward unease upon the old desk.

"Napoleon was a great man," he said with a forceful emphasis that was the stronger because he had preceded it by a pause.

The class waited for more.

"Great men are rare—as distinguished from men who think themselves great. Napoleon belonged to the first category, the

The Silence of History 199

rare one, and therein lies the reason why he has entranced many historians, scholars, poets, and novelists, why so many outstanding men have found such a fascination in the career, the character, and the very working of the mind of Napoleon Bonaparte. Lord Acton, the nineteenth-century British historian, said in a lecture: 'No intellectual exercise, for instance, can be more invigorating than to watch the working of the mind of Napoleon, the most entirely known as well as the ablest of historic men.'"

Professor Carleton gave Lord Acton's quotation from memory, and this was a source of passing pride and pleasure to him. He hoped that some of the members of the class would notice how frequently he could give a quotation from memory. And in teaching he was, in his more humble way, attempting to show the students something of what Lord Acton had said about Napoleon, to give them an example of a mind at work upon problems and periods of history, and to arouse their minds by his example as well as by the subject matter and content of his lectures.

And the image of Napoleon was reawakened in his own mind with the fascination that he had so often felt in studying the Emperor ever since his first freshman course in history. Now he could understand why he had fallen as though under the spell of Napoleon, and greatness had more meaning and significance to him than it could have had when he had been a mere freshman, like the young people sitting before him as he lectured. The example of greatness, of the working of a great mind and personality in the affairs of history, that was, in the affairs of men, instructive, as well as captivating, fascinating.

Professor Carleton had sidetracked himself from what he had planned to say in the lecture, and he was more interested in going on about the greatness and qualities of Napoleon, than in giving his exposition of why it was necessary for Napoleon to fight England by imposing a Continental System on all of Europe. But he roused himself and explained that this was essential because of England's sea power, and the blockade which England could impose on Europe. The only alternative to the Continental System would have been an invasion of England,

and her defeat on her own island. Napoleon had gone to Egypt with the hope of reaching India and by this means bringing England to her knees.

He counterposed for the class the greatness of Napoleon and the necessities imposed on a great man.

"Perhaps he had to lose," Professor Carleton said just as the class bell ended the hour.

And he spoke with regret, as he had first felt regret when he had read of Napoleon as a freshman at Harvard. He spoke in the tones of a regret similar to that which Eddie Ryan felt, listening to the lecture and grasping out to absorb the full meaning and implication of every word the young professor uttered.

That was on the morning of the day Professor Carleton proposed to Ramona, and was accepted. But in the midst of his joy and happiness, he wondered if that day had been his own Waterloo, and did all men meet a Waterloo? Was Waterloo the symbol of men's history, Waterloo and St. Helena?

And Eddie Ryan, also, during the remainder of the course, kept thinking and brooding about Waterloo and the Island of St. Helena.

During the last weeks of the course, the class took up Bismarck, the hero of Germany, and the development of the system of alliances which led to the World War in 1914. Eddie began to think bitterly of the war as having been one "for steel and gold."

He came out of the course with such thoughts, Waterloo, St. Helena, "for steel and gold," and these were the questions which he was pondering as the new year began, and he took courses in Political Economy and Political Science. What was the purpose of war in history? And what did fame and success and glory mean?

He was developing a brooding and saddened bitterness, and a sharpened feeling about life as struggle to the last minute, struggle to the grave. And when you struggle to that last minute, and right into your grave, what would it all mean if you became famous and remembered?

He studied with greater intensity and desperation, and with a less clear conception of a goal and of why he should go on driving himself in a hunger for some kind of future. He must do this, and he must go on doing it, he told himself, and possibly it was all only to end up at his own Waterloo and on his own St. Helena.

Chapter Thirteen

I

The winter days seemed to pass very slowly, as though time itself were bogged down in the snow. Eddie saw much more of darkness than of daylight. Usually he awakened before daylight or "at the break of day," a phrase his grandmother was fond of using. And the darkness came fairly quickly after he had reported to work at the station, relieving Corlin. Business was sometimes a bit brisk in the afternoon, and there were chores or tasks he had to perform, cleaning to be done, and, on some days, snow to be shoveled from the drive and station grounds. Thus, it would seem that he had scarcely come to work than the day was gone, and the night had begun to set in. His spirit and morale were affected and Eddie was called on to use more force of will in order to keep up his intense pace of study. He was taking two courses in Political Economy, and the reading on this subject was more difficult and slower than in history. The subject matter was not as exciting either, and he would feel more in the mood for reading and less in that of studying than he had during the two previous quarters. And once the darkness began to set in, and the day was fast waning, the corner station was very lonely. He made time pass and studied, but with an effort. He spent many intense hours alone with himself and his own mind. He was his own companion to such a degree that a seemingly permanent sense of the solitude of life was being fixed into his character, and he began to feel with growing poignancy the loneliness of living in general, and concretely and immediately, the loneliness of his own life.

The Silence of History

This loneliness was emphasized by the nighttime scene at dusk, the dark corner that was full of fleeting shadows, with the street lights pale against such shadows.

He suffered from more eyestrain and used his eyes most under electric light, and the slowly passing quiet winter evenings were accompanied by burning pain in his eyes and an aching head. He drank more coffee and took aspirin liberally, hoping to blot out the pain, and to be able to go on studying without discomfort. In consequence, he would have a sour stomach and heartburn, and this added to his anxieties, as well as to his discomforts. Eddie did not know on what morning he'd awaken with strained and aching eyes, or a troubled stomach, and he lived not only with this immediate worry of distress but also with the more disturbing anxiety that his health was not good, that his eyes were too weak for the burden he must place upon them, and that, perhaps, there was something wrong with his heart.

If he should see a doctor, he feared that he would be told to quit or let up, and he couldn't do this, and live out a hopeless and ignorant future. Dr. Stanford, the eye specialist, had frightened him with the fear of blindness and he had carried and fought this fear for over a year, defying it when it was flagrantly pressing upon him through the burning strain he felt in his eyes and head, and forgetting it as much as he could, assuming or hoping that the doctor's prediction would turn out wrong, or that some new discovery would save him in time.

But after a good start at the new station with Bill Corlin as a partner, the winter had set in, and it was as though cold winds were blown roughly through him to shake and shatter, if not to freeze his morale.

The days came. The days went. He and Peter Moore still walked to classes whenever the weather permitted, but they had to be ready earlier in order to catch a bus and make their eight-o'clock classes if the weather was too inclement for walking. He went to classes from eight to eleven and then he would go directly home, or else spend an hour at the library on campus. Between one-fifteen and one-thirty, he would leave for work, either by bus or elevated train. At nine o'clock, he closed up the station, turned the key in the time clock as he left, and hurried to an elevated train. Then, he usually studied until he could not remain awake any longer, and he'd drop into bed and into a heavy sleep of exhaustion. He'd hardly seem to have fallen off into sleep when the alarm clock would shrill into his ears, and he would awaken, one big lump of being, heavy with tiredness and depressed from the tiredness and the need of more sleep.

He'd drag himself out of bed, and try to wake up by sticking his face into a bowl of cold water, and then he'd soak up coffee which his grandmother would have ready for him. At the end of the third successive class, Eddie would be weary again and he faced more work, and the long continuation of the day and most of the night. After the bell of his ten-o'clock class would ring at ten minutes to eleven, he would sag into a let-down, and would feel his full weariness, and with this, he'd become morose with depression and an emotional feeling of hopelessness which was the outgrowth of fatigue.

Eddie had passed the half-year mark as a student at the University, and the change in his hopes and attitudes was becoming more conscious on his part. He was losing his concern about social aspiration and ambition, but not about a girl, and his hankering to go out for athletics persisted. His respect for a life of the mind, and his desire to live such a life, unhampered and unrestricted, was growing upon him, and his perspective of the future was changing from the idea of success to that of the life of the mind. But he was also beginning to see with increasing clarity that the life of the mind was not separated from life, but was part of all living, and that life itself, and everything within it, was part of the field of knowledge. The life of the mind meant speaking the truth, and sometimes fighting for the truth, and since he was pretty well convinced of this, he wasn't thinking any more of success, of money, of getting rich. He might not get rich, and he might not be a worldly success if he tried to live what he had come to call the life of the mind. Learning as he hoped to learn, and studying as he was studying, wasn't necessary to be a success in life, if you measured your advance merely in terms of dollars. The biographies of many successful and self-made men didn't tell of studying as he was doing, and of the kind of sacrifice he was enduring, and the risks that he was taking. Even though Eddie had his depressions and his flashing seconds of despondency and weariness, he was full of hope. There was so much to be done in the world, and so much, now, that could be done. With education and science, scientific method applied to life, with reason and truth brought like new light into the world, there was a better and more just world to be, a world that was more technical and was run by the principles of right and justice. This hope was stronger in him than the passing despairs and low moments when he thought that he didn't care, and that all he wanted was to quit, to give up, to forget, and find some kind of successful peace like a contented fattened cow.

After all, he couldn't be Socrates.

And even though he couldn't, he harbored as a shameful secret ambition the hope and the desire that he could be Socrates. He dared not tell this thought to anyone, for if he did, he'd be laughed at more than ever in his life, and he'd seem crazy, like someone who thought he was or could be Napoleon.

His generation was the one that should go into politics and make the fight for reason and truth. This idea was growing in his thoughts, and he was beginning to think of it as one of the ones he'd adopt, as a lighthouse of his future.

But this meant he must learn, learn, always learn. He'd tell this to himself, thinking of the famous words of Danton:

L'audace, toujours l'audace, encore l'audace.

And the sight of girls in fur coats, wearing black galoshes and silk stockings, their faces young and unlined, their eyes transparently shining with life that was recently born, their smiles and laughter, and the beauty which he saw in so many of them, the sight of girls on those winter days put a look of hunger into his eyes and filled his spirit with yearning and thoughts of love and poetry.

He was a hungry young man, carrying a battered briefcase stuffed with books, looking at the world with weak and bloodshot eyes which sought the wonder of life. And the laughing girls with soft-rosy faces did not see the hunger and wonder of those bloodshot eyes cast upon them.

The days were passing. Dark days. January would go into February, and he would be twenty-two years old and still so much was unaccomplished; he lived as though in the silence of his own hopes and dreams. However, he couldn't accomplish much yet. He was not ready.

Eddie found the first weeks of the winter quarter to be different, and there were days when he took punishment.

"Son, you're workin' too hard," his grandmother began to say to him with increasing frequency.

"Oh, I'll be all right, Mother. I'm young and in pretty good health."

"Sure and when a lad is young, he doesn't know how strong he is, and to hear him tell it, he's stronger than a giant. Didn't I hear them sayin' how strong they were in the old country? But be careful, son, and watch your health. The Lord gave us health to watch over it, and not be abusin' it."

"I'll watch it. I'm all right, Mother."

But was he?

"Eddie, aren't you going at study too hard, driving yourself too much?" Peter Moore asked.

They were walking over the crusted and graying snow, beyond the lagoon and on the flat stretch which extended toward Cottage Grove, toward low knobs called hills, and toward the summer meeting place of the Bug Club. It was another dim morning, unpleasantly cold but short of rawness. The snap in the air was almost pleasantly invigorating. But the clouds were low and dark like polar dirt transplanted to hang over Chicago and give Chicagoans another depressing day.

"I don't think so," Eddie said so quickly as to have almost snapped out his answer.

But he wanted to admit to his friend that he tormented himself with worries that he was overdoing it, and he did fear for his health and his nerves, for his heart, and, most of all, for his eyes. And since all this was true, it was inevitable that he would sometimes begin to fear, and then to believe that he would live only a short life. And even if he did have a long life, would his eyes hold up? This question could darken him with a despair that was sheer Hell.

"I don't want to sound like an apostle of dissipation, Eddie, which I am as far from as I can be, but all work and no play, Eddie, it isn't making you dull, I can see that—but is it good for you?"

"I look all right, don't I?"

"Yes, I admit that."

"As long as I'm doing it, and not suffering, I'm sure I'm all right, Peter."

"That's a sensible answer. But strain creeps up on a person without his knowing it. You ought to watch yourself for any strain, Eddie."

"There's so much to learn," Eddie said.

"You or I can't learn everything, or be everything."

Eddie didn't answer quickly. He agreed that there was no evidence, no grounds for assuming that either could expect to achieve big things in the future, but he didn't want to admit this. If he wasn't going to try to achieve big, why achieve at all?

"We'd better shake our hoofs. It's getting on toward eight and if we drag along, we'll be late for our classes," Peter said.

They hastened their pace. Peter wanted to run, but Eddie said they'd make it to their classes merely by stepping on it. Running would tire him out too much. He'd had less than six hours' sleep the night before.

They strode on, with Peter Moore, who'd been a high school runner, getting ahead of Eddie, and then waiting a second or so for his companion to catch up with him.

Eddie was glad that they had become silent. He didn't want to talk any more, much as he respected, liked, and trusted Peter Moore. The conversation depressed him, and he could be worried and fearful all day, thinking about himself and his health. Worry of this kind couldn't be controlled by the mind, not always, and once it started, you were in the merry-go-round-going mood, and around and around your mind could go, around and around in the same circle.

As Eddie kept pace with Peter along 57th Street, he suddenly told himself that if he didn't have hopes, strong hopes, he wouldn't be at the University. His depression began to lift.

II

Eddie carried through those wintry days, sticking to his course and rebounding swiftly from each round of depression and anxiety, as well as from his periods of fatigue and eyestrain. By the end of January, he found the days easier to get through, and he had, thus, managed to come through a crisis of a kind. But Eddie was not simply acquiring more knowledge, collecting facts, and expanding his acquisition of ideas. He was continuing as he had been since the first class day of the previous June; he was developing, and at a pace which was becoming increasingly faster. The size of the world within his mind was continuing to grow. This experience brought him the opposite of his morbid and melancholy state, that is, moods of exhilaration, of intellectual excitement and intensity of emotion about some idea, some passage in a book which he read, some idea which was new to him.

Eddie had become a young man who was not still within himself. His thoughts and dreams, like his moods, were rapid, crowding upon one another, and his entire life had become, not chaotic, but thick; it was thickening as much as it could without becoming chaos. Especially after the winter quarter had begun, and he took a course in Political Economy, Political Science 101, and Social Control, an advanced course in Political Economy which he'd had to get permission to take, since he hadn't the necessary prerequisites, he had become more aware about life itself as the field of knowledge, the real subject of study. The filling station, and the Express Company office in which he had worked prior to coming to Rawlinson, the daily newspaper, his neighborhood and the characters in it, his family, his childhood and high school days, all of these were extensions of what he was studying in his courses and reading in textbooks and other books. He also made himself the object of his own study. As a filling station attendant, he was an

The Silence of History

economic man, and his pay, his commissions, his petty grafting were economic facts.

Eddie became both more alive and more nervous. However, he wasn't heavy, pompous, solemnly seeking in his working life; he didn't go about as though with a metaphorical net, ready to chase every butterfly of fact that he glimpsed. He saw and grasped relationships and connections. He knew that Rawlinson was buying his time with the idea of getting profit from its purchase, and of gaining good will. He practiced the principle of *caveat emptor.*

Eddie's going to the University didn't mean much to old friends, and if he saw any of his high school classmates, as he did occasionally, mostly by accident, they asked few questions about his courses and progress, and little was said of it in his family. Some of the older neighborhood fellows, meeting him on the street, warned him that he'd better be careful because if you read too many books, you might be locked up as a nut just the same as you might be given a bum's rush to the booby hatch if you pulled your pudding a lot. Thus he was gradually set apart because he was a student at the University; he was made an object of suspicion, and was even told that he had a goddamned nerve going to that atheist ANA University, thinking he could learn something, and who the hell did he think he was? This increased especially when word got around that he was doing very well and if he continued to do as well as he had already done, he would set some kind of scholastic record. This went to show what kind of a place it was over there on the Midway, and a couple of the fellows argued that they weren't honest, them professors over there, and they were giving young Ryan them fancy marks because he was an Irish Catholic boy from the Catholic schools, and you watch and see if they didn't get him away from the Church with them methods.

"It's ignorance. You understand it as well as I do, Eddie," Peter said, walking to classes on a morning of February thaw when Washington Park was squashy with mud, puddles, and soiled melting snow.

"It doesn't bother me any. I should ask anybody what kind of a future I want to make for myself?"

"I don't know what it is, but there are so many people afraid to crack a book."

"My Uncle Larry gets books out of a rental library downtown, but he has them wrapped in packages that don't look like books so nobody will know it," Eddie said.

"We don't have many books at home, except for my textbooks, and a few I bought," Peter said.

Eddie stepped over a puddle of water. It was depressing to know there were many, all over Chicago and America, many who hated and feared books and what was to be found in them.

Couldn't it be that he dreamed pipe dreams when he looked ahead and thought of fellows such as Peter and himself, and others like them, learning and then changing people, by convincing them more and more of the truth, and of the method of finding out the truth, testing and correcting, changing and revising it. What he meant was saving men, and Peter would usually ask him how much can you save men, and for what?

Eddie put the same question to himself in his own thinking, and often he didn't have great hopes for the salvation of mankind.

And that was God's job, anyway, wasn't it?

However, these thoughts about hope, about truth, about ignorance, occupied Eddie far beyond their importance as causes for what he was doing. For whether or not the truth could make all men, or other men, free, it would be Eddie Ryan's means of liberation.

He had already gone more than far enough at the University to have perceived this. How others acted or might say to him could not deflect him from what was becoming his direction in life.

He was trying to educate himself, primarily, for himself, and not for others, and he had come to understand that he would, himself, have to be ignorant and prejudiced if he did not get an education, and he had also developed to the stage where he distinguished between success and truth. The purpose of

The Silence of History

education should be to look for the truth and to learn the means of finding out the truth, and this didn't at all mean any guarantee of becoming a success in life, getting a better job than you might otherwise have gotten, and becoming rich.

These thoughts had come to him as a reaction to the atmosphere of his whole life, which had been saturated with an emphasis on success and money. His father, sick and dying, had urged him to get an education, in order that he might make something out of himself and have a better life.

"If you grow old with nothing in this world, you're nothing," his old man had said.

At the Express Company, drivers and chauffeurs and the route inspectors and wagon dispatchers had all spoken the same way, and he'd frequently heard them say that they wished they'd had more sense when they were young fellows and had gotten themselves an education instead of running around and pissing away their time and their dough, because if they had, they could have made something out of themselves in this man's world. This was the common idea of the meaning of an education, and it represented what Eddie had believed when he'd determined to make something of himself by getting a college education.

"What does depress me, Ed, is that fellows like you and I, we're half cut off from our own by learning," Peter once said.

Eddie did not reply to this. Later, he thought again of Peter's remark, sitting in his station, and looking up from his book out through the window at snow falling in big flakes in the dark night.

He was changing. He was growing away from others as much as others could grow away from himself. He was becoming a different person. More than that, he wanted to become a different person, to make himself over into more than he was.

Eddie watched the snow coming down more heavily, charging the air with life and movement and changing the aspect of the night in total silence. He was enthralled with the simple beauty of falling snow on a dreary corner. He went outside for a few moments to feel the snow wet upon his face, to smell the dampness of the enlivened air.

Then it was time to close up the station.

He left, carrying his briefcase. He passed rickety wooden houses with pale lights in some of the windows. His feet, warm and dry in galoshes, crushed the wet, sticky snow. The flakes fell on his face and coated his glasses, and he felt himself to be vastly free and in touch with the silent strength of the far-off and darkened sky out of which came the snowstorms to crush down upon the city. He thought of himself as a child of such a storm.

He rode to 58th Street in a dismally lit elevated train, thinking that sometime in the future he wanted to feel as free as he just had, while walking in the storm to the elevated station.

Chapter Fourteen

I

The life of those at a great University might be seemingly dull when it is dramatic, and apparently dramatic when it is banal. The dramatic, the significant, the important, even the spectacular are related to time and unfold in time, and in different sequences of time, some longer than others. Unless the living sequences of time can be filled in and revealed at their adequate pace, the dramatic and historic must be needlessly distorted in order to make false conflict and drama, and the falsity of history becomes inescapable. The life of a great University is full of many kinds of drama which unfold in time, and so it was in those days when Eddie Ryan was a student. Many who were part of the life of the University were preparing to better history, and the quiet drama of their days and their preparation grew in importance and interest through the years.

Eddie Ryan had already, before the Winter quarter of 1926, come to see himself as contending with his destiny, and he was living through the beginning of a destiny, day by day, and minute by minute, in a manner which must unfold according to its sequence of time.

Eddie's drama, then, was in himself. It was a drama of sacrifice and risk about which almost no one knew very much. Even in terms of will and physical effort and exertion, the meanings of what Eddie was doing and what others were doing fell into their respective time patterns, and stood out in contrasts.

There was Lonesome Larry Royal, who took the same course as Eddie in the winter quarter of January 1926. At the end of the previous football season, he had been elected football captain for the next fall. His picture had been printed in the rotogravure section of the *Chicago Sunday Record Herald*, as the most handsome football captain in the Middle West, and one of the most handsome college gridiron stars in the nation.

He was first called Lonesome Larry by a classmate in a South Side Chicago high school, where he had been a fullback and a ball player. In his third year, when he had run seventy-five yards to make the winning touchdown in the South Side title game among public schools, Larry had been at a dance, and a fraternity brother had said:

—Look, Larry's lonesome, only four flappers ready to faint in his arms.

"Lonesome Larry" became his nickname after that evening, and he didn't mind being kidded and was a good sport. Lonesome Larry was merely one of the brothers at his fraternity house, and everyone who knew him among the students was ready to agree with one of his fraternity brothers, who had said:

—Lonesome Larry Royal is as regular as a straight line.

He was very solidly built, of good muscle and frame, one of the best to be found on a young man in Chicago. But he had the kind of face that girls wished other girls would forget, a Roman god's head, with the most perfect and sunny head of blond marcelled hair and regular, Nordic, handsome features. Lonesome Larry would never be lonesome.

Thus was he written up in the press.

Larry Royal was manly, handsome, earnest, a courageous football player who was technically very good but inclined to be rigidly repetitive in what he did, and who needed a good line and blockers in order to play up to his best potential. Lonesome Larry was not incapable of thinking; that was not his difficulty. He could think, but it took him a little more time than it did others, thinking did. On the football field, beneath the marcelled blond hair that was something superior to the statue of Apollo Belvedere, something went on—that is in the gray matter. But what went on wasn't always fast enough for football, nor for examinations; it had almost caused the fatality of ineligibility.

In January, Lonesome Larry appeared on the first day for one of the Political Economy classes which Eddie took. There were some girls, but not too many. They looked at him with the look girls have when they are that way. The next day, he appeared; the girls looked. On the fifth class day, after the bell had rung, Lonesome Larry went to Professor Traynor and said:

"Say, sir, do you know if I took this class before?"

"No, sir, I don't," Professor Traynor answered with an irony that was both amused and barbed.

"I can't remember, sir, if I did, or if I didn't."

"I don't remember that you did, sir."

"Then I must have taken another course."

He stayed in the class, and morning after morning, he showed up, and listened with an air of concentrated seriousness that was pathos, but pathos in slowed-down time.

Lonesome Larry didn't make friends with any strangers in class, but often said "Hello" to those who said "Hello" to him. He passed with a C, thanks to the help of his fraternity brothers, and retained his eligibility.

The previous fall, he'd gone off tackle for thirty-six yards to win a conference game on Stagg Field when the shadows of autumn stretched the ghosted memories of first greats, including Walter Eckersall. More or less, thus was the drama of Lonesome Larry's feat described in one of the downtown papers.

And there were those whom Eddie met outside class. One was Henry Oldering, a small youth with large tortoise-shell glasses, whom Eddie had seen often and had come to regard as an intellectual and, probably, a brilliant student. Peter Moore brought them together for a quick lunch in Commons one chilly but sunny day in early February. Oldering was majoring in Political Economy. Eddie shrugged his shoulders at his wrong guess, for he'd believed that this quiet, modest, but well-composed young man was majoring in philosophy.

"Yes, I'm majoring in Political Economy, because that's the basic subject for achieving social justice."

"I don't know how far I go along with that," Peter said. "Economics, Political Economy, can't be any more basic than psychology and ethics, Political Science, other subjects."

"There's a unity of subjects. We divide them up for working purposes, but they overlap, and knowledge and study is divided up into these subjects for purposes of, for . . . for purposes of convenience."

Eddie was pleased with his remark, because it had been intelligent, and pretty well expressed.

"If you read Henry George's *Progress and Poverty* . . ." Henry began.

"I have—that is, part of it—the beginning," Eddie said.

"You should finish it, because that's where you get the meat, nearest the bone. But you can't afford to miss as much as a single word of the book," Henry explained.

Eddie was eager, but not completely certain of himself because he might make a mistake, and might know far less than Henry Oldering knew about Henry George. Still, he was convinced that he was right, basically, in his criticism and rejection of the theory. For a moment he wanted to sidetrack any discussion because of his fear that he couldn't talk well, but he told Henry Oldering that the theory of Henry George was one-sided.

The Commons began to get noisier as the lunch hour crowd started coming. Henry and Eddie continued to disagree about Henry George's theory of the single tax, but their voices were sometimes not clearly distinguishable to one another because of the rising roar of other voices, the clinking and clatter of glasses and crockery, and other noises.

But Henry didn't mind the noises, and he persisted, quietly, with a stubbornness marked by the gentleness of his manner and the even modulation of his voice. He was too tolerant in manner, too even in temperament, too friendly, unmenacing and inoffensive to seem like a fanatic. However, he was rigid as steel, and made no concessions to Eddie, and continued to state, assert, and reinforce the same statements about the theory of the single tax. At several moments, he appeared to have gained an intellectual advantage, but Eddie was stubborn, and clung to his position.

"Scientifically, no explanation is an explanation," Eddie said over the coffee.

Henry began talking of Newton's laws of gravity and motion, but was soon back with the theory of Henry George.

Neither convinced the other. They got nowhere, but liked one another, and hoped to meet again.

Henry Oldering was nineteen, and suggestively lady-faced in his innocence, but his was a very intelligent face and expression. His air of a student was reinforced by his glasses and briefcase. And he could have been a better student than he was, B, and B minus, if he were interested in more subjects and applied himself with some added diligence. But he concentrated on the theory of the single tax, and indefatigably sought converts. The fact that he failed with regularity did not discourage him. His earnestness was thorough, like armor without a weakness or opening; his manner was sweet, tolerant, and bore what would be called the marks of sincerity. His was an importunable conviction, but without the force to win adherents by intimidation. He sought to convince, but was not convincing.

Eddie went to work, unwillingly bowing to necessity, and Henry Oldering wandered off by himself, crossing and recrossing campus instead of going to Harper Library as he'd intended.

He was seeking someone to convert.

II

Donald W. Torman was a little man, born in Cleveland, Ohio, and thirty-eight years old. He was an Assistant Professor of Political Science, a Republican, a Mason, and by intention, desire, and effort, he was a scholar. He allowed neither his Masonic membership nor his Republican sympathies and voting record to interfere with scholarship and scholarly truth. Thus, he always raised the question for his Political Science 101 freshman classes:

"What difference, if any, can you people find between the

platforms of the two parties, especially in the 1924 Presidential election?"

And he usually helped the class to arrive at the conclusion that there were no significant differences.

Professor Torman, however, believed that the period was a temporary and preliminary one of change for the better by growth rather than through a return to normalcy. It was but the beginning, the pre-Galileo stage of scientific politics, when the future was chartered, the course was planned, and the method was available. This was scientific method.

Professor Torman believed in scientific methods more actively than he did in God.

Professor Torman's lectures were clear and simple, but full of questions, posed as such, which cut into the false sanctities of editorial-page political thinking and would dissolve the glitter of "glittering generalities" which had been sanctified as the political Biblicalism of America.

Eddie Ryan caught his attention very quickly, within two weeks. He regarded him as one of the best students he'd had in some moons, asked him many questions in class, and was pleased by the answers.

Eddie got an A in the Political Science course of Donald W. Torman.

III

Eddie Ryan was registered for three more classes for the spring quarter, another full schedule for a quarter. He reread *Lockesley Hall* by Tennyson, and parts of *In Memoriam*, and he quoted many times to himself:

'Tis better to have loved and lost
Than never to have loved at all.

And he read Shelley's *One Word Is Too Often Profaned*, and Keats' sonnet, *When I Have Fears That I May Cease to Be*, and he quoted lines from it to himself, especially the ending:

*. . . then on the shore
Of the wide world I stand alone, and think
Till Love and Fame to nothingness do sink.*

And he also quoted:

My name is writ on waters.

He now needed an outlet within himself, because it was becoming necessary for Eddie to tell himself more of what he was thinking as a consequence of the education he had so far gained for himself; that is, he was feeling a pressure to articulate, at least for himself, what he thought and believed. Growing had meant changing, and he did not know the meaning of the change that had been transpiring in his mind. He was internally nervous with his own growth and change.

Thus was Eddie Ryan at that period, the beginning of spring 1926, and his fourth straight quarter as a student of the University.

Chapter Fifteen

Peter Moore was doing quite a lot of thinking. You couldn't help it, if you went to the University in such times as the present. But why did he tell himself, or think to himself, which was the same thing, that he couldn't help thinking a lot? Should you try not to think a lot?

Peter knew what he meant when he beat around the bush like this about thinking, and not being able to help thinking a lot.

It was in *Hamlet,* wasn't it, that Shakespeare wrote that *thinking* "does make cowards of us all?" And wasn't it—*thinking,* or *conscience?*—"sicklied o'er with the pale cast of thought?"

Yes, it was.

And yes, he was thinking a lot. He was getting *sicklied o'er with the pale cast of thought,* he guessed.

Peter did not want to be a coward, nor did he want to be *sicklied o'er,* nor did he want to think anything but the truth.

But the truth, sir, forsooth sir, what is the truth?

Nor was it that the truth made a coward of you because you were afraid to face it, and accept it, and even to proclaim it in public. It was something else, in his case anyway, and he guessed it was or it would be the same in the case of others like him. That was, as far as general situation and background were concerned, cases where you were the first, or one of the first, to get an education in your family, among their friends and your friends. You find out that getting an education is not—not necessarily, anyway—being as you were before and merely knowing more than they did, the way in which one person knows more than another about an automobile engine and how it runs, its mechanisms, and principles and whatever else you could learn about automobile engines. No, it wasn't like that.

As he saw it, it wasn't just an education, a liberal education, so that when you finished with it, you'd be ending up with something of a liberal mind.

That was one of the benefits he hoped to take away with him from the University when he was finished. The other was his legal education.

It was funny that he hadn't thought of anything so simple and easy to infer: if you got an education, that did something, brought some changes in your mind, and you'd be changed, *ipso facto,* because your mind had changed. But it was the simple things that were so often overlooked.

He was starting to have a lot of moods, more than he knew were normal and average for him. He was becoming moody, that was what it all added up to.

It added up to something else, also, and there was the rub.

In sum, it added up to what was trouble. That was why he was getting more moody.

Peter began wondering how Eddie thought, because Eddie could have the same problem as he, and judging from little things and comments which he had made, Peter imagined that Eddie was coming to these problems, just as he had. Peter decided that he'd talk to Eddie.

He laughed, and bent over the plain and much-used old kitchen table which he used as a desk. It had more surface room than most desks, and he liked it better. Peter's sense of order and neatness with his things dated back to childhood.

He chuckled, almost without making a sound. He didn't have to decide that he'd talk to Eddie. What the hell, he'd talk, that's all. There was no difficulty about such a matter.

But there was.

What was he going to talk about, clearly, in detail? This question wasn't the basic one in his mind. What did he mean? That question was in the center. It was a key question.

And even to Eddie, revealing his doubts could be a difficult procedure. Once he thought of it, he was in a quandary. It was a pickle, then, and he was in it. He was in an intellectual pickle.

Did he doubt, or didn't he? What, and how much?

On several nights, Peter had begun exploring this question, but only so far as to realize that he was thinking his way into a pickle. Then, he'd decided that he should study his assignments, rather than to think about what he guessed he wasn't ready to think about.

Perhaps he was rationalizing, one way, the other way, both ways. Ever since he'd read James Harvey Robinson's *Mind in the Making*, he'd been on the lookout for signs of possible rationalizing in his own thinking. It could get very confusing, and sometimes it did. For instance, that book on the *History of the Warfare of Science with Theology in Christendom*, by Andrew D. White. He had been given a big jolt by that book, yes, quite a darned big jolt. It came as that because he had had such different ideas, or better, notions and rationalizations. There had been so much ignorance and prejudice around, so much in the circumstances of his own life, that he had not been aware of the attitudes and the ways in which many men think and try to solve problems and advance knowledge, and all the rest of it. Without realizing it, he had picked up so much more ignorance and prejudice than he could have imagined, and without your ever knowing it, prejudice and ignorance could make you conceited, making you believe that you were so right, and that right and justice were all with you, and on your side, and just that *God Loves the Irish*.

That was the title of a book Eddie Ryan had lent him, and whenever he thought of it, Peter smiled. It wasn't a good book, and probably Eddie didn't think it was either, but Eddie sometimes laughed about it, and must think much the same as he did about it. He guessed that they both half-wished that the book were true in the sense that *God Loves the Irish*.

But what all his thinking amounted to at the present time was

The Silence of History

that the world seemed to be all askew, out of joint, off-kilter. It was as the character Juno, of the play *Juno and the Paycock*, by Sean O'Casey, said when he and Eddie saw it together, one night during the last Christmas holidays:

—*And I tell you, Joxer, the world is in a terrible state of chassis.*

Toward the end of the winter quarter Eddie had said, with something bitter in his voice:

—Peter, I'm going to make a study one day of Woodrow Wilson.

—Why Woodrow Wilson?

—The war of steel and gold, Eddie had said. It was a war of steel and gold, not a war to make the world safe for democracy. And I had started at the U thinking that he was the greatest President since Abraham Lincoln.

—Yes, I understand, Eddie. Everything gets unsettled.

That was a conversation they'd had walking to school toward the end of the last quarter.

—*The world is in a terrible state of chassis*, Peter had quoted.

—That was a funny line, a hell of a one, Peter. And the characters, Juno and Joxer and the Paycock.

—I could understand it—the people, they're our own.

—Yes, Eddie had said, thoughtful, and perhaps kind of hurt. His voice had sounded that way.

On Saturdays, Peter helped clean the house, and did work on the building. He didn't mind it, and sometimes he kind of liked it. That kind of work left your mind free, and you could think and put a few pieces of the puzzle in the right place. At least he tried to, but the pieces he got in the right place on one Saturday, so he'd think, would be in the wrong place in a week, or a couple of weeks, a month, or during the next quarter.

Peter knew what he wanted to become in life, and why he was at the University. He had often told himself that he had no grandiose dreams. He was ambitious to get ahead, to be respected and to make money, enough to live comfortably, and he thought that he could help people, too, once he was educated and out in the world, as a lawyer and politician.

He'd learned enough to know that much of the trouble of this world was caused by ignorance and poverty. And if he believed this and had come to see the need for tolerance, then he should be tolerant once he had an education and success in the outside world.

One morning in January, he and Eddie had been walking across Washington Park to classes, with the snow crusted over the ground, the sun dazzling, and an invigorating zing in the cold and the wind. He loved to run, and had a strong desire to run for the mere fun of it. He had had such a feeling of health and of being in good condition, of tone to his body, his muscles and his nerves. Eddie hadn't wanted to run much, and wearing a long overcoat, and carrying a briefcase heavy with books, he couldn't very well have.

They'd walked fast, their feet crushing the snow. Eddie spoke of the French Revolution and said of St. Just, one of the leaders who'd been guillotined:

—He was scarcely older than we are now, and he wrote a letter, saying "I feel—I could ride the crest of this century."

Eddie had told him this, hoping that he'd like it too. He was aware of that, because he knew Eddie quite well. He hadn't, however, responded as Eddie had expected and probably had hoped he would respond.

Ride the crest of this century.

What young fellow their age wouldn't want to, if he had the ability and opportunity? But Peter didn't think it was for him to dream in this way and harbor such thoughts and ambitions. Theoretically, any person born in the United States could be President, and look at the case of Abraham Lincoln. But as the boys around 58th Street and Prairie Avenue said when the question of looking for work arose:

—Jobs is scarce, and good men is plentiful.

A couple of times, he had thought of this in passing in an effort to reason out why he hadn't responded with enthusiasm to Eddie's quote of St. Just. If you tried to do that, ride the crest of this present twentieth century, you stood a big chance of getting drowned. Maybe it could make him seem like a coward if he said what he thought, but you couldn't talk indiscriminately, and you couldn't even talk to many people about how you felt and what thoughts you had. You could only talk to a very few. Most people couldn't understand. This was his impression, on the basis of the people he knew, and he was inclined to regard them as sufficiently representative of people everywhere, or at least everywhere in America. What they couldn't understand was too much of the truth, given to them too fast. And they couldn't understand young fellows like himself and Eddie Ryan, getting too smart and educated in a hurry, and showing too much ambition, especially if they didn't believe, or pretended to believe, in religion, the *mores*, all that you were expected to believe in.

Peter knew that here was the really troubling question that he had to keep wrestling with in his mind. If he should give up his faith, what would happen? There would be hell to pay and more than that at home, and he'd never hear the end of it. Day after day, he'd get it from all sides, especially from his two cousins, Al and Jerry. And they'd influence his Aunt Kate. He was living in their home, and Aunt Kate, who owned the six-flat, three-story buildings, was their mother. They both treated him all right, decently and with friendly feeling. In fact, they were a little proud about his going to college, especially Al, who wanted to get into politics, and was the unpaid helper of Mr. Herkowitz, the precinct captain. But at the same time, they also were suspicious because he was a student of the University, which they had heard was against Catholics, and even worse, against religion.

—Don't be comin' home here an atheist or anything like that, Al had said on a recent Saturday night at the dinner table. And this was a theme song of Al's, and some of the older fellows in the neighborhood. Jerry sometimes picked up the tune.

—Mother of God, that's what I hear tell they do to boys like Peter at that place, his Aunt Kate had said.

—I don't have much confidence in Eddie Ryan next door, Al said.

—And him with an old grandmother, and a dead father, God spare that.

Aunt Kate, he was pretty sure, had been thinking, also, of his own dead mother, and of "Pop." And she had brought a choke to his throat, reminding him of the sadness about which he couldn't talk to anyone. She'd been saying, too, how much she and his uncle, who died a year ago, had done for him. They had done much, which he appreciated, and when Aunt Kate said anything alluding to the years he'd lived with them, he never took offense. The choke in his throat and the rising of sadness in him came because of his dead mother, and poor "Pop." It was not his sadness only, but that of his family, and that was the sadness of life. He knew that he had to accept this, and he did. He couldn't call back his mother and the years gone by, and now he was a man, with his twenty-first birthday behind him.

—Don't be lettin' Eddie Ryan or anyone be takin' your faith away, Peter, for the sake of your dear mother, may her soul rest in peace.

—Don't worry, Aunt Kate, I'm not going to let them lock me up in any of the towers over on the University campus, and keep me there until I sign an oath to be an atheist.

—This isn't a joking matter, Al said loudly, but then he let the subject drop, and talked about how it wasn't going to be so easy for "us" to win the next election, not with the Mayor down in the Hall. Peter restrained his smiles, but he was very tolerantly amused. Cousin Al talked a big game of politics.

"Too much reform doesn't get votes, that's what I say."

"Human nature gets the votes, Al," Jerry said.

Al was twenty-five and Jerry was almost twenty-four. Jerry worked irregularly, sometimes at the Express Company, and drank with the boys on the corner. Al had used to yell at him but didn't any more, and through Herkowitz, Al was getting Jerry a political job.

Aunt Kate was disappointed in Jerry, and often she'd sat up worrying, but he was her baby. Al was steady, and caused her no worry. But she loved Peter, too, and he loved her.

He couldn't wound her by saying that he'd lost his religion, but he was afraid that he was losing it. And if he did, living

The Silence of History

at home might be intolerable. And all of them would feel disgraced and hurt, especially Aunt Kate and his Pop.

He didn't want to be a hypocrite, but he didn't want to cause a commotion about matters which none of them understood, and to make himself the talk of the neighborhood. Maybe he was thinking of his career, and of having clients and getting votes some day in the future, but if he didn't think of his future, who would?

And now that he was at the University, and had begun reading and studying, he could begin to understand why they were all so lost in prejudice and how they paid for the poverty and ignorance of the past. They weren't poor now, and the value of Aunt Kate's buildings was going up. It was the poverty of the past and her poverty in the old country. With most of the people in the neighborhood, especially the Irish, it was the same. They were almost all better off and the neighborhood was full of those who'd come up in the world, a little way up, at least.

Eddie Ryan had made a funny remark which applied to many of the people in the neighborhood. It had cut as sharp as a knife, and was uncharacteristic of Eddie as he'd been a few years ago.

—Peter, Eddie had said, they are doing one of two things. They're either forgetting that their old man and old lady had pigs in the parlor, or else they remember it with a bitterness that even Napoleon couldn't feel about Waterloo.

Weren't they the victims of their background, the product of environment? Take Aunt Kate and his uncle, Dan Nolan. She had come here the year before the World's Fair of 1893, and was married that year. Uncle Dan had saved up enough money to be in on a partnership in a saloon while he worked as an insurance collector, and had lived in a boardinghouse, saving his money, dollar by dollar. He sold out at a small profit, and went back to insurance collecting, and then went to school nights and learned bookkeeping, and he saved and got enough to buy stocks. He was lucky, became a contractor, and bought the buildings, which were side by side, when the neighborhood was not yet built up much. He was satisfied.

His place in society was settled, and he and Aunt Kate were fixed for life. But neither of them had come to America with any money to speak of, a few pounds each, and they were "low Irish." That must have affected them.

That world was going. That was why he was studying, acquiring an education. It was all different, a time of progress. However he was pondering, now and then, about progress, what it was and what it meant. He was wondering about many things, about Negroes, and dagoes, and Jews, and about economics and politics, about almost everything that he used to believe.

What should he turn these beliefs over for? The desire to save the world wasn't in him, not strongly, because he didn't believe that the world could be saved. That wasn't correct, either. He was in a period when he didn't know what he actually believed, or what he would believe in a few years.

Until he knew, should he sound off? The sensible course of action for him would be to wait until he knew what he believed and thought.

However, Peter had reached such a conclusion more than once; his doubts and questionings had been recurrent and progressive. Once you doubted and began to look about you and to think, this was how it must be, he thought. But then, if it were, where was the point at which you would stop? Could there be any point? Or must you go on until you believed in nothing? That was what many thought, others besides his cousins, or fellows like that, who didn't think but merely repeated what they had heard said by others who repeated what they had heard. But how many were there like his cousins and Aunt Kate, and the rest of his family? And how many had lived in the same believing way? His mother had. All of his people, back across the Atlantic in Ireland. And Eddie Ryan's people, and hundreds, thousands, millions and more and more millions, living and dying, and hadn't they ever known the truth? And *the truth shall make ye free,* he thought. The sadness of seeing things from this light was too compelling for Peter to be ironical. It filled him with a hush of awe. It endowed the very idea of life, of people succeeding one another, from generation to generation, with the

The Silence of History

dignity of sorrows, and a scope of numbers and of time. When there had been so many, over so many years and generations, everything took on a different kind of meaning.

This was what he had told himself on a winter Saturday night when he stood at the parlor window. The room was dark, and the apartment behind him was silent. The shade was pulled up, and he was looking out at Washington Park at night, a scene which was so familiar to him, but which had suddenly become so strange. The snow, seen in spots through the outline of the wire fencing about the courts, was bluish, and the trees behind the court were stark and bare and dark. The night was a little hazy, bluish also. Automobiles passed on the street separating his side of South Park Avenue from the park boundary, and a few people passed by on the sidewalk. Strangers in the night. The night was strange, too, with life. All of the history of man had so far led up to this moment when he, Peter Moore, was standing by the window and looking out, seeing snow like a blue shield of the light of the moon, and trees bare as death, the shadowiness waking everything like an unfinished background of an unfinished scene. He saw in this the world and behind it was not only space and earth of which he knew every fact, but also the past, and all that was yesterday, and seven thousand yesterdays. More than seven thousand yesterdays. But they all, the total sum, all of them, were yesterday. For all of the past was the same. It was not time any more. Time was only the present. Looking both before and after, we didn't look at time. Eternity was like that. It was without time. It was like the past, except that it was the future beyond the living future.

Was it like the past? Was it only the past as it was now, except that it was the past when the last man had breathed his last, and there was no one to look, as he now was looking?

If that were the truth and there were no God, nor any Hereafter, then there would be no one to remember. Who remembered what Indians once did on the spot of ground across the street or on the ground on which Aunt Kate's building here had been constructed?

He was blue. Now he wasn't thinking about the truth, but brooding over what it might be, or might not be, no one knew.

No one came back. And the reason he was blue was that he was brooding about the truth he did not know, and that, maybe, no one knew.

Could the same scene across the street, the moonlight on the snow, happen and happen and happen many times with no one to see it, no one on earth, and with all that man had been and done only a memory when there was no one to remember it?

His mother would be nothing, like all the dead. How many times as a boy had he gone to Confession and received Communion, prayed, been good for her, for his mother up in Heaven to know that he was being a good boy—for her.

Peter hadn't cried in years. He couldn't cry now. He was crying without crying.

He turned away from the window.

"Is that you, Peter?" Aunt Kate called from the kitchen.

"Yes, Aunt Kate."

She was lonely, too.

Every day it was more difficult for her to walk. He went to Mass on Sundays with her, almost every Sunday, so that he could save her from being embarrassed as a result of how slowly she walked. She weighed about two hundred and ten pounds, a lot to carry on her feet, what with her rheumatism.

—Ah Peter, it's the feet that will be the death of me.

—Your feet will get better.

—A person's feet can get better, but the years don't get better. Peter, you're a good boy. Your mother'd be the proud one if she was here to be seeing you now.

—I hope so.

—Well, I try to be proud of you for her.

—I'd like to make you proud of me, Aunt Kate.

—Let God, Our Lord, help you, Peter. Ah, me feet, they ache like the punishment of sin.

Aunt Kate wore black. She'd worn black before Uncle Dan had passed away. She walked with strained slowness, and he remained by her side. He didn't mind it. Going to Sunday Mass did her too much good. She didn't talk solely of her feet. She spoke of the people she saw, and always asked who anyone was

The Silence of History

whom she didn't recognize or didn't know. She liked being greeted, spoken to, and she'd remark on the looks and appearance of those she knew.

—There's Mrs. Dunne. She doesn't look a day older than the first day I set eyes upon her. Look at her, she walks like a bird. She's so little, Peter.

—Yes, she's the talk of the neighborhood, Aunt Kate.

—And how and what in the name of the Lord Almighty have they to be saying about her, the old get-outs and gossips?

—Oh, I didn't mean that there's gossip and backbiting about her, I mean people know her and like her, and talk about how she flits along the street.

—I see. It's a sin to backbite a good woman, and she's a good woman.

—Yes, she is.

—She knows what trials and tribulations are, and it's long years since she buried her man, long years.

Mrs. Dunne disappeared ahead of them, turning the corner of 60th and South Park Avenue.

Slowly, they made their way to church, almost seven blocks.

Could he say he didn't believe and not accompany Aunt Kate to church for Sunday Mass?

That question which Peter asked himself was of heart and sentiment, not of truth and belief. And he felt it as such. Could he hurt his Aunt Kate by proclaiming disbelief which she could not understand, and could only regard as betrayal, ingratitude, and scandalous disgrace of her and of his father, and of her whole family, and the good names of Nolan and Moore? Could he repay her love and care of him, as she looked upon his years in her home, by denying the belief which she believed to be the sustenance of her life, and the consolation of old age which brought its thoughts of death and its fears of the awful hour when death would come upon her like a thief in the night, and she would tremble before Almighty God, and might even have to answer to God, Himself, for the sin of Pride and the sin of his becoming a heathen atheist? Could he leave a wound in her heart which might never heal? Could he hurt her so? And could he hurt his father, too? And throw the family into bitter anger and a violence of indignation that would be lifelong? For he was sure that this would happen if he were to become a black sheep.

And what would he gain? What would he achieve? What good would he do for his fellow man, and for himself?

Peter did not need to ask himself these questions. They were all like seeds covered by the shell of the big question he had asked himself.

Once, on their way to church, while Aunt Kate labored across every sidewalk square, Peter was seduced into a spell of illusion and a trapping net of guilt. He believed that he had done it, said it, crossed the Rubicon from his past to a future as a heretic, and that the reactions to this deed would be thrust upon him at any second.

—It was better that you was dead.

He could hear Aunt Kate saying that in anger and on the verge of tears. But she wouldn't cry. There was as much hardness as kindness in her character, and if she cried, she cried alone. Aunt Kate was not a woman to be demonstrative.

—Look good and long 'pon this sleeve, she often said, holding up her left arm as she spoke. Look long upon it and tell me if Kate Moore Nolan wears her heart there upon it?

There would be the flash of conquering pride in her gray eyes, and her round face, which had grown massive with the years, would hide her sadness in a look of flint. But she'd cry alone.

When he'd had these thoughts about Aunt Kate, they'd been on their way to High Mass, at eleven o'clock. She liked going to High Mass. It took longer, and he'd get restless, but would usually be able to maintain sufficient self-control so as not to make it too apparent. He tried not to be bored at Mass, but that was a long-standing problem in his religious life. During all his years of going to Mass on Sunday, the struggle with boredom had interfered with his concentration on the symbolic meanings of the Mass, on his prayers, on Heavenly things and scenes, on what was religious and relevant instead of mundane and irrelevant.

Of late, he had not been helping souls in Purgatory, or his own soul, by exiling the mundane from his mental intentions.

The Silence of History

That Sunday morning, in particular, he mused over the mundane while Father McGee, a man of somewhat plump proportions, bald on top but with fringes of gray hair on the sides of the large head which featured a very ruddy face, took his time saying High Mass.

Peter and his aunt followed the Mass, kneeling, sitting, rising in the crowded church which was so familiar and full of memory and nostalgia for them because they had been coming to it for so many years of their lives. Aunt Kate had grown old during these years, while Peter had grown from boy to young man. The sadness of years lived and lost was upon Aunt Kate.

Mrs. Nolan felt the years in her feet and ankles and "in my heart." And now, the years had passed, swift as a bird on the wing. Her man was gone, and others were gone, too, and her family was raised, and her nephew beside her here in church, Peter, had grown up into such a fine, clean young man. She was praying for him after all she had heard tell of that University where he went.

She prayed, bowing her head, but, now and then, looked up to gaze at the altar in the front of the church, with the candles lit in three rows on both sides of the Tabernacle, and Father McGee and the three altar boys in their black cassocks, and the Holy Mass going on. Father McGee wore green vestments, and it meant something, the color of the vestments the priest could be after wearing when he said Mass, but she didn't know the meaning of the colors, except for gold and black, and there were parts of the Mass she didn't know what could be their meaning, or she'd forgotten, but she loved the Holy Mass, with the singing, the Latin, with her knowing hardly a word of what it was meaning, except for a few that had been told her, but it wasn't the knowing the Latin, not for the likes of herself, or the likes of most she knew.

But she had long been accustomed to hearing Latin in church, and it was both familiar and mysterious; it was soothing and a comfort and a solace to the heart. She was always thinking that the angels sang in Latin. Oh, God, have mercy on her poor soul, *Hail Mary, full of grace, the Lord is with thee* . . .

She whispered *Hail Marys* with her head slightly bowed, and the singing made sadness like happiness, and fear like hope. It was like gold, flowing through the church and pouring into her.

Father McGee singsonged more than he sang, and with a recognizable touch of brogue. The chorus consisted of three men, and that pretty Peg Lawlor played the organ so lovely and sang so pure, just like innocence. She should be married, and a pity it was, what a pity, that she wasn't, Peg Lawlor. You'd think the men would be at her doorbell and hoping to be the lucky one. If her Al should come home and say, "Ma, I'm engaged to Peg Lawlor," there'd be nothing out of her to oppose the wedding.

But she couldn't be thinking like that, not in church at Holy Mass.

Our Father Who art in Heaven . . .

She said *Our Fathers* and listened to Peg Lawlor sing the *Credo.*

And Peter heard mumbled sounds coming from her lips. He knelt, now and then moving his lips as though in silent prayer, or in actual prayer. His ruddy face was a blank of solemnity.

His eyes moved with the smallest movements of his head, and he took within his stare, one of masked curiosity, as many people as he could. So many he knew. He could say, though, that there were more he couldn't recognize than there were he knew, including parishioners known only by sight. But how did it come that he was having such dull thoughts? Eeny-meeny-miney-mo. Aunt Kate was puffing, breathing a little heavy. And he could hear rustlings of her dress, little sounds of little movements. Where had his thoughts been? There was a mental pause before he recalled his thoughts about doubt and belief and himself, and the sadness that had come upon him here in church when Father McGee had begun to say this High Mass. A depression of new sadness was coming back. But he didn't feel it as much as he had before. He didn't actually feel it. It couldn't, therefore, be sadness. He was dull, that is, he was feeling dull to himself, and the thoughts he'd had, and dull about the people around him. It was almost a strange feeling; it was strange, but not a

The Silence of History

feeling. A state of mind, a state that was the antonym of a state of feeling.

An indistinct smile played about Peter's wide lips, and was reflected in his eyes. There weren't many of the boys from the street at Mass this morning, the topers. He hadn't been around the corner of 58th and Prairie late enough to see them staggering about in their Saturday night ritual. But there must have been some. If there hadn't been, 58th Street and Prairie wouldn't be the same. His brother Johnny or Cousin Jerry hadn't been drunk last night. They'd seen a movie and Jerry got home early enough to go to ten-o'clock Mass.

They all rose with much shuffling. Aunt Kate was slow.

For years, every Sunday, he'd done this, and these others here, about five hundred, had done the same thing. The sadness of the past changed into the monotony of Masses which he had gone to. This was a monotony of remembering, and few individual Masses came to mind. Almost all of these Masses were recomposed into a few, some clear, some vague, and about them there was also a large blur, like a changing but permanent fog. From them, he had acquired only strands of association with the emotions of memory, found in nostalgia, poignancy, flooding sunlights of happy moments and hours, and all that had become the residue of what his boyhood and all of his past years had been in the meaning of his inner self, the true Peter Moore. From Masses, his spirit had but rarely drunk rich cream or sour milk, but only watery skim milk.

Since he'd been a public school boy, he'd usually been alone in church during his grammar school days, and had preferred eight-o'clock Mass to the nine, which the parochial school kids went to. He'd used to like to avoid the Catholic school kids, but not because there was any reason to be afraid that they might jump him; he didn't like to stand out, alone and different, and he thought that he would at nine-o'clock Mass, when the two pews, by the center aisle, would be full with them. Aunt Kate and Uncle Dan thought that he could get all the education he needed at public school, and this hadn't made him ashamed or afraid of being thought about as a poor kid. He liked Carter School better. It had more for a kid, the playground with a place to play indoor ball in the school yard, school ball teams, a chance to play basketball and wrestle, manual training, track team and track meets, and the kids at St. Michael's, which was the name of the parish, had none of this.

And his aunt and uncle had not just believed that a public school was good enough for him. They'd thought the same about their own sons, Al and Jerry, and had also sent them to Carter School.

He'd wanted to stand out in sports at school, but not so much in classes that the other kids would think he was too smart to be a regular kid. But he'd liked good averages, between 80 and 90, and that made it easier for him at his aunt's, and his father was happy and proud of him.

It was a mortal sin to miss Mass on Sundays, and the only times he'd missed was when he'd been sick, as for instance during the epidemic of Spanish influenza in 1918 when the war was still going on. He hadn't wanted mortal sins on his soul. He strove to be a good Catholic. How silly and what a silly, bad risk it was, to take the chance of burning in Hell for less than an hour, a half hour, give a minute or a few this way or that.

At Mass, he'd pray for the repose of the soul of his mother, and once every month or six weeks, at least, he'd receive Holy Communion, as an offering to God for her and her soul. He'd imagine her, beautiful in Heaven, even as beautiful as the Blessed Virgin Mary. Prayers, especially on Sunday mornings when he was receiving the Blessed Sacrament, brought him close to her. He'd feel it. He couldn't say how, not precisely, but he'd feel it. Heaven seemed to be almost behind the altar; it was that near. Part of this feeling was in the movement of his prayers. This was vague, but yet convincingly real to him. The vagueness was in the inner vision of the mind's eye. His prayers moved through the gray air with a kind of thickness like dust, although there was no dust. From his mind, as though there were eyes in it, he saw this air, and what he felt was a kind of sense of movement of the prayers through that air. The prayers would move, thus, beyond the altar, and on into Heaven which was fantastically nearby.

The Silence of History

The prayers, he knew, not knew but believed, not believed either but, at all events, the prayers floated into Heaven, and piled up as on a floor, becoming something valuable and piling into riches, but he didn't know just what the prayers became, or became like, or took the shape of, although he would assume that it was gold, but he was guessing, and his mind couldn't conceive what it exactly was.

His mother knew though, and she was pleased. She sent back love to him, but he couldn't feel this as he did the prayers in motion. There was a contradiction in all of this, because he could see his mother, in white, not clearly, not distinctly, and he could not see her face, that is, see in his mind, which is to imagine, but he did imagine her, a white-clothed figure, more vague than clear. He almost never could envisage her face distinctly, and most of the times when he knelt there, a little, freckle-faced boy in short pants, the face was lost behind gray air, but he would know that she was smiling behind the gray air, and her smile was like an angel's smile, and it was for him. She smiled at him, from Heaven to earth, to St. Michael's Church on earth. At him.

It was after Peter had taken Sunday school instructions and made his First Holy Communion that he began to have such imaginary experiences at Mass. He was eight years old. He had reached the age of reason, could sin, and be punished for his sins in the next world. He could go to Hell. He would have to watch his conscience or he would when he died. He knew people died. Everybody living was supposed to die, sometime. But that was when they got old, for most of them. And it was a long, long, long, long time before a boy of eight got old. He had to grow up first and become a man, and that was a long, long, long, long time, too. But people died. His mother, she was dead. She died. He had never even seen her. She was in Heaven. He wanted to see her. She was his mother. He had to go to Heaven to see her. He couldn't see her if God said he had to go to Hell. He couldn't, never, never, never for never. That was, never see her. You burned in Hell. He wasn't going to burn, not if he could help it. It hurt too much, even sunburn. He had tender skin. He sunburned easy. They said that about him. Aunt Kate said it. Being burned hurt. It blistered you. Yes, he had to watch his conscience.

Peter made his first confession on a sunny Saturday afternoon in May. He went to church by himself, going early in order to be the first and get confession over with.

He looked as though he had been scrubbed very clean, and with his freckles, he also looked unmistakably Irish. There was a clarity of innocence in his eyes; he shifted them constantly, with the speed of his curiosity. His Uncle Dan had growled and cursed in a cranky mood while cutting Peter's hair. He'd snipped the curls all away, and had given his nephew a very close haircut. That didn't matter to him. But it was funny, Uncle Dan grumbling and growling, cursing some, and Aunt Kate coming out to the kitchen, and saying to Uncle Dan:

—And maybe it's you what should be going to church to make your first confession, and not the boy, there.

—What's ailin' you now, woman? Uncle Dan said.

—Nothin' aching me, Aunt Kate told him.

It had been funny. He thought so, walking to church. But anyway, he had gotten his hair cut by Uncle Dan.

It was strange, going to his first confession. He was more bewildered than he was afraid. He shouldn't be afraid, but he was. There was nothing to be afraid of, he'd been told, it was something everybody did, that is, everybody who was a Catholic. Lots weren't Catholics. They weren't lucky, as he was. Because they didn't have the true religion. He did. That was why he was doing what he was doing, making his first confession.

He ought to feel swelled up some, because he was doing what he was doing. He was. Maybe he was not swelled up, not swell-headed, but he was something, because he had reached the age of reason and he was something more now than he used to be. It was like he was getting bigger.

He wished he could grow up faster.

That's what he'd pray to God for, to make him grow up faster.

Peter was more proud of himself than he was bewildered and afraid.

The Silence of History

He walked along, doing things a boy did. He jumped over a low iron railing, and then jumped back. He laughed as he looked at the sign inside the railing.

> KEEP OFF THE GRASS

There was no grass.

The low railing fenced in a small plot of ground, almost square, in front of a gray stone building. There was no grass. It was dirt. They should have changed the sign.

> KEEP
> OFF
> THE
> DIRT

He hopped, he stepped on the lines of sidewalk squares, he didn't step on the lines, he picked up a stone and flung it easily into the street at nothing, he put his hands in his pockets and took them out of his pockets, he gazed at the sky that was big, far away, as it stood up there, hiding Heaven from Earth, and he wished he could be one of the clouds up there, and float by, looking way down here on earth, and floating until maybe he would float into Heaven.

And he wiggled his ears. That was something he did good, and funny. He made kids laugh when he did that.

He spoke to people on the sidewalk. Aunt Kate and other grown-up people said never speak to strangers, but he didn't know why not, because after you spoke to them, and they spoke back to you, they weren't strangers any more. Sometimes, he spoke to people, to some person, maybe a man, maybe a lady, who was ailin' and achin', he guessed, because they would be cross and cranky, grouchy, and they would growl at him, or curse him, call him names that he wasn't, that is, he wasn't the name they called him, like, for instance, a "dirty little beggar." He liked to be clean, but of course he got dirty playing, but he always cleaned himself up, and he never begged. Even when some old lady or another person wanted to give him something, a penny or a nickel, or maybe even a dime, which could buy two chocolate sodas, and he liked chocolate sodas with the ice cream and syrup and soda water and all, he would always refuse to accept any money from people like that. He didn't talk to strangers because he was a little beggar, he said "Hello" to them because he liked to talk to them, and hear them talk, and let him ask them questions.

He spoke to a couple of old ladies, and a big man with a black mustache, but the man told him to "Shut up," and said it with a voice like he was a foreigner.

And he walked to church, doing the things he always did when he was walking by himself on the street. He forgot to be worried and afraid, and he forgot about what he was going to do when he got to church.

But when he came to the church, he did think about it, and all that he let himself forget came back, and worse. He wished he didn't have to go up the stone steps, open the big, heavy door, and go up into the church and he had what he guessed was meant by "a sinking feeling," that is, a kind of feeling that must be fainting when you didn't faint.

So Peter Moore, the little boy with the gray-green eyes which were so open with a clarity of innocence, walked up the steps of St. Michael's Church, and he went inside, and the church seemed to him big, big as he didn't know what. If he could have stopped breathing, he would have.

Peter quickly and automatically went forward, reached up to put his fingers in the holy water fountain to the right, blessed himself, got into the last pew, knelt down, and blessed himself again. He had neglected to genuflect before the Blessed Sacrament, on the center altar.

There were other children, boys and girls, scattered around the church kneeling in pews, while a few had already formed a line before the confessional boxes, two in the rear, and one up front on the left. He knew what to do. First, he must pray and examine his conscience, and be sorry for all his sins, or get himself to be sorry if he wasn't already. He lowered his head and began doing this first thing.

The doors close behind him kept swinging, and more children were coming into church. If he could get in line quick, it wouldn't take so long.

The Silence of History

He was soon in line in the back, with his conscience examined. Four were ahead of him, three boys and a little light-haired girl who looked more scared than anyone he ever saw. Seeing her that way made him not so scared as he had just been.

There was only a very short wait for Peter and the other children who had come early. A few moments, Peter thought of them as jiffies, a couple of jiffies, after he had taken his place in line, Father Waters showed up. A current of excitement went through the church when he opened the side door on the left, by Father McGee's confessional box, and in a flash of sunlight, he came into the church, closed the door, cutting off the flash of sunlight, crossed in front of the altar, with a quick genuflection before the center altar, and walked like a marching man up the side aisle to the confessional box before the chair where Peter waited in line.

Father Waters was about thirty-eight and had come to the parish with Father McGee in 1900, when it was started. He was a big-boned man, small and broad, who would have looked very insensitive but for his large soft brown eyes, which suggested a tenderness of feeling and character. When he looked at parishioners, his eyes almost caressed them with kindness. His lips were very thick and his face and head appeared to be unusually big because of a prominent jaw. But his modest, restrained smile, along with his eyes, usually left an impression of kindness and goodness of character rather than homely irregularity of features.

—That man is almost a saint, Mrs. Nolan had said one Sunday at the dinner table.

Peter had changed his mind and wanted to get into the confessional box after he saw Father Waters. He couldn't be afraid when it was Father Waters who smiled at him and spoke to him when Aunt Kate and his uncle took him to church.

The wait was brief. When he knelt inside the confessional, with the slot closed, and heard mumbling from behind it, Peter was he-didn't-know-what-he-was. He was a boy full of awe.

Then the slot opened, and Peter saw the priest, but indistinctly, through the wire screening. Words took hold of Peter, and they came out, surprising him, as though he were doing something he didn't know he could do.

"Bless me, Father, for I sinned. This is my first confession."

"Yes," the priest whispered.

Peter confessed all he thought were his sins, looking around and thinking of playing when he was in church, a few disobediences or wishes to be disobedient, a few curse words like "hell" and "damn," wishing one morning that school would burn down, and bad thoughts of wondering where babies came from and how they came. Father Waters told him, in whisper, that this was a happy day for God in Heaven, because it was a chance for God to be made happy by a boy like him being a very good boy and trying not to sin. He asked Peter to say the Act of Contrition and be sorry for his sins. Peter remembered this prayer, which he had memorized, and said it perfectly, without a mistake. In mumbling whispers, the priest pronounced the words of absolution in Latin. He gave Peter three Our Fathers and three Hail Marys for penance.

"When you are tempted to sin, pray to our Lord and He will help you to be a good boy."

The slot closed. Peter felt good. He rose and stepped out of the confessional, thinking he could fly as good as an angel if he only had wings. He said his penance quickly, and was soon outside in the sunshine, and his freckled face was beaming with smiles. He felt that good.

He went home, doing and thinking the things of a boy.

The next morning, Peter felt very important, especially because he couldn't have breakfast, or even touch a drop of water until he received Holy Communion. Then, he would come back home and, boy, would he eat. He wore a new blue suit, and a Buster Brown collar, with a big white silk bow tie. He was uncomfortable about his clothes, and would be glad to get back home and change, because he didn't like a collar and tie like those. Aunt Kate spoke of how sweet he looked, and he liked and didn't like hearing that.

He went to Mass. The Host tasted dry and flat. He swallowed it easily.

That was something he had been a little worried about. He

The Silence of History

ate a big breakfast, afterward. Then he changed his shirt, and went out into the backyard and stood there, wishing he could play and not worry about his clothes, his Sunday suit.

His father came for Sunday dinner and gave him a half dollar.

—You're a fine lad, Peter, a fine one indeed, his father said.

But his father was sad. He just knew it. And he heard his father saying something to Aunt Kate about his mother, and Peter was sad.

—She'd be proud of him, Kate, if the Lord had spared her to be with me today, his father had said.

It was for about three or four years after he had received his first Holy Communion that Peter used to pray at Mass as though his prayers spoke to his dead mother, and traveled through thickish mists of air and space to fall into Heaven as gifts, like gold or jewels. Sometimes this would happen often, sometimes less often. But once Peter was outside the church again, with the Mass finished, he did not dwell upon these experiences. They were for church alone, just as the Mass was. They were not real outside of church, in the outside world. Church was one thing. The outside world was another. In the same sense, the Host was not food. This separation was the way Peter took life in, saw it, when he was still too young to reason things out; it was the way he responded, the way he was.

He was the happiest and unhappiest of boys. Daily, his unhappiness was lost in what he saw and did, in play and fooling among boys his age. Almost orphaned, he had the feeling of being a stranger, and caution had grown in him as though it were a protective instinct. He'd had to face rivalry of older cousins into whose home he had been placed, and he seemed to mind his own business and to be cheerful and undemanding. His aunt and uncle were not very sociable, and they lived very much to themselves. They had been immigrants, classed as greenhorns, and their pride was in their buildings and the protection it gave them in Chicago, so far away from the County Cork. They clung to what they had in their defensive pride, and kept to themselves and their own. Similarly they clung to their religion. Without it, and without the protection of money which made them not-beholden, they would have been at the mercy of strangers, and they would have nothing to show for their lives and their having come out to America. Waste was a sin in their eyes, and they tempered their faith with a frugal materialism. Having acquired their property, they were safe, and their temperaments seemed to flatten out. They were not, however, exceptional. Many others in the neighborhood, or in nearby ones, were similar. There were not many parties given by such adults, much going out, or traveling. The wonder of life and America was that they had acquired property, a home in which to live, a building in which they had their home and from which they drew income in rent. They lived with this wonder. They lived for small comforts, and hopes of Heaven when they died, and believed that their children would be much the same as they.

The world for Peter was mostly what he had been told that it was, and the attitudes he had were formed unconsciously. He had already absorbed much of the hard common sense of his uncle and aunt. This kept things in their places. He kept his experiences at Mass in place, and to himself. He played mostly with Carter School boys, and only a few of them were Irish Catholics too. Religion did not form one of the features of play and was not almost constantly present in his environment or mind as it was in the case of some parochial school boys. Mass was on Sunday. He didn't have catechism lessons. The stuff of his thoughts and dreams was not saturated with religion. Religion and school were separated.

He was most absorbed in the things of a boy, and in doing these things. He could forget what was beyond his own understanding, and what bewildered him, confused him, made him fear, caused him torment. He did not understand what happened when he prayed at Mass. Then, he began to think that it was not real and true; it must be only some kind of imagining of his. Then, he stopped imagining. Then, he couldn't sum up what he had used to imagine. Then, he forgot and these experiences sank away from his memory, and only occasionally did they come back in his thoughts, but when they did, he could be very, very sad. He didn't like to press more sadness upon himself by remembering the sorrow whose only cure was to forget. He had

The Silence of History

heard it said from his early childhood that you've got to make the best of things, and he kept trying to do just that. He'd succeeded, too, and had grown up making the best of things.

He kept out of trouble. He never cut school. Before he'd graduated from grammar school in 1919, he'd come to see that education was opportunity, a means for him to get ahead and make something of himself. His aunt and uncle didn't understand why he had to get more education, but offered no opposition, and when his father spoke with them all, Aunt Kate and Uncle Dan favored the idea.

—Kate, things are better and times is better, sure it's becoming a different world every day. Sure he's smart and a good boy.

—He's a good boy, I can say that, Aunt Kate said.

—He is, and it's with the help of God and Aunt Kate, the father said.

—Yes, 'tis so, the uncle said.

—I heard what you've been saying, Al said, coming into the kitchen. Every word you said is true, damned true.

—Al, Aunt Kate said.

—Mother, I couldn't swear before you. Damn—that's not swearing.

—You're damned right, it isn't, Aunt Kate said.

They all laughed.

—Peter's about the smartest boy in this man's neck of the woods, and if he goes and puts his nose to the grindstone, studies, graduates from high school, and then takes law at night school, he can make somebody out of himself and make us all proud. He can be somebody in the political game, and our family ain't gone all the way that it ought to go. The kid's younger, and different, a new generation, and we'll all be proud of him some day.

They all liked that.

And Jerry came in. He was plump, but hard of muscle. Supposedly a tough, fighting kid in boyhood, Jerry wasn't as tough as his reputation had been. It was the same with most of the boys he ran around with. He hated school, and his feeling about work was almost as strong. He didn't really need to rush into a job. The family had enough, and in time to come, he'd get his share, and why shouldn't he have his fun while the fun was for the having. You were only young once. As Timothy Gorman said:

—Early to bed and early to rise was for the Boy Scouts and you got as much chance of meeting a regular guy as that Greek philosopher had of meeting an honest man.

Tim Gorman was Al's age and had an easy political job because of his old man's drag. The old man was a police sergeant, who ought to become a police captain one day not too far off.

Jerry was good-natured, and not tough at all when it came to fighting. He didn't like to snub anyone, and he hung around the pool room with his gang, and liked sitting around, shooting craps, maybe picking up a nursemaid in Washington Park when he could, or a tramp, and taking a shot of booze. He was congenial, friendly, and not looking for fights even though he wasn't afraid of a guy.

Someday when he got older, something would pop up, easy money, easy cash, and he'd settle down a little. Stocky Tabor was the same kind of a guy, and so was the rest of his bunch.

But, also, he'd come to like Peter.

—We don't want Peter to be another punk, bumming around. If I ever catch him gettin' himself into trouble, and going to hell, I'll punch his nose in. Sure thing, he ought to go to high school. He likes it, and is smart, and he ain't no sissy.

—Maybe he needs more schoolin', it could be a fine thing, Aunt Kate said.

—Lots of boys his age is lookin' for work. There ain't places for 'em all, Peter's father said. And there's good free high schools and who are they for if not boys like Peter?

Peter went to high school. He was one of the best students, with an average of around ninety. He applied himself with a dogged perseverance, and would sometimes read the same assignment three times. For understanding did not always come easily, and he believed himself to be a plugger, rather than a quick, smart student who could get a lesson in no time and race through his lessons like a whirlwind, always knowing what he studied and coming up with averages of 95 and even higher.

Peter plugged, persevered and sacrificed himself into the

The Silence of History

distinction of becoming one of the high-level students in his school, Sherman High. He had been quick in arithmetic, but when he got to geometry, he had difficulties in understanding many theorems, and in trigonometry it was worse. But he spent many hours in his small back bedroom, sitting at an old kitchen table, going over the same lesson twice, three times, and in some instances struggling on through a fourth and fifth effort. Likewise, he would stay with problems until he could prove them and was confident that his solutions were correct. He faltered and gave up on some evenings, and on others, he went to a movie, or for a walk, sometimes by himself, at other times with friends, and especially with Freddie Morris, a grammar school classmate who was working for a cousin, the owner of a furniture store. Usually, he'd be refreshed and study better after knocking off. Also, he made track at Sherman High, running and high-jumping. Peter scored in almost every high school track meet, but he got few firsts. He was a fraction of an inch taller than Eddie Ryan, and lacked the height and long legs to become outstanding at the high jump. Fred Morris, for instance, was always about two inches ahead of him, if not more. Overcoming the disadvantages of his size would have been an exceptional feat, and this was an ambition which had become fixed with him. He daydreamed, aspired, and worked for the day he'd go over the precisely balanced, but so easily upset bar, at six feet. Spurred on by this aim, he practiced for long hours, and no failure halted him. When he was off-form, Peter brooded.

If he were only able to decide that high-jumping didn't matter enough to let himself get into a state of unhappiness . . . His aim in life was not to be a great high jumper, so great that he'd break the world's record, and to go up to 6:09 or 6:10. If he could make that, what would it matter?

Peter was subject to moods of this character only rarely. And while they were upon him, he didn't deceive himself, really. But he knew it was a fact that he was disappointed as hell.

And while he'd be in the worst of his gloom, the dump of dumps, he'd get the sort of sneaking thought that he couldn't be feeling as bad as he thought, and, therefore, he must be putting it on too thick. That was a means of excusing himself, wasn't it? And maybe that was what he was doing.

Peter often took long walks with Fred Morris, and they would tell each other what was on their minds. They talked a lot about track, running, and high-jumping, and Fred was better for Peter than many coaches might have been. He told him that much practice was needed, and added the wish that he himself could go on with athletics. He'd like to play football, and high jump, and he wouldn't mind playing basketball, either. Such a remark struck notes of sadness in both of them. Peter, whose mother was dead, and Fred, whose father had died when he was about four years old. For a moment or two, they would lapse into silence, and they'd feel very silent inside of themselves as well. The hurt of childhood and boyhood, the hurt that was long-standing with them, would come back, and there was something beyond expression in their sadness, although they did not feel sorry for themselves in the sense of self-pity. Often, they had ached from a sense of loss that other kids, as they grew through adolescence, never realized. They did not speak of this to one another but it drew them silently together in their quiet moods. When they would be walking through Washington Park, or along South Park Avenue or on another street, they often talked.

"That's right, Fred. And there are so many people in the world who have plenty more to worry about than I have."

"You're good, Pete, you know that, and what you need to do is to keep going and trying. Sometimes you are off-stride, when you start for the bar. You don't get off easy and in stride."

"Yes, I've been working on that, and it's better now, but that has been one of my faults. I used to take a couple of steps too many, and I couldn't get up the pace and speed I needed for the jump."

"It's buck fever, Peter, and the only cure is practice and experience," Fred said.

"I guess so."

But both of them doubted Fred's statement the second after they had agreed about it.

"There's more to it than that," Fred said.

The Silence of History

"I was just going to say the same thing, Fred."

"There's attitude—what is called psychology, isn't that it, Peter?"

"Psychology. Yes."

"Buck fever—that's real psychology, I guess."

"I suppose it is—it's attitude. If your attitude isn't right you tighten up, and think about what you're trying to do, instead of going ahead and doing it."

"That's a good way of putting it. You can't be loose if you worry and think you can't make it, and your form is not right, or your stride is off, or you aren't leaving the ground at the right spot or any one of a hundred things—but you know all that, Peter."

"Yes, and too much, I'd say."

"You got to get over there, Peter, get it out of your system. Just tell yourself you don't give a damn if you make it or not, that's what I used to do, and so, I wouldn't worry or have attitudes. I'd just get in position on the right side, stand and go and jump. Hell, I wouldn't know what I'd done, and I'd be over that bar, and landing on the other side. Then, I'd tell myself, 'Morris, you made it, you did, Morris.'"

"That's what I want to be able to do, but when you aren't doing something right and you don't clear the bar, time and time again, that's when you start worrying."

"The more you eat, the more you want. The more you worry, the more you still worry, Peter."

"Yes, that's so," Peter agreed thoughtfully.

That night they stopped at the drugstore at 58th and Prairie and sat in one of the booths on the left side, to have malted milks.

Peter sipped out of a straw, looking down at the foamed-up chocolate, liking the taste as he sucked it up, and suddenly he knew that he was out of his spell and that he'd be back in form the next week when he went out for practice, and jumped. This was the way it happened, that is, coming out of a bad period such as the one he'd been having. You just came out of it, and your whole attitude changed, and you knew you were going to do better. Failing was part of the way you developed.

"Say, look at that, Peter."

Fred was referring to a full-bodied young girl with a big bust shaping her pink dress.

Peter looked. He guessed that he must be feeling the same as Fred. You saw a girl like that one, with such breasts and a figure, and you were tantalized, and wondered why you couldn't be like most guys and get a girl, satisfy yourself, and find out what it was like.

"I'll bet she done something to get tits like that, boy, oh, boy," Fred said.

"They must have just grown that way."

"The hell they did," Fred said. "She just got that way, and grew 'em big by getting herself laid plenty, that's what I say, Peter."

Peter didn't comment. The image of the girl and her big breasts was still hanging in his mind. All the boys looked at a girl like that when she walked along a street, and every one of them would have the same thought. He did. He supposed he shouldn't, but he did, just as Fred did.

He was afraid he'd blush, and was ashamed.

Wasn't a girl like that ashamed, too? The way her breasts stuck out, she must know the boys all looked at her, and thought of her big breasts and the rest.

"Who is she? Do you know who she is? I never saw her before. Did you?"

"No, Fred—not that I can remember. She must be new around here."

He didn't know. Didn't know? He agreed all right, with Fred, but he couldn't help it, the way his desiring was mixed with shame and sorrow for himself and everyone because they all had these same wishes and desires.

One thing about sports, and about high-jumping—you forgot to be ashamed of your body. Then it was wonderful to have one, and it gave you a thrill and you would sometimes have a strong sense of purity.

A number of the boys in the neighborhood would agree with him. As the girl with the large bosom left, some of the boys

The Silence of History

who were just hanging around the front of the store were saying something and laughing. He was curious to know what.

Sometimes when you saw a girl, oh, you just wanted nothing else but to feel her, and see her and, and . . .

"Yes, I was thinking, God, I'd like to get my hands on those tits of hers," Fred said.

And yes—that was what he meant, Peter told himself.

Scenes like that one, talks and walks with Fred, track, studies, watching the boys on the corner, all that went on, filling the minutes and hours through the years while he'd been growing up, these were all part of yesterday, when he'd believed, when he hadn't had any idea that living could be different and better, and in those years and years, had he learned much? How much?

Aunt Kate mumbled prayers and breathed with a noise that was not loud, yet audible enough for Peter to hear; there was rustling, and other evidences of movement and people, some coughing and sneezing, a man beside him on his left, hissing prayers nervously, and the singing and chanting, and the movement on the altar, and all the people, kneeling, and who sang and chanted Latin, and they, all of these people, like himself, and most of them for much longer, had been living the minutes of life, living for what?

The Latin swelled in sadness and a dignity that was like death given dignity through the centuries, and Peter wanted to believe with these people, and with his dead mother, and the dead of his family, and the dead of the centuries. He wanted to believe when he heard the soprano voice of Peg Lawlor.

Agnus Dei,
Qui tollis, peccata mundi,

The *Agnus Dei* restored to him those peculiar emotions of consolation, that sadness that was full of sleeping softness, that sense of littleness before God and bigness in belief, that melting of self into the long years of the continuity of the Church from the birth of Christ on to the successive events of Christ's life, to the triumphal entry into Jerusalem, the Last Supper, the dark night of Gethsemane when the sweat on Christ's face was like blood oozing from the mark of men's future sins, to the Way of

Calvary, the agony of sunless daylight hours on the Cross, the burial, the Resurrection, and Ascension, and the long, slow centuries, the recurrence of the Sacrifice of the Mass, through the generations, the eternity of incorruptible feelings of the Lamb of God who washeth away the sins of the world and the corruptibility of those who shared in incorruptibility, that is, the life of the world, the flesh, the Devil and the way of life of eternal penance beyond that world, the flesh and the Devil.

After the singing of the *Agnus Dei*, Peter heard the voice of Peg Lawlor, as though disembodied, a soul whose humility was rich and softly mellowed, gently echoing in a plea of the stricken soul that was poor for pity and was rich in a gold of sound. It was the voice of a sinful soul and of woman as angel, singing:

*Oh, Lord, I am not worthy
That Thou shouldst come to me
But speak the words of pity
And my spirit healed shall be.*

The bell tinkled from the altar, heads were bowed, the Latin prayers of Father McGee were a faint, very faint mumble, and Peg sang for all, the plea of the sinner who was lifted by Christ, and the most solemn moment of the Mass came and went while all knelt, and almost all bowed their heads, and many tapped their breasts lightly with closed hand.

And an unleavened wafer and wine became body and blood of Christ in a Mystery of Mysteries.

Peter, with his head bowed and his eyes closed, did not think of the transubstantiation, but of the triumph of permanence which came to him in an imagined image of Jesus Christ.

Then, the Mass continued and it was as though Peter's emotions were silent with solemn awe. The silence of his emotions ended, he felt that he was his precise self once more, he wanted to get outside, the sacred parts of the Mass were over, a few left, and the church was full of people whose nerves were alerted and who controlled themselves in a final few moments of patience, and Father McGee chanted in a suddenly clear voice:

Ita Missa est.

A quick and very amused smile broke on Peter's face. For it was almost an experience to be in church at the end of Mass, especially High Mass. He was thinking of the rush to get out of the church as fast as possible. And his smile was all the more amusing because he wanted to get out just as much as everybody else, everybody except maybe one, or a couple of people, mainly women. But he couldn't join the exit rush because of Aunt Kate.

He didn't mind that. He could wait and watch, and he found that an enjoyable, interesting occupation for a few minutes. Watching people was fascinating. He never failed to have his interest aroused, his curiosity awakened, and often, his mind would be stimulated. Sometimes, pretty often, he would find unexpected humor in watching people just passing by him on a street or somewhere. In church, there wasn't so much humor, except the alacrity with which the people got out at the end of the Mass. And that of course wasn't really funny.

Only a few got out in a hurry, before the aisles became crowded, and progress was slow, and he'd have to wait, also.

The choir was singing, but stopped before the crowd had emptied out of the church.

Mrs. Nolan sat with an air of stoic resignation, but her curious eyes were taking in the slowly moving crowd which was close to packed in the aisles. Peter stood at her left, also searching, but maintaining an air of reserve proper for one in the House of God. He smiled with restraint at those he knew.

The church was soon almost empty, and they could leave. Aunt Kate labored to the back of the church, and did not attempt to genuflect when she blessed herself by the holy water font. Peter patiently helped her down the steps in front of the church. She wobbled and waddled as she slowly struggled along. Her eyes were cast upon Peter in a wonderment of near unbelief. To think that he was her nephew, and her brother's boy. Now, and wasn't it that he was a man? His poor mother, Lord have mercy of her poor soul. Mrs. Nolan looked on Peter, now, almost as her own, and was proud of him, because he was a good, clean boy, as good as her own. And her own were good, because she knew that Jerry would settle himself down because he wasn't a bad boy. If that University didn't ruin Peter, he'd be a good one, too, oh, she prayed that God would save him from what she heard tell that place could do to a good young Catholic boy.

But Mrs. Nolan had other concerns on her mind. Her feet. They would be aching by the time she got home, and she would have to sit soaking them in hot water. It was the hard stone of the sidewalk that did it. And the walk was long. It seemed longer from church to home than the other way around, harder on her poor old feet. The people at Mass were all gone ahead, and there weren't so many on the streets. A loneliness came over her, and she grew sad with the heaviness of all her years. She was but flesh getting on in life. The desire to be back in her own home was strong in her, because then she could be where she was used to everything, and the sadness lying upon her heart would not be so heavy. There would be things to do, the Sunday dinner to finish cooking, and plenty to keep her mind occupied and off thinking of so many days gone by, more gone than there were others to come in her life.

She held onto Peter's arm, and he walked with patient slowness, making certain not to go faster than her poor legs would allow. They were beginning to ache, and she knew that they were swelling. The walk home would be hard on her, it would give her a bad time. But she'd do it and not complain, just like she'd done it before. After a soaking in warm water, the pain would go out of them, and she'd be more comfortable. And whatever aching and suffering she did, that was to her credit because it had been for going to Mass. Her brother, Mike, always told her, sure and she should go and come in a taxicab, or buy an automobile, and let one of the boys, Al or Jerry or Peter, drive her, but she had gotten along all of these years without an automobile, and she could get on more years without one. An automobile was expensive, a waste of good money. And if she bought one, Jerry might be driving it and have an accident, and even be killed, for nowadays the driving was fierce.

They had been walking in silence. Peter seemed so quiet, he usually talked to cheer her up, she wondered was there something on his mind? A girl? One of them girls from over at the

The Silence of History

University, Protestant, sinful, she didn't know what? She feared those she heard about even more than the professors she heard tell would try to take a Catholic boy's faith. Plenty there were with no decency at all, and the Devil was at work all of the time. Yes, she worried about Peter and the girls, knowing full well what a decent, clean boy he was. No one ever could tell when some girl would turn the head of one as young as Peter. It wasn't the way it had been when she was a girl.

They had walked on along 61st Street, past the store fronts, almost all of which were closed.

"How are you feeling, Aunt Kate?" Peter suddenly asked, after thinking that he'd let too much time elapse without speaking to her.

"Oh, I'm all right, except for my feet."

"We'll go more slowly."

"I can't be walkin' much more slow, and as 'tis, I don't know when I'll be gettin' back home."

"You'll get there all right."

"With the help of God, and you, Peter."

"Yes, with the help of God, Aunt Kate," he said, in a voice full of kindness and patience.

But why was it that God was always thought of most in sadness, in sad hours, in time of sad misfortune?

This question framed itself in his mind as though by its own will. He had never thought of God before in precisely this light. Yet it seemed true. And didn't this mean fear more than love, sorrow more than joy? But didn't it console sadness and calm fear, and did not that lead more to the possibility of happiness? And take it away, faith in God and Church, would there be less fear and less sorrow? He didn't think so.

But perhaps he was not certain, convinced, ready to know what he thought. And what he thought on this morning was with the lingering effect of the Mass influencing him. His memory of those times at Mass when he was eight and he'd made his First Communion had come back to him, full and complete, and the blind or ignorant sorrow of his early boyhood was changed to memories of something he wished to have back again. Wasn't that enough truth for the Church?

But he was going to study to be a lawyer, not a theologian. He didn't want to think any more of doubt and faith, not then, not for Sunday.

The walk home with Aunt Kate was painfully slow, but Peter tried to make conversation, to help her and himself, also, forget some of the sadness of life.

Let well enough be well enough, Peter decided. His thoughts and doubts about Faith could rest. But they did not rest. They came back and he kept going around the same circles in his mind, believing and not-believing, in a suspension of uncertainty. He wanted to preserve his belief. But he could neither convince himself that he was doing this, nor could he abandon it. On several nights, he took lonely walks in Washington Park, and looked at the stars in mute appeal, as though they had a voice and could tell him what he was unable to tell himself. They were silent with the eloquence of beauty, but that silent eloquence stirred him to the depths, and the mute grandeur of the silver jewelry of all the heavens raised his spirits. Such nights of harmony beyond beauty, of a music that played on all his spirits, could not be accident of matter. And yet they were as silent as tombstones.

Peter remembered all these thoughts and emotions as he stood looking out of the window at Washington Park in the snow.

Chapter Sixteen

My thoughts began to explode like cannon crackers. I probably seemed very angry, and there was some anger in me, but I was more excited than angry. Almost every day, I was changing my mind about something that I had previously accepted, believed. I didn't think through these changes of mind and view, but jumped to them according to occasion, occurrence, observation, stimulus, and class assignments. Anger and intensity were inescapable under such circumstances. Had I shown slackness of temperament, calmness, a lack of the emotion which was the source of energy for my anger and intensity, then my education would have been meaningless, and I would have been more a human parrot than a young man who was learning. I had taken my studies seriously, and ideas had meaning to me. Ideas were the means we used to understand the world. Understanding the world was finding out the truth. That was what education was, a study of the truth. This I believed even before I had known it, back in my short-pants days as a kid in parochial school. The sisters were teaching the truth. So they believed; so I believed. I carried this belief into college, and when I learned, I was learning the truth.

Then also, the conditions of my life and my struggle to attend the University could only have predicated an intensity that was seriousness, and a possibility of finding anger which, likewise, was seriousness. I couldn't be bland as were some of the fraternity boys and the students from well-to-do or rich homes. A young man couldn't drive himself as I did and be casual or bland, restraining his enthusiasm, softening his manner of expression and neutralizing his choice of words in saying or writing what he thought. You don't do that and work a seven-day week, carry on for sixteen, seventeen, or eighteen hours a day, suffer eyestrain, and even fear that you can go blind. It couldn't have been otherwise in my case. What I did was necessary, essential, if I wished to educate myself. And I not only wished it—I had determined that I would get an education.

The consequence was that I was, without awareness of this fact, separating myself from others. I never went to lunch on the campus without my black briefcase, stuffed with books and notebooks. I didn't have time to see my old friends, and my lack of social life, dates, and much relaxation, permitted greater concentration on study, more intensive assimilation, a constant growth in my knowledge, and greater rapidity in my thinking. I kept gathering and generating more intellectual energy. I was developing habits of self-stimulation, and thinking about many questions, conditions, and circumstances. I was asking myself questions, and posing issues beyond the immediate work I was doing in my various classes. I believed that I was learning about life and the world, past and present, and I was trying to apply what I was learning. My questions and the issues about which I would think were connected with the world and with my studies. Many of them were economic. For instance, I thought about acquisitiveness, and the parts of that book of the British scholar, R. W. H. Tawney, *The Sickness of an Acquisitive Society*, which I'd read. In America, the title had been changed, I'd learned, to *An Acquisitive Society*, because the original English title might have been considered too offensive. The very phrase, "acquisitive society," had been full of many meanings for me, the meanings of truth. For when I first heard it mentioned, which had been in a classroom, I had instantly recognized truth in the phrase itself, and I had felt a protesting anger and sadness. Several times I had thought that, yes, it was an acquisitive society and it was sick.

I grasped this as truth instantaneously. From both my reading up to that time, and my personal experiences and observations,

The Silence of History

I had a background of facts, ideas, and reflections for my acceptance. I did not think of these at the time. I had no need to. We do not carry or retain our knowledge consciously and call upon all of it every time we reach a conclusion, or recognize in the words of someone else a statement which we know is truth. Only when we have need to bring up and order our facts and reasons do we usually do so. We know by absorption and assimilation, and a newly discovered truth becomes a discovery which leads us to revalue and alter our interpretations of what was and what is, an alteration of what we are and where we are going in life, remaking the person we were.

When I began to study at night school, and then at the University, I wanted success in life, and hoped to make money as a goal of success. I was ambitious for such success. But I was pursuing an aim, taking a means and finding a road which was leading to something else. I was not living to succeed as I believed, but to the contrary, to abandon what I regarded to be success as my goal in life. I was not a young man with the stuff of Babbittry in my character, and I was not the young fellow that Pat Keefe or Mr. Wood thought me to be.

We are like living histories, and as we live on, we go through successive mutations. When we plan, our plans "gang aft a-gley" in the full sense that Robert Burns meant when he wrote:

The best laid schemes o' mice an' men
Gang aft a-gley.

For not only do circumstances, difficulties, the unforseen and fortuitous developments and forces outside of our control "gang aft a-gley," but so do our own minds if our thoughts be measured against those which we held at a previous time when we decided upon and formulated the sense and purpose of a life ambition and planned to go ahead and fulfill this ambition. One of the great unknowns in the lives of many is the caliber and quality of their minds. How will our minds grow, or fail to grow? What will be our limits of understanding? And what are we seeking with our minds as possibly distinct from our ambitions?

Of this we often know little, and we are filled with illusions which we take for knowing.

The paradoxes and contradictions of all of us, of our natures, are often most poignant in youth. Then, we feel our own past, our childhood, with the pain of loss more acutely, just as we feel all of life with the hard points of immediacy. In youth, we find and live a pathos, and our growing pains are felt in the heart. The cruelty of a change of mind, of a sweeping acceptance of new ideas which makes life, the world, the future, all new for us, the ruthlessness of our rejections, are accompanied by melancholy thoughts of life and death, and by pains which, like Oscar Wilde's love, dare not speak their name. The joy of youth is also the sorrow of youth. That sorrow is of and for the past and the future.

And in this joy and sorrow, we are often at war. If we think and feel, then we are most certainly engaged in battle, and could like Rastignac in Balzac's *Père Goriot*, shake our fists at Paris, at all of the cities, at all of the world, and declare:

"Henceforth, there is war between us."

We learn and are taught in life, even though we may have but meager formal education. We change through learning, and through failure to learn just as definitely as our bodies change. And what is interim change but a change of the meaning of life, which is change not only of what we are thinking at any moment of present time, but also of what we thought at past moments.

And when we give our energies to educating ourselves, we are acting to change the past, that is, our own past. That personal past, which is the used-up portion of our lives, is not, however, a limited and strictly history of personal events, including such events as dreams, wishes, thoughts, facts, beliefs, impressions, ideas about the world and all of the history and past of the world. For us the world is what we know it to be, and what it has done to us, that is, what has happened to us. Belief in God, faith in a religion, acceptance of the Santa Claus myth, or belief that babies are brought by storks, these are experiences of the personal past of many of us. And fear that any violation of the Ten Commandments, neglect of

The Silence of History

the obligations of the Catholic Church, if we are Catholic, or commission of any or all of the Seven Deadly Sins will bring us eternal damnation, this is implanted in our personal past. And also that the world was created in seven days by God, as this fact is recorded in Genesis. And that George Washington never told a lie. And that the United States is the greatest country in history. And that wobblies, or members of the IWW were I Won't Work's and I Want Whiskey's. And that St. Patrick drove the snakes out of Ireland. And that white men are superior to black men. And that Christians were better than Jews, Catholics better than Protestants, and the Irish better than any other race or nationality. And that priests were especially smart and learned and know more about theology than atheist, bigotted Protestant professors. And that pluck is luck, and where there is a will, there is a way, and if you wish for something hard enough and long enough, you'll get it. And that there is injustice in the social and economic system as it had become known and as it operated. And that the United States fought the Central Powers in order to "make the world safe for democracy," in order to defend freedom of the seas, and in order that Kaiser Bill wouldn't send his goosestepping Huns across the Atlantic to conquer us. And that an alderman with a Neanderthal mind and an "itching palm" was a big shot. And that the U. S. Constitution was the greatest political document written by man, along with the Declaration of Independence, a document in which nothing contradicted the Constitution of the United States. And that the Day of Judgment, as foretold, would surely come in God's time, and when it did, you would arise from the grave, in your mortal flesh which was recognizable, and that on that Day, you would be Judged and the Judgment would tell you and every one who had ever lived if you were among the saved or the damned. And that the world you lived in was just about the best of all possible worlds short of Heaven. And that James Whitcomb Riley's *An Old Sweetheart of Mine* was poetry, immortal poetry. And that if you worked your way through college, studied with diligence, had stick-to-it-iveness, plus the other virtues needed for becoming a success in Life, you would become a Success, and that you'd be admired for studying with this aim in view. And that the One, Holy, Roman, Apostolic Church was the true Church, the only true Church. And that death is the purpose of life. And that there were ghosts and the bogey man. And that maybe God did love the Irish, with a particular love. And that for every boy who is on the level, there is a girl who is on the square, and everyone was made for someone, and would find that someone, sometime. And that your soul would burn in eternal fires if you committed sins of the flesh and were not absolved of these sins before you died. And that every line of Rudyard Kipling's *If* was a true motto for success and that if you could fill that unforgiving minute full of sixty seconds' worth of distance run, you'd be a success in life, and a man. And that Darwin said we came from monkeys, the *Titanic* sank because the builders or someone else had painted on the engines, or somewhere on the ship that "There is no God," and that right was right and wrong was wrong and the Church was right. And much, much else was part of the personal past of some of us. It was part of mine. What I had done or was, this was influenced by the acceptance of all this as truths, and while the influence of each proposition, statement, assertion, principle, was of different strength in the changing formation that was myself, the influences were real as such, and some supported stronger influences, thereby giving strength of effect by association, by linkage with other influences, and there were elements of past experience, and past experience was the past of my own life, the content of my yesterdays, the constellation of my interior life.

From the past I often wished to recapture lost feelings, as well as lost experiences and lost time. As I abandoned what I had acquired in the past and had regarded to be truth and principle, I did not think that I was changing my past, and that I was thus, seeing a past that was new because it had changed. I was changing my mind. I was finding out what I had not known.

I did not appreciate that learning was an experience and acquisition which was brought into the continuity of myself.

The Silence of History

Thus, I did not realize that my life was not learning now for today and tomorrow alone, but also for yesterday.

My past, in terms of reading and of knowing something of what the world was like, was bare as compared with the successive quarters which I had spent at the University. The bareness was felt in my lack of more knowledge, of references from my past which could serve me in my studying.

Concerning the subject matter of my courses, these were beyond what was in my personal background of living, or that of my family, and of most of those whom I knew. In history courses, this was obvious, and the idea did not occur to me that it should have been different. Ireland had come into the modern history course only as an occasional and passing reference, and then in relationship to Britain. The course of history had not run through the Green Isle of my forbears, and I had no fancies that any of my ancestors could have seen or participated in the historic events I had read of and that Professor Carleton discussed and analyzed in class. History had happened. History had been made. History had been lived by men and women who had their time and their day, and they had all been different from what my own ancestors had been. The latter did not belong to history, and I did not think of them. I was studying what was far away from me in time and these once real characters were socially far away from me too.

In the Middle Ages there had been more to recognize, because of the dominant role played by the Church. I felt an emotional richness as contrasted with later periods, and in that richness, there was more of the familiar. I had been feeling the ages of the past through the Church since I had been a little boy, and, this had especially been so at Mass, on feast days such as Christmas and Easter, and during Holy Week. The continuity of the Church since Christ was taught to me, and, I, like many millions before me, had knelt and looked toward an altar with holy candles, had heard the singing and chanted Latin prayers and liturgical words, and like them, I had known what these meant, and had showed through the representation of symbol, the life and passion and suffering of Jesus Christ, our Lord. For such was the meaning of the Mass.

There had been nuns in convents in the Middle Ages, and I had been taught by nuns, dressed in their black habits, and living in convent homes where they spent hours in prayer. I had heard the echo of the nuns at prayer in their chapel at the yellow brick convent home on the Indiana Avenue side of the grounds, and at a right angle to the back of the building which housed our parish church and school classrooms. The echo of women's voices in unison of sound, that of prayer and song, had stirred me with emotions I did not understand, but knew in their immediate truthfulness, with their true but almost quelling sadness. I couldn't begin to give this sadness a name, but it was related to the heart of life, to the trueness of hearts, and to the timed and yet forever important life of Christ on Earth, which was the sacred ceremonial repetition of the Church, the meaning it expressed in a poetry of the centuries which I could not recognize as such, but which was the first poetry of my life.

Lantum ergo, Sacramentum
Veneremur cernui

That feeling of sadness of emotion is focused, without hindrance, upon life and death, responsive to awe to the tormenting fears of Hell. Knowledge of death, awareness of the mortality of the flesh, the expanding devotion for one's prayers toward the physical destiny of clay into dust. Time in the crumbled relics of man and generations, monuments and civilizations, the pathos and thwarted yearning to live before and after, to speak with those whose voices are dead dust and those who are the voiceless unborn. Death. Death and the somber beauty of the world which we cannot know forever, the silence of stars, the lavish feel of moonlight with its many colors, and its contrasting nervous shimmer in uncontrolled joy. The soul of man which can only live in time for the wonders of the world, even though he grieves in the agony of a world which will lose the sun and the perfume of spring flowers, the storm and calm of a world which man sees as the image of his commanding impulse for joy that is excitement as well as sleep, and the future that becomes the fact of death. Man, forgetting all of

The Silence of History

this that appears as ever and eternally recurring, a music of the world beyond even Beethoven's power, the persuading suggestion that man can find what *even* music will not give him, all of this could be softened into the surceaseful sorrow of the chanted Latin, and during the long, slow years of those changeless long Middle Ages, the slings and arrows of more than fortune which must have been infinite in number. The bruises and wounds from these slings and arrows which must have been less painful.

Attitudes and feelings such as these were a survival from my past which grew roots in the History of the Middle Ages. It was in Professor Kraft's class, of course. Now and then, after the course had finished, I happened to turn toward some aspect of life in the Middle Ages. It was a consoling dream to think of myself living back in the stillness of those centuries, enjoying a simplicity, and free of the tiredness and strain that I felt so often and which would sometimes leave me weary, both physically and spiritually. I would be *all alone*, bewailing my *outcast fate*. Before the *to be or not to be* of life and death, there was the *to be* or the *not* of life, my life, my future. I would return to thoughts of the dead centuries of medieval life and of the Holy Roman Empire as one in which there was not the struggle for life and success that was so predominantly a characteristic of 1925 and 1926. I was nostalgic for those dead centuries. My wish to have been alive in those centuries was, like so many daydreams, not completely sincere. I wanted to be alive in the present, as I was. But also, I was indulging myself and giving way to fancy involved in elements of self-pity. I had my moods of feeling sorry for myself.

However, those daydreams of the Middle Ages as a time of almost Heavenly Peace on Earth were but a string of moments, partial lapses from my more constant preoccupations. They were far from being pure daydreams, and more than a wish for the peacefulness of release was involved in their generation and the feeling which accompanied them. I desired to get closer to the past, to make the past real, to make it live in me, to know it with all of my senses; I wanted to live what I had learned.

Who hasn't wanted the sun? Is that what I got out of going to the University?

It was not the commonplace that I wanted, not the generalizations about men and the past, but contact with the living reality. It was a reality for places in time, and its peace was more peaceful than peace could be around me, while romance was more romantic than any romance I could ever hope to find. It seemed changeless, and peace of the spirit and happiness were in the changeless. Change was not only life, but also, change was death. And this was part of the meaning of my feelings and emotions, and my aspirations and desires were often pulled into these meanings. Then I would have a most poignant sense of the pathos of the past.

I had been learning against the background of the past, and learning that background more than I had known it before. My emotions grew more roots in the past, and from these stemmed the pathos of that past. It was as though I had both lived and never lived in the past, and I hungered for it because its emptiness should have been full.

I had begun at the University with history, but this seemed more a coincidence than any act of choice. Among the courses I had to take were several in history. I wanted to take these, because I was aware that I must learn more of history. I had not thought that the progress and process of my education in college would be centered in the question of relationship—myself and history. I did not come to know this at the time, or to use any such phrase as this one. But the words of understanding come long after that understanding has been lived through and experienced. And it was more than a question or a problem that I was coping with, it was my living and reliving from the past and finding reality beyond the immediate reality in which I had lived and grown up. For it was the reality which constituted the world. That was "the outside world," where things were done, where things happened, where news was made, where events of importance transpired, and where history would be made. There, then, was the reality that counted. It was the reality of the present which linked up with the reality of the past. Both past and present were the world beyond my own. Of course, this was the same for almost all other students at the University, and was a condition of learning. But the concrete meanings, emotions and thoughts, the way I learned, the changes in myself were all specific and their significance was personal, individual to myself. The reality of that world beyond changed from what I had thought it to be as I was growing up and prior to my matriculation at the University. But we are not separable from ideas and beliefs, as we seem to think, nor from our world. The change in what I regarded as the reality of that world beyond was a change in me. It was also a change in my memory, and a change in memory is a change in the person. What happened in my memory was of importance, for here was the exciting drama of myself played in many a way. Memory was becoming more than a source of nostalgia, a fairyland of what had been and of what I had wanted and even still wanted. In my memory, there were dreams and the dreams of dreams.

But the three quarters at the University had awakened my memory and stimulated it into alertness. My personal past was becoming more rich than I could have believed possible or understood a year before. I was beginning to draw it for understanding, and to find in any experiences, thoughts which helped me to learn, and which added to the basis of my understanding.

My jobs could be seen in a new light once I had begun to study economics. The time clock at the Express Company, the overtime slips of drivers which I had once worked on, the time lock on the door of the gas station where I worked, the pressure to sell which was placed upon attendants, the hierarchy of authority in the Express Company and at Rawlinson's, the life and death of my father, the many things about salesmanship, mark-ups, hot numbers, of which my uncles had spoken, the odds and ends of fact about the hotel business which my aunt had mentioned over the years, the meaning of Christmas in business, a novel, *It Pays to Advertise*, which my uncle had bought years ago, and which I had read, the peddlers who came around to my station, the short-change artists who had caught me napping twice—all this was involved in the process of economics, and gradually came to my mind as I read about industrial society, feudal society, the Industrial Revolution, social control in industry, the doctrines of contributory negligence and *caveat emptor*, Bismarck's social laws, Napoleon's Continental System, Beard's *An Economic Interpretation of the United States Constitution* . . .

These all were facts of my experience, related to economics. They were known incidents which formed part of the meaning of the economic process.

I had used to hear many remarks about supply and demand, and it almost seemed that this law was the explanation of economics on a plane with Newton's law of gravity and motion. But I first began to wonder and then to disbelieve, that the law of supply and demand explained all that it was supposed to. It was acquisitiveness. And I could well respond to Tawney's phrase and title, *The Sickness of an Acquisitive Society*. This was an exciting recognition of my own thoughts, and it came one day in the classroom of Professor Dorland, a serious, bald-headed, sharp-nosed man, whose features, when seen quickly and as a composed unit, suggested unpleasantness. There was a sharpness in the line of his oversized nose, and his thick, tortoise-shell glasses were placed low on his nose, so that he often looked over his glasses, and it was this which could be cited as the reason for calling him smart, mean, or annoying. But the look was not one of superiority and contempt, as I had at first supposed. He looked like advance notice of bad grades, sarcastic exposure of your weakness, and had a slow but corrosive, taunting manner which would make each day dreadful, because you were sure he would taunt you without mercy. But he was quite different. He spoke quietly, but with firmness, although his words came out in a sharp rasp. He was thin and a fraction above medium height, but I had the recurring impression that he was tall.

It means little, usually nothing, to state that a man does not look like a college professor, but the first week in the classroom with Professor Dorland, I had difficulty in believing that he belonged up at a desk, and felt that he must be a case of mistaken identity.

The reason was Professor Dorland's undistinguished appear-

The Silence of History

ance. He was undistinguished, but somehow he wasn't. There was something anomalous about him. And anomalous isn't the right word. He should have looked ordinary but he just didn't quite. His nose was a little too long and sharp. And his face could suggest the imminence of humor.

He came and went and didn't have much to do with us, other than to lecture, which he did in an easygoing, conventional manner, and, at the beginning, it didn't seem as though he was saying anything of consequence, but I'd keep listening, and most of the other students would do likewise, and our interest would grow. Once Professor Dorland got going, he had a dry wit, and used it to our amusement and for his own pleasure at the expense of orthodox economists, and what he called sundry gentlemen of means who are possessed of the peculiar delusion that the stork brought Adam Smith, trailing clouds of wealth, only yesterday morning.

A good number of us laughed at the joke, when Professor Dorland told us that it was not a matter fit for laughter. But he was half-smiling himself.

He continued lecturing in a dry, wry voice. Sitting near a window, on the right side of the door, I took notes as I listened, but the title of Tawney's book was also in my mind. *The Sickness of an Acquisitive Society*, the phrase was liberating and clarifying. Deep walls of fogs, which hung between me and "the outside world," were penetrated and dissolved; I could see the social structure and organization of modern society and modern life. I could see through and behind, see where there was nothing and yet more than an emptiness, because there was a beyond in the unseen. I knew many things with one thought. A phrase of six words described for me, revealed to me, informed me about the cause of what had been dissatisfying to me and the reason for a long, slow-growing anger. I had come to understand. And what I understood was a great wrongness. This was in people, and it was like a fever that burned them when they thought that they were cool. They were hurting themselves, and leading themselves into a swamp where the germs of their own illness proliferated. But they were hurting others more than themselves. And they had hurt me. They could hurt me in to crippled permanence unless I saved myself, along with those others who would cure the malady. They were hurting the world with sickness but they called it the most healthful state of health. They were going on thinking this, deluding themselves, deluding others that the sickness wasn't sickness, preaching that every day and in every way, things would get better, when in point of fact the sickness would get worse and worse.

This was not a beginning in my revolt, but it was a crystallizing moment of great consequence. Nor was Tawney's book the only influencing one; there were many others.

I thought with dire, deathlike foreboding that there would be another World War, and a cyclic depression. And did the acquisitive sickness have much to do with what was to come?

Chapter Seventeen

Eddie and Peter still walked to school on most mornings, and their walks were very enjoyable, with the park green and shining, and the morning sun bright with the spring. The dew was still on the grass, with the shine of the morning sunlight, birds were singing, the world seemed to be so full of the urge to live and to love.

On some of these mornings, usually the finest, Peter and Eddie would be melancholy. It was as though they shared the same feeling of deprivation. Neither complained to the other about the emptiness which they both felt.

It was the look of a girl, and it was more than that. There was so little in the personal lives they led, and they would, on occasion, think that they were getting far less out of living than was actually the case. They would reach moods full of wistfulness and poignancy. They would both be soaking into themselves the richness of the world, but they were walking through scenes of that richness like strangers. During the passing weeks and months of a year not yet half over, they had been living in a world that was growing steadily more strange to both of them. They bore the unhappiness of changing minds and with this unhappiness they carried the memory of lost years of their boyhood. The mornings seemed to induce these moods of nostalgia, and to remind them both of a loss, so that they were filled with regrets for what was already gone of their lives, not only those years of boyhood, but also its innocence and sense of the perpetual wonder of life. Never had this wonder been more appealing to them in their boyhood days than when they had happened to be in Washington Park when the sun was rising. That wonder of the sun, then, had also been the promise of life, and it was as though the world belonged to them and they would live in the sun forever. It had roused in them both dreams which they could not remember, or could but slightly recall; dreams, however, which they did not try to bring back in memory. Their dreams vaguely resembled music, and they were songs which had been singing in them.

Peter and Eddie had known the morning park separately as boys, although they had occasionally taken their Airedales out on a summer morning; they both had Airedales, females, who didn't get along or play well together. Freedom was Eddie's dog, and Beauty the one that Peter and his father had owned. Now and then, especially on the morning walks in the park, Eddie would remember Freedom, and sometimes Beauty also. The thought of his dog, and the times he would take her to the park was one of the saddest of the memories that would come to him. Freedom, a shaggy, friendly dog, had wanted to jump on anyone she saw, and be petted and played with, and now she was dead, she was nothing, there was no more Freedom, his dog. The thought of this could be a crushing heartache, and the dog as though betrayed. For she had not known of her death, and could never have known, and they had kept her cooped up most of the time, and dogs, particularly Airedales, hunting dogs, and good fighters, should be outside, running and sniffing, out in the air and space. And when Freedom did get out, she'd be overexcited. But how different a dog she'd be, wagging and waving her cut stub of a tail, running wildly, without purpose, or should he say with a purpose of sheer animal joy and energy. When she had been a puppy, she had been like all young dogs, full of such joy and energy, running, jumping up on everyone, playing all the time that she wasn't sleeping or eating, playing with her tail, tearing around and around the back yard, always hungry for food, affection, and attention, and that mutt's look

The Silence of History

of appeal would almost break his heart. But there was nothing of all that left, nothing but what he remembered.

Energy did not vanish, only breathing life. But there was a new energy in the world with each morning, and those spring mornings in the park had awakened in song and sunshine as though they, too, were forever, just as it seemed that his dog Freedom had been forever.

The spring mornings when Freedom had run in the park like a crazy puppy, and those when Peter had taken Beauty to the park, also, these were gone, and that was all that was forever, that which was gone. Forever was nothing, was all that had once been and was no more. And we only remembered a small part of all that was forever. We carried a little of forever in our minds and memories.

Eddie no longer believed. He did not believe in the faith of his boyhood. He did not believe in the God of his boyhood. He did not believe.

That belief had, also, gone into what he had called forever. It was gone, as his dog, Freedom, was gone.

The idea of the impermanence of life crept through him, and his anger was a form of impotence, of the powerlessness, not only of himself, but of men, all who had ever been, and all who ever would be.

The creeping gradualness of the dark meanings of impermanence did not anger him because of his beliefs, not only about religion, but also about the society of men. He knew many moments of joyous hope, and he would look forward to a future of work and effort, of gaining knowledge, with the thought that he would contribute by helping to cure some of the ills of life from which men suffered. More personally, he was free of many of the fears that had hurt him, and he could, while he lived, try to be more consistent. He could live without fear, and he would learn to face death and to die, also, without fear. And he wouldn't live the pitiful sacrifice to the gods that be, nor to the acquisitiveness that caused the sickness of society. Before they died, men should live and feel the world as a quickened pulse of love and joy and whatever was beautiful in life.

His moods jumped from light to darkness, from the gloom of midnight to the glory of a morning dawn. His thinking helped to condition, or possibly to cause them.

His was not a fine life, but it was the road to freedom, the only one for him. He had learned that freedom demanded knowledge, and this he must acquire, and acquire, and acquire. To be lonely, however, was like being a failure, having something wrong with you, possessing a character with gross flaws. He couldn't admit to any such feelings, not even to Peter. It wasn't necessary, because Peter knew, and often had the same feelings himself.

"Maybe it's better to be working, as you are, Eddie," Peter said on one of the fine mornings when they walked to school.

At first, Eddie didn't understand why Peter should make such a statement. Peter was more free by not having to work.

"You don't feel so set apart from the world, if you're able to get away from campus, out into the world."

But Eddie, while no longer surprised, remained a little uncomprehending of Peter's dissatisfaction.

"It's a secluded life," Peter said.

"But what's wrong with that, Peter?"

"You're out in the world, working, that makes a difference. Just going to the University is not doing anything, all preparation, and in a kind of isolated world that could be miles away from Chicago from the way it seems, once you get accustomed to hanging around the campus as much as I do.

"I'd be glad if I could do just that."

"What, Ed?"

"Hang around campus and study more and not have to work in my gas station."

They turned the bend, around the new, yellow shrubbery, and were on the graveled walk where the lagoon came to a shore line. The water, so calm, was dancing with golden little sprites. The scene almost made them catch their breath for a second or two.

There were three rowboats visible.

Eddie had a strong urge to rent a rowboat and to go with

smooth efficiency over the dancing sprites on the water's surface.

They took an eastward angle, away from the edge of the lagoon; Eddie had a feeling of hungering pathos.

He looked back at the dancing sun spots upon the water, tantalizing with the illusion of life.

"Pretty, isn't it?"

"Yes, it is. It gets you with a choke in the throat, doesn't it, Eddie?"

And more than a choking up in the throat, a wrench of the heart, and the pain of distance and non-communicability.

"That's why I doubt my doubting. Ed, I don't know if I am or am not an agnostic."

Peter had spoken resolutely, with an emphasis of determination in his words.

They walked in silence for some paces in the grass and they carried their spirits as a heavy burden, and the heaviness kept pressing on both of them.

"No, there isn't anything," Eddie said, after they had gone some yards across the grass, and their shoes were becoming wet.

"But how can anybody know. There might be. There isn't any proof that there isn't," Peter said.

"Or that there is," Eddie answered.

"I grant that, too, there isn't either way."

The chirp and song of birds, the croak of a frog, the bark of a dog in the distance somewhere behind them, the fresh smell of the spring morning, sky, and sun, all the greenness, and their own beating pulses, all seemed to press a cry upon them, but they did not cry out. They wanted to cry out, speak out to the sky, and the sun, and the clouds, and the newness of the world, and to be spoken to.

There was no noise, but only the voiceless voice of the universe. And they both thought that there was something wonderful in such mornings, and they wanted to feel that this wonderfulness, this wonderful something and they themselves, were part of a plan and purpose. They had the habit of God and of God's design, or of design attributed to God, even though

Eddie said that there was nothing, and Peter that he didn't know for sure.

With denial and doubt leaving a painful dolor in their minds, they received the morning world as they always had, as the same world they had known for years, a world of plan, of God's design. They were close to this world and with it in spirit, sadly, but nevertheless close to all that the shining sun brought into shape and color and a singing kind of visibility.

"No, there's nothing, Pete."

"What?"

"It's all empty and it happened like this; we're all accidents that happened, too, that's all."

Peter was shaken and couldn't get past his doubts. He was slow to speak.

"Then what's it all for?" Peter asked as they were getting on, closer to the Cottage Grove boundary of the park.

"Chance and chaos, I guess," Eddie said.

"Then what difference does anything make? What difference is—what we do?"

"None—but the truth. We should learn the truth."

"Don't laugh, Ed—but what is the truth?"

"Confirmed data, facts, and . . ."

Eddie's answer broke off.

There were problems that he yet must study, and he had been cut short by his unsureness, not of his new and basic disbelief, but of his ability to express it in all its possible ramifications.

They walked on, and the world was the same world, the sky the same kind of sky, but theirs was the sadness of seeing that same old sameness with new outbursts, with new and old feelings.

The dust of the stars becoming through time's mutation the dust and ashes of death. This thought came to move Eddie, like a line of poetry, as they left the park.

"There are other questions, besides God and religion, Ed, and I wonder if these aren't more important," Peter said, after they had crossed Cottage Grove Avenue.

"Yeah?"

The Silence of History

"Tolerance and prejudice, for instance, the Anglo-Saxon myth of superiority and the belief that the Nordic is a superior race, or even that the Caucasians, that is, the white race is superior by birth and heredity."

"The Irish aren't so superior."

"No, I wouldn't say we are."

"You are superior if you've got something up here," Eddie said, pointing to his head.

"Yes, that's true enough."

The thought stirred Eddie into exhilaration, and there was no darkening gleam of disbelief in him at that moment, when he and Peter walked along the north sidewalk of 57th Street. The buildings looked dull and old, and Eddie guessed that they must have been built around the time of the World's Fair or Columbian Exhibition of 1893. There was a glare to some of the yellow bricks. But Eddie noticed no more. He and Peter went on talking and Eddie's interest in talking with Peter was becoming ever keener. He liked what Peter had said, the way that Peter had agreed with him.

"The Irish are most prejudiced of all," Eddie said.

"But are they, Eddie?"

"Aren't they?"

Eddie was a bit carried away.

"What about some of the fraternity boys and campus big men or the club girls over here?"

Eddie held back answering for a few seconds because he didn't like admitting to his having been snubbed a number of times, too many times.

"They're no worse, I guess. They're the Nordic myth, goddamn it," Eddie said.

Peter's laugh was like praise and flattery to Eddie.

"Yes, Ed, our people have their ignorance, God knows, and narrow-mindedness—they don't know any better. But I don't know if I'm prejudiced—more prejudiced than others."

Eddie thought of his grandmother, his mother, of Peter's aunt, and he could understand them. He felt as Peter did.

But how he felt was not the important thing. It was how he reasoned, and according to the truth. That was what counted.

They crossed the street at a big diagonal, and began walking faster, because it was almost eight o'clock.

Eddie's faith in the religion of his childhood and in God, had just about gone. His belief in the social system and the economy of that system was gone, and he believed that socialism was inevitable. But he had still to learn more about socialism, and he tended to be confused, attributing to Marx a rigid iron law of wages, which was obviously not correct, because if it were, he wouldn't be getting one hundred and forty dollars a month, plus commissions, would he?

In his public speaking class, which was held in Mandel Hall at nine o'clock, and was given by Professor Swanson, one of the subjects for a four-minute talk had been Marx, and he had declared that one of the weaknesses of Marx's doctrine was a belief in the iron law of wages, while a second was dialectical materialism.

Eddie knew that he was still in his preparatory stage, not by reasoning things out, and any analysis of himself and of his situation, but more directly, by awareness, by a quick and immediate grasp of his situation and his development. He still needed more, not of the world, but of books and ideas, and his feelings ran opposite to those which were stirring in his friend, Peter Moore. The outside world was irking him, and he could not have stopped a growing and deeply sinking resentment of it, and, specifically, of his job at Rawlinson's, even though he had developed more resolution than he had ever known before, and hardened his will beyond any imagination he could have had of his own potential strength of will power. It was inevitable that he should get resentfully fed up with the station and its day-by-day grind. His ambition was lost for Rawlinson O&R, his interests had shifted, and his ambitions were detached and as though on the prowl. He was carried along by his inner drive and his feelings seemed to be, in a sense, possessed. He could not as easily force any interest in the work he did at the filling station, and he had begun to get increasingly careless about its condition. Cleaning up was becoming more difficult, and it was almost as though he had to draw upon close to the fullest resources of his will power

The Silence of History

to do any such thing as wash windows. Corlin was slowly getting fed up and he believed that Eddie was taking advantage of him, letting him do too much of the dirty work about the station. He made occasional indirect cracks about this, and about Eddie, but not more, Eddie let these remarks go without comment, and Corlin couldn't work himself up to having a showdown. He liked the guy, and you couldn't help liking him, Corlin would keep telling himself. But this wasn't the reason why Corlin did not have a showdown. At least, he didn't think it was. He wasn't afraid of Eddie physically, if it should come to a fist fight, but this had not entered either of their minds. Somehow, Corlin sensed that it would do no good to have a showdown with Eddie. It was Ryan's will or something, he wasn't the kind of a guy you could talk or argue into doing something. Maybe it was that, Corlin reflected.

Deacon, however, did not have the same notion, and he had begun riding Eddie, as well as complaining to Mr. Wood. Deacon found fault whenever he could, and with every possible small detail. Deacon was too smart to go at Eddie without cause, for he knew how high Eddie stood with the Boss, and Ryan did keep selling well, considering the volume of business and location of the station. But he snatched at any excuse he could find, and he knew how to speak to Mr. Wood and mask any ill will toward Eddie, pretending that he was in a quandary about this fellow, Ryan, and he didn't know what to do, but he was trying most sympathetically and fair-mindedly to keep the young fellow. He was only doing his own duty, and had to consider all the men under his supervision and their morale, and not Ryan alone. He did not make his case too strong because he only had petty criticisms to make.

Eddie knew very little of this; he only knew that he wasn't getting along well with that sonofabitch, Deacon, and that the guy was turning in lousy reports about him. He imagined that these would weigh against him, and accepted as fact the notion that he couldn't beat Deacon by going over the s.o.b.'s head.

But this wasn't the point at all, because Eddie did not believe that he was a good filling station attendant, as good as he could be, and he knew that he wasn't giving the company his all. He couldn't argue with his heart in his words, and say that Deacon was a sonofabitch, that is, from the standpoint of Rawlinson O&R. He didn't and couldn't have the right attitude for the job any more, as he'd more or less had it when he'd begun working with Rawlinson just a little over a year previously. Then, he'd believed in much that he now rejected, from God to Arthur Brisbane to Deacon to he didn't know what all.

The idea of giving any of his time to anything but himself was beginning to rile and anger the living hell out of him. It was not reasonable, and he knew it, but what was he going to do about it. His life was at stake, and his life was time, and that was what he wanted and needed, time, his own time, the time of his own life. That was what he was selling by work, and what he was beginning to resent.

The basis of freedom, for him was freedom of his own time.

The result of what he thought and felt came out in daily moments, thoughts, occurrences, and frequently, he would discover what he thought by what he said or what popped up in his mind. The development and discovery of what he saw in time and freedom came in this way.

This was happening to Eddie with a sense of sadness about life. There was depth and feeling for him in all of life and anything that could have meaning, a new, sudden, and strange meaning that he had never thought of before. He had been discovering the world in study and he was in movement toward it.

He believed that somehow there would be big storms ahead in the world and in his own life. And more than believing this, he seemed to sense it.

The days were going by. These were the days of spring. And they were days of hope and hopelessness. The reading and studying which he had done had led him to see that the world had no purpose and would one day come to an end. And man himself would end with all of his dreams and expectations, all of his works, and even fame would die as man did, and life would become death, and time would end in a world as cold as ice.

There was no God who would one day judge men for what they did; there was only thermodynamic reckoning.

This little gap of time we called our lives was lit by but a spark and then there was nothing but frozen blackness. There would be a night without time, a stagnant stillness of the darkness, and that was eternity.

And Eddie Ryan was only twenty-two. This was what he must accept in order to hope and work and struggle. Everything was not to be seen against that big void which would one day be all there was, all the hopes and dreams and thoughts that there had ever been. All remembering and forgetting would end, and there would only be a silence in the world, a silence in the sky, a silence of the stars, a silence of the planets, a silence that would fill the sightless vastness of an empty space. The rocks would be as empty as the air. And the emptiness of all emptiness would be the memory of man.

For a little while—

For a little while he would think, walking through the dewy grass of Washington Park with Peter when the sun was new and the birds were singing and chattering.

For a little while, he would think, riding to work on the bus or an elevated train.

For a little while, he would think at the filling station, as he serviced a car, or studied, or took a bawling out from Deacon or from Howell, the other supervisor.

For a little while, he would think, going home at night on the elevated train, with the sun gone down, and the night penetrated by the silent sadness of moonlight.

For a little while, he would think, at home, in the parlor, studying, in weariness, with eyes aching and his stomach heavy and nervous from drinking too much coffee in order to rob himself of sleep.

For a little while—that was all, that was life, all of the life there was or ever would be—only for a little while.

Chapter Eighteen

I

Eddie had not known who Thelma Carson was on the gay and sunny morning when she had smiled at him across the room during Miss Patrick's English Composition class. He had wondered who she was, and what kind of a family she came from, what her parents were like, and what her father did for a living. He had put many other questions about her to himself and had supplied imaginary answers. His main guess, however, was that her father was a businessman. Most of the students had fathers who were in business, and he'd bet that few of them were, like Peter and himself, the sons of workingmen.

If she knew, would his chances wither? The thought forced itself on Eddie on a dull, rainy Sunday afternoon, with darkness gathering rapidly to rush in a dirt-colored night. It had rained most of the day, and the rain came down to splatter the blackened streets, and to fall monotonously onto the damp, graveled dirt of the service station driveway. Loneliness was wet and black on the corner, and the factory opposite him was like a huge abandoned tomb of solitude, a ruins where the quiet bones of all emperors and chancellors of Hope were housed in the final foreverness of stillness.

Eddie was reading a book on the Italian Duce, Benito Mussolini, and he had looked up with a grin of amusement. The author, an American journalist, had compared Mussolini to Theodore Roosevelt. Eddie recalled reading Peter Dunne's "Book Review" in which Mr. Dooley discussed Teddy Roosevelt's

The Silence of History

history of the Rough Riders regiment which played a riproaring, significant role in the taking of Santiago during the Spanish-American War. "Teddy Roosevelt," Mr. Dooley had said, "should have called his book, *Alone in Cuba!*" Eddie grinned, and then he thought of Thelma, and of his father. Yes, would she lose interest in him if she should learn that his father had been a workingman most of his life, and had died just about pauperized?

Staring out of the service station windows, which were dirty with rain and dust, Eddie felt that he was looking at the thickest shadows of hopelessness in his whole life.

Suppose he was smart, bright, even more. What of it?

Here he was with more than three quarters behind him at the University, and just look how happy he was.

Before he had imagined what Thelma Carson might think, he had just about turned his dreams and all of his feelings and yearnings and all that was in him to her. And then he'd just about turned all of this into a ghost, and then he'd put the ghost out of its misery. The ghost had died. Ryan had murdered Hope. Lay in Sweet Stuff and damned with worms and crazy quantum worms he who first cried:

—Hope! Hope! I hope!

The loneliness of the night was in Eddie, impressed into him. He continued, for a few moments, to stare out at the corner; it was dreary, so dreary that it seemed to have been deserted by all of the living. Except himself.

He was alone in the world. Each man was though, wasn't he? Alone in a world with a dream of a world, that was just about it, each man's life. Was it only life, or shouldn't it be called fate, destiny?

She wouldn't be so interested in him if she found out who he was, what he was. It was not only his father, but all of his family.

Eddie had thought this with a suddenness like that which marks the making of quick and right decisions, decisions based on the way things were, and on what had to be done. This gave an added strength to his conclusion. His mood became one of even darker melancholy, which also meant that he felt even more, more fully and profoundly, the loneliness that was wrapped about him and that fell carelessly, to drape and hang over all that he could see before and about him. The ultimate of life was loneliness, this loneliness. And wasn't it the loneliness of man, knowing that he would have to die, and that he faced life, condemned to die and leave it, alone?

Yes, she wouldn't care for him because of what he had been and what his family had been. What he and they had been, yes, and what they were.

Eddie did not press his thoughts further, but rather he allowed them to sink into his mood. He turned back to the book on his desk.

Eddie sat reading, with his fountain pen in hand, and a large-sized, loose-leaf notebook at his right on the low, scratched desk. And the rain fell, almost in straight, thin gray lines, liquid threads dropping through the heavy obscurity of darkness and the shadows where the spreading glare of the station lights disintegrated into that obscurity. Even the buildings seemed unwanted, structures built where they stood because there was no other place where they could have been built. The corner was superfluous with dreariness. If the dead could build in deathliness, they might have built such a corner. It was a city scene fragmented off by the range of vision, a corner that was lonelier than are the dead in the minds of the living.

Eddie was bent over a book, a lonely figure in this lonely scene.

Only the living could feel loneliness as though it were anguished pulsing death. And he felt . . .

He read.

He wanted to cry out through the wet darkness of the chilled, wet Sunday night. There was no one to cry out to, nothing but blind darkness, empty with air.

Maybe she would love him.

And maybe the sun would be shining in the morning.

And he was young, and he could live before he died.

Yes, he might walk home with Thelma in greenness and sunlight, and he might kiss her.

Yes, he might, and could live by crying out the tears of the past. The sufferings of the past were dead with all that had died.

The Silence of History

And there was only now and tomorrow. Now was wet and dark, and tomorrow could be dry with sun and light.

He read until it was time to close up.

As he turned the key in the keyhole of the time lock, he felt cold raindrops on his cheek and head. Then he walked off in the rainy darkness, carrying his stuffed briefcase.

He had more hours of study tonight.

Everything around him was soaked, soaked with rain and dismalness.

—Why did Mussolini have Matteotti killed? he asked himself.

The thin gray lines of rain fell on him, and about him. Most of the houses were dark. In some, dim lights from kerosene lamps wavered against the window panes. The dimness was more mean than the darkness.

He walked on.

—Yes, he killed Matteotti, and the trains ran on time! he told himself.

The past was a dark pit of strangled agonies. And the trains ran on time. And strangled agony was dead in the dead silence of dead time.

He walked to the elevated station, as usual, climbed the steps, paid his fare, went up to the platform, and waited for the next southbound elevated train.

He was as tired as the Sunday night was dreary. It was more than physical fatigue. The day's work had been very easy, and he'd had very few customers. It was the tiredness of being alone, and being lonely. It was the tiredness of day after day. It was a tiredness of self, a tiredness that was himself, and the weight of himself.

—Heavy, heavy hangs over thy head.

Words from a boyhood game, tin-tin.

—What shall the owner do to redeem it?

More words from the same game.

Heavy, heavy hangs life over thy head and what shall thou do to redeem it, thy life?

It was that kind of tiredness that hung, heavy, heavy, over an unredeemed life.

And Eddie's mind began to splash away, a rain of melancholy

in a fog of pity. The dreary night changed as he did. He began to see in it a somber beauty which had pressed down to close all the horizon and, as it were, bring the world's end, and life's end, very close to him. The darkness was so silent that it was all softness, and softly, with a softness that itself was beauty, the darkness had come over the dead gray of the damply depressing day, and had seeped over all the meanness of the streets where yesterday's life was forgotten.

He heard an express approach in a rising volume of sound that became a hurtling roaring and grinding. It passed on, headed downtown. He saw few heads inside, against the lighted windows.

A moment or so afterward, his own train came, a Jackson Park local. Eddie boarded it, taking a seat by the window. There were about eight other passengers, all men, and seven of them were colored. Their faces were dull with work and tiredness, and they wore old suits and overalls. Often, Eddie saw a similar human sight, the stupor or boredom of men going home from work at night. He felt what he saw, and wanted to sink away into the same state. His wish was like a sentimental yearning.

Just to sink through stupor and into sleep, sleep, "sore labour's bath" forgetting, forgetful sleep, the sleep that dreams are made of.

The car swayed and jerked.

Eddie opened his briefcase and drew out a copy of *The Picture of Dorian Gray* in a green leather-bound edition.

The local elevated train seemed to creep along, slowly, but compensating with loudness for its lack of speed. He was very conscious of the wheels going around on the track below him. He read with difficulty, and thought of putting the book away and of merely sitting in tired reverie and daydreams and thoughts, or even dozing off, until he should reach 58th Street. So much of his boyhood and of his life was associated with the elevated trains and even the various stations, and streets for which the stations were named. It was like pressure within him to remember.

The conductor, who was sitting in the other car, in front of the last one where Eddie sat reading, called out "Thirty-fifth Street" in a loud voice of rasped boredom. A Negro got off, a tall, young fellow wearing blue overalls. There was a hard, surly expression in his eyes. He walked slowly out of the car and as though his body were full of angry power ready to be unleashed.

Eddie didn't notice him. His eyes were fixed closely on the pages of Oscar Wilde's novel. He didn't see the young Negro, and yet he did see and sense the big fellow. There was a quick movement of the eyes, and an almost physical sensation of hostility and danger.

He had always, since his early childhood, been seeing, sensing, absorbing more than he could realize. But his sensibilities had begun to grow, to increase and multiply.

And he was learning, sometimes, to do more than one thing at a time. He'd read that Julius Caesar had been able to do that. You had to, or you couldn't get anywhere in the world. You couldn't learn very much, you couldn't become important and have the knowledge to do many things.

Eddie still, at that time, was lacking in awareness of how much awareness he had. Then, too, his memory was far beyond what he had ever thought it to be. Only slowly was he learning about his faculty to remember. He'd had no need to know how much he remembered, prior to his studying. Memory, sensibility, all traits and faculties, function with use and purpose.

And thus, Eddie didn't see, yet he did see the big, surly young Negro worker in overalls give him a glance of hostility and anger, as he walked out of the car.

And he went on reading Oscar Wilde's *The Picture of Dorian Gray*.

The train moved on.

The Picture of Dorian Gray wasn't gripping him, but he didn't have the word for what it did, the drip of nostalgia, a dainty, yellow flower, dithering the ladies, a flower, flowers, and the style—was Wilde's style an example of fine writing, beautiful writing? Eddie couldn't say for sure. But one reason why he was reading Oscar Wilde's book was to find the answer to such a question, to learn about good, fine, beautiful writing. He guessed that was one reason why he tried to crowd into his reading some novels and stories. There were books he ought to read, and he wanted some day to write, although this wasn't the only ambition he had. But if he didn't read the best novels, how could he learn to write himself?

The Oscar Wilde novel wasn't exciting him; the idea of the story, the character, the writing, it all didn't come together to pull him up into the world of a book and hold him so enthralled that he was almost a prisoner of what he was reading.

The style—he wasn't able to describe what it was in the style that bothered him. He kept changing his mind, blowing hot and cold about the book. It was clever, with a clever idea all right. Maybe he did like it a lot.

But Eddie almost rode past 58th Street. He rushed out of the train with an opened and flapping briefcase. He had become interested in the novel, and had forgotten where he was.

The rain had stopped, and a gray fog was drifting over the roofs of 58th Street. Immediately in front of the elevated station, there were the low roofs of the line of stores on the north side of the street. But there were three-story buildings along Calumet Avenue, and seen from the rear, they were lost in a vague, indistinct evenness of shape. The scattering of lights from windows made no pattern, and were repulsed by darkness and fog. They were soulless signals without meaning, which in "dizzy foolishness" of hope became blunted, lost lights in the foggy futility of a darkness that was sterile to the impotent moon.

He closed his briefcase, looked about and thought:

—Oh, the sterile beauty of the world.

II

He awoke while the dawn was vague and gray, and his eyes and muscles were as heavy as the stupor of his sleep.

There was a jarring insistency in the ringing of the alarm clock.

Listlessly, he sat up, reached to his right, and shut off the clock. He heard his grandmother in the kitchen. She was up and getting his breakfast. He was dreary with half-awakeness. But the

The Silence of History

day was new. The dawn was new. The morning was as new and young as any morning had ever been or ever would be.

He got out of bed as though his body were heavy with iron chains. He wanted to groan and moan because of how he felt. But he knew that in a few moments he would be awake and alert, and it would be as though he could never be tired, never be old, as though he and the world would never die.

He heard his grandmother calling to him about his breakfast as he walked into the bathroom, near his own room, and on the left of the hall between the front and back of the apartment.

He began singing in a low and pitchless voice: *There's a Long, Long Trail A-Winding*. Until the day that he would be marching down the long, long trail that was winding—the long, long trail of life—the long, long trail of his life? Would it be long?

And maybe it would be, long, long and winding, and would it be lonely?

Today, he hoped that Thelma . . .

And maybe he would have to be going down that long and winding, long trail alone, and lonely.

Men marched the long, long, winding trail of history.

And every day the world began. Every dawn was new, and the trail, the winding trail was a long one through all of the new dawns of the new days.

Eddie was wide awake when he went out into the kitchen for breakfast.

His thoughts had turned prosaic. It was just another day of the same grind, wasn't it, another day to go on, as he had been during all of those other days.

The dawn was growing lighter beyond the curtained glass of the kitchen door.

"It's going to be a nice day, son. Here's your coffee, drink it down and I'll have your bacon and eggs in a jiffy."

She served him the coffee, and he smelled the aroma, and he smelled the bacon which she had sizzling in a frying pan on the stove.

"All of the years of me life that I got up to cook breakfast, gettin' me men off with the buses, and gettin' me children off to school and to work, and now here I am gettin' me grandson off to be a scholar," she said, standing over the stove.

More than fifty, more than fifty-five years ago, she had stood over a stove, early in the morning, earlier than now.

His emotion was formless; it did not have the shape of an idea, of meaning. He didn't know what to think of this fact.

"And even before I married Pa, there was me lady in Brooklyn, and a fine lady she was, oh, she was a lady, a big, fine lady, Mrs. Barton. The day I heard tell in the bakery that Mr. Lincoln was shot, sure I was up early, and makin' breakfast for Mrs. Barton, and Mr. Barton, before he went to his office. The day they shot Mr. Lincoln. Sure he must have been a good man, wasn't he, Edward?"

"Yes."

But Eddie didn't know for sure and certain, not on the basis of the facts. He had to read more, learn more facts and what they meant, because he couldn't go by what he used to believe and think. He guessed that Abraham Lincoln must have been a great man, but he'd have to wait until he knew what he thought of Lincoln. It was the same with many men in history, many problems and issues and ideas.

"Here's your breakfast, son, now eat it while it's hot. Do you want more coffee?"

"Yes, Mother," he said softly.

She took his cup and saucer. As he began eating the bacon and eggs, he saw that the sun was coming out.

It would be another good day. He wanted to daydream of the girl Thelma, and he wanted his dreams all to come true, today.

"Oh, and sometimes, it's like it wasn't but yesterday that I walked into the bakery in Brooklyn for me lady, and I was hearing that Mr. Lincoln was shot dead, killed by a bullet, and sure it's almost all the years of me life," his grandmother said, talking to herself as much as to him.

All of the years of a life, going day by day. The time when dreams could come true wasn't very long. Not long, not too long, Eddie thought as he ate fast. He had to hurry and be ready, as usual, when Peter whistled for him.

Chapter Nineteen

I

Since he was ten years old, Eddie had been living in a world that was war-corrupted, and the effects upon people were so many, so varied, yet usually went unrealized for what they were. It was like breathing in befouled air when the atmosphere is thought to be pure.

The effects of the War, which had begun back in 1914, had been more indirect than direct, and many had been taken for granted as natural and normal and not to be given a first, let alone a second, thought. Far away, miles away from Chicago, in Europe, killing had gone on, day after day, and when one side killed, it was noble, while it was beastly and Hunnish when the other side did the same thing. The lies of propaganda had been deliberately spread, by word of mouth and in print. The increased brutality and the decreased value of human life became a fact of the history of the world during these years of Eddie's. He had daydreamed of killing Germans heroically, mowing them down with a machine gun, surprising them by crawling through the shell-torn darkness, the holes, craters, the black shrouded earth of No-Man's Land, and of blowing up machine-gun nests of Germans who were stationed in front of the enemy trenches, in advance posts established in shell holes.

The Germans were indistinct of feature in his mind, difficult to picture except as the German soldiers in some of the moving pictures he had seen, usually on a Friday night, a Saturday or a Sunday afternoon. He had, after the American Declaration of War, gone to a public library, a half mile or so from home, and had taken out two books, one about the rape and devastation of Belgium, and the other about the movies. The author of the first was a Catholic priest, and he had written even of women as old as his grandmother being raped by the invading German soldiers. And this had all happened because the Beast of Berlin, Kaiser Bill, wanted to conquer the world. Once his army of Huns, like the barbarians of Genghis Khan, had beaten France and England, should this happen, the Kaiser would send his beasts across the Atlantic Ocean to invade the United States, and if we were unprepared, ours would be the fate of poor little Catholic Belgium, of France and of England. He had imagined this happening, and of America becoming war-torn, shell-torn, with ruins in villages, towns, and cities, until Americans, who were the bravest of the brave, the most heroic of all heroes, would rally, perhaps in a stand at Chicago, making of his own city a bigger and more heroic Verdun, and the hero, and saviour of Chicago would be none other than Eddie Ryan.

On a November day, after darkness had set in with its decisive finality, Eddie had been alone with his sister Clara and grandmother. That had been in 1917. It was one of those nights when your life stopped still, and you studied, daydreamed, did what best you could to pass the time until the next morning's sunshine would be all over the streets and all over everything. And the sunshine would be in your heart, and you would be full of those dreams you dared not admit to anyone, those dreams you hugged to yourself. Those dreams of yourself as a hero, brave, fearless, as heroic as any hero who ever lived, more heroic than all of the heroes who had ever been. And his heroism was all for Gertrude Dawson, whom he was too shy to speak to, to say "Hello" to, and of whom he thought, day after day.

Brooding and dreamy, Eddie sat at the back-parlor table where he was later to study about the War, to study until his weariness was almost like an invasion of death into his body and mind and he would drag himself to bed, like a drunk who could not control his movements.

The Silence of History

Eddie was trying to get his homework done, but something was happening to him, something that he couldn't really, exactly say what it was, but he knew what it was. It was school and everything. Some of the kids didn't want to play with him, and had ditched him twice last week, and he didn't like Sister Martha, the seventh- and eight-grade teacher, but that wasn't what he meant, because you shouldn't dislike a nun, a nun was holy; it was she who didn't like him, and thought he was a roughneck, and that he wasn't good for anything but fighting. Once, twice, three times, he didn't care how many times a week it was, she made him kneel up in front of the room by the window-side of the seventh- and eighth-grade classroom, and she'd say to him:

—Edward Ryan, you'll come to a bad end.

He was only thirteen, too young to be a soldier and fight in France. Would the War last long enough for him to become a soldier?

Opening his books was like he couldn't say what it was like. He didn't want to, and what was the use?

But he knew that there was a use, all right. Much as a kid hated it, he had to get some education.

Eddie sat, glumly slumped in a chair, staring at his school books as though he might be looking at castor oil that he must take. He hated homework; he hated going to school; he hated sitting from nine to twelve, and from one to three in the classroom. And Sister Martha.

No, he couldn't hate her, because she was a nun.

Did he have to like her?

The way she screamed, and socked kids around, almost none of the kids liked her, Mauling Martha, that's what they called her.

But why had she taken such a dislike to him? He didn't act worse than others.

Eddie didn't pursue his question.

—Edward Ryan, the only thing you're good for is fighting.

That was a kind of compliment, or should be, in the eyes of the kids. But why did his own bunch ditch him?

He wished they'd move to a new neighborhood.

And he wished that he was old enough to join the Army, or the Marines, the Devil Dogs. He could be a hero, come back to Chicago, and then, he'd be in all of his glory, all right. He thought of this, but his mood did not change any, except that he was beginning to feel awful restless. Then, he heard the excited shouts of "Extra Papers" from the streets, down toward the corner. The shouts came nearer, and were louder, and he could make out something about the first youths killed in France.

Eddie got the money from his grandmother, pulled a sweater over his head, and bolted out of the front door, leaving it open so he could get right back in again. He was almost holding his breath, it was like that, like he was holding his breath to find out what the news was all about, if the news was terrible and if the Germans were beating the Americans. His fear was like a gun ready to go off, to be fired inside him. And there was already in him the accumulated fear of over three years of the menace of the German goosesteppers, of the danger they were to America, and of the possibility that they would win in Europe, conquer it, and come over here to America to conquer it, the way that they had conquered Belgium. He thumped down the front steps of the building, almost losing his balance and pitching down head first.

Eddie was panicky, and on the verge of giving way to that panic. He was not sure about anything pertaining to the War, and he did not believe in his own confidence that America couldn't be beaten. His sureness was seriously cracked in the formulations of himself and of what America meant to him and was in his own heart.

Six or seven men, with voices as rough and tough as they were loud, were shouting, hollering the news of the first Yanks, the first Americans, to be killed fighting Germany. He didn't know where these men came from. Their faces weren't familiar, and he wasn't certain that he'd ever seen them before. They were selling the Extra Edition. The volume of loudness of their voices made them tough and mean in his eyes.

They kept bellowing out the cries of "Extra Papers."

A couple of kids of his own age were also shouting and, like the men, they had a bundle of newspapers under their arms.

The Silence of History

Eddie didn't know the kids, either. These men and the boys were like an invasion of South Park Avenue.

A kid walked up the steps to the front porch of the building, pulling out a copy of the newspapers which he was selling, and the strange boy's voice, itself, was a bullying intimidation.

"Extree papee?"

Eddie was in a trance. It was sort of like being awake and watching himself standing asleep on his feet. He was conscious, and was helpless; the shouts were reverberating in his head like wild, loud explosions of sound in a canyon.

The scene was as familiar as months of reseeing could produce familiarity. It was like a picture seen so frequently that he could see it in his mind with his eyes closed. South Park Avenue. Pole lights from lampposts. The darkened solidity of shrubbery, wire-fenced tennis courts, and trees which bounded the park, and absorbed the end of daylight. The low whizz of wind through the branches of the trees and the leafless shrubbery. The shadowed irregularity and remoteness of the regular lines of the wire-fencing of the tennis courts. The sidewalk and street with the usual play of light and shadow upon it. The immediate outside world of his home, which was almost a part of home, as sunken into a possessed permanence of objects as was the kitchen of the flat in which they lived. It was a small fragment of street, of the city, of the world, which was a continuation of home, and the sudden noisy invasion of the men and kids selling Extra editions of the newspapers was a penetration from the far-off world, practically, into his own home.

The excitement was brief. Eddie gave the kid a dime and put his hand out for change. He became tense with unhappy determination and hurt resolution. The kid looked tough; he was a little bigger than Eddie; the kid wore old clothes which, in themselves, showed the signs that he was poor. Eddie quickly sensed that the kid would try to cheat him by running off with the dime. And the kid had been about to scurry around, jump down the front stairs, and rush on to sell more of the Extra papers. But when Eddie put out his hand for change, the kid's face went blank, and looked strange in the shadowed light. Eddie was afraid that he would have to fight. He stiffened in nervous readiness. The kid moved his lips to talk, but said nothing. He dug a dirty hand into his pocket, fished out a nickel, handed it to Eddie, and bolted down the stairs, almost losing his balance and falling on his face on the cement.

Eddie looked at the big headlines. The first American soldiers had been killed in France.

The pack was moving away, toward 59th Street, and the din which they made was gradually declining.

Eddie was glum with a cheated feeling of false excitement. And, yes, he was sad, very sad. He looked at the bare trees across the street. Darkness. They were killed, the first ones, American soldiers.

He looked at the sky, far away, at the bare trees again, at the sky again, at the sidewalk. He was sad because he didn't like death.

Eddie went back upstairs, silently saying a prayer for the souls of the first American soldiers killed in action in France.

II

There was no wartime suffering in Eddie's family, nor did he know of any in the neighborhood. Among older fellows who joined up, only one died, a tough kid named Laughing Jack. He had played indoor ball in the Washington Park playground, but Eddie knew nothing about his family; he lived some blocks away, around Garfield Boulevard and Wentworth Avenue. He went into the Navy, and was washed overboard in a storm: he drowned.

Nor was there any violence except that a couple of Jewish kids, regarded as sissies, were clouted, but not savagely. Kids dug trenches and played war, and there were signs in windows which indicated that Liberty Bonds had been bought. Before America got in, there was a popular song, *I Didn't Raise My Boy to Be a Soldier*, but after the American Declaration of War, it was not heard much, and one of the wartime songs was *America, Here's My Boy*. One night, a Liberty Bond Drive meeting was held in a vacant lot, and many songs were sung. Eddie liked that. In the newspapers, he read about the Huns, and the Kaiser, and,

The Silence of History

now and then, about repressions in America. He didn't pay much attention to these, and didn't understand them except as pro-German sabotage and helping Kaiser Bill. There were other war songs, and the one that he liked best of all was *Over There*. It made him want to march and to be a Yank, also, going over, over there, a youth who would be brave and devil-may-care, and who would be rum-tum-tumming everywhere, over there.

He daydreamed a lot of going over, Over There, and of becoming a hero, winning medals, and he'd imagine his name being in the Chicago newspapers, and everyone who knew him reading of his feats.

But there was always a fear behind such daydreams, because he could be killed, and he didn't want to die young. He would imagine himself as a hero who escaped death, but that was only imagining and supposing, and if he really were in the Army and fighting, he could be one of those who went first, maybe before he could even get over-the-top.

He couldn't think of the War, the fighting going on Over There, without, also, thinking of death.

And he did not think of death in general, but as of individuals dying, soldiers, young fellows who had grown up from being kids like himself and the kids he knew. And, also, of ball players, his heroes, such as Eddie Collins, or men like his Uncle Larry, or even his older brother John, who was seventeen when war was declared against Imperial Germany. And he thought of himself. If he were older and a Sammy Boy, or a doughboy, he'd face death himself, and he could never be a hero except at the risk of his life. Would he be a coward? He was afraid that he was afraid, because he didn't want to die so young, before he had really ever lived. This thought grew in his mind all through the last phase of the War, after the United States had gone in. His dreams of heroism became very concrete and sometimes very troubling and distressing.

The worst thing you could be was yellow, a yellowbelly. He didn't want to be that, a coward, to be afraid. He was worried about his own courage, and, often, he would sink into the doldrums, because he didn't think that he had courage. No kid had ever called him "yellow," and he hadn't run away from fights, if he saw that he must fight. But he didn't like fighting, and didn't go about picking fights. He was supposed to be one of the best fighters in the neighborhood, and he guessed that he was. He was good, and he was a good boxer, and when he'd put on boxing gloves, he'd been good, even with kids ten or fifteen pounds heavier than himself. He had had a couple of hard fights, and he'd beaten kids bigger and heavier than himself. When he fought or boxed, he never lost his head, but always knew what he was doing, and was quick to find a weakness or an opening and take advantage of it. None of the kids noticed how he would use his dukes, and they didn't know that he thought and watched as he did. They merely said that Eddie Ryan could fight, and that Ed Ryan was tough, or don't tangle with that goof, Ryan, he can fight and use his dukes, or something like that.

So, he wasn't considered yellow, and while he was razzed and kidded a lot, kids didn't pick fights with him, they didn't challenge him and say, Come on, fight! Once or twice, bigger kids had kept razzing him, he had lost his temper, but not by getting sore as hell, and blindly swinging or yelling. Instead he had become cold and hard with a fury of determination, and once he had picked up a rock and thrown it straight at the head of the big kid who was picking on him. But Eddie had to be provoked until he felt desperately driven before he would act in this way.

Eddie wanted to have courage, and could only see this in terms of risk and fighting. The idea of sacrifice was involved, also, because of the teachings and story of the Church, as he had learned these in school. The early Christian martyrs had given up their lives for the faith, and this was one of the noblest acts that could be performed. The martyrs were with the Communion of Saints in Heaven, and they had been during their long timeless minute of eternity ever since the days when they had been living and breathing as he was. Because they were Christians, they had been seized by the pagan soldiers of pagan Rome, and after being cast into dungeons, they were brought into the grounds of the Coliseum, and to make a circus for the Roman populace, they were torn to pieces and eaten by hungry lions.

The Silence of History

When Eddie thought of these martyrs, he would shudder, especially if he were in bed in darkness at night. The lion, roaring monarch of the jungle, taking one leap, with big and sharp bared teeth, grinding into the helpless flesh of a Christian, perhaps a girl, a beautiful girl, tearing her flesh off and eating it. To imagine this sacrifice, with the Romans cheering, would make him quiver and shudder in such helplessness that he'd have a moment of sick horror. The bite of the bared teeth, how much had that hurt? And those who had been put to death by the sword, or crucified, and Christ, Our Lord, suffering on the Way to Calvary, the Stations of the Cross, carrying His heavy cross, with the mobs of people jeering and spitting at Him, spitting into His face, falling under the weight of the Cross, and then nailed to that Cross, and dying for three hours on Mount Calvary, while the sun was lost in a Blackness that came over the world, and the crown of thorns pierced into His head, and once He had cried out:

My God, My God! Why hast thou forsaken me?

And again He had said:

Father, forgive them, for they know not what they do.

The idea of martyrdom and sacrifice was planted in Eddie's thoughts. A soldier was a martyr of his country. If he died, it was a glorious death, wasn't it? Eddie was willing to die as a soldier, but he feared that he would be afraid in the actual trial of battle. He was a kid, still, and he didn't have to face a soldier's trial of courage, and maybe he wouldn't have to, because the German Huns would be licked before he was old enough to become a soldier. But the War remained in his daydreams; he lived with it in imagination.

This was part of Eddie's private, internal life, a dream life of imagination, which was, also, punctuated by questions, thoughts, small stretches of reasoning, but these were left hanging in air, as it were.

All of this drifted in and out of his mind, and left seeds that were slow-growing and would not be manifest for years to come. He was a boy like other boys, wanting to run and play, and interested in games and fun, movies, spinning his top, playing marbles, doing what the other kids did. He was more shy and intense than most boys, and he showed a greater capacity than was noticed by anyone for being by himself, playing games alone, dreaming dreams, brooding and losing himself in his own thoughts.

It is these fancies, these chance thoughts, which are often the true preparatory and vital seeds of growth in a boy, and they were in Eddie. Here were the seeds of growth which went unsensed, the feelings which were seeds lying in a fertile darkness below the surface of his mind.

Nineteen seventeen became nineteen eighteen. He was having his worst year in grammar school, and often he couldn't study. His will lost the power of command. He was thirteen and fourteen that year, and he sulked within himself, and went to school, thinking that he hated it, but wishing for it to be different, and hoping that it would be.

At times, he would be painfully shy, awkward, and ashamed of his inability to overcome this condition. The days were slow, until they seemed to mope. He thought he was not going to pass, and was surprised when Sister Martha did pass him to the eighth grade. By the spring of 1918, there was a large American Expeditionary Force in France, and the War became a brutal slaughter. Eddie read of the course of battle in the newspapers, almost every day, and he absorbed a sense of the terribleness of the fighting. When the Second Battle of the Marne was fought, he was nervous, worried, afraid, because the Germans had begun an advance and maybe they'd win, maybe they'd beat the American doughboys. Eddie couldn't believe it but he did fear that it might happen. The war stories often emphasized how many Germans had been killed, and, of course, they were Germans, Huns, and they had to be beaten, or else we'd be beaten and they'd come over here, and invade us with the aim of doing the same to us that they had to Belgium.

But they had been killed, and they'd never go home, never see their wives and children, never go to work at whatever work they did before the War, never breathe again. They were Germans, but weren't they men? They got killed fighting for the

The Silence of History

Kaiser and the Fatherland, *Deutschland Ueber Alles*. But it was still so, they had been killed.

And they killed Americans, too, as well as French Poilus, and British Tommies, and Scots. They had lost the Second Battle of the Marne, and the Americans had helped save France at Château-Thierry, and the Americans were killing Germans and advancing.

But it had seemed that the War would go on for a long time. It had passed its fourth year. He'd be going at eighteen, younger if he could get in, and fighting.

He didn't want to die so young.

He'd be afraid.

He'd be going and he'd pray to God not to let him be a coward, he'd go as soon as he could get in, he'd go, he'd be a Sammy Boy, Over There, Over There, he'd go over, he'd be going over, and he wouldn't be coming back until it was over, Over There. And maybe, he wouldn't be coming back.

War was Hell, just as General Sherman said.

He was afraid his father, or Uncle Dick, or his brother would be drafted, and would go over and not come back.

—I'm not going Over There and be a hero, killing my fellow man, Uncle Larry said at supper one night.

—Don't let them take you, Larry, Grandmother said, in a heat of anger.

—Uncle Sam decides, we don't, Uncle Dick said.

—Not Uncle Sam, Jesus Christ, Uncle Larry said.

—Tell 'em, Larry, Grandmother said.

—They're not getting me to kill my fellow man. Let them read *The Sermon on the Mount* and the *Ten Commandments*. Doesn't it say *Thou Shalt Not Kill?* Uncle Larry asked.

—It's different—it's war, and a soldier of his country . . .

—Soldier, my ass, Uncle Larry said, interrupting Uncle Dick.

—But there's the draft from eighteen to forty-five, Eddie said.

—Let the drafters and the grafters go. Not me. I wouldn't register for their draft to kill my fellow man, Uncle Larry said.

There was silence at the table, the silence of fear as if they had to be silent, or they didn't know what would happen.

—Good for you, Larry, Grandmother said.

—They can put you in jail, Uncle Dick said.
—Let them goddamn try, Uncle Larry said.
—Good for you, Larry, if they come around here, I'll close the door in their faces, Grandmother said.
—They can't touch me. I did nothing criminal. What in hell have I got to do with them warriors and war lords, the Kaiser, and kings? This is America, and I'm staying here in America, minding my own business, Uncle Larry said.
—Bully for you, Larry, Grandmother said.

An expression of angry triumph came upon Uncle Larry's weak face.

Eddie was afraid that his Uncle Larry would be caught, and sent to jail, but he did not condemn him. But Uncle Larry wasn't caught or picked up.

The end of the war in November of 1918 brought the outburst of the Armistice Day celebrations, but Eddie didn't see them; he only read of what had happened in the newspapers. These outbursts came as a total surprise to him. He had not known, had not suspected that people felt that way, and had that much steam to let off in celebrating the news of Peace and Victory.

Fourteen years old, Eddie was living in the promise of the future, of growing up and he was happier at school with a different nun teaching him in the eighth grade.

III

The War had lasted from July 28, 1914, to November 11, 1918. Out of the killing, the many sufferings of millions, new hope had sprung from hearts tormented even beyond the edges of sadness and sorrow. The world grew into the bright dawn of the end of "the war to end all wars," the war "to make the world safe for democracy." It was a dawn of the spirit that came upon the world when Eddie Ryan was still yet a boy. It was morning in history, and Eddie had not grown beyond the full morning of his own life.

When the War ended, it became history to Eddie, history finished and ready to be written into a history book for kids to study one day, as he had studied the Spanish-American and Civil

The Silence of History

Wars, and other American wars. And he was relieved, quietly happy in his unspoken self, the self of Eddie Ryan that only he knew and was in communication with. He couldn't grow up to be a hero in khaki, and to return home with medals on his chest. But, also, he wouldn't end up in Flanders Field, where poppies bloomed in the springtime. He'd never seen a poppy, not to his knowledge, but poppies blooming in Flanders Field were beautiful and sad, a field of flowers growing over an earth once soaked with blood, over graves, over the greatness of yesterday's heroism. He would not have a Sammy Boy's "rendezvous with destiny." Of course, he had some "Rendezvous with Destiny," on big-league ball diamonds. But not one which would end with a smashing zing of a bullet heard, possibly by buddies, and penetrating his forehead before, or as he heard the *zing*.

But the War was over, and Old Glory had not been hauled down. America still had not lost a war. American pride and confidence sank into him in new doses. With the War over, he began feeling a nostalgia for it, and for Over There, wishing that he had been one of the heroes who with devil-may-care and double-dare courage had helped to achieve history. This, however, was a matter of moments. He was growing, hoping, and the War was memory and history. History was what had happened—in History. It was what was happening that was important.

And History was closed. It was finished. He knew what some of History meant, including the War. Wars ended, and they were settled by the winner getting the aims of the war, and that was the way it happened. President Wilson went to Paris to the Peace Conference, and he guessed the President would know what to say, and what ought to be done. He was the greatest President we had had, since Abraham Lincoln, and he'd given America the Federal Reserve System, hadn't he?

And the days passed, happier than the years before, because he liked school. His thoughts were on school, and fun, and Gertrude Dawson, and the coming baseball season, and Sister Josephine who treated him as a favorite and understood him, and playing, seeing movies once or twice a week, and on high school, and on whatever the passing day brought. He dreamed and hoped, and he dreamed and hoped to get Gertrude as his girl, and he spent his happiest year in St. Basil's, which he had entered in 1915. By spring, 1919, the War had receded in Eddie's memory and his thoughts of it were getting less and less frequent.

The War was over. The Bolsheviks in Russia, with men named Lenin and Trotsky running them, were running the country, but they were having trouble and ought to be getting the boot any day.

The War was History.

Eddie was fifteen, and he found interest in what, for him, was today, and not yesterday and yesterday's history.

Things were the same as they had been, pretty much, and more than pretty much. There had been an unbroken continuity of life. With the War over, everything would go on as before. The ballplayers would be back, those who had been in the service, and the others who went into shipyards. Older fellows, like Dick Ennis, who was an usher in church, and was quite a dresser and dated lots of girls, he was back, passing the collection at Sunday Mass. There was another new priest, Father Leclos, from a French family in the neighborhood. They owned a milk business. He was almost like a sissy, but he was pretty good with kids, and interested in baseball, and he only seemed like a sissy, he wasn't really one. He was young and popular, delivered good sermons and said his Masses fast. Father Waters was the other priest, and he was also popular.

But the changes of face and person on a small scale were not disruptions of the continuity of living from day-to-day, in the parish and neighborhood.

And Eddie, as so many others, had not felt or smelled the stinging, foul wounds of the War in late 1918 and early 1919, not to their knowledge.

The War was history, but only in the sense of the end of the actions upon the battlefield. The War was but feebly known history as far as the consequences were felt and the meanings known. Spiritually, the War had filled the world with slow-working poisons. It had disrupted the patterns of life of nations and individuals, and with shot and shell, with a violent bloody surgery

The Silence of History

of historical action, a blind man's surgery, it had operated upon the society of mankind. What had been was no more. The dead would not awaken. And the living could not live as they had before the time when the dead had been awake.

The world was dislocated, and people did not know what they saw, nor their own hearts and minds as they believed they did. The world had been filled with lies, with false propaganda, with the result of twisted, contrived, and often tormented thoughts. Life had been made very cheap, and truth even cheaper. High hopes and ideals had crashed and smashed. Bitter despair, cynicism, and brutality had been given force and momentum. The world was very sick. History was sick.

But to Eddie Ryan, this was all unknown. Nor was it any different to others in his neighborhood, and in other neighborhoods and cities. And there was forgetfulness in energy, in many escapes. With the end of the War, there were outbursts of gaiety.

However, Eddie Ryan's life did not follow any such pattern. He was too young, and too full of innocence and dreams. He graduated, and played ball all summer, and hoped to see Gertrude Dawson and have her become his sweetheart. He wasn't a man and didn't think that he was. Men ran the world, and the men who ran America had to run it pretty good, because it was America, God's country, although a lot of the politicians were crooks and grafters, so many people said, and a lot of their talk was just "political talk" which, like "newspaper talk," was something pretty common that he'd heard used very often, almost since he could remember.

Eddie had shifted back from thinking of war heroism to the heroism and fame and glory of the baseball diamond. But, nevertheless, he remembered the heroism of the War, especially of Château-Thierry, and of the Marines, the Devil Dogs. He remembered the War, from time to time, but he was occupied in his interests and dreams of the moment, of his time and years and situation, and he accepted what he read and was told as a matter of course. When there was danger, he worried, but hoped for the best, and for an end to the danger. There was much to interest him, and feed his dreams, and he was a boy who might often be and was, in fact, unhappy, but he was rarely bored or without something to do. Just as he had invented a game of war and battle with playing cards, and had spent hours alone playing this game, with atlas, pencil, and paper before him, so did he do likewise with two baseball games his Uncle Dick had bought him, one in 1913, and the other in 1916. He played big-league games by himself, keeping the score in composition books. This he had used to do with his older brother, Johnny. John had grown bored with games, or pretended to be, and didn't come around as much, even though in 1918, his father had been promoted at the Express Company, and the Ryans had been able to move, for the first time, to a flat with an inside toilet and steam heat, and to have a gas stove for cooking, and electricity for lighting the home, instead of kerosene lamps, and stoves burning wood and coal. The family lived a block and a half away on Calumet Avenue. But John, who had gone to high school for almost two years, had been put to work by his father. He had a job with the Express Company, in an office having something to do with the wagons. That was all Eddie knew about the job at the time, except that it was good pay, eighty-five dollars a month. Eventually, he learned that John had begun as a clerk, or telephone clerk, in the Wagon Department, just as Eddie later did.

After Jack Dempsey knocked out Jess Willard at Toledo, Ohio, on July 4, 1919, Eddie made up a prize fight game with playing cards, similar to the war game, and he used to play this, imagining that Jack Dempsey was, more or less, himself; he kept the record of all the fights. And he set out to have Dempsey fight every heavyweight of even slight importance. Sometimes he stacked the cards for Dempsey to win.

He could play games like this for hours when he was alone, and by the summer of 1919, he had been doing so for about six years. He had a football game, and a basketball game, and with these he did likewise. But always, he wanted to play whole schedules, seasons, successive seasons of his favorite team, imagining what was happening as he played. He pretended that this was all real, and that he was in the center of it all, a player, manager, or all of the players, the sports writers, um-

The Silence of History

pires, and referees, and the eyes of history and the future, seeing this happening, these games and conquests and victories, and both being there and in them, involved, and at the same time being people in the future, posterity, hearing about these games and records, being told of them, so that he was telling himself from present to future, and he was making the present, recording it, and he was the posterity of tomorrow for whom it was recorded.

Eddie was happier than he knew, especially for a lonely boy, and he had become that with an implanted depth of loneliness within himself. Loneliness is a phenomenon of size, the size of the world. And this size is different from person to person, but in a subjective inner sense. The size of the world inside a human being's head is a determinant of loneliness, of its extent, of its very existence in the sense of emotions being existent. All people are not lonely. Time as well as space are crushed into too much smallness for them to be lonely in time and in space. Loneliness is a condition of imagination. When time and space are big, and we find ourselves lonely within their extent and complexity, then we are living with our imagination. And only by feeding it can we ease the burden of loneliness. But achieving that, we gain a happiness.

This Eddie did in his growing boyhood and adolescence. Thus was he happier than it seemed. For he counted, as is often done, the hours of unappeased imagination. During these times, Eddie could do little to keep his confidence and pride in himself, and to ease the shame he felt about whatever seemed to be bothering him. Often, it was loneliness. He wasn't liked, or he had been ignored, or he was looked down upon, or he wasn't thought to be as good or his folks weren't as good or as rich as they might be, and he wasn't wanted and popular, and maybe he was talked about and laughed at behind his back. If only he could be different, and more like other kids, he'd feel better and happier. If only the real Eddie Ryan could be known by someone, by Gertrude Dawson, then he wouldn't have such times when he was hurt. He wanted to be different persons, and to achieve different destinations at one or another time, but he was always living with this in mind, in the back of his mind.

Like older Americans, he didn't think that he, himself, that other people, that Chicago, that America, and that the world was going to change the way it did change, or that the changes were already going on, as day by day the time between the disappearing present and November 11, the day of the Armistice, was getting slowly greater.

There would always be crosses, white crosses, in France, Over There, Somewhere in France, the Argonne Forest, Chemin des Dames, Arras, Château-Thierry. They would never know life, the white crosses, silent, and sad as the sad brooding of November, the crosses of the dead who died to make that very brooding day, November 11, 1918, and all the days to come, his days. Their name was on a white cross, more silent now than the silent night. And the name of Eddie Ryan?

Somewhere, Over There in the days beyond and to come, there was going to be his name, Eddie Ryan. So he thought on that November 11. In his saddened loneliness, he could not help it, he became suddenly happy. He was happy in the gloom of twilight which had begun to sink into the park as he walked about. He felt happy, but he remained sad. Many had gone West. Gone West where the gloom was more silent than the twilight, more silent than those white crosses, gone West into the silence of the Armistice with eternity.

A cross, a name, a memory, like a ray of twilight in the darkness, a ray of twilight silent but forever falling through the darkness, that was name and fame. To go West in twilight, or in no light, that was fame or oblivion.

He wandered about, and the sun fell behind the West, beyond and beyond in a hazy sky, and dim twilight seemed to leave shadows of all the years that were and had been across hard earth and over withered grass. The twilight and shadows were lonely, and he was more than lonely, because he was happy with thoughts of tomorrow's sun. Today, and yesterday and yesterdays that had gone West since the first yesterday, these were all part of the twilight that never was smothered out in dark oblivion. There was a twilight reserved for those who earned it and that was what you left when you went falling through the world, going West where there were no more sounds than

The Silence of History

among the crosses Over There. He was more than lonely because he carried the twilight of the white crosses, and the twilight of many yesterdays when those who died and never died were as he was at twilight on November 11, 1918. The world always waited for the sun, and the sun left the glow, lovely as a prayer, lovely as love, rest over the black night of all the dead of all of history.

He was waiting for tomorrow and sunshine while he walked in the twilight that hid the sun of the dead yesterdays that never died because they left the faded but glowing, grayed softness of the light which darkness never strangled. That was memory and fame. And that was what Eddie Ryan wanted.

And it grew dark on November 11, 1918. Eddie went home to supper.

"Sure and I'll say me rosary for those poor boys that'll never see their mother again," his grandmother said at dinner.

"Oh, such a celebration," Aunt Jenny said.

"It was time—damned well time they stopped. God and Jesus Christ never meant us to kill our fellow men," Uncle Larry declared.

"But they were Germans, see what they did," Clara said.

"Who's been givin' you that stuff?" Uncle Larry asked with hurt sharpness, looking across the table at his niece.

"Everybody says it—it's been in the papers, so many times," Clara answered.

"It's peace now—let's not quarrel. We can have an armistice, too, and think of the good to come," Uncle Dick said. "And now, things will get back to normal. That's what we need."

"They sure better. It's like New Year's Eve celebration in the Loop right now," Aunt Jenny said.

"You don't say?" said Eddie's grandmother.

It was dark outside. The day was gone now. Eddie had a sour stomach and a feeling that a holiday was ending, and that it was like New Year's Eve, only bigger, and that maybe more than just a year had ended. But he didn't think further of this; he sat and ate, slowly for a change. He had a feeling that was kind of strange to him; he didn't know what it was.

Then, as he jabbed a fork into a piece of pork chop, he guessed that he was sad.

He didn't want to be sad. But he just was. He was very sad.

"Larry, Larry, will they hang the Kaiser now?" the grandmother asked.

"Is that all you can think about, hanging? Can't you think of something happy, on the good side of life?" Uncle Larry wanted to know.

"I'll hang him if they let me," the grandmother stated. "All those men killed. Indeed I will, if they'll let me."

"I don't want to hear any talk of death and all that stuff. I want to hear talk of the good things and the happiness of life," Uncle Larry said, sulking.

"I guess we'll have to leave things to President Wilson," Uncle Dick said. "Smart man, he has a vocabulary of over five or fifteen thousand words. Some fellow was telling me, its one of the next largest vocabularies after Shakespeare."

"Christ didn't need no fifteen thousand words to say *Love Thy neighbor*," Uncle Larry said.

"Ah, give me a rope, and I'll word me your words, a rope, that'll be me words," the grandmother insisted.

"Nobody said a word about the supper I cooked after working hard all day, getting up at six this morning," Aunt Jenny complained threateningly.

"It was elegant, swellelegant, Princess," Uncle Dick quickly said.

"Rope is cheap. Ah, but what do I care. I'm an old woman and me bones are old, and I should be carin' if they're fightin' and killin', and killin' and fightin', but mind me words—because I say a rope is cheap."

"Cripes, let's be happy, there's peace on earth," Uncle Larry said.

Eddie feared that one of the regular rows at the dinner table would start, and these distressed him very much. But none broke out. Supper on that evening of November 11, 1918, passed in nervous family peacefulness.

After supper, Eddie was moody and restless. The night was

The Silence of History

historic. He tried to think of this, of what it meant and of how he felt, but he kept telling himself that the night was historic. He played checkers with his uncles, successively, and won two out of three games from each of them, and then, he played solitaire for about a half hour. He began yawning and was sleepy. He went to bed. The day was gone. The war was over. He slept well, and when he awoke, he forgot what he had dreamed of during the night.

He went to school. His boy's life continued as before, far away from *Over There*.

Chapter Twenty

I

There was an old song that he had used to hear and used to play on the Victrola when he was a little boy, *Genevieve.* The Victrola was almost fifteen years old now, and it was scratched and needed new varnish, and he never played it, but his grandmother still did. She'd sometimes sit alone in the parlor, playing records, especially Irish songs sung by John McCormack, the famous Irish tenor. John McCormack and Enrico Caruso were the two great singers at the time the Victrola was bought for a hundred dollars, when he was a boy of seven, and Caruso was supposed to be the greatest singer in the world. Caruso was dead now.

He'd used to like to hear Caruso sing, and McCormack also. Caruso sang Italian opera, and he wasn't able, of course, to understand a word of the songs, but he'd liked to hear them. So did his grandmother, and when he was a kid, before they'd moved to the 58th Street neighborhood, he'd used to play the Caruso and McCormack records for her, and for himself. They would both sit, listening, the boy and the little old grandmother, with her hair still brown and thick, and her quick brown eyes lost in a dream. She'd be remembering the past, he'd guessed, remembering Ireland and her girlhood there. She must have been remembering love, the feelings she had, and this used to make Eddie feel a sadness for her, and a sadness to think that people had to grow old. It was the sadness of being hurt by what used to be and never could be, the sadness of

The Silence of History 313

the dreams that came true and of the dreams that had never come true in days gone by. And that song, *Genevieve,* had always been sad for him in the same way. Yes, *the days may come, the days may go, but Genevieve,* and the days had come, the days had gone, the days were coming, the days were going, and there was no *Genevieve,* no love, for him, except in his daydreaming, and in his wishes, his hopes, his expectations. *But Genevieve, my Genevieve,* he had no Genevieve. And why, what was it in him?

Eddie was asking himself the same question that he'd asked himself many times, and for many years now.

Walking across Washington Park alone in the morning sunshine, the question came again, suggested by his thoughts and memories, and by Thelma Carson. Singing *Genevieve* silently to himself, he thought of her, and wished that her name were Genevieve.

Eddie was going to classes alone because Peter had pulled a muscle in his leg, practicing in track, and couldn't walk the distance to campus. Once again, it was a wonderful morning, a soft morning, shining clean and new across the world and upon Eddie. He quoted Tennyson:

In the spring a young man's fancy lightly turns to thought of love.

But this line did not awaken the nerves of emotion in Eddie. It went flat and dead as he thought of it. His feelings, his reaching out, his pathos of need and readiness to become exalted, all this was not his fancy lightly turning to thoughts of love in the springtime, just because it was the springtime and he was a young man.

Eddie read poetry and listened to songs and music as though he were living them. And he had found so much frustration and disappointment in daydreaming, and in songs and poetry about love and his hopes of love, that he had become self-conscious about himself concerning Thelma Carson.

He was hoping. He was ready to see her in a trance of beauty, to imagine her as Shelley would have, or Keats, if he only had their lyric gifts; he was ready to love her as an image of perfect beauty, to feel worshipful and adoring, but this readiness was latent in him, a seed that had not burst up to flame like a field of flowers in spring days. He had:

　. . . eyes to wonder . . .

But lacked

　. . . tongue to praise.

And, thus, he felt

　. . . in the chronicle of wasted time

He walked on, hearing the chattering, chirping sparrows, the song of birds in trees, robins, he guessed, the croak of a frog from the lagoon, hearing the silent loudness of the morning, still wet with dew, like some song of love and life that the sun had sung for ages and would sing for ages to come.

The sun and dawn, the sun when it made such mornings, and such days, was never silent, never lost in the vanity of history.

He thought this and he wanted to think it, and he doubted his thought.

All this wasn't real, fully real; it was desire above and beyond desire.

No, it wasn't real, and it was still the feeling within him that he associated with love. It was what he wanted to be real, real in some way.

He wanted it, once again, to be real, as he walked to school, alone, carrying his overladen briefcase which had become worn with daily use.

Coming out of the park, he again thought of "the chronicle of wasted time," and of the song, *Genevieve*.

II

On that morning, he got back his term paper on Mussolini and Fascism, with an A and the comment:

The Silence of History

Excellent. Incisive logic, and the promise of psychological insight. Far above average, and if such work is continued, the results in a few years can be brilliant.

Mr. Torman had given Eddie a look of recognition when he handed back the ten-page paper, and had said, in his overcultivated voice:

"Very good. You tear Odon Por apart."

"I didn't agree with him."

"That's very evident," Mr. Torman told him, with traces of a smile on his sharp and intelligent face.

"Castor oil isn't the river of time," Eddie said.

Mr. Torman laughed, somewhat down in his throat, and with a subtle irony, a superior laugh of one who had studied and knew the subject and was laughing with an equal at all the hogwash that was currently being ladled out about it. Eddie caught this, and was complimented into speechlessness. He was so below Mr. Torman's level, but he had been reading Mr. Torman's doctoral thesis on propaganda during the World War, and he wanted to tell the instructor that he was doing so, but he was shy; and he didn't want to seem to be buttering up Mr. Torman.

Eddie stood by the desk with nothing more to say. Most of the students had left the classroom. The remaining ones and Mr. Torman left. Eddie followed them.

He was lonely and quietly triumphant. The term paper on Fascism and Mussolini, and Mr. Torman's reaction to it, the praise and grade which he'd received, all this was involved in one more victory, heading him forward. If he could share this, speak of it and be admired for it, by Thelma Carson!

Nervously, he swept his eyes about the crowd of students in front of Cobb Hall; he sought a face and a smile, someone with whom to talk a moment or two. He saw no such face, and walked off, taking quick steps because he didn't want anyone noticing him to suspect that he was as lonely as he was. But he quickly slowed down his pace. He walked at a diagonal angle toward Mandel Hall for the Public Speaking class.

Eddie was struggling with himself because he was ill-at-ease. His pride of triumph and progress, marked by Mr. Torman's praise of his term paper, had been like vapor in the indolent and lazy loveliness of the morning, and he was hurt, as though with guilt, because of what he didn't have, and feared that he couldn't get because there must be something wrong with him, something clumsy, awkward, goofy.

It was Thelma Carson. She was on his mind. He'd never get anywhere if he didn't try, and he was struggling with himself because he thought that he ought to try today, that is, he ought to ask her if he might walk home with her. What if he should be turned down?

Better than ask, only say to her after class that he was going in her direction. He didn't have to say why. It could be to meet someone. It could be on a date.

If she said why not walk with her, what would he talk about? This, more than being turned down, troubled him.

He didn't know her.

He didn't know girls.

Eddie reached Mandel Hall, and, taking a seat alone, he started to read his term paper. But he only read a couple of sentences when class began.

He was impatient for the next class, and his impatience seemed to be turning into determination, even desperation. He had to sit and listen to others make speeches. He wouldn't be called upon.

And few of the members of the class ever had anything much to say.

Why couldn't it be he, and not some other guy, who was the one she'd fall for, no, he meant love.

The summer was coming, and hadn't he earned some fun? And she was beautiful. He had a distant look in his eyes. She was in his mind's eye.

—There is no forever, he suddenly told himself, while a lean, blond, gray-suited student named Carlton Lawrence was giving a four-minute speech on why the American Way of Life was the best way of life man had ever thought up.

III

Professor Arnold R. Carson enjoyed a reputation as a distinguished historian and teacher, and he was liked by those who knew him for his sweetness, simplicity, and honesty. His had been the life of a scholar, and he was one of the men of his time who had engaged himself in the quest for the truth. Born in North Carolina, his family had moved to Virginia, and his father, a lawyer, had left a farm of several hundred acres. Arnold's father was a man of character, which was manifested in the intellectual contradictions and seeming contradictions of his thinking, his career, and his conduct. He had served as an officer with Stonewall Jackson, and had been a brave soldier, and while he had fought courageously, often heading cavalry charges, and undergoing heartbreaking experiences of defeat before the cavalry of General Sheridan, he had only high regard for Mr. Lincoln. He had been influenced by the ideas and writings of Jefferson and Calhoun, and was cynical and harsh in his law practice, but was otherwise idealistic. His influence was, probably, the determining one in the decision of his son, Arnold, to become a scholar, a historian. Arnold went to the University of Virginia and then took postgraduate work at the University of Chicago. Also, he studied two years in Germany, and read the German historians, especially Ranke. But he concerned himself almost exclusively with American history, and, in the main, with the South. He made studies of the Old or pre-Civil War South which were broad in scope, for they encompassed cultural trends and attitudes, as well as politics and economics. An ideal and a faith motivated Arnold Carson, so that his works led to an affirmation, not of the Old South alone, but of the Union, of America. And this faith and ideal were to be found in the blessings of liberty, gained and preserved under conditions of slow and orderly progress. A mild, conservative but humanistic social Darwinism was wedded to this conception, and he quoted John Fiske with almost undue frequency. Although he did not possess a great style, he wrote with some charm as well as clarity, and his books, monographs, and articles were honestly felt, and truthfully expressed. There was no greatness, no brilliance to Arnold Carson's work, but there was sincerity which was generated by an inner force, and serious readers, especially colleagues, could not miss the value and persistence of these qualities.

He studied the culture of a period, as well as its politics and economy, and he saw in the ensemble a striving toward something beyond, which was, in his view, liberty and truth. His books stimulated others to pursue further studies, and won the praise of professors, and then of the president of Princeton University, Woodrow Wilson.

Arnold Carson married young, while he was a postgraduate student, and his bride, small and pretty, was strong of mind and feeling, gracious, and devoted to him. She was intelligent, but any opportunity for a career on her part was sacrificed to his fame, as well as to family happiness and the welfare of the children, Thelma and her brother, John Thomas, who was a year older than Thelma. Thelma and John Thomas grew up together, in an environment which both later came to regard as sheltered. They played much together as children, and were close in spirit, sharing their thoughts and hopes, as well as their dissatisfaction with their lives. These, while vague, were recurrent. Neither of them wanted to be so sheltered, and they often felt deprived of the happiness and fun of less protected children. As they reached their college years, they both feared that they had missed most of the joy and freedom of childhood. Their childhood had not been severe and restrained, and their parents had not forbidden them from playing with children whose parents might be, or might seem to be, from the hoi polloi. They were different and set apart. Both were precocious, especially John Thomas, and they avoided the games most kids play. Thelma was quickly bored with the idea of dolls and doll houses, or so she thought. And John Thomas did not relish the rough-and-tumble of boys, and he turned out to be very poor at most games. They both wanted to play, but some affected attitude which they had gradually acquired held them back from doing what they secretly wished to do,

The Silence of History

and could even be on pins-and-needles to do. The parents gave them some encouragement, but when neither responded, they were allowed to follow their own bent. Children could develop young, and show more intelligence than teachers and the adult world, as a whole, realized. That was the father's view, which he frequently stated. Children were human beings, not brats and nuisances, to be seen and not heard.

The family life of the Carsons was social and cultivated. Distinguished men and women, mostly in academic life, but also poets, novelists, artists, political men, and others of note and attainments came to the Carson home, and the conversation was always serious and frequently very intelligent. There was a sense of purpose and dedication in the life of Professor Arnold Carson, which affected the atmosphere of the family home, and was continuously, day by day, influencing the brother and sister, in ways indirect and direct. Purpose, itself, is a positive factor in a family life, and is reflected in the attitudes toward living, society, and the world which children absorb. When the father lives for a high and self-respecting purpose, and one which is virtually cast in the light of eternity, the days can become both laden with meaning and immediately meaningless, because the real meaning is postponed into the future, and even into eternity. Life becomes rich and poor in paradoxical simultaneity. The present is saturated with purpose, yet it is a purpose that leads on and on and on. The future absorbs the unfulfilled present, which is too gravid, too saturated. One can be living in order to live, until living for living is a confusion of mind and senses.

And furthermore, the Carson home lay upon the greatness of man's past. The future, for which the family so frequently seemed to be living, was already lodged in the greatness of the great men of the past. The dead breathed life through today into a distant tomorrow, and reality borrowed much from before and after. The dead were more living than the living. Who could be Thomas Jefferson, or near to him in caliber? By understanding his greatness, there would be a greatness in some tomorrow perhaps.

Thelma and John Thomas came to feel, and sometimes

strongly, that they were living *before* and *after,* and not in the present, but they did not think of it in such a way. The present was less than the past, beneath it. The future would be the past, in some way made in the future. *Before* them, the great had lived; *after* them, posterity would think something that almost no one could judge now, except possibly a few. This something that would be thought *After*, and about what was *Before*, involved judging, but it would also be something more than judging. And, in consequence, something was lacking in the lives of both of the Carson children as they grew up. There was a deficiency, but not in themselves or their parents; it was in the very present, itself. They were only children, and, then, adolescents. They could not live off a past greater than the present; they could not find in the superiority of yesterday that which they needed in their own growing todays. They were still too young to gain what their father could from history, and from his work as a scholar and teacher of history. Nor could they grow up joyfully for posterity and the days when they would be dead, and the glory and greatness of Thomas Jefferson, and of Woodrow Wilson, would gain a fullness and resplendency in the progress of truth and a high morality of truth. But neither could know what caused this almost vaporized dissatisfaction, their doubt about their own value and the value of all who were alive and of their years, their precocious understanding without joy and sorrow, without the spraying warmth and softening of their own emotions. The University atmosphere, so permeating their family life, was the space of air surrounding the rigid solemnity of gray, Gothic beauty, embodied in stone which weighed unending tons, which was wrought into a setting where today could be but the tribute paid to yesterday. The dissatisfactions which accumulated for both of them were soothed and quieted by the pleasantness of their lives, and the happiness which was in their home and was nourished by their mother as well as their father. Mrs. Carson was a pretty little woman who managed all of the practical details of the family, and spread cheerfulness and love through the days.

Then, they were growing up.

The Silence of History

Revolt was not simmering in them; it slept a sleep of pseudo-peace, troubled only by strange dreams which were forgotten with each new dawn.

John Thomas early decided to follow in his father's path. He would study history, write history, teach history. He became bookish at an early age, as did Thelma, and in school he was, by far and with obvious certainty, the best pupil in his class. His gentleness, intellectual seriousness, timidity, and superiority did offend the great majority of the other boys and girls and made him unpopular, not because he was aggressively competitive, but because he was seeking to get and to hold what the other children did in play and in their whole lives. That was the world, a full and safe entry into reality, the losing of the growing self in reality.

With Thelma, it was the same. She, also, sought the world, the reality of the minutes which passed, and the reality that was to be the minutes of her future as she grew. She, more than John Thomas, was imbued with some set attitude of superiority. It was a part of what she was. She saw herself as superior. She had been growing that way. She looked up to her father and brother, was quiet, sensitive, a pretty girl with the promise of beauty in her features and growing form, and father, mother, and brother all encouraged her to read, to think, to write poems, and to be one of the happy unit of their home.

But because Professor Carson was a historian, and because he was so plunged into the South and knew such contrasts and changes, the conversation at the family table, and in the evenings, especially after the War, touched much on politics and economics. Thelma didn't respond to this, much as she wished to. She went looking for herself, and read novels and short stories, many by nineteenth-century Russians, and one day, she came upon Nietzsche's *The Antichrist*, translated by H. L. Mencken. She felt more than she understood of this work, because she had not read any of the German philosophers. But *The Antichrist* was a strong wind of the present to her, like a strong wind off Lake Michigan that rose above the wild pounding waves, scratching off the breaking whitecaps, splashing sprays of water like sprays of life on anyone nearby. And the wind swept over and beyond the break, with a wild new song, full of the strength of life. And on that she could let it all fill her and give her the wild, wild strength of the wild, wild wind.

The dead, like Thomas Jefferson, lay in graves and vaults, but the wind could never be buried, and today it was the wild, wild wind, just as it had been in all the days of the years of the century gone by. It was wild and young and she was young, and wild with being young. The wind sang a howling wildness of power. The wind was like Antichrist.

Her father would often read aloud from the Bible, using the King James version, and he tried to encourage his children to do likewise. They were Presbyterians, but not churchly and sanctimonious.

Thelma didn't like the Bible; she didn't like to hear it read; it would bore her or irritate her. And when her father read passages aloud, at the table after dinner, or on other occasions, she usually slipped away to her own room, where she read Nietzche's *The Antichrist* or nineteenth- and early twentieth-century Russian fiction including writings of Chekhov and Gorky and other literature. Her bright room, lined with books and with pictures of her father, her mother, her grandparents, Woodrow Wilson, General Lee, Lord Byron, and George Washington, was her virginal sanctuary, but as she read, she would sometimes suddenly have the crazy wish for the wind to smash the windows, knock her down, turn into a god and violate her maidenliness with the strength of a god.

That was bad, a "sin." No, there was no "sin," but only life and yes, and Death and "no." She was young, and she wanted to say "yes" to life, and "Yes," and "Yes," and she would become more excited than dreamy, with her body sometimes trembling to be made strong by a strong violation.

A sense of the present, without any lack or deficiency, would be ready to quiver in all of her nerves, and she would believe that any minute, any second, such a present would come. Growing more calm, Thelma would be resolute, knowing that

The Silence of History

the moment she awaited would come, and she would become like a woman of the gods, a woman of destiny.

But she was too young; she was only a girl. She must wait, even though she might grow impatient to the degree of resentfulness, still, she must wait. In a few more moments, Thelma would relish in gladness her home, her girlhood, her virginity, her protected life. She could be safe and yet know that her day would come when safety would be ripped out of her life, and she would begin to be and to live as a woman, one who would become as remembered with familiarity as the very names she heard mentioned, downstairs at dinner or in the front room. The day was not yet to be, and she could go on as she was, but with a happiness all her own because she knew that she waited for her day, when all values would be transformed and she would live in the world of men who were of the present, of this day, of tomorrow, men who were the supreme makers of history, Antichrists. The dead were dead. And she would not live with the shadows of graves stretching too far, stretching over her like the night did when she lay herself down to sleep.

An illusion, a belief, a feeling stronger than the most certain indication, spoke in a silent, wordless confidence to her, and told her that she was not living for the dead, for Samson and Rebecca, and the daughters of Ashkelon, and the wives of Solomon, all Jews, too, and she had nothing against the Jews, except that their women had the wrong values, and from the daughters of Solomon they had become like Mrs. Berger, the fat wife of Mr. Berger, who owned the butcher shop on 57th Street, near Harper. Oh, how she always wanted to be young and beautiful, with a strong beauty, Helen and Cleopatra and . . . . and Thelma Carson.

There would be the soft face of her father, reading, or his voice, and that of her mother, her lovely mother, and of John Thomas. She might hear a remark, or a passage from the Bible.

"Without railroads, what would the North have done? Particularly when General McClellan was a textbook Napoleon?"

"We would have lost, Dad?" from her brother.

"And how. We're both, the gray and the blue, the Union. What magnificence of simplicity in the words:

"'With malice toward none, with charity for all . . .'"

Or she might hear her father read in a voice which changed, changed almost into a poet's voice; perhaps he would be reading from the Psalms, which were among his most favored parts of the Bible. Perhaps:

Let integrity and uprightness preserve me; for I wait on Thee.
Redeem Israel, O God, of all his troubles.

She sometimes wanted to think of redemption, but she knew, after reading *The Antichrist*, that there must be a revolution. She would think:

". . . from today? Transvaluation of all Values! . . ."

This was life, life in her day, and the Bible was the past. She was finding the ideas of the way to life and she would find Life, Life, just as life would find her. But the Russians told her of life as nothing else did. She could find *The Lower Depths* of Gorky, and *Lisa* of Turgenev, and *Family Happiness* of Tolstoy, and *After the Theatre* of Chekhov, and feel it as close and immediate, as right now, almost happening today, more than she could feel anything happening, say, on 57th Street.

Thelma found the University far more to her liking than U. High, which she'd attended, and which was run by the University and had sometimes been called "Jun High." But this was only natural. She was becoming a beautiful young woman, and yet she remained a girl in the flower of her first bodily bloom.

Thelma was not without shyness, but her reticence and good manners, learned, like second nature, from her parents, gave an impression of much greater shyness than was actually true. Her virginity, her young years, and her pride were sources of this shyness. And she was a girl of very limited experience and contact with the youth of her own generation. As a freshman, she was pitched, for the first time, among a variety of young students which was much too extended to be reduced to classifiable types. During her first freshman quarters, beginning

The Silence of History

in the fall of 1925, Thelma encountered a number, girls as well as male students, to whom she had little and even nothing to say. She realized that many were from backgrounds—racially, religiously, geographically, socially—of which she had only heard in talk that didn't interest her. As such, they were curiosities, young people whom she never expected to see as actual persons in the flesh, talking in English, laughing, acting very normal and like others, those who were recognizable and quickly identifiable. Those who seemed strange usually dressed like and looked somewhat like those who didn't. In a number of instances, the names alone were cause for her feeling of strangeness. It would be an Irish, Polish, or Italian name mentioned in a classroom, a name that suggested an origin different from her own.

But this reaction was superficial and of short duration. She came readily to accept, in her own mind, and as a fact, the bigger world that existed beyond what she had known. It was an exciting fact, and the University was but a suggestion of the real big world of doing and of Destiny. The thought and belief—for it was both—persisted that she would be a Woman of Destiny. But she held back from this bigger world, even in thought. She didn't know it, and she did not want, really, to know a large part of it; she looked down with aloofness at vast slices of life. She believed, not in life, life in the raw, but in literature, which was higher than life, was a criticism of life, and was life at its best, its most beautiful, its topmost peaks.

Thelma was majoring in English; her brother had selected History, as he had decided long before his matriculation.

They both had decided on what they wanted to do in life. John Thomas would be a historian, a scholar, and a teacher; Thelma would write. And both of them believed that they were doing what they had decided upon doing. Rather than conceit, this belief was like a reflex of their lives, and the environment in which their lives had been unfolding. They did not know what failure was; they did not understand it. They did not encompass defeat within their imagination. It was not that they were full of premature vanities about themselves and their abilities;

they were not saturated with a sense of themselves as superior, as vastly better than their contemporaries. Rather, they knew a little world which seemed to be superior. They belonged to this little world. It was in them; they were in it.

The University was part of that world, its center, its heart, and they were of the University and in it, before they matriculated as students. They remained in the same world while they went to classes, day-after-day. At the beginning of their campus lives, they both knew more members of the faculty than they did students, and they knew professors, instructors, and others officially associated with the University better than they were likely to know most students whom they would meet. There was no mystery, no wonder to college for them. Nor was there fear about themselves. And from the beginning, they had done well.

Thelma was in her second year when she took Miss Patrick's course in English Composition, 103. Thelma had delayed taking English Composition 103 until the spring quarter. It would be better, she had reasoned, to wait until she wanted to write, and, even more than that, until she wanted an easy course, for her to take English Composition 103. She could get her parents, her brother, and family friends on the faculty to read something that she wrote or would write, and she was even in correspondence with H. L. Mencken, who would read anything good she might write, and consider it for publication. Thelma had written to Mencken after having read *The Antichrist*, while she'd still been in high school. Mencken had answered, briefly but promptly, and most graciously, like a true gentleman. She wrote occasional letters, and, regularly, received the same kind of replies which, usually, were dictated on the same day that her letters were received. The great editor urged her to write, and assured her that she had a definite talent for writing of a certain delicacy of perception.

Such praise was virtually equivalent to a guarantee of eventual publication, and of a future. Her thrill, on first reading the editor's letter, had been one of slow-reaction, and, then, of being lifted up through air. She had looked down, to see and tell herself that she, Thelma Carson, was coming up to where

The Silence of History

she, Thelma Carson, was risen. It was as though she had seen the future, knew it, and could look back into her present and watch herself moving into her future.

Her family, of course, had been more than delighted; they had all been proud of Thelma, but they were not surprised, for they believed that she would show talent as well as be a beautiful young woman. The pride of the family was restrained by conventions and the good manners which all four of the Carsons had, as though by instinct.

And love and respect, long expressed and satisfied, is frequently, in fact usually, restrained. That was not only the way the Carsons were together, but, what they regarded as the way people should behave in a family. The response of quiet and underplayed pride was belief and feeling expressed in direct reaction. It afforded some moments of happiness added to all of the ones which had been theirs through the years. It was a continuation of the process of accumulation of the blessings of life.

"Isn't that a wonderful letter, Thelma," her mother said.

"Why that's fine, Thelma," her father told her, after reading the letter from Mencken; and he gave her a paternal kiss on the forehead and took her hand and patted it.

"I won't say 'Sis' or 'Sister,' I'll say Young Lady, you are not going to walk slowly through the golden gates, you will waft into the Promised Land, meaning you'll be flying to Fame without wings, swimming through the sun without burn, no Swinburne, no swallow, but sweller for swallow," her brother said.

He laughed.

"That was like a stutter of congratulation, Thelma, but it was almost clever, and it was meant to be a peripatetic, beating-around-the-bush way of going through the straight path and saying, Good, *Benum, beno, beni,* you know what I mean. Good going, girl."

Thelma liked the near-nonsense of her brother's compliment, because it was not nonsense and it meant that he was as pleased as he could be at any good fortune of his own. It was looney, brotherly sign language.

"It's only encouragement, nothing more, but I'm happy. I'll try to live up to the value of such encouragement," she said.

"You will, no doubt," the father said, adding a German phrase which none of them understood, with jocular preciousness.

This was a scene before dinner as a day was fading, and a beam of sunlight, mellowed as though to purity of perfection, fell through the window upon the white tablecloth and the warm wine-red of the old rug.

And this was suggestive of the pattern and slowly flowing current of their family life. It was happy, but in the sense of contentment. Thelma and John Thomas both missed something, wanted something, expected something in the future that they had never as yet known. They thought of "something" by word, because they looked ahead to what was new. Thelma was still under the spell of Nietzsche in her first college days, and she wanted to wish that the Antichrist would come, but she knew that this was a poetic idea, not a truly real one. But she looked ahead and, on occasions of irregular frequency, she imagined that the new tomorrow, or the tomorrow of tomorrows, would be the world just as though the Antichrist had come. The transvaluation of values would be effected, real . . . something, a something that had happened. The values of life, those were the ones that would be transvalued. She believed in this, in part of it, in some of the things, or something. She believed, that meant, she didn't—she disbelieved in sin. Sin, of course, as it was defined in church, and in the Bible, and by most people. In this matter, she knew what she meant, and often thought of it, walking to school, or to Harper Library, or at other times. She meant sex. When sex reared its ugly head, that wasn't sin, it wasn't rearing an ugly head, and she knew she wanted it, the experience, the flight, so to speak, the flight of transvaluing, the, oh, the poetry and wonder of Nietzsche's writing and what it did to her, only felt down there in . . . the well of herself, and not up in her brain, not above up there. Vagina, she thought, was an unpleasant, unpoetic word.

However, for Thelma, sex could not be a hope, an expectation, was not the goal of all transvaluation, not sex alone. Of course she was going to become a writer, she was going to try to, that she had decided upon, and fame, success, that was something, and more than something, because she knew what fame, success, doing things in literature meant. But still, there was something undefined, undescribed to herself, not yet experienced, that she wanted, expected, counted upon, and she was waiting for the day when it would happen, when it would be real to her Destiny. And then she would know what she meant, and had been becoming all along, for a long time; something was being a *femme fatale*. But just not that with this one, or that one, because she meant a *femme fatale* who would be remembered, and that was like never growing old. She would like to write as beautifully as Elinor Wylie did in *Jennifer Lorn*, and she would like to be as beautiful a rose in autumn as a rose was beautiful in the spring. That was something, and she would, if she could, she could, yes, yes, she could sketch something by her "own sweet skill."

She knew and she didn't know what her something was. But yes, yes, her "own sweet skill!"

Thelma believed in all of this, and in herself, but she was within a protected sphere of life; she did not know the unprotected world.

IV

Thelma believed herself to be more mature than most of the young male students on campus, and she felt older, mentally, in her thinking, as well as in experience. She had met so many older and distinguished men at her home, and had heard so much talk and discussion, and she could only have this feeling about herself as being older than most of the young fellows on campus. Now and then, she had been drawn to one or another, but she pressed down the attraction, and told herself that she wasn't really interested, not seriously. He was too young, the particular student toward whom she was drawn. He hadn't read as much as she, and wasn't interested in literature, or he wasn't seriously enough interested, or he didn't have any personality to speak of, or there wasn't any real attraction in him, after all, and it had been an imaginary attraction.

She had decided thus, and several times. There had been a number of dates and encounters, walks in Jackson Park, shows, meetings in the Coffee Shop of the Reynolds Club, automobile rides with students who had autos, and invitations to her own home. They, the fellows, were young males who were looking, making the chase in the manner of college boys of the times. And Thelma was ripened with readiness to be looked for and chased, after the manner of college girls and young women of the same times.

She had been kissed, and she had even necked a little, which was hot kissing, passionate or, perhaps, she thought, sensuous osculation. That was, she hadn't fallen in love; she hadn't surrendered her virginity. Such was what "serious" connoted for Thelma. None of this had yet been serious, and "serious" was her own word, the one she used when she thought or merely happened to remember one or another date or encounter. But she hadn't gone behind the meanings of the word for herself, and discovered whether or not she was afraid to let any "seriousness" occur.

Shouldn't she accept the body, and the needs of the body, if she were going to live by the ideas of Nietzsche? Was *The Antichrist* just another book?

Thelma had just put these questions to herself, but she hadn't pressed any awareness out of herself. And she didn't need to answer these questions in her mind. She was answering them by protecting herself with seriousness. She was not ready to be unconventional in conduct, but only in mind. *The Antichrist* was, so to speak, the dreaming fulfillment of her serious, sleeping self, of her idea and image of herself, and of the future for that self, and not merely of physical desires, or of acting against convention. She was in her protected world, and it was the source of what confidence she possessed in her abilities and her future. She was not ready to emerge from her protected position, and she couldn't take that risk. She couldn't physiologically or psychologically. A strong desire to take the risk would take hold of her, only to be met by resistance

The Silence of History

that couldn't be overcome. This was the substance of Thelma's caution, but not as she herself precisely viewed it. Thelma was not seeking any serious experience; to give herself to any man was serious. She could be serious if she met someone about whom, well, someone who made her serious, just had that kind of effect on her.

But she didn't expect to meet anyone who would make her serious, not for a while. She wanted to get her college education, and presumed she was probably selfish. She wanted her life and privacy, especially the privacy of her mind. Seriousness might violate her privacy. And she didn't meet anyone who was worth that.

There were times when it could be so easy to give in, because that was what it was, giving in to men, and giving in to herself. There were times when it was easy and she wanted to give in. She wanted to find out. She wanted to know. She wanted to be able to think of herself as one of those young girls, young women, who knew. There were times when she just wanted to, she wanted to with her body, with passion ready to escape control and burn her into a loss of all her will power, but she did not lose her self-control, which was her will.

However, Thelma had only rarely desired to such a degree. More often, her self-control, curiosity, and interest in books carried young men along without any rising sex on their part.

Within a couple of days of the beginning of the spring quarter in 1926, Thelma was becoming bored in the English Composition 103 class of Miss Patrick. She quickly knew that she was too much advanced beyond the class, and decided that it could only be boring for her, and what was the use of that, letting herself be held in such a class like a bird in a cage? Why not change to some other course? She still had time. And she decided to switch to another course, but the next morning, she had changed her decision; she'd stay on in English Comp. 103; a dull, easy course would be good for the spring, and especially since she was certain that she'd get an A for the course.

The students all seemed to her to be—not stupid, she couldn't tell that so early—but average, and non-literary.

—Thelma, since when is this any different?

Life had to be that way. Most people had to be average. Who would do all the boring kinds of work if the whole human race were above average, and even above that?

There were no free spirits in English Comp. 103. Thelma was not thinking of herself, but of the other students.

They looked, oh, they looked like a filled-cup classroom. Some of the girls were pretty virgins, like the one with the large, rather large breasts and blond bobbed hair. She looked healthy as butter, newly churned butter. Yes, a pretty girl. And no, she didn't envy the butter beauty. Thick like butter. And the way they looked at her B beauty.

They meant the male students. And it didn't make her jealous. Enough of them made eyes at her.

There were other good-looking and pretty girls; among the men, some, quite a fair number at that, were definitely good-looking, or that plus, and a few even had sex appeal.

Sex appeal!

No, she didn't like the phrase.

Animal instinct appeal?

Better. Yes, better, definitely.

The reason she was taking English Comp. 103 was not that of being initiated into that appeal. Her aim was credit, not discredit. Yet, some male animal magnetism didn't spoil a class, not for her. This wasn't the reason she was staying in the class, though, and the appeal of these boys, three or four of them, was comparative. Her heart didn't speed up.

She had noticed him as one of many. Just one of the students in whom Thelma had seen and felt animal magnetism, physical appeal.

She had noticed him as one of many. Just one of the students in class.

The mornings were turned over and another April was torn away from the wall.

Thelma happened to turn across the room toward Eddie as he answered a question. His voice was soft, soft and sincere. And he had curly hair. He seemed so eager, and he was intelligent, she guessed; he sounded intelligent.

She had become aware of Eddie, and then he of her. Thelma

The Silence of History

grew more interested in Eddie as the days went by, but it was her curiosity, rather than an emotional interest.

He was Irish. Ryan. What were the Irish like? Really like, together in their homes and by themselves? Of course, they were all Catholics, with a few exceptions. The Ryan boy couldn't be a free spirit, could he? She didn't think he was. Sometimes when he spoke about a composition that Miss Patrick had read aloud in the classroom, his remarks made her mad. The way he'd say:

—I don't like it; it's no good.

—It's not true.

That was what he'd said about some poor student's paper on Mussolini, the Italian.

He didn't always enlarge. He would praise sometimes by saying he liked a composition. His own, well, she couldn't say whether she liked them or not. He'd written sarcastically about Arthur Brisbane, and Babbitts, but he didn't seem to have any poetry in him.

Well, he was better than she thought, better than most of the class. That made the time go a little faster.

Eddie looked over at Thelma often, and now and then she'd return the look and smile, not always, only now and then.

Thelma's interest in Eddie was growing, but it remained the same, that of curiosity. That's what she believed true. Yes, it was, and she was convinced that she was right. However, she did manifest a growing interest in Eddie Ryan, and, more than certainly, he did in Thelma Carson.

Chapter Twenty-One

I

Thelma Carson was seventeen and Eddie Ryan was twenty-two, and they were both innocent of life. Their innocence was not a simple lack of the physical experience of sex, but of understanding, and of the fruits of experience, which is a feel and sense, an awareness which is like intuition. In their hearts, their feelings, their being, the world was wonder, life was wonder. The future was all of this wonder of the world and of life, and it was going to come true for them; it was going to be life, all of life for them. But this was hope, and only partly recognized in their own minds. It was covered over by shy shame and by all of the fears of scorn and laughter which are cast, and which they were afraid would be cast upon them by many others if they but admitted to their faith in knowing and living the astonishment of the glory of the world.

"Oh, what a Heavenly day!" Thelma said.

"Yeah," Eddie exclaimed, wanting to say more; he couldn't.

They were walking slowly across campus toward University Avenue, and Eddie writhed inwardly with the silence of distressed shyness. His mouth was dry, and he was becoming more and more self-conscious. It was his old shyness.

After class, Eddie had drifted outside after her. She had turned and smiled, showing such even and fine white teeth. There was more delicacy in her, her face and features, than he had realized.

She smiled, but it was vague.

The Silence of History

Eddie grinned, and he didn't know what it was like. He knew how he felt. That was awkward.

He had stood talking with her, saying it was a nice day, while she called the morning lovely. Nothing of much interest had happened in class, which had just ended. Miss Patrick had read several papers turned in under an assignment to do a descriptive composition. These were dull, badly written, and full of grammatical lapses. Miss Patrick had told the students that such poor writing was inexcusable, and that if they could not express themselves correctly, how could they ever hope to regard themselves as educated persons? If you didn't know your native language, what could you know? Could you know yourself, or could anyone know you, fully, as well as they might? No, she scarcely thought so.

"Those compositions were so boring, weren't they?" Thelma had asked, as they stood by the edge of a crowd of students on the sidewalk.

"Yes, they were pretty bad."

"The subjects," Thelma had remarked with curiosity and an insinuating suggestion of friendliness toward Eddie. "'My Dog,' and . . . I forget the others already."

"'How the Team Won the County Title.' That was one," Eddie said, glad of a chance to talk.

"Oh, yes. That was the mixed-up football game."

"Yeah."

Then they stood, about two feet apart, silent for a number of those seconds in which there seem to be deep hollows of words and contact.

The discomfort of his silence sharpened his self-consciousness. He must be awkward, as graceless as an elephant. He almost felt like an elephant falling down head first.

However, Eddie did not actually mean all this. He didn't know what to say, and Thelma was too close to him, too beautiful and the spring morning was like Thelma. She was in bud, and the morning was also as in bud.

She watched him with her face framed and raised in curiosity, as though she were trying to figure him out. Holding her books and a black loose-leaf notebook with both arms, Thelma looked as calm as any calmness of the scene and the late morning. Thelma didn't have time for many thoughts, because the pause of silence between them was, in fact, so brief. The tempo of her thoughts was slower than Eddie's. And she was not desperate with her own needs. There was something she liked about him, something very sweet, and something else that warned her to be careful, something which made her uncertain. Maybe there was that sweetness in him, this . . . Ryan, Edward Ryan, that was his name, and . . . Her thought was interrupted by Eddie finding his tongue.

He asked what she was doing, and where she was going now. He was surprised, a little, by his own questions, but encouraged at his escape from inarticulateness.

Thelma told him that she was going home, and he said he was going in her direction. She asked him if he didn't want to walk her home.

He was walking her home, going across campus, at the beginning of the first walk with her, as he thought. And his thoughts were hopes. Thoughts and hopes had gone so long in unfulfillment that Eddie was full of inner pathos. This strolling walk with Thelma Carson had to mean so much more than it could, and Eddie became the victim of his own wishes, was confused by his own needs, and was stricken wordless.

They strolled on, and Eddie had nothing to say.

Was she waiting for him to speak? Hell, a foolish question. His plight of silence became all the worse.

But it was the same old story with him. It had happened before.

He was tempted to despair, because he felt hopeless, hopeless about himself.

This situation, for it was such rather than a mood, had quickly sprung up in him, and he and Thelma had not taken many steps before Eddie thought it could seem impossible for so much to have transpired in his mind in the brief minutes following the end of the class hour, the meeting outside, and the mere beginning of the walk. But thoughts and feelings can come swiftly, and crowd into condensation; they can be compressed and known without all the words which designate them

The Silence of History

coming into the light of full awareness. They are linked to the experience and the many memories of past days, and we know many thoughts and feelings from our yesterdays, and do not need them to be placed in our minds, or to come in images at a particular moment when they are part of the changing structure of the lights and shadows of our consciousness. Our conditions and states of mind and mood are full of the unstated but known, and of images unseen in the eyes of many and yet before us as though they were being seen. We are an inner universe of mobility and movement. A few minutes can be full of much or of little. Eddie's minutes were full of much.

And thus, they had begun to walk and were strolling on, Thelma and Eddie. The chimes had tolled the hour, eleven o'clock. There had been those who walked by, those who strolled. Many had disappeared into the various buildings, mostly for eleven-o'clock classes. The campus atmosphere had subtly changed, and it was one of lazy-shiny islanded indolence.

Eddie thought of how rare it was for him to walk as he was, with a girl, without any pressure to hurry, and with a sad desire to be lazy, to stroll in the sunshine with her as though Time were of no consequence, and its passage was as lazy as the slowly drifting clouds.

But he had no time for this kind of life, no time in which to do with Thelma the things that others did when they were in love.

"Do you want to write?" Thelma asked him.

"Sometimes, someday, that is."

The question flattered him, but she had pronounced that "you" with a hardness of tone which jabbed like a frozen needle of sound. Thelma didn't think why she did this, but knew she had. And Eddie knew it, he knew that there was something behind the way she had given a curt emphasis to the pronoun "you."

It was like saying:

"Jenkins, do you . . ."

It didn't matter what.

"What do you want to write?" she asked, but this time, she

pronounced the "you" in her normal voice; it was a soft, quiet voice.

He must have been oversensitive, and was relieved, almost gratefully so. There was a strain in taking offense over little things. That's what he'd probably done.

"Everything," Eddie said.

Their pace had slowed, and they could have been taken for a young couple in love, or falling in love. On Eddie's face, there was much more emotion than he realized; it was expressed in the eagerness, the aliveness, the happiness playing upon his round face.

"How can you write everything?"

It was like running in good form and suddenly tripping, falling flat on your face, spilling stupidly on all fours; his feelings were like that. He had tripped over his own feet, and pitched comically into sand or dirt.

"I don't know. I've got to learn."

"Can anyone learn how to write? Be taught?"

Eddie didn't know.

"You learn—somehow."

"I don't think it can be taught."

"I'm coming to think you teach yourself."

Thelma swung her head toward him and tilted it slightly upward, since he was taller. She stared at him, momentarily, in curiosity that was like an expression of wonder, and she seemed as lovely to Eddie as any young girl ever had. Her skin had the texture of smooth softness, and her light, very light blue eyes, becoming expressive, had a pale loveliness which appeared to be looking wondrously at the first new wonder of the world.

"How can you be taught to write everything?"

Eddie had been choking up with too many feelings, too much of the effect of Thelma upon him. How could he know what to say?

"I don't know if I can write—I mean I'd like to, I want to."

"Oh!"

Her exclamation could have meant much, or nothing. He didn't know. And she had exclaimed an "Oh," because she didn't have any clear idea of him. She couldn't place him, put her finger on what he was like, or think either about his becoming able to write.

They had passed the circle in the center of the campus, and continued on the walk, with 58th Street ahead of them, beyond University Avenue.

"You're majoring in English, aren't you?"

"No, in Social Science." Eddie failed to catch the face she made, one of disappointment, superiority, and then boredom. "Yes, I plan to study law, but that's not all I want to do."

"No?" she asked, her voice and manner beginning to change, taking on a note of superiority.

He wanted to tell her of his plans and hopes, and to win her admiration because he could hope and plan so much, but he was hesitant. She might laugh, think him crazy, conceited and vain.

And suddenly, hopes were shooting up high in him, and he had plan upon plan.

"What else do you want to do?"

Thelma had forgotten his name, and struggled to recall it. But it had gone clear out of her mind. It was an Irish name. She was certain of that. But what was it?

"I want to read and know a lot, as much as I can."

"Is it all worth knowing?"

Still she couldn't remember his name. Rolan? She ran through other names while Eddie spoke.

"And I want to teach, and write, and maybe get into politics."

They had reached University Avenue. Two cars, driven by students, passed; one was an open Ford which shook and rattled. A tow-headed student, sitting by the driver, waved at Thelma.

Jealousy, fear of losing Thelma before he had her, went suddenly fluttering through his mind, taking him by surprise as might a huge and noisy dark bird, suddenly coming at him as though from nowhere.

The cars went on; they crossed the street.

Politics!

And Beauty, how could he appreciate the Beautiful?

And as Thelma so thought, Eddie's mood became very, very soft. But his mood was no softer than the late morning, than the balmy air, than the serenity of the sky, than the repose which was like a spirit that had drowsed the world. He could feel the days to come in the air and in himself, and these would be his days, and his time. He could pet and caress the world, the loveliness of the world.

She was part of the world's loveliness. And he was with her, walking her home.

He felt his hopes as the future that was to be, and that would be. It would happen, his dreams would come true, and he'd be happy. This summer, he'd be free from classes, and he could have dates and . . . He looked at Thelma from the corner of his eye.

His feelings were welling up and he took this as a sign that he was in love with her. He saw her now as the girl he loved, the girl he had lived to find for twenty-two years plus a few months.

He saw her profile and face as pensive and poetic, a face of dreams and the loveliness of the springtime.

Lovely and loveliness, these words were becoming fixed in his mind.

She was all the dreams of all the girls he had loved, that he'd thought he loved, and in her, he'd found all the hopes he'd had for all those girls. If . . .

Suddenly, it was as though he had become breathless, and would grow faint and dizzy. Eddie seemed to be breathless without losing his breath, and dizzy without dizziness. This condition came as the state caused by If . . .

If . . . The first step forward, the beginning of progress through If gained, achieved, accomplished, attained, gone through, If she should give him a date.

They crossed Woodlawn Avenue, still strolling, not talking, and Eddie was in struggle with himself to ask her.

His state was anything but unfamiliar. It was as it had been four years ago when he had needed a date, and had been stricken with fearful hesitancy about making a telephone call and asking for a date. There had been a whole series of girls, and he had phoned and failed, one after the other, in his efforts to get a date. And so often, he'd felt as he did walking on past Woodlawn

The Silence of History

Avenue with Thelma Carson, thinking that no girl could be lovelier than she was, and wanting to get a date with her, to see her and have the chance of winning her love.

They had gone more than a block without speaking, but not in a silence of common mood, not because they were linked in feelings which needed no expression. With Eddie, there was a hungering wish, and with Thelma, there was the wish to wish. For she had been wishing and hoping to know him, and to find in him, oh, to find in him, she didn't know if she had wanted to love him, because she didn't know that she wanted to love yet, and surely not some Irish boy who went kneeling before the priests whom Nietzsche condemned in such poetry of cursing, or poetic cursing. She wanted to love someone who was thinking "with a hammer" in the days of the fading "twilight of the idols," some who would be an approach to Antichrist.

No, he wasn't.

She could see that she'd been a little foolish. He was nice, serious and gentle, and even though disappointed in him, Thelma wouldn't say that she disliked him.

They had passed fraternity houses, professors' homes, and Thelma turned up toward 57th Street at Kimbark Avenue.

Eddie's conviction of his awkwardness was growing more strongly discouraging by the second. It was his second year of college, and still, couldn't he talk to a girl? But this was a self-deception that didn't deceive. There was no need to talk. The sun, the morning, spoke the eloquence of life, and that was what they would both have felt if they could. Their thoughts were like puffs of smoke, blown slowly off into some meaningless distance. They were shy with life, shy with the sun and the morning, shy with an urge to kiss and cling as though kissing and clinging to life and the sunshine of a new soaring day, when Love itself seemed to have become new in the noiseless calm of drifting clouds.

The morning spoke to itself in the recesses of themselves. That was what love seemed like, and it also seemed like an urge to rise, to float and fly, and to be as vast as the blue heavens of sun and cloud. Desire came upon them both as they strolled along, and they were suddenly overwhelmed into inarticulateness. They felt for themselves, as much as they did for each other, a caressing desire, as though they were a sun with warming rays and a warmth of finger tips and hands and lips. And they felt for the very air, for the smell and touch and sight along their way. They were dazed, as if they had suddenly awakened into a place of wonder that was almost Heaven. And while they were in a state of languorous happiness, a state of half-awake and half-dreaming ecstasy, each feared feeling more than the other. They both had been waiting so eagerly to find and know such moments that when they did and were knowing them, they were so incredulous that they couldn't find release in speech. Were they alone in a secluded spot, in Jackson or Washington Park, any place where they would have dared, then Thelma would have reached into his arms, drawn tight against him, and relaxed as though falling slightly backward, while she kissed and was kissed passionately and until it was an exciting, clinging kiss of desperate, unwavering goodness and was an aching joy of kissing and of content, of the hard and straining pressing of body to body, so that it would almost have been as if she were lying down for him and her eyes were on the sky and every hurt and pressure was the sky streaked with flashes of lightning and bolts of thunder. She even wished he could take her in the middle of the street, as though he were Antichrist! This flushed her cheeks, and she looked off at the dull red brick of a flat building.

—He can hurt me until I scream, he can drive into me like driving a spike in me, he can . . . have me and break me up.

—Ooh, I know what it is. I know, I know.

She could act. She could take her clothes off, or let him tear them off. She wanted to be ripped and hurt until it was wonderful and the sky was a merry-go-round.

But she couldn't talk.

And Eddie bulged in discomfort. Discomfort that stung, had power. He wanted to grab her, no, hold her slowly, slowly, tightly, more, more tightly, until he was having and plowing her like a field when the crazy sun skipped high and crazily in the crazy, cockeyed sky.

His breath came in jerks. Thelma and Eddie felt, but they

The Silence of History

still did not speak of what had gushed up within them, love of love itself. A few moments before their drift up Kimbark to 57th Street, they had, each, been repressed in restless confinement within the thickness of their personalities. There was more than shyness, innocence, the inexperienced feelings, and the consuming, grasping, swallowing impulse to gulp down the world if one could. It was more than love which was motivating both Eddie and Thelma, more than love that they were seeking. They couldn't know this with their inexperience of the world, of its ways, and of the struggles and processes of the world, the "outside world." They had but dim intimations of this world they were hoping and planning one day to enter, and to be part of, but these were sufficient to add to their shyness, and to sound inner warnings of hesitancy when their feelings and desires awakened into active and urgent need.

Thus they were on their walk from campus. The immediate moments, seconds passing like each of their strolling steps, were controlled, but there were pressures and images of themselves, hopes of what they wanted to become, or of what they thought they did, their whole growing selves, behind the immediate moments.

Thus, they strolled, wanting to be more in love and more sure about being in love than they were, and in each of them, but especially in Eddie, there was an intensifying desperation which threatened all self-control, and made of the need to say or to do something a source of growing, silent anguish.

They had not noticed much around them. They had been self-absorbed, or mutually absorbed, since the moment they had faced one another after the end of the morning class. Yet they had both been very sensitive to the atmosphere and its quality, the sun, the campus, and street scenes, as they had strolled along, just as any two students of opposite sex might. Thelma walked to and from home to school and had been coming and going to the campus for so long that she carried the outer scenes inside herself in fixed memories, and could, as it were, see memories as well as the fixed features, the buildings and grass and streets and sidewalks, super-numerous, small details. Eddie was so used to city streets that he didn't notice, or rather, didn't think he noticed, many of the random details of streets and buildings, nor many of the strangers whom he saw for a moment on the streets. Life was awake; the world was awake, and they were as awake as life and the world. This was more or less how they wanted to feel, and how they did, to a far greater extent than they were able to realize.

They turned the corner at 57th. Across the street was the old dull building of St. Hilda's, a Catholic high school for girls. Eddie remembered St. Hilda girls who had gone to parties and dances a few years back, that is in 1923 and 1924, and he asked himself, what would these girls think if they saw him now, walking with Thelma Carson? Mary Rourke, Grace Marion Scully, Clara Lonigan, and that girl from 69th Street and Nomad, Maggie McGee, but everybody called her "Maggie the Wop."

The nostalgia of these names and memories was like hot steam rising fast and becoming like lost air that finally creeps into the clouds. His nostalgia was gone. It was felt like wet steam for a moment only.

The answer to his nostalgia was Thelma Carson, plus what he would do in life, his struggle to make himself into somebody.

To be famous!

Would she laugh at him because of his ambition?

Asking this question of himself, Eddie looked at Thelma, hoping with all of his hopes congested together and ready to find quick and immediate fulfillment in a smile, a glance, a word from her.

She was beautiful and she could be everything to him, for him.

Thelma was aware of his look, but she didn't turn to respond to it. He was smitten, she knew for a certainty. This gave Thelma more of an aching relief than pride, although she was proud of having affected him this much. It gave her a power over him, something that she was familiar with, and could enjoy, regardless of who the smitten fellow was, or of what he was like. This was natural, normal, as she should be. It was a female's will to power, she guessed. No, she didn't merely guess. She accepted it; she knew it was that.

They were walking on at the same slow pace. There were more people and more students on 57th Street than there had been on

The Silence of History

58th, and Eddie found this an intrusion upon the mood which, he believed, had been growing fast between them. The spell of poetry was broken, and then supplanted by casual prose. The silent intensity of their mood and their emotion was lost. They were both quite calm, but with disappointment. There was unsureness in both of them, for each was ignorant of what the other thought.

Students passed. One was big, a husky in a maroon sweater with white numerals, 1929, sewn on the chest. That was for freshman athletics in some sport, perhaps football. If only he had the time for sports! No, he was better off without it.

"Do you like football?" he asked.

"No, not enough to get excited about. Do you?"

"I used to. I used to play in high school."

She turned to face him, opening her mouth slightly, staring with an expression of curiosity which caused him a fast fluttering of dismay.

"You aren't big enough for football, are you—Ed?"

By calling him "Ed," she had taken out what would have been a sting to him. But he wished that there had been more in her voice, and in what she had said. More of, well, many things. Tenderness, compliments, softened interest, admiration, acceptance, more of just feeling for him.

"I managed," Eddie said, not wishing to add that he had long arms and big shoulders, because he often feared that he was graceless on account of the length of his arms and the breadth of his shoulders.

They both glanced at the books on display in the windows of Oldering's Book Store. They wanted to stop and look at the books, many of which were but recently published. But Eddie was shy of asking Thelma to stop with him.

He had so much to learn. He didn't want to seem ignorant.

They walked on. Thelma mentioned Walter Pater.

"He's wonderful."

"Do you know his writing?"

"A little of it. His *Conclusion to the Renaissance*. If we can live like that, and give the best quality of our minutes . . ."

"But that's only done in art—not Social Science."

Eddie didn't say what he wanted to say. He didn't say that, perhaps, he could not be an artist, and that many couldn't, even if he could. And he had a living to earn, and was life worth living? And what about love?

He wanted to fall in love with Thelma and know the best quality of every minute with her, and to burn while she burned with a "gem-like flame."

"Do you like the Russians?"

"Who? I've got to learn about them. I read a History by Milyukov."

"I mean the writers."

"I know *Smoke* by Turgenev. I like it."

"*Smoke?*"

"Yes."

"I never read it. I like Dostoevsky."

"I like Gorky's *Twenty-six Men and a Girl.*"

"I don't know it. I like Tolstoy."

"I've got to read him."

They were unself-consciously interested and went on saying what books they liked or didn't like. Eddie parted from her at the green-painted gate in front of the wide old wooden house on Harper Avenue. He wished she'd invite him in.

She was beautiful.

She smiled with restraint as she said goodbye. Her teeth were so even, so white, ivory-white.

Eddie mumbled his goodbye. He was enchanted by the sight of her.

She walked slowly up the front steps, turned and waved a hasty farewell with her left hand. She was gone, inside the screen door.

She was beautiful.

Eddie turned, and walked slowly toward 57th Street, in a dazed joy of his emotions. He was vague with euphoria, in a world where euphoria was moving with time to a euphoristic future. During the stroll, at the end of it, and also during the days which had led up to the moments of the walk, Thelma had been growing into a luring enticement, leading him to a helplessness of dreamlike craving that had had the cooperation of years of yearning and dreaming. A few steps on the sidewalk, away from the green gate, and he was in a haze of happiness. His brain was like a fog of vaporized rose petals whose perfumed odor became an odorless caress. He walked through a few moments and over a few squares of cement with the lightness of the reflected light of almost noon upon it while he was blissfully smiling with a bliss that was like ecstasy.

But then his head cleared again, like a stage become lit by the clarity of daylight, and Thelma Carson stood in the culmination of his own experiences of a young man's lifetime. He thought he loved her, the real Thelma, and in heedlessness of where he was, he walked in a rolling, almost floundering manner, thinking that the image in his mind was the reflection of the real Thelma, and he loved her.

His love was real, and it was for Thelma, but it was also a love of the drugged and drowsy ecstasy. And those who had loved and felt and had been loved with the first pure loveliness of love, they had known no more than he.

His mind cleared gradually as this strangely familiar and familiarly strange state gave way to a lessened purity of recollection of those moments just vanished, and an impatient hoping for the moments to come, when his arms would pass her into a warm stiffness of desire as compelling as his own, and in the excited contact of their bodies, they would kiss and hug, and clutch more tightly as though each were the totality of living for the other. And he imagined himself demanding, and she silently hugging in wildly lost control, and then, having her body, which was mystery become an awakened ecstasy, impetuously joyful.

The corner of 57th and Harper. A drugstore. A real estate office. A flat building with latticed, rough-edged stone below the first floor. The gathering rush of the swift humming and rattle of clicking wheels upon trucks, an I.C. train, southbound. To be coming here often, day and night.

She walked into his life with the grace of a singing spring morning, and they then walked through life together, with arms curled together, knowing one another and loving with the best of the quality of each moment pressing into moment into moment.

He was in love again.

And this time with a girl more beautiful than all of the beautiful girls he knew, the beautiful girls he'd gone out with, usually once, the girls with whom he had been in the thawed moments of yesteryear.

Villon again.

Simply, he told himself, Thelma Carson was a beautiful girl and he wanted to go out with her, and maybe, yes, he wanted in a hoping way to see the future with her.

He thought he would take her out, and soon, and he thought that he could, and that was what Eddie wanted to think with the belief that it would come true.

It was time that his dreams came true, more than double time plus.

He walked on at a brisk pace, sweating from the exertion. He had to get home and eat, and not be late.

But he was a half-hour late, and Corlin was sore. Eddie had promised to relieve Corlin an hour earlier, at one o'clock, because Corlin had promised to meet his missus and go somewhere with her; he'd make the hour up whenever Eddie wanted him to do it.

Corlin was "sore enough to bust my guts," and Eddie could only meekly say how sorry he was, and, with his apology, repeat the remark several times, that he didn't know how it had happened that he had forgotten about his promise to let Corlin off at one o'clock.

Corlin finally cooled off, and said they'd forget it.

But Howell came around and got sore because the air compressor was dirty. He threatened Eddie with loss of his privilege of reading, and of his job. When Howell finished bawling him out, Eddie couldn't speak. The wound of humiliation slashed in him was too deep.

He stood, pale, with his lips tight, and his teeth pressed tightly together. Eddie wanted to say something; he wanted to talk back. He couldn't because he had been so offended. Losing his head would have been foolish; he couldn't do it, couldn't flare

The Silence of History

up in temper. Howell had started sounding off at him with such suddenness that he was thrown completely off his psychological balance, caught by surprise, and the first effects of the tirade were of shock as well as hurt humiliation.

Howell had said that he was asking Mr. Wood to rescind the privilege, withdraw the privilege, and cancel the privilege given Eddie to read.

And he ordered Eddie to stop loafin' on the job with books, to stop readin', to cut it out, stallin' and pretendin' he had to sit on his can with all of them books. He had told Eddie that he was sick and tired, goddamned well tired of Ryan, because Ryan caused him more trouble than any other attendant in the whole city, and he couldn't be coming around all the time, just to check up on Eddie Ryan, there were better fellas walking the streets, a damned sight better ones, and whose eyes did he think he was pulling the wool over, anyway, and what in the goddamned fucking hell did he think the Rawlinson Oil and Refining Company was? Howell, even when not angry, did not have an easy time getting out words to make more than average sense and when he got burned up, then his words choked together.

His face became red, and redder. He seemed to bestow an angry pity upon himself, and his voice would betray a whine as well as its cruel brutality.

Actually, Howell was sort of funny, except that your boss was never very funny unless you were laughing with him, not against him.

A curling sarcastic smile asserted itself around Eddie's lips. It had come irrepressibly. Howell was disconcerted into a new rage.

"You watch your goddamn ass," Howell shouted, shaking a finger at Eddie.

The sarcastic smile was gone in a new blanched intensity of expression and of waiting and expecting.

But for what?

For Howell to stop howling.

"You laugh, you smile, you take it goddamn serious."

And Eddie gave this remark silence.

"You can leave any time."

What Eddie couldn't do before, he wouldn't do later. And that was to speak. He thought:

—You piston-lunged sonofabitch.

Then, when Eddie waited on a gasoline customer, Howell was flat as a deflated balloon. And he wanted to get out of the station. Joe Deacon had more or less talked Howell into bawling out Ryan mercilessly. Remembering his talk with Deacon, Howell stopped for a moment, as he was going through the station doorway. Hadn't he been too hard on Ryan? Maybe he had. He kinda felt so.

But he was a boss, a supervisor, and he had to stand by what he did.

—You've got to be decisive!

Hadn't Mr. Wood said that?

"Get the air compressor clean, Ryan," Howell ordered, but in a modified tone of voice.

He left the station in the company Ford coupe.

Eddie's anger was slowly pushing up to the surface. He was sore as hell by himself, but only for a few moments. His anger changed to concern and worry, worried depression of his spirits, and then, fear. He'd lose his job. Would he? And what about his education? His mother?

Eddie went into the toilet to get the can of Kitchen Cleanser used for cleaning the air compressor. Howell, the blubber bastard, had gotten his tongue twisted on that, air compressor. Howell, compressed hot air. But the guy was his boss.

—Handwriting on my fate, Eddie told himself.

What would he do?

He needed his job. His youngest brother? His youngest sister?

He came out from the toilet with the can in his left hand, and got a dry rag from a bin in a corner. He moved close to the air compressor. It was a low, side-bellied machine with a gauge, a belt, and an automatic pump, an ugly-looking machine. The tap was greasy and oily as well as dirty. Yes, it needed to be cleaned and polished up.

But Eddie couldn't do it. He couldn't, and he wouldn't. He didn't know. Which was it? Both?

Just Howell.

The Silence of History

He had been bullied and threatened.

Eddie put the can of Kitchen Cleanser back in the toilet and stuck the rag in the back pocket of his overalls.

Eddie determined that he wouldn't touch the air compressor. Let it stay dirty.

He was frightened but also determined. His determination won out over fear. There was more than stubborn determination in Eddie; there was defiance. He was defying, in grimness of spirit. He wouldn't, and goddamn it, he wouldn't touch the air compresser on that day, not after the kind of treatment Howell had dished out to him.

And he didn't.

He opened up his briefcase for books, sat down at the desk and began studying.

And Thelma. The charm and loveliness of his morning walk with her returned in the pathos of memory.

Dreaming of love, studying, full of sentiment and defiance, there was Eddie in the station and the May afternoon sunshine faded away in the dusty street with pounding trucks, the quiet and loveliness of the sunset blending the last colors of the day before it was lost to darkness, with the earth turning on its axis, and Eddie on that earth, turning and turning his mind and his heart.

And on that day, Eddie thought, as though by chance, that the struggle of his life would be harder and more bitter than he could have known before. He gave this little heed, less than a minute's reflection. There grew, in him, this knowledge.

Not only knowledge, but courage, will, determination, and defiance—without these he was lost.

With Howell and Deacon, there were two banks of a Rubicon, his and theirs. Right through life and the world, there would be two banks of a Rubicon.

It stuck to his thoughts and seeped through them. He had almost always known this. And now he knew that he knew it. No man crossed the Rubicon of his life and returned, except if he carried head, and heart and soul to be surrendered in servility.

He had crossed.

Eddie looked out upon the blue end of twilight, the pale lights, the irregular coagulating of shadows, the thick forms of blackness where the buildings were, and yes, he had waded over.

Night was coming.

He loved Thelma. He wanted to love her. He wanted her to love him. Night was coming. Night was darkness, and death was the darkest night of all. This darkness was behind him on his side of his Rubicon.

Now he must learn to change from fear of that darkness to contempt for it, contempt for death. He must learn, gain, find, pull from life, by the roots, a high and laughing courage as well as a bitter courage.

And could he walk with Thelma by him, her hand in his?

He thought no more of his Rubicon of Life. But he knew that he knew that he had crossed it.

He had some minutes of agitation. Then, his yearning for Thelma was like pain, the pain of loss. And it was like a terror of mystery. She who could be so vivid in his mind, where was she? Clutching the empty air, gulping and gorging upon the empty air, and, yes, struggling against the empty air, all because of some dream he called Beauty, and of the dream that man named Love, he must find and make and do in that empty air. The empty air of light was tomorrow. The empty air of no light was the night of tomorrow and tomorrow and tomorrow and the darkness that was at the end of tomorrow's light of day.

Sometimes, his words were the poetry he couldn't write; they were like a substitute for that poetry. One didn't live poetry, though, not in a world of howling Howells. The encounter with Howell, his bawling out, that seemed to have happened more than merely a few hours ago; it happened at some indefinite time in the past, in the dead and buried past. How could it be serious? Eddie couldn't regard that visit of Howell's as important. It wasn't the end of the world, it wasn't anything but a lot of steam, blown out by a boss way down on the lower rungs of the ladder of Success.

But it was serious, serious enough for him to lose his job, and his chance for an education, because with him it was—No Job, No Education.

There were other jobs to be gotten, but Eddie couldn't think of any to match what he had. And even though times were good and prosperous, there were probably two and a half to three million out of work.

Eddie knew that he was far, very far from the freedom which he sought, wanted, and which he would have.

There was still time to clean the air compressor.

He wouldn't do it. He tormented himself with apprehension, fears of losing his job. Two of his brothers, who lived with his mother, went to work every day and did their jobs. Hundreds of thousands did the same thing. They, too, many of them, had the living hell bawled out of them by bosses. That happened plenty of times.

But the men took it.

You had to take it. If you couldn't take it, how could you dish it out, if you should have to do that? If you didn't take it, what kind of a man were you? Didn't a man take his medicine?

No, he wouldn't take it. Eddie told that to himself, and he was determined not to take it. He was apprehensive lest he should turn coward, and melt his determined will. He wouldn't take it. When Eddie locked up, the air compressor was still not cleaned.

He was afraid, though, about his job. However, with the day's work ended, he quickly went from fear to forgetfulness. There was Thelma to think of, and tomorrow, and more tomorrows without any worry about the "petty pace" and *Macbeth*. And he had not merely been afraid. Hadn't he shown some guts? And what would she think? But he wouldn't want to tell her. The idea of his even being bawled out was harder to take because of her; it could lower his dignity in her eyes. Because of Thelma, he had been more hurt, more affected by Howell than he might otherwise have been. There was a strengthened reason to feel his dignity; he hoped for her to love him, if she didn't already, after their walk. Normally, you got sore, and laughed it off or bragged about it when you got a lacing from one of your bosses. But you didn't like it, even if you played a good game of pretense.

And Eddie hadn't liked it.

He could forget that evening, and Howell's howling, and think of the walk home with Thelma. And he could grow soft in dreaminess thinking of her, loving her, being loved by her, wandering, strolling.

Eddie studied with more difficulty that night. Thelma had distracted him more than Howell had done. It was as if he could reach out and touch her, but she wasn't there, nor any place nearby.

The last days of the spring quarter of 1926 were darkly trying for Eddie. He lived in double uncertainty. He didn't know if he'd keep his job, nor could he be any more certain about Thelma Carson, and he lost his weak confidence in his chances of winning her, by imagining that he was winning her, and that he had won her.

He went to classes each morning hoping, and he went to work dreading.

Eddie had hoped that she would wish him to walk her home the next day after class let out. She did not go home at eleven every day, but only rarely. Eddie had been lucky in catching her on that sunny morning which was already enshrined in his dreams.

Eddie couldn't make out what Thelma thought of him, and he anguished with impatience and impetuosity. Waiting was a recurring pressure upon him. And he couldn't understand, or rather, he did not allow himself to understand delay, or a slow growing in the heart, the affections. This troubled him, and often caused distortions of his actions and speech.

Love must be sure and swift to reveal itself. That was how Eddie thought of, and wanted love. If it were slow in growing, uncertain, unrevealed, Eddie would begin to know a torment of indefiniteness.

And this was his disappointment, after that walk home with Thelma.

The need for love was a cry of his heart, and of all of himself;

The Silence of History

he had sought, but sought in vain, and so many times he had loved or wanted to love, but he had lost.

Disappointment was like being stabbed, and he could not wait with calmness while love grew, because he feared new stabs of disappointment.

On the morning after their walk, he'd begun by taking his time when the period ended, and then he'd hastened outside. He didn't immediately believe her gone when he failed to catch her in a fast, surveying glance. She had gone.

The awful feeling of being stood up on a date had settled in his brain with a leadenness of depression. And the fact that Thelma Carson did not have a date with Eddie, this did not save him from his feelings, including those of shame and humiliation. He had taken for granted that he would again walk Thelma home after class. If she loved him, if she were falling in love with him, wouldn't she have waited to see him? He was persuaded of this logic because he believed it to be true. As he grew up, he had come to absorb an image of girls and women who would give value to this notion. Eddie believed in the truth of these popular ideas about girls and women, far more than he knew. These notions constituted a sort of men's tales, and were concerned with the wisdom of knocking 'em dead, not literally, but figuratively, and of managing them. And if they didn't go for you, then you hadn't, quite obviously, knocked 'em dead. If they went for you, they'd really go, they'd go ga-ga for you. When they didn't, where were you with them, if not just about nowhere? And the absorbed result of all this would make Eddie the suffering victim of the delusion that there was something wrong with him, because he hadn't, and he didn't, knock 'em dead. But he didn't know this, and his oversensitivity would produce moody spells because he had no girl. He was close to raw and tender to the touch about his lack of ability to impress girls and win their love, almost to win undying love at the first sight. This was acquired habit, as it were, and in Eddie's case, he had been affected not only in sensibility, but in dreaminess, the naïveté of his feelings about truth, and other factors as well. As a city boy, he had grown up withstanding the assaults upon the nerves of all the new noises of life which are so much the atmosphere in urban life that they are taken as though they were more natural, more a product of the natural phenomena of the universe, than the rumbling roar of thunder, the song of the birds, or the unplacated monotony of autumn winds.

Eddie suffered, not only from an absence of the kisses he wanted with all the need of one famished for the food of affections and emotions, but also from a deprivation of the senses. A calm loveliness, which seemed to be mystical because it was uncapturable in words, this was the harmony of all of the harmonization of life, the finality of happiness which gave one a suggested sense of peace in perfection. And for Eddie, such was the quality of happiness that would come with love. Nature, in its finished harmonies, this was the glory of the world. And that glory was associated with love, felt more stirringly and wonderfully, known more intimately, because of love. And love and beauty and that glory of the world could be found and felt in beautiful girls and women. Once, he had believed that girls and women were superior to boys and men, more perfect and pure, more noble, and love was the bond of beauty. This was, in fact, more than merely believed; it was an ingrained attitude, which collected about itself wishes and desires, dreams and hopes, all that he had looked forward to as the source and center of the greatest of joys and happiness. He had looked upon girls with worship and adoration. And these attitudes had not all been abandoned, nor had Eddie lost all of the habits of mind and feeling which he had developed through his growing years. He wanted them to be as he had dreamed them; he wanted them to be the loveliest creatures in the world.

He was full of sunken contradictions of attitudes, wishing and feeling about girls, and he was hurt as a consequence of these contradictions. These were inmeshed, were part of the reason why he had so often felt so lonely. He wanted too much out of love, just as he did out of life in everything important, and he could not find in life all of the satisfaction and returns that he required. Nor did love promise him the fulfillment and the many joys and blisses that he sought from it, yearned for with undiminished hope, despite setback after setback. The longing in his spirit sank his loneliness to great depths, and overcast it with a somberness that darkened the clouds of his melancholy. At times, love seemed to be a lie, and his daydreams turned to bitter anguish, as well as shame of self because of his profound silliness in imagining that the impossibly unreal could become real, and give him bliss beyond measure. He wanted girls, a girl, to create with him a love and to live with him all the feeling and passions of poems. Shelley and Keats, Byron, Browning, Tennyson, Wordsworth, and Shakespeare's sonnets. He sought a girl who would be flesh, young, new flesh, the unharmed flesh of a virgin, and who would be dream, music, the ethereal, mysterious and unattainable beauty of music which spoke to the spirit, though without one word, of a grandeur which was its own finality of fulfillment.

He had sexual desires, and he knew the physical discomfort of such desires, when they are unfulfilled. He looked at legs and their shapeliness and the shimmering neatness of the silk stockings which covered these legs. He looked at the dent of dresses between the thighs, as a girl walked.

And Thelma!

It must be she.

II

That fine morning after the day of their walk to Thelma's home, he sank into a sickened weakness of despair.

Again!

The sun was shining in a mockery of warm glory. The grass was green with mocking indifference. The gray Gothic, the towers on the gray chunky-looking buildings, were dead with stone but designed into mimicries of beauty, unfeeling, unmoving, imitating aspirations. The campus was beautifully quiet in deadness for Eddie Ryan.

He looked about, and waited, peered in all directions, and tried to fight down a growing, rising pressure of nervousness, which threatened to make him panicky.

And he had missed her, and he had to spend the day with himself, worriedly waiting for tomorrow.

Eddie started trudging home.

The disappointment he felt was because of the expectations he had nurtured. She might have gone off, thinking that he was avoiding her. He didn't know the facts, and would torment himself by trying to guess and speculate. He tried not to do this, but failed to reason away his disconsolate mood. Approaching home, Eddie was in low spirits. It well could have been no slight this time, but next time, there might be a slight. Something told him that Thelma and he would make the right kind of a couple. But he remained disconsolate.

Could he work, could he study or would he moon and think, moon away the afternoon?

And Howell might be back.

Why was it his lot to be so unhappy, more unhappy than most of those of his own age, most of those he knew?

A premonition of failure, and of unhappiness to come, stuck in his mind. The struggle which he was making did not win him much appreciation.

The fast-sprouting hope for Thelma had been an illusion, a foolish one.

The battle would have to be made, to be waged on, alone.

But Thelma remained a confusion to him.

And when he couldn't know, he was the prey of his own moods and thoughts. He couldn't know.

Eddie rode to work on the elevated, expecting to have a bad day.

Corlin had cleaned the top and surface of the air compressor. He said little to Eddie, and was cool; he was in a hurry to get away. Howell showed up, looked around, said that he hoped Ryan was turning over a new leaf, and drove away. Time dragged on Eddie's shift. His mind was tossed and pitched in new uncertainties.

May passed into June and the quarter was coming to its end. Eddie was forced to fight the growing restlessness which beset him. He thought of Thelma Carson and the summer, and he found his job more irksome and aggravatingly unpleasant. He was stale on the job, and kept wishing he didn't have to have it. And Deacon kept coming around in June, watching and checking up on him. Deacon made Eddie nervous. He always had something he wanted Eddie to do, or there was something that wasn't right, and Deacon would say so with a sarcastic edge to his words. Deacon was making the job almost unbearable. Eddie's resentment was getting steadily stronger.

Eddie walked home with Thelma Carson once more, but the magic of their first walk was not recaptured. Thelma was matter-of-fact and seemed to treat the walk as the most casual of experiences. She didn't talk much, and what she said was most casual, giving Eddie no easy opening to say anything that might bring them closer toward one another. And Eddie believed that he must say something to get closer to her. But what? Between a word or a sentence, there would be yards of walking in silence, or even a half-block of it.

The walk became a strain upon Eddie, making him tense. He lost his thoughts and was a discomfort and burden to himself. He felt foolish, and feared that he'd make himself look or sound foolish to Thelma. He felt an awkwardness of inferiority and inexperience, and an emptiness on his part which left him with almost nothing to draw upon and talk about. Not to Thelma. How could he talk and say anything when at her home so many men of the world of ideas, writers, musicians had come, and she had heard them at the supper table, and afterward in the parlor.

For Thelma had mentioned, in front of class, on the previous day, that she knew many of the faculty members because they had been to her home, and she had heard them discussing many subjects with her father and other guests.

This was paralyzing to Eddie because he knew that he knew so little, that he had only begun, and if he talked of what he knew and thought, he'd only seem to be spouting, like a beginning student, part of what men who knew and could teach him had said, and better, in Thelma's home. He'd sound pretentious, smart-alecky, wouldn't he? And he'd bore her, wouldn't he? He'd sound as if he were showing off, and on so little.

This was another source of his paralysis.

The family had even taken her to Europe one summer, and she

had seen as well as heard what he must see and hear and learn about.

His realization of his ignorance, of the vast knowledge he must acquire, and his earnestness and the eagerness he wanted to preserve, develop, and never lose, this stole away his tongue even more.

They were walking past a fenced-in yard in front of a wooden frame house that spread sidewise, and he saw purple flowers on tall stems, whiffed their odor, more a perfume than perfume, and saw in them a blooming glory. He said they were lovely; but he didn't know what kind of flowers they were, what their names were. She asked him did he like hollyhocks? He said that he did, without revealing that he had but just discovered what hollyhocks looked like.

Soon they would go to the farm in Virginia, she said, and she couldn't wait, she was looking forward to this with so much desire. She'd ride a horse, work on the farm, collect information about the darkies, and in the nights, silver with moonlight, and sensuous and full of the mystery of the earth, they'd talk, her family, and she'd remember when she was a little girl.

"Oh, that's grand, lovely, I love it," she said.

"It must be," he said, his words scarcely audible.

The country, what did he know of it and of nature?

He felt a resentful inferiority, not against Thelma and her family, but against his own past. What had he grown up with? What had he missed? What must be sacrificed of his time to make up for the spent years of growing up?

His mind became active, but locked up within himself, and it was more difficult for him to talk than it had been when this walk had begun.

And Thelma, she was more beautiful than he'd seen before, lovely, so lovely. She was at his side, walking in a simplicity of grace and beauty, and he wanted to touch her, take her arm, kiss her, and he wanted her, all of her, for himself, in the Virginia moonlight, and he wanted to tell her, and she walked at his side, she walked in grace, such grace, she was beautiful, she was lovely, and he was choked up with a confusion because she was lovely.

In a few minutes, they said goodbye at her gate, and she disappeared through the screen door.

The sun bathed the street in the loveliest glory of infinity. Under such a sun, he walked home before going to work.

Chapter Twenty-Two

I

I remember the day in July 1926, when I quit my job as a filling station attendant of the Rawlinson Oil and Refining Company. Mr. Wood, my boss, Superintendent of the Service Station Department, had given me new evidence of his faith and confidence in me. Deacon and Howell, the supervisors, had been riding me, and turning in reports which gave me demerits. That was when I read, for the first time, Bertrand Russell's essay on "A Free Man's Worship," from his book, *Mysticism and Logic*.

It was not by chance that I went to the library after quitting my job, but it could be chance that I should have read the Russell essay. For it and my action in quitting my job were a climax, an ending and a beginning for me in a youth which may seem abnormal because it was so much devoted to study and preparation for the future—for my future—and in that youth so much dedication was given to some of those virtues which are hailed far and wide in America.

That July day was like the end of an act in a drama of mind and spirit, but it was an undramatic drama because there was no slugging conflict, no victor and no defeat. Nor did this act end with a promise of love and happiness, or with the loss of love. It merely ended in decision and realization; it was merely my day of choice, of resolution to face the greater unhappiness that may come in tragedy, and to face it openly and simply, rather than to devote myself to the lesser unhappiness

The Silence of History

of taking one more step on the climb up Horatio Alger's ladder, where I might go slap-happy, might break an ankle, or might shove my feet into somebody's nose and squash it.

The climax of that day is, alas, not of the stuff that books are made of; it is only of the stuff of which lives are made or unmade. The man who takes a chance and speculates in money, that's the stuff that is dramatic; the man or youth who takes a chance and speculates on his freedom and destiny merely makes a decision, so who cares? And who should care?

I made my decision to quit casually and as though on impulse. It was impulse. But impulse is not whim, divorced from character, and always willfully irrational and irresponsible. It is that to those who make easy decisions look like hard choices while they surrender to the allurements of a slow or fast upward movement on that Horatio Alger ladder.

Mr. Wood was fair and a gentleman, but he could not understand my decision. Nor could I explain it to him. He told me that he had lost his faith in human nature. He would have been kind to me, had I stayed, just as he had been kind before that day. And my interview with him had already amounted to a tacit slap in the faces of Deacon and Howell, who had been riding me. For I was not bawled out as they might have wished, and as they needed me to be, following their reports on me, and in prospect of the future reports which they might have written had I stayed on. No, Mr. Wood had not given me a lacing-down, he had not talked cruelly or coldly. The agreement to a vacation which came readily and with quick sympathy was a concession by Mr. Wood; this was not company policy.

I couldn't have helped it—that is, I could not have done otherwise. I had to do it by necessity, a necessity which was essential for ambition's freedom, inner freedom, freedom of my soul and spirit.

In March 1925, I had gone to work for Rawlinson. In June 1925, I matriculated at the University. All through that period, and even prior to March 1925, I rarely lived as youth was living, as most of my generation, especially my friends and acquaintances, were living. In their terms, I was making a sacrifice, and perhaps I was. Possibly I was giving up much of my youth. But I had learned quickly that this did not matter. Saturday nights came and went, and I sat studying, hearing no horns blowing, dancing with no wonderful one who was love's lovelight, and a keen mama to boot. It became harder to get a date when I tried. And with time passing, that didn't matter so much. There was an accretion of something else. It was in myself. It was the force of will.

Warnings came to me, some friendly, some not so friendly, some contemptuous.

—You're overdoing it.
—All work and no play . . .
—You'll end up in the booby hatch.
—You got to have fun.

I didn't despise or disdain fun. But I was not of that class, race, type, and status which easily advances in the world. I had to make extreme efforts. There was no other alternative. Had I been less extreme and not taken risks, I should only have been playing at gaining an education.

And I had overdone it before. On the high school gridiron, I'd taken risks. That was fighting spirit. I'd drunk with the boys, and almost killed myself. That was wild stuff, and Ryan could drink himself under the table.

I began overdoing it in another way, for another reason, and with another end in view.

—Ryan, you don't have to kill yourself.

Men had killed themselves with knife and fork, in the stock market, in business offices, by giving more than they could afford of health to working for companies.

I had, then, been overdoing it for almost two years, overdoing it by study, by loss of sleep, by almost ceaseless observation and thought. There had been strain and worry. Tiredness. Nervousness. But I had slowly learned how to carry some of these strains.

That had been the choice I was required to make—overdo it, or fail to develop.

II

When I sat in Mr. Wood's office, I had had behind me those two years. My seemingly impulsive action had come out of the changes within me growing out of that overdoing it; out of that I had learned and come to believe what the probable future would be. I did not need to think that what I had already given thought and study to, and I did not need to think at length about what I must do to go on. I could act on impulse. In this case, impulse was the decision to continue on the road that was mine, and not on one that was paved to lead me away from where I would go.

However, there was no explaining this. I respected and was grateful to Mr. Wood, but I believed that his ideals would betray me, and they might also betray him. I had worked for two big corporations, controlled by men who did not know me and who were far away. I did not know what they would do, and I couldn't study, as I did study, in order for them to find me and lift me up some rungs on their ladder. And I was not seeking to learn what they would have required. Men such as they spoke of more and more prosperity. I read of this in the newspapers. I didn't believe them. I was already convinced that the prosperity we were enjoying would go tumbling down in a new cyclical depression. I was beginning to see, by anticipation, a future quite different from that in which Mr. Wood believed. Not only was there to be a cyclical depression, but also war would come, a second World War. That I believed as though it were knowledge. More personally, competition and rising in the world would mean my contending with fellows like Deacon and Howell. I should only have had trouble and more trouble with such guys.

There was no discussion of these questions with Mr. Wood, and I knew there couldn't be.

For I was no longer seeking Success as it was viewed in business.

Out of such views and prognostications my decision had come. Thus, I did quit on an impulse.

III

For the first time since my graduation from high school, I was out of work. It was of my own choosing. It was a consequence of, an act of my own will. I had done it. I had put myself out of work.

But in fact I had retreated when I could do so easily. I should have found this more difficult had I waited. This is how my action of that July day seems when it is viewed in retrospect.

Yet, it was serious. It was as serious as the burning pits of Hell are to a sinner.

Without work, what was I, and what could I do? How could I continue my education? And I must become educated, or my soul would die. This I knew.

There were no doubts in my mind about the seriousness of my situation. But I had risked. And I had been right in risking.

This conclusion settled in my mind, and I remained convinced of it even though I was not equally sure of my stamina and character. I could be right and yet I could fail. There was doubt in me, ominous, portentous, a silently threatening doubt which was stalking the edges of my mind, and which could spring upon my confidence and courage and devour them.

It was most fortunate that I was alone, and remained alone, going to the library to read. I escaped the diversion of having someone else drive my doubt howling upon my courage, and perhaps of weakening or confusing me. I could more easily clasp and hug my conviction that I was right, that I had taken the right action, without having to explain or defend it to anyone. My loneliness of the previous months was my protection, my sense of added strength. I was able to believe that I had acted with courage and to lift up my own morale.

I knew that I had done more than merely quit a job. My act was an assertion, an irrevocable step toward freedom. It placed me more on my own and without protection; but also, it put me in a situation which called upon me to struggle with more driving grimness and more will than ever yet I had.

The Silence of History

I was fed up with my job at Rawlinson's. When I had begun, I had believed in a future in business and corporation law. I had believed in stick-to-it-iveness, in the victory of merit and loyalty, hard work, and intelligence. I had seen a future in the oil industry such as there was not at the Express Company. I had believed that businessmen were smart, brainy, clever, worthy of admiration, and able to control and manage what they were doing. I had believed in the practical and in experience, as well as in knowledge. One without the other would be insufficient. My whole experience had tended to confirm this belief. I couldn't be a carpenter, fix things with my hands, and I had no experience of any consequence in trying to do such things. There had been no manual training in parochial schools. But I had had a physical, athletic boyhood, not a withdrawn one because of lack of ability or of timidity, for I was not athletically timid. In sports, I had learned to do innumerable things with my body, to use it or parts of it as an instrument, and mostly I had taught myself. From the age of seven on, I had thought about the sports I liked. The amount of thought I gave to sports in boyhood and up to about the age of eighteen was really vast. And then, I had absorbed a considerable body of details about business. Half-listening when my uncles talked about the shoe game, and selling, I had picked up fact after fact. These facts, about selling, mark-ups, prices, advertising, turnover, good and bad seasons had, as it were, entered one ear but they had not gone out by the other. My Aunt Jenny had spoken of hotels where she worked, and my father about the Express Company. Then I had worked at the Express Company, before getting my job at Rawlinson's.

I was a young man of twenty-two, a person, not a category called student, or another category called gas station attendant, nor a type called young blood, nor a division in parts, one part worker, one part student with ambition, one part young fellow who wants girl, and one or more additional parts that belonged to the notions and prejudices of anyone else. I was no one's type, no one's allegory, no one's illustration of any kind of preconception, trade-marked capsule or anything else.

I was myself.

And I had lived without the grace of plotted graphs and all the other methods and means that the erudite, the knowing, and the unknowing who think they are the knowing, find and use so as not to know what human beings are like, and what they can do.

What affected me was what had come into my life, what had reached my awareness and consciousness, what had been received by and through one of my senses. I had been offended by what had so been absorbed.

And gradually, I had used and drawn on my experiences and memories outside of the University, trying to correlate what I remembered with the ideas and the contents of the subjects I had studied, and with the books I read. I had not merely been studying subjects; through these, rather, I had been studying life. Life was in books and it was in all of my years and memories. There were lies in books, and there were also lies outside books.

I used what I remembered, and I tested what I used from memory. I had not had highbrow prejudices against business and businessmen when I matriculated at the University. But I came to see later that I had quit Rawlinson because I had changed my views and values, and did not see my future in any way associated with business. Perhaps it would have been more immediately if I had taken a poke at Deacon and been fired. But it would have been a far less significant action than the one I took; it would have been without, or with few consequences in my self-development, and with little to help me find its meaning.

IV

Sitting high up in the Crerar Library, I was full of wistful pathos for freedom. If I could spend long hours in libraries, reading, I would perhaps become an educated man. I envied those about me, mostly males, students apparently, but some were older men. They sat poring over books, and some were taking notes. I ought to take notes too, I guessed, but there

The Silence of History

was so much more pleasure in reading. The hell with notes!

Once I had started reading in the Library on that July day, my perspective of myself as well as my immediate concerns changed. The Rawlinson Oil and Refining Company shrank out of my mind, and my sense of myself faded in concentration upon the open pages of the book before me on the table, where I sat alone. The reading room was smaller and quieter than the large main reading room of the Chicago Public Library across the street; there was less shuffling of feet and movement of people; the windows were to my back, and they were opaque. From far down on the street below, the sounds of traffic rose, but it was too early for nervous drivers to be jabbing their horns, and the reading room was veritably quiet.

I was free. I felt free and my wish and need of freedom were a poignancy of yearning. And after quitting Rawlinson, I needed freedom, more than ever. For I had gone so far in change—change of values, change of purpose—that I must go on, or I would be guilty of self-betrayal. I had taken a direction which must lead me on and on along a hard road. It was one where I would have to go unprotected, except by myself. Knowledge was my protection. I must have the time and freedom to gain it.

All of this I did not foresee in sharply outlined clarity and with a decisive, prophetic logic. I sensed, I knew, I guessed, I realized this. It was apparent. I had chosen to fight, because in my mind and in my heart I had said "No" to the values, even the sacred ones, of my times.

Thus it was. Thus I was.

And I read.

"A Free Man's Worship," from *Mysticism and Logic*, by Bertrand Russell.

I lost myself in this essay and in thoughts, not of my fate, but of man's fate.

Yes, I thought, I must try to live to the end with "unyielding despair."

And yes, I thought, "a long march through the night," and yes, to be "proudly defiant" until "the slow, sure doom" should "fall."

Yes, even though the final doom be an oblivion of static energy in the clockless waste and eternity of entropy, it still could be, and it would be, and it was, that man had had the pride and bravery of aspiration and truth, even in the face of utter doom.

I could accept the struggle with fate, I could march through the night, knowing that beyond the last darkened horizon, there would only be a flattened waste of energy in that clockless eternity of entropy. And to accept that fate and to go forward—that was victory enough. That was victory without reward, without pay; it was victory with only the honor of the soul of man.

Chapter Twenty-Three

Eddie received a letter from the University on the morning after he had quit his job with Rawlinson Oil and Refining Company. Before he tore the envelope open, he was certain that he knew what information the letter would contain. He was correct.

He was informed that he had won a Freshman Honor Scholarship as one of twenty students with the highest grades.

And five days later, he got a job as a service station attendant with the National Oil Company of Illinois, thanks to the intervention of Mr. Leeson.

He began trying to write, and sending out a few manuscripts, mostly satirical pieces.

In the fall, when he saw Thelma Carson on campus . . . what?

He asked himself this question often.

The summer of 1926 passed. Eddie was assigned to a new station at 47th Street and Bishop Street, at the southwestern boundary of the Union Stockyards. The air stank on hot days, and swarms of flies invaded the station. Eddie fought them with a Flit gun. There was little business. Traffic pounded and shot by on 47th Street.

Eddie read books, dreamed, fought flies, and the air was often sick with the stale odors of the stale blood and intestines of slaughtered hogs. Sometimes he shot craps across the street in the dirty candy store of a Bohemian who used loaded dice. On his first Saturday night of work, a drunken Polish stockyards worker slashed his wife with a razor, and was taken away by the cops in a paddy wagon.

The days passed.

He read *Les Misérables* by Victor Hugo.

Killing flies with the Flit gun, he wondered and pondered— If it had not rained on June 17, 1815.

The summer seemed slowly to pass.